THE UNITED NATIONS:
Past, Present, and Future

The

UNITED
NATIONS

Past, Present, and Future

EDITED BY JAMES BARROS

Erindale College
University of Toronto

Fp THE FREE PRESS, NEW YORK
COLLIER-MACMILLAN LIMITED, LONDON

212503

The Free Press
A Division of The Macmillan Company
866 Third Avenue, New York, New York 10022

Collier-Macmillan Canada Ltd., Toronto, Ontario

Library of Congress Catalog Card Number: 72–075159

printing number
1   2   3   4   5   6   7   8   9   10

The Contributors

Leland M. Goodrich

JAMES T. SHOTWELL PROFESSOR EMERITUS
COLUMBIA UNIVERSITY

Stephen G. Xydis

PROFESSOR, DEPARTMENT OF POLITICAL SCIENCE
HUNTER COLLEGE, CITY UNIVERSITY OF NEW YORK

Leon Gordenker

PROFESSOR, DEPARTMENT OF POLITICS
PRINCETON UNIVERSITY

David A. Kay

PROFESSOR, DEPARTMENT OF POLITICAL SCIENCE
UNIVERSITY OF WISCONSIN, MADISON, WISCONSIN

Leo Gross

PROFESSOR, FLETCHER SCHOOL OF LAW AND DIPLOMACY
TUFTS UNIVERSITY

Robert W. Gregg

DEAN
AMERICAN UNIVERSITY, WASHINGTON, D.C.

Contents

INTRODUCTION

The six essays that follow are an attempt to examine the evolution and workings of the United Nations during the past quarter century. They are also an attempt to examine the effectiveness of the world organization as an instrument for conflict resolution and cooperation in a world political system dominated by nation-states. Each essay deals with a principal organ of the United Nations. The first three essays concentrate on the Security Council, the General Assembly, and the Secretariat (secretary-general) while the last three essays deal with the Trusteeship Council, the International Court of Justice, and the Economic and Social Council by examining the decolonization process and the development of international law through the United Nations as well as the United Nations economic, social, and technical activities. Thus the pages that follow will be of particular interest to students of international organization, international law, and international relations.

What these essays show quite clearly is that during the past quarter century the United Nations has displayed a capacity for survival which must impress even its most vociferous critics. Part of this capacity for survival can be traced to a world balance of forces in which the two powerful blocs tacitly agree that an all-out war between them is unthinkable. But it can also be traced to a United Nations Charter that is flexible enough to allow the organization to handle situations and questions never envisaged by the signatories at San Francisco in 1945.

Unfortunately, both of these factors were absent during the League of Nations period—especially during its last decade. Their absence helps explain the demise of that organization. Though the external forces were no more under the control of the League than they are under the United Nations, certain constitutional flaws which hindered the operations of the League were avoided at San Francisco when the United Nations Charter was negotiated. In any comparison of the League Covenant and the United Nations Charter, one is immediately struck by the sharper division of function and responsibility among the principal organs of the United Nations than in the League. Thus the jurisdictional difficulties that some-

1

times developed between the League Council and the League Assembly during the interwar period have been less of a problem under the United Nations—with one noticeable exception, the General Assembly's "Uniting for Peace" Resolution, to be discussed shortly.

The United Nations Charter also accepts the imperfect nature of a world community composed of sovereign states. A multilateral treaty negotiated by states and accepted as such by governments, the Charter specifically recognizes "the principle of the sovereign equality" [1] of the member states, even though in its preamble it speaks of "We the Peoples of the United Nations." Likewise, the Charter contains a provision re- stricting the United Nations from intervening in "matters which are es- sentially within the domestic jurisdiction of any state" [2]—a looser provision than the corresponding one contained in the League Covenant.[3]

The Charter, unlike the Covenant, takes a practical rather than legalistic approach to maintaining the peace. The League Covenant, for example, did not prohibit a state's recourse to war. It merely attempted to circumscribe and restrict this traditional right. The Charter, on the other hand, admonishes member states of the United Nations to eschew the use of force or threats in their relations with other states or in any way in- consistent with the purposes of the organization[4]—a concept far broader and more encompassing than the narrower legal concept of war, especially as it was interpreted during the League period.[5] This wider, more practical, and less legalistic approach is mirrored in the wide powers for main- taining the peace given in the Charter specifically to the Security Council and with qualifications—the power merely to recommend—to the General Assembly. On the whole, however, the similarities between the League and the United Nations are far greater than the differences,[6] but these dif- ferences, when added to a changed external setting, have made possible the survival—indeed, one might say the active use—of the United Nations.

Of the Charter's six principal organs (General Assembly, Security Council, Economic and Social Council, Trusteeship Council, International Court of Justice, and Secretariat), it is the Security Council which is saddled with the most important task—"primary responsibility for the maintenance of international peace and security." [7] This specific and sharply defined role is then riveted to the premise that power goes hand in hand with responsibility and that to maintain the peace there must be a consensus among the great powers. The premise is realistic and based in large part on the experience of European inter-state relations during the preceding centuries and by the interwar experience and World War II. The outward and legal reflection of this premise is the Charter's stipulation that a unanimous agreement of the Security Council's permanent members— a euphemism for the Great Powers—is necessary on all substantive ques- tions. Naturally, this procedure concedes that no substantive action can be taken against a great power, or any state allied to a great power.

This built-in constitutional "veto" by any great power of any sub- stantive action by the Security Council has been used by the Soviet Union less irresponsibly than commonly supposed. Of the 109 vetoes cast in the Security Council and tabulated to 1967, 104 were cast by the Soviet Union. However, if one examines these vetoes carefully, he will discover that 51 were cast in connection with seventeen membership applications, several were cast in connection with appointing the secretary-general, and the rest were cast against proposals where the possibility of amendment did not exist and the Security Council had either to accept or reject the proffered resolution.[8] The veto, however, is both realistic and sound in an international community based upon nation-states where some states, to borrow a phrase from George Orwell, are more equal than others. Indeed, in comparison with the procedure of the League Council it is a step forward, which few critics of the veto appear to notice or acknowledge, for in that institution a negative vote by *any* state was sufficient to thwart substantive action by the League Council.

One disadvantage of the veto formula, however, is the enumeration of the Security Council's five permanent members—the Republic of China, France, the Soviet Union, Great Britain, and the United States.[9] At the San Francisco Conference the question was raised as to why France or China were ever included as permanent members of the Security Council. France, for the great power she was, and China, for the great power she would be, some wit answered. Nevertheless, the rigid composition of the Security Council's permanent membership in a world political system which is never static and often sees the rise and fall of the power of states, is a constitutional defect in the Charter which raises the specter of future difficulties. The question of Communist China's representation in the United Nations, as recent events have shown, was largely procedural. However, the difficulties would be vast if it were felt that Japan or some other state was entitled to permanent membership in the Security Council. In that situation an amendment of the Charter—requiring the concurrence of the permanent members of the Security Council—would be necessary.[10] In fact, even the amendment of the Charter increasing the nonpermanent membership of the Security Council from six to ten proposed in 1956—following a great influx in membership—was accomplished in 1965 only when the continued expansion of the organization's membership made agreement on the selection of the six nonpermanent members of the Security Council more and more difficult.[11] This, as we shall see, has been only one of the problems produced by the increase of the organization's membership.

Because of the Security Council's composition, its role in the world body is largely determined by the membership of the organization and especially by the permanent members of the Security Council. Political division and a lack of consensus among the great powers outside the organization leads to political division and a lack of consensus inside the organization and in the Security Council this lack of consensus is manifested by use of the veto.

Such was the situation in the years immediately following the establishment of the world organization when there was a division of the world between two power blocs, each led by a superpower. Though the struggle was political and based upon the conflicting strategic and military desires of the contesting groups, it was on the whole falsely projected as an ideological struggle. Labeled the "cold war," this lack of consensus by the Great Powers reached its zenith with the Berlin blockade and the North Korean attack on South Korea in the summer of 1950. The Security Council's decision recommending that aid and assistance be given to South Korea was made possible only because of the fortuitous absence of the Russian delegate. The subsequent return of the Soviet Union to the Security Council and its use of the veto in the Korean question resulted in the adoption by the General Assembly of the Uniting for Peace Resolution in the autumn of 1950. This was an American-initiated attempt to circumvent the Soviet Union's use of the veto in the Security Council, as in the Korean question, and thus give the General Assembly a larger role in maintaining peace and security. The resolution was pressed by the United States despite British advice, namely, that the future composition of the General Assembly might change—it was dominated by the West during this period—and the resolution might then become dangerous.[12] Prophetic advice, in retrospect.

It was, of course, argued by some—especially by the Soviet Union —that the Uniting for Peace Resolution was contrary to the spirit of the Charter. They contended that the Charter placed primary responsibility for the maintenance of international peace and security on the Security Council rather than on the General Assembly. Moreover, it was pointed out that the General Assembly's action in adopting the Uniting for Peace Resolution was merely a recommendation. Therefore, the resolution was not binding on the member states, regardless of the moral or political influence that it might generate. In essence, by accepting the resolution, the General Assembly undermined the centralized system envisaged by the Charter. by the Security Council on the question of maintaining the peace and pre-Under this system states would be legally obligated to execute a decision serving security. The General Assembly's alternate system would be somewhat akin to that of the League Covenant in which decisions on maintaining peace and security were decentralized.

The reply to this was that the Uniting for Peace Resolution was justified under the letter of the Charter because Articles 10 and 11 gave the General Assembly extensive powers to discuss and recommend anything within the purview of the Charter, including the maintenance of international peace and security. Furthermore, though the Security Council had primary responsibility for maintaining the peace it did not necessarily have exclusive responsibility. In actual practice, the collective military measures envisaged in the Uniting for Peace Resolution have never been invoked though other provisions of the resolution contributed to the General Assembly's handling of the Suez crisis of 1956 and the Lebanese crisis of 1958. On the whole, passage of the Uniting for Peace Resolution probably had the effect of giving the General Assembly a wider view of the role that it could play in the world organization.[13] This wider view was accepted more and more as the expanding membership of the United Nations changed both the composition and the character of the General Assembly.

The rapid expansion of the United Nations membership was not to commence, however, until 1955, so that Western dominance in the General Assembly rendered it an attractive instrument, as far as the United States and its allies were concerned, to circumvent the Russian veto in the Security Council. Meetings of the Security Council declined during these years while meetings as well as agenda items of the General Assembly increased. During this period the General Assembly was manipulated by the United States and its allies to support their positions and their policies in the cold war. The "package deal" of December 1955 was the first break in the static membership of the world organization during the 1950–1955 period. Though not fully realized at the time, it was the beginning of a veritable flood of new states into the world body. The high point in the admission of new states was in 1960 and only recently have membership applications begun to ebb. The increase in membership soon changed the General Assembly from a Western-dominated organ to one dominated by states from Africa and Southeast Asia. Its character changed. Some of the similarities among these new states—former colonial possessions, nonwhite, and less developed economically—cement them together whenever questions dealing with colonialism, racial discrimination, and economic development surface in the debates of the General Assembly or in other organs of the United Nations.

Initially, as membership in the organization expanded and its character changed, the Soviet Union likewise saw that the General Assembly could be used as a convenient forum for promoting its policies and for undermining the position of the United States and its allies. The Soviet Union's own response to the Uniting for Peace Resolution was a systematic support of the new states in their drive to remove the last vestiges of colonial domination under whatever form disguised and wherever found. The campaign culminated in December 1960 with the General Assembly resolution entitled Declaration on Granting Independence to Colonial Countries and Peoples. It was followed a year later with the establishment of a Special Committee on Colonialism to examine the declaration's implementation. However, from this point on in the early 1960s, the Soviet Union, like the United States after 1955, soon discovered that the new states could not be indiscriminately manipulated or used as instruments of Russian foreign policy in the General Assembly. They too had drives, attitudes, and values which did not necessarily dovetail with those of the Soviet Union. The struggle to increase the nonpermanent membership in the Security Council from six to ten as well as the membership of the Economic and Social Council from eighteen to twenty-seven was only one such conflict. Rejected as unacceptable to the Afro-Asian states was the Soviet Union's challenge to Secretary-General Dag Hammarskjöld's handling of the Congo crisis. Likewise rejected as unacceptable was Moscow's proposal that Hammarskjöld be dismissed from the office and that the secretary-general's office be reorganized into a three-man body representing Western, Eastern, and Afro-Asian interests—the so-called "troika" principle.[14] Moscow was further disenchanted with the General Assembly by the general resistance offered by the Afro-Asian states to the Soviet Union's policy during the Congo crisis. Finally, the Soviet Union was reticent to give the type of support that the African states desired on the questions of the Portuguese possessions in Africa, the racial policies of the South African government, and the white minority government in Southern Rhodesia which had unilaterally declared its independence from Great Britain.

Therefore, the Great Powers, by competing for the support of the new Afro-Asian states in the years after 1955 and encouraging these states with their permissive admissions policies which accepted all applicants for membership to the United Nations, although some clearly did not fulfill the qualifications stipulated in Article 4 of the Charter,[15] have produced a General Assembly whose composition is very different and whose character has radically changed from that which had passed the Uniting for Peace Resolution in 1950. In a sense, it was only in the 1960s that this membership increase produced a United Nations that could really be called a world organization encompassing all the areas of the globe.

The mutual aversion of the United States and the Soviet Union to an Afro-Asian–dominated General Assembly led in the early 1960s to a renewed use by the Great Powers of the Security Council which both sides had at different times abandoned. However, some major issues, vestiges of World War II, continued to be discussed outside the Security Council and the United Nations. The question of Germany is a good example. Other crucial issues have been tacitly ignored—the Vietnam war, for one, and the Nigerian civil war, for another. On the other hand, crises which the Great Powers mutually desire to control—the Middle East and direct Arab-Israeli confrontations—they attempt to maintain in the Security Council or in discussions among the Great Powers outside the Security Council.

The Great Powers' return to an increased use of the Security Council has led to a General Assembly where prime political issues involving immediate crises are submitted less and less often. This is not to say, however, that all important political questions are excluded from the General Assembly's consideration. The General Assembly can be expected in the course of its work to discuss many important international irritants such as racial discrimination and colonialism—issues of obvious interest to the Afro-Asian states. Naturally, economic and technical questions are virtual monopolies of the General Assembly—again, of obvious interest to the underdeveloped Afro-Asia states—since the Charter gives it paramount responsibility through its control of the Economic and Social Council. In this situation, however, regardless of the issues being considered by the General Assembly, the jockeying by states for votes—with vote trading and bloc voting—continues. These devices, which are strikingly applied by the Afro-Asian states but not restricted solely to them, have been used since the first meeting of the General Assembly in 1946 and especially by the Western bloc in the early 1950s when they dominated the General Assembly.

Judging from recent developments—witness the Security Council's discussions of the Indo-Pakistan conflict—it would be safe to assume that the trend of raising important political issues before the Security Council will continue. This trend will probably not re-create exactly the type of Security Council envisaged in the Charter. But it may well lead to a Security Council in which the Great Powers, anxious to keep world violence at an acceptable level for themselves, and assuming their interests are not directly involved, will come to agreements to control situations where violence threatens or has erupted. This cooperation by the Great Powers in the Security Council would most likely occur in areas outside the European theater. The admitted inability of the Security Council to function in the manner hoped for in the Charter has not been due to any intrinsic weakness or malfunction of the Charter's articles, but to political factors of the United Nations external setting. Indeed, one can argue that the occasional limited success that the Security Council and the United Nations have been able to achieve reinforces the basic premise made prior to and during the San Francisco Conference in 1945: that power goes hand in hand with responsibility and that any successful functioning of such a world body as the United Nations would stand or fall on the ability of the Great Powers to arrive at a consensus both inside and outside the United Nations.

As to the General Assembly, in the future it will undoubtedly expand its activities and shift its attention to questions which it can rightly claim are intended by the Charter for its supervision. The General Assembly's wide powers to discuss and recommend will allow that organ to expand its economic and technical assistance programs already in operation and to open new ones which by no stretch of the imagination can be considered concerns of the Security Council. One immediate question is worldwide pollution, especially of the seas and oceans, whether these are considered territorial waters or high seas. The General Assembly's decision to convene a conference at Stockholm in June 1972 to examine the question is an example of the type of action which it can initiate to focus world public attention on an issue little thought of in past years. Weather control is likely to be another issue which the General Assembly will sooner or later have to tackle. Of course, the difficulties that most General Assembly actions face is that, unlike national legislatures, its recommendations are not binding on the member states of the United Nations. However, by airing an issue and passing a recommendation on it, the General Assembly expresses the mind and informs the world community—attributes which Walter Bagehot ascribed to the British House of Commons[16] and by inference to all national legislatures.

During this quarter century of activity, the position of the secretary-general has developed far beyond what was envisaged at San Francisco in 1945. Under the Charter and especially under Article 99, the secretary-general is given the opportunity for public political initiatives which his predecessors in the League lacked. Even under the League, however, the secretary-general was active behind the scenes. Recent evidence tends to show that this was true in the case of the League's first secretary-general, Sir Eric Drummond. It was certainly true in the case of Drummond's successor, the Frenchman Joseph Avenol, though his actions generally hastened the upsurge of Nazi Germany and Fascist Italy and the demise of the very organization he served.[17] If the secretary-general of the United Nations is active both behind the scenes and in public, this is due not so much to the added constitutional power that he has under the Charter as to the political configuration of the world since 1945. The political division of the world and the growth of bipolarity, as well as the emergence of the Afro-Asian or nonaligned world, has led to a greater delegation of authority and power to the secretary-general by the constituent organs of the United Nations. This has, in turn, allowed the secretary-general to assume stances and undertake initiatives which would have been unheard of for the secretaries-general of the League.

It was expected by all during the course of the San Francisco Conference that the secretary-general would play a more active role in the United Nations than his counterpart had in the League. Correspondingly, it became understood that no one should be selected as secretary-general who did not have the confidence of all the permanent members of the Security Council. The Security Council veto, therefore, applies in selecting the secretary-general. His actual selection, however, really occurs outside the United Nations setting in official and sometimes unofficial consultations until a consensus is reached on a particular person. The selection of Norway's Trygve Lie as first secretary-general of the United Nations is a case in point. Since the prospective candidates of Moscow were unacceptable to Washington and those of Washington unacceptable to Moscow, compromise was necessary and agreement was finally reached on Lie. As he was a citizen of a state which was friendly to the Anglo-Americans, there appeared to be no reason for objection to his candidature from that quarter. To the Soviet Union, Lie's youthful and strong Marxist orientation and his seeming sympathy and sensitivity to its interests in northern Europe made him equally acceptable. In fact, it can be argued that during the early days of the United Nations Lie's actions, on the whole, were friendlier to the Soviet Union than they were to the United States and its allies. His support of the South Koreans following the North Korean attack in the summer of 1950, however, so infuriated the Soviet Union that Moscow would not agree to his reappointment as secretary-general for another five-year term.[18] The extension of Lie's contract by the General Assembly, against the Soviet Union's objections, was legally questionable but his continuance in office was in no way politically productive because Moscow refused to recognize or deal with him and, if we may borrow another phrase from George Orwell, considered him an un-person. Any secretary-general placed in a position of direct confrontation with a permanent member of the Security Council will expose himself to Lie's fate. He will be able to finish his contractual term, but his political value will be greatly diminished.

A similar fate befell Dag Hammarskjöld during his second term when his initiatives and activities during the Congo crisis were unacceptable to the Soviet Union. Hammarskjöld's interpretation of his office as somewhat akin to that of the president of the United States—namely, that the office contained certain implied powers and that this allowed him to undertake political initiatives—might be traced in part to his prior training and position as a senior civil servant of the Swedish government.[19] Certainly, however, in the Congo crisis as in other situations the support that he sought and received from the rapidly forming Afro-Asian bloc in the United Nations gave him a political base or constituency which permitted him to become involved in the substance of political questions more so than Trygve Lie.

The question that might be posed is whether the secretary-general's assumption of political initiatives is necessarily desirable. He could, of course, be considered an exceptionally situated actor in the international system like the bishop of Rome.[20] But the Hammarskjöld model which is uppermost in many people's minds is in fact the exception rather than the rule. In comparison with the others who have held the post Hammarskjöld was a very superior secretary-general. He was an unusual individual whose personal qualities are not likely to be found in most candidates for that high office. Indeed, selection of an individual to serve as secretary-general is based not on his intelligence or experience but on political expediency.

A miscalculation by a secretary-general can cause great harm. A good example of this is U Thant's abrupt withdrawal of the United Nations Emergency Force in Egypt prior to the 1967 Middle East conflict—an action for which he has been strongly criticized. One can ask whether so delicately balanced a world can afford uncontrolled political initiatives by a secretary-general and whether the good that he can do is not far outweighed by the harm that he can cause. Greater cooperation among the Great Powers inside the United Nations and especially in the Security Council will undoubtedly go far in limiting and directing the political endeavors of the secretary-general. His selection in the future, however, is no longer likely to be essentially a Security Council operation. If strongly opposed to a particular individual, the Afro-Asian states can probably mount a one-third blocking vote in the General Assembly. Thus Afro-Asian attitudes toward any future candidate will have to be taken into account by the permanent members of the Security Council even if they themselves agree on a particular candidate.

The political process of conflict resolution employing the political organs of the United Nations has been assisted by the continuing development of international law under the aegis of the world body and the varied economic and technical assistance programs mounted through the organization.

During the interwar period under the League of Nations there was a concerted effort both to develop and to codify international law. The establishment by the League of Nations of the Permanent Court of International Justice at The Hague, the cases that it adjudicated, and the advisory opinions that it rendered to the League, contributed in no small way to the development of international law. The establishment of international legal norms is important in governing inter-state relations. These legal norms are rights which states recognize exist, which they invoke, and which they admit they are obligated to observe. Their violation does not erase them anymore than an individual can erase municipal law by violating it. Indeed, like the individuals who violate municipal law, states do not claim they are above the law. They may defend their acts in various ways, but never on the grounds that international law does not exist or that it is not binding on them.

The process of developing international law has been given far greater impetus under the United Nations. Naturally, the task of establishing international law norms through the United Nations in what is a decentralized international system fragmented into well over one hundred units depends upon the range of agreement that can be secured within the system; or, to put it another way, it depends on the consensus that can be achieved among the states comprising the system.

Unfortunately, the division of the international community into two blocs during the years following World War II has hindered the process. To the Soviet Union and its allies many aspects of international law are unacceptable. Ideologically, they view it as a legal system which was largely developed during the capitalist period and hence tends to reflect and promote the values of that economic system.[21] Moreover, the process was further hindered by the proliferation of Afro-Asian states that entered the United Nations after 1955. Many of these Afro-Asian states view international law essentially as a group of legal norms devised by their former colonial masters to maintain and protect the status quo. As revolutionary states, they find this unacceptable since they are committed to overthrow the status quo in those non-Western areas still dominated by Western powers. These revolutionary Afro-Asian states, committed to the independence of other Afro-Asian Western-dominated areas and to sweeping social changes within these areas as well as in their own countries, by their very actions at first isolate themselves from other members of the world community.

After some years as independent states, there is a lessening of revolutionary fervor and the consolidation of internal power as well as economic development soon leads to an appreciation of the utility of international law as an instrument for regulating conduct between members of the world community. Something of a reversal soon sets in and the Afro-Asian states find themselves pragmatically—like the Soviet Union—invoking the norms of the very legal system that they at one time condemned.[22]

The United States has also hindered the development of international law by its sweeping reservation accepting the International Court of Justice's compulsory jurisdiction under Article 36, paragraph 2, of the Statute of the Court. According to the American reservation, the so-called Connally amendment, no dispute in which the United States is a party can come before the Court "with regard to matters which are essentially within the domestic jurisdiction of the United States as determined by the United States of America." Unfortunately, this reservation has set an example which has been followed by other states and has contributed to a political climate in which states have refused to take issues to the Court, thus reducing the use of the Court's facilities.

In spite of all this, the actions of the Security Council and especially those of the General Assembly and the latter's establishment of the International Law Commission, the work of the commission, and the Assembly's own resolutions and declarations, not to mention the cases adjudicated and the advisory opinions handed down by the International Court of Justice at The Hague, have contributed to the law's development.

The varied economic and technical assistance programs undertaken by the United Nations are no sudden departure from prior practice under the League.[23] Indeed, during the League's later years there was an attempt by the second secretary-general, Joseph Avenol, to concentrate the organization's activities on these programs and to attempt whenever possible to expand them. Avenol's approach was based on the mistaken notion that by depoliticizing the League and making it a great center for technical and economic cooperation it would entice back into the organization the important states that had already left it: Japan, Germany, and Italy.[24]

The difference, however, between the activities of the League and those of the United Nations in these economic and technical assistance programs is that they are far broader under the United Nations, more varied in content, deal with more states, and are coordinated with similar activities mounted by the specialized agencies founded after World War II. The League and United Nations programs in these fields also differ in one other respect. The nature and complexity of the United Nations programs involves the organization in far more direct administration than was the case under the League. This, in turn, partially explains the increase in the number of personnel in the United Nations Secretariat when compared with its League counterpart.

Just before World War II, the League was moving in the direction of expanding its nonpolitical activities. Without commenting on Avenol's notion of a depoliticized League, a committee established by the League Council and presided over by Stanley Bruce of Australia recommended not only that these economic and technical activities be expanded but that they be centered in a new organ which was to be responsible to the League

Assembly and called the Central Committee for Economic and Social Questions.[25]

The commencement of World War II only days after the Bruce Report was issued and the years of warfare that followed did not lead to the obliteration of the Bruce Report. Its recommendations were remembered and accepted by those who wrote the United Nations Charter. Many believed that the rise of anti–status quo states which led to World War II could in large measure be traced to the economic and social dislocation in those countries during the interwar years. Thus international arrangements which might assist in curbing or controlling these economic and social dislocations would be desirable. The end result was the establishment of the Economic and Social Council which carries out its duties under the auspices of the General Assembly. Alongside the Economic and Social Council were also established a host of specialized agencies, legally independent from the United Nations but closely allied to it, to handle certain specific areas of concern to the international community: world health, food and agriculture, postal matters, and so on.

Initially, these nonpolitical activities of the United Nations and the specialized agencies were of interest and concern only to the United States and its allies and were on the whole ignored by the Soviet Union. However, because of the increase after 1955 of member states that would obviously profit from the technical and economic assistance that might be rendered by and through the United Nations and the specialized agencies, Russian interest developed in these nonpolitical activities.[26]

This interest by the Soviet Union was largely an attempt to achieve propaganda advantages with the Afro-Asian states against the West and to proclaim to them the advantages of centralized Marxist planning for economic development as practiced in the Soviet Union. In time, increased Afro-Asian membership in the world organization saw a successful drive by these states to expand the membership of the Economic and Social Council in an attempt to control it and hence to channel more aid and assistance to them through the agency of the United Nations. Whereas before the nonpolitical activities of the United Nations had been split by the East-West conflict, now the demands of the Afro-Asian underdeveloped world have produced a split along a North-South axis. Since the increased aid and assistance programs that these states desire can be funded only by the more affluent Western states, a struggle has developed in which demands are made, programs devised, and attempts then made to acquire the necessary Western financial support to implement them. In dispensing technical and financial support, states are more likely to give assistance on a bilateral basis since from such agreements reciprocal political concessions are likely to accrue.

In fact, the expansion and proliferation of programs under the United Nations has neither been efficient nor has it led to rapid economic development. This is due in large measure to the unrealistic expectations placed on international technical and financial assistance programs. Much of the

United Nations' work in this field comprises feasibility studies, resource surveys, and so on. This is not to say that successes in such programs have not been achieved, programs completed, and invaluable assistance rendered. But, at most, these programs can only marginally assist an underdeveloped state in developing economically and thus socially. In large measure, economic development must be based on internal forces and actions. The mixed successes achieved should not, however, make us lose sight of the fact that certain nonpolitical problems can be approached only within an international context. The questions of pollution and overpopulation or of trade restrictions, for example, obviously fall into this category. Even if political considerations may be a factor in some of these problems, certainly an attack upon them is best mounted through the economic, social, and technical facilities offered by the United Nations and the specialized agencies.

As one reads the following essays, one will be struck by the adaptive qualities of the United Nations and its ability to adjust to a changing international context. It has survived the worst days of the cold war and gone on to accommodate itself with the influx of the Afro-Asian states to drastic changes in composition and character. Indeed, the most startling transformation that the organization has gone through has been the increase in membership during the last decade and a half. The impact of the Afro-Asians continues and has touched almost every facet of the organization's work. This has produced unavoidable strains and tensions, but it has also produced a United Nations which is truly international and more reflective of the forces and desires of the world community. How the Afro-Asian states will affect the United Nations in the future is hard to say. But no one will deny that they have a role to play in the world organization. There is the likelihood, however, that their seeming unity in the world body will be disrupted and that competing blocs will be formed, especially as they develop economically and the enthusiasm for independence subsides. If this should occur, new configurations will form within the United Nations and a new period of activity will commence for all its organs.

James Barros

NOTES

1. UN Charter, Article 2, paragraph 1.
2. *Ibid.*, Article 2, paragraph 7.
3. League of Nations Covenant, Article 15, paragraph 8. On this point see Leland M. Goodrich, "The United Nations and Domestic Jurisdiction," *International Organization,* III, No. 1 (February 1949), 14–28.
4. UN Charter, Article 2, paragraph 4.
5. For a discussion see Leland M. Goodrich, Edvard Hambro, and Anne Simons, *Charter of the United Nations: Commentary and Documents,* 3rd rev. ed. (New York: Columbia University Press, 1969), pp. 43–55.
6. Leland M. Goodrich, "From League of Nations to United Nations," *International Organization,* I, No. 1 (February 1947), 3–21. See also Leo

Gross, "The Charter of the United Nations and the Lodge Reservations," *American Journal of International Law,* XLI, No. 3 (July 1947), 531–554.

7. UN Charter, Article 24, paragraph 1.

8. Sydney D. Bailey, *Voting in the Security Council* (Bloomington: Indiana University Press, 1969), pp. 27–32.

9. UN Charter, Article 23, paragraph 1.

10. *Ibid.,* Article 108.

11. Goodrich, Hambro, and Simons, *Charter of United Nations,* pp. 641–642.

12. Dean Acheson, *Present at the Creation: My Years in the State Department* (New York: Norton, 1969), p. 450.

13. For a discussion of the Uniting for Peace Resolution, see Inis L. Claude, Jr., *Swords into Plowshares,* 4th ed. (New York: Random House, 1971), pp. 268–272; Goodrich, Hambro, and Simons, *Charter of United Nations* pp. 122–125; Leland M. Goodrich, *The United Nations* (New York: Crowell, 1959), pp. 178–181.

14. Sydney D. Bailey, "The Troika and the Future of the United Nations," *International Conciliation,* No. 538 (1962).

15. UN Charter, Article 4, paragraph 1.

16. Walter Bagehot, *The English Constitution* (Ithaca, N.Y.: Cornell University Press, 1966), pp. 151–152.

17. James Barros, *The Corfu Incident of 1923: Mussolini and the League of Nations* (Princeton: Princeton University Press, 1965); James Barros, *The Aland Islands Question: Its Settlement by the League of Nations* (New Haven: Yale University Press, 1968); James Barros, *The League of Nations and the Great Powers: The Greek-Bulgarian Incident, 1925* (Oxford: Clarendon Press, 1970); and James Barros, *Betrayal from Within: Joseph Avenol, Secretary-General of the League of Nations, 1933–1940* (New Haven: Yale University Press, 1969).

18. James Barros, "Trygve Lie: De Mortuis nil nisi bonum," *International Journal,* XXV, No. 2 (Spring 1970), 405–413.

19. Prior to his appointment as secretary-general, Hammarskjöld had served as undersecretary in the Ministry of Finance and undersecretary as well as secretary-general in the Ministry of Foreign Affairs. In 1951 he was appointed deputy foreign minister. According to one student of the Swedish constitutional system, the "undersecretaries are the highest officials in each department immediately under the minister, and the law itself defines their function as 'political.'" Dankwart A. Rustow, *The Politics of Compromise: A Study of Parties and Cabinet Government in Sweden* (Princeton: Princeton University Press, 1955), p. 176. See also Neil C. M. Elder, *Government in Sweden* (Oxford: Pergamon Press, 1970), pp. 81–87.

20. J. David Murphy, "The Papacy and the Secretary-Generalship: A Study of the Role of the Exceptionally-Situated Individual in the International System," *Co-Existence,* VII, 165–181.

21. See Oliver J. Lissitzyn, "International Law in a Divided World," *International Conciliation,* No. 542 (1963).

22. *Ibid.;* Richard A. Falk, "Revolutionary Nations and the Quality of International Legal Order," in Morton A. Kaplan (ed.), *The Revolution in World Politics* (New York: John Wiley, 1962), pp. 310–331.

23. Arthur Sweetser, "The Non-Political Achievements of the League," *Foreign Affairs,* XIX, No. 1 (October 1940), 179–192.

24. Barros, *Betrayal from Within,* p. 146 and passim.

25. League of Nations, *League of Nations Publications, General 1939,* No. 3.

26. Alvin Z. Rubinstein, *The Soviets in International Organizations: Changing Policy Toward Developing Countries, 1953–1963* (Princeton: Princeton University Press, 1964); Harold K. Jacobson, *The USSR and the UN's Economic and Social Activities* (Notre Dame: University of Notre Dame Press, 1963).

Leland M. Goodrich

THE UN SECURITY COUNCIL

That the United Nations has been conspicuously unsuccessful in the performance of its principal task, the maintenance of international peace and security, is a widely accepted view. That this view is so commonly held and with so much apparent justification becomes particularly serious in its implications when we consider that when the Charter was written it was the promised effectiveness of the new organization in maintaining international peace and security, in contrast to the discredited League of Nations, that was made a principal argument in its support. It was emphasized that the new organization, by virtue of its power to take military measures, if necessary, to enforce its will, had a capacity for effective action which the League had lacked. The Security Council was the specific organ which by virtue of its composition and powers gave to the new organization its promise of greater effectiveness in saving "succeeding generations from the scourge of war." [1]

The primacy of the peace and security function of the United Nations and the Security Council's special responsibility for its discharge give a special importance to the analysis of the role of that organ in the work of the United Nations and its promise for the future. What was the original thinking of those who wrote the Charter on the organization of international peace and security? How did they justify vesting in an organ with the composition, voting procedure, and powers of the Security Council the primary responsibility for the maintenance of peace? Was not the requirement of the concurrence of the permanent members in all decisions on nonprocedural questions an invitation to deadlock and futility, given the likely development of relations among major allies after victory had been attained? What, in fact, has been the Council's record during the past twenty-five years? Has its role in the organization greatly changed? What have been the factors contributing to this development? What of the future? These are some of the questions that we need to consider in formulating our conclusions on the past, present, and future of this much publicized and much criticized organ of the United Nations.

THE CHARTER PRESCRIPTION FOR
PEACE AND SECURITY

The peace and security provisions of the Charter, which have their organizational focus in the Security Council, were initially prepared and adopted under the influence of the League experience, the events leading up to World War II, and the experience of the war itself.

Considerations Influencing the Charter Makers

Under the Covenant of the League of Nations, members undertook not to "resort to war" under specified conditions and to utilize methods of peaceful settlement.[2] The Council, with limited membership—permanent members plus nonpermanent members elected by the Assembly—was given broad powers to discuss and recommend action with respect to any matter "affecting the peace of the world." [3] No effort was made to differentiate the overall responsibilities of the Council from those of the Assembly. Each member had the duty to apply economic and financial sanctions against any state resorting to war in violation of its Covenant obligations.[4] The individual member had the responsibility for deciding whether this act had been committed. In sum, the League system of collective security was based on the legal commitment of each member state to apply sweeping economic and financial sanctions against the aggressor and an additional, less clearly defined commitment to adopt military measures, if necessary, to preserve the political independence and territorial integrity of members against external aggression.[5] The Council was to serve as an organ of mediation and conciliation and, in the case of aggression, might recommend measures, including military, to be taken by members. The rule of unanimity was generally followed in its decisions.[6]

From the experience of the interwar period, the drafters of the Charter appear to have concluded that the League system, as conceived and as it developed in practice, had shown deficiencies that needed to be remedied in the new organization.[7] The League had never become a truly universal organization and suffered particularly from the absence of the United States. While those initially responsible for the drafting of the Covenant clearly had in mind that the Council should assume a special responsibility for the prevention of war, in actual practice, for a variety of reasons including the absence of the United States and the failure of the United Kingdom and France to harmonize their policies, this result was not consistently achieved. To be sure, the Council rather than the Assembly was the League organ to which recourse was normally had in any specific situation where peaceful relations were endangered. However, the Council's effectiveness was greatly reduced by the absence of major powers. Furthermore, as the number of nonpermanent members was increased from the original four to eleven, the attractiveness of the Council to the major powers that were members of it and its value to them for considering vital questions of peace and war declined.

A most serious deficiency of the League system, in the opinion of many observers, was the highly legalistic and unrealistic nature of its sanctions arrangements. The unreality of the League system became particularly apparent after the United States refused to join. Members saw the need to substantially reduce their commitment to apply economic and financial sanctions. The need to coordinate the individual actions of members was also recognized.[8] However, the Covenant did not give either Council or Assembly power to order effective coordination. Furthermore, even though members recognized the legal commitment to apply economic and financial sanctions, their obligation to take military measures, if necessary to defeat aggression, was at most a moral one. The Council's authority was limited to recommendation only. As the experience with sanctions against Italy[9] showed, economic and financial sanctions may depend for their effectiveness upon the likelihood, if not certainty, that military measures will be taken if necessary. Furthermore, the Italian experience pointed to the practical difficulty of making sanctions effective against a major power without a major war, and the need in any case of having the full cooperation of all other major powers in such an undertaking.

The experience of the years immediately preceding the outbreak of World War II yielded still another lesson that was seriously taken to heart by the drafters of the Charter. The Covenant had stressed disarmament—the agreed reduction and limitation of national armaments—as an independent road to world peace.[10] The record of the League in actually achieving results was negative.[11] Nevertheless, partially as the result of limited agreements reached outside the League and the strength of demands within many countries that armaments should be reduced, the challenge offered by regimes openly basing their aggressive policies on readiness to use armed force was not met in timely fashion. As a result, it came to be widely believed that peace depended upon the availability of armaments to keep the peace even more than upon the limitation and reduction of armaments that might be used to disturb the peace. This line of thought supported and strengthened the conclusion that the major "peace-loving" military powers had a special responsibility for keeping the peace and that this principle should be implemented in the constitution of the new organization.

Finally, the war itself created a situation in which with some justification the major victors could lay claim to having a special responsibility. The fact that the mobilization and use of their superior military power had been necessary to defeat Axis aggression pointed to the need of having their military forces available to keep the peace after the war was over, particularly since there was an understandable inclination at the time to see future threats to and violations of the peace as coming from the same sources as in the immediate past and present. Furthermore, the fact that the defeat of the Axis powers had only been possible as the result of cooperation between the United States, the United Kingdom, and the Soviet Union emphasized the need for basing a future peace organization on the cooperation of those countries.

The procedure by which the Charter was prepared as well as the facts of international life gave assurance that the peace and security provisions of the Charter would reflect the special interests of the major powers and would be based upon a full recognition of the importance of the power factor in international relations. The initial preparatory work was done in the United States Department of State[12] where a draft plan was prepared which was submitted to the governments of the United Kingdom, the Soviet Union, and the Republic of China, and was accepted by them as the basis for the discussions at Dumbarton Oaks in the summer and early fall of 1944.[13] The Dumbarton Oaks Proposals,[14] representing the agreement of the four participating governments, with some additions, were submitted to the participants in the San Francisco Conference and were accepted as the basis of the discussions there. The work of the San Francisco Conference, from beginning to end, was governed by the basic principle that any proposal which was unacceptable to the major powers—the permanent-members-to-be of the Security Council—would not be adopted, as their membership in the organization was considered essential.[15]

The Charter provisions relating to peace and security, and particularly those having to do with the responsibilities, functions, powers, membership, and procedure of the Security Council, are to be understood and judged in the light of these considerations.

Charter Provisions on Structure and Role of Security Council

The Charter lists the maintenance of international peace and security as the first purpose of the organization.[16] It prescribes two principal approaches to the achievement of this purpose: collective measures for preventing or removing threats to the peace and suppressing acts of aggression and breaches of the peace; and adjustment or settlement of international disputes or situations by peaceful means. The regulation of armaments is made a subsidiary approach, to be undertaken after the effectiveness of the system of peace enforcement has been assured by the placing of necessary armed forces and facilities at the disposal of the Security Council. One declared purpose of the regulation of armaments is stated to be "the least diversion for armaments of the world's human and economic resources," [17] consistent with the requirements of international peace and security.

The primary responsibility for the maintenance of international peace and security is placed on the Security Council.[18] Until amended in 1965, the Charter provided that the Security Council should consist of five permanent members and six other members elected by the General Assembly for two-year terms, three members being elected each year.[19] The names of the five permanent members were listed in the Charter, thus introducing an element of rigidity that did not exist in the case of the League Council.[20] The principle professedly followed in determining the permanent members was that those members of the organization who had made major contributions to the winning of the war and who consequently would be expected to make the major contributions to keeping the peace should be in position to exercise corresponding influence on substantive decisions of the Council.[21] Clearly, however, other considerations than these dictated the inclusion of France and the Republic of China, neither of whom, at the time the Charter was written, gave promise of having this capability in the near future.[22]

Following the League precedent, it was decided at San Francisco that there should be nonpermanent members of the Security Council elected by the General Assembly. When the Covenant was being drafted in Paris at the end of World War I, initial plans called for a Council limited in membership to the Principal Allied and Associated Powers,[23] following the practice of the European Concert. Strong opposition to this proposal, reflecting the view that it did not give recognition to the legitimate interests and possible contributions of the smaller powers, led to the adoption of a plan under which the Council would be composed of five permanent members, and four nonpermanent members elected by the Assembly.[24] In drafting the Charter, the principle of nonpermanent membership to give the smaller states representation and assured participation in the work of the Security Council was readily accepted. Roosevelt and Churchill had played with the idea of a great power directorate, but in Department of State planning and in the intergovernmental discussions from Dumbarton Oaks on this idea was not seriously considered. At San Francisco, however, there was strong support for introducing into the Charter some criteria for guidance of the General Assembly in the election of nonpermanent members to assure representation of the "middle powers," those members whose contributions to the work of the United Nations in the maintenance of peace could be expected to be substantial, though less than that of the permanent members of the Council. To satisfy this demand, an amendment to the Dumbarton Oaks Proposals was adopted providing that "due regard" shall be "specially paid" by the General Assembly, in the exercise of its electoral function, "in the first instance to the contribution of Members of the United Nations to the maintenance of international peace and security and to the other purposes of the Organization, and also to equitable geographical distribution." [25]

The powers given to the Security Council under the Charter were considered sufficiently extensive to permit it to effectively discharge its primary responsibility for the maintenance of international peace and security. Furthermore, an effort was also made to so define and differentiate these powers from the more general and less coercive powers of the General Assembly as to make it clear that the Security Council was not only to take initial action but also to take exclusive action in some areas. This differentiation between the responsibilities and powers of the two organs was regarded as one of the strengths of the new organization. By this means what was thought to be one of the serious defects of the League— the lack of a clear placing of responsibility—was to be remedied.

The powers given the Security Council are set forth in general terms in Article 24 of the Charter which provides that "in order to ensure prompt and effective action by the United Nations, its Members confer on the Security Council primary responsibility for the maintenance of international peace and security, and agree that in carrying out its duties under this responsibility the Security Council acts on their behalf." The same article provides that in discharging its duties the Council shall act in accordance with "the Purposes and Principles" of the United Nations. The paragraph further provides that the specific powers granted for the discharge of these duties are laid down in Chapters VI, VII, VIII, and XII of the Charter.

At San Francisco an attempt was made by some delegates from smaller states to place additional restrictions upon the Security Council in the discharge of its responsibilities either by defining in greater detail the circumstances under which it was to exercise powers of enforcement action or by giving the General Assembly power to review any action of the Security Council and hold it to account for failing to perform its duties properly. All of these efforts were in vain as the Sponsoring Governments and France insisted upon vesting in the Council wide discretionary powers which could be exercised subject only to a factual report to the General Assembly.[26]

In addition to the powers vested in the Council by Article 24 and Chapters VI, VII, VIII, and XII of the Charter, the Charter gives to the Security Council certain additional powers, chiefly of a constituent character, relating indirectly to the maintenance of peace. Under Article 4, the admission of new members to the organization is made conditional upon the recommendation of the Security Council. This contrasts with the Covenant provision which gave the Assembly exclusive power to admit new members.[27] The Charter association of the Council with the General Assembly in the admission of new members was based on the ground that an important condition of membership was the willingness and ability of the state in question to carry out the obligations of membership in the maintenance of peace and security. Furthermore, the rights and privileges of a member can be suspended by the General Assembly only on the recommendation of the Security Council.[28] Also, the Security Council's recommendation is similarly required for the expulsion of a member for persistent violation of the "Principles" of the Charter.[29] Due to the responsibilities given to the secretary-general in connection with the maintenance of peace and security, his appointment by the General Assembly is made conditional on the recommendation of the Security Council.[30] The League Covenant provided that the secretary-general be appointed by the Council with the approval of the Assembly.[31] At San Francisco there was some insistence on the part of the smaller states that the secretary-general should be elected by the General Assembly. The Sponsoring Governments and France, however, insisted that in the light of his increased powers in the peace and security field it was important that he have the confidence of the major powers, and that therefore the Security Council should be associated with the General Assembly in his appointment.

The same reasoning does not explain the provision of the Statute of the International Court of Justice (ICJ) which gives the Security Council a concurrent role with the General Assembly in the election of judges.[32] This arrangement was originally adopted in the drafting of the Statute of the Permanent Court of International Justice, the predecessor of the ICJ, as a means of harmonizing the conflicting claims of the large and small states which had blocked the establishment of a court at The Hague Conference of 1907. It had worked satisfactorily in practice and was adopted at San Francisco without discussion.

The powers of the Security Council in dealing with disputes and situations which may endanger the maintenance of international peace and security are the logical consequence of the "primary responsibility" conferred under Article 24. The specific powers given the Council by Chapters VI and VII [33] can be conveniently grouped under two heads: those powers that the organ may exercise for the purpose of bringing about a peaceful settlement or adjustment of a dispute or situation, and those which the Council may exercise for the purpose of maintaining or restoring international peace and security once there is a threat to the peace or a breach of the peace. Under the first heading, the Charter gives the Security Council a range of specific powers that it may exercise with respect to any dispute or situation likely to lead to international friction submitted to it by a member or nonmember state. It may, in the first instance, when a particular dispute or situation has been brought to its attention, conduct an investigation to determine whether it is sufficiently serious to endanger the maintenance of international peace and security.[34] If it finds that the continuance of the dispute is likely to endanger international peace, it may call upon the parties to settle their dispute by peaceful means in accordance with their undertakings under Article 2, paragraph 3, and Article 33 of the Charter. Additionally, the Council may recommend proper procedures or methods of adjustment, taking into account any procedures that the parties have already agreed to and also taking into consideration that legal disputes should generally be referred to the International Court of Justice.[35] Should the parties to the dispute fail to settle it by means of their own choice, the Council may recommend such terms of settlement as it may consider appropriate.[36] If the Council finds that the dispute is of a local nature which could most appropriately be settled by a regional agency, it shall encourage the parties to follow that course without, however, impairing its right to consider the matter if the parties so request.[37]

When a dispute or situation assumes a serious character with one or more of the parties involved threatening to use force, or actually engaged in doing so, or when there is thought to be a danger that a violation of the peace will occur, the Council may determine the existence of a "threat to the peace, breach of the peace or act of aggression," [38] and proceed to deal with the critical matter in such manner as it may decide is most appropriate, with three broad alternative courses of action open to it. These may be followed in any order or combination that the Council decides.[39] First of all, by the terms of Article 39 of the Charter, it may make recommendations to the parties. Normally, they would be made under Chapter VI for the purpose of achieving some peaceful settlement or accommodation. If there has been some threatening movement of armed forces or an actual military attack or some action that is likely to lead to the worsening of the situation, the Council may call upon the parties to adopt provisional measures with a view to preventing any aggravation of the situation.[40] Such provisional measures are adopted without prejudicing the rights or position of the parties, though any failure of one or both of the parties to accept and carry out such measures may be taken into account by the Council in determining its subsequent course of action.

In a situation of flagrant aggression where the time factor is important, the Security Council may decide that, instead of adopting either of these alternatives, it is necessary to proceed immediately to the use of collective measures of coercion under Articles 41 and 42 for the purpose of restraining the aggression and restoring peace and security. The measures that the Security Council may order range from the interruption of economic relations and the severance of diplomatic relations under Article 41 to the use of air, sea, and land forces under Article 42. Decisions taken by the Council under either of these articles are binding upon member states though the obligation to use military measures under Article 42 is dependent upon the conclusion of special agreements under Article 43 between the Security Council and member states, by which members undertake to place at the disposal of the Council specific forces and facilities. While the language of certain articles[41] would give some support to the view that decisions under Article 42 are binding in the absence of special agreements, Article 106 makes it clear that the binding force of Council decisions to use military measures is dependent upon the conclusion of such agreements and this interpretation has been accepted in practice.[42]

In addition to authorizing the Council to deal with disputes and situations endangering the peace, the Charter recognizes that the maintenance of international peace and security will be facilitated by regulating the level of national armaments. The Security Council is responsible for formulating, with the assistance of the Military Staff Committee, plans for "the establishment of a system for the regulation of armaments" to be submitted to the members of the organization for their acceptance.[43] However, the Security Council is not the only organ which has responsibilities in connection with disarmament since the General Assembly is also authorized under the Charter to discuss "the principles governing disarmament and the regulation of armaments," and to make recommendations to the member states and to the Council.[44]

In the exercise of its powers under the Charter, the Security Council takes its decisions by qualified majority votes. Here again the Charter departs in a significant respect from the Covenant which provided that decisions, not only of the Council but also of the Assembly, should be taken by unanimous vote. In an attempt to get away from the principle of unanimity which had been a serious obstacle in certain instances to decisions by the League, while at the same time safeguarding the rights of the major powers, the authors of the Charter provided that all decisions on nonprocedural matters should be taken by a majority of seven affirmative votes with the concurrence of the permanent members.[45] The only exception made to this rule was that, in any decisions taken under Chapter VI relating to the peaceful settlement of disputes, the parties to the dispute should abstain from voting. Decisions on procedural questions, however, did not require the concurrence of the permanent members and could be taken by seven affirmative votes without any special requirement as to the composition of this majority.[46]

At San Francisco this formula for determining the Security Council's voting procedure—which had been agreed to by President Roosevelt, Prime Minister Churchill, and Premier Stalin at Yalta—came under attack on the ground that it gave to the permanent members of the Security Council an excessive influence over decisions of that organ. There was little inclination to question the propriety of requiring the agreement of the permanent members for decisions under Chapter VII on "preventive or enforcement action" but there was widespread sentiment that the right of veto should not apply to decisions taken under Chapter VI for the peaceful settlement of disputes. In spite of strong insistence on the part of the smaller states that the requirement of great power concurrence should be restricted in its application, the Sponsoring Governments and France firmly adhered to the position that it should apply to all nonprocedural decisions of the Council. In a statement presented to the conference by the Sponsoring Governments and France,[47] which was not, however, approved by the Conference, this interpretation was based upon the theory that all steps, from the decision to carry out an investigation down to the decision to take military measures, constituted one continuous chain of events, and that each decision in this chain of events had possible consequences which justified the requirement of concurrence of the permanent members all along the line. Furthermore, in this statement it was made clear that the question of whether a particular matter was procedural or substantive should be treated as a substantive question, likewise requiring the concurrence of the permanent members. This is the basis of the "double veto."

While the voting formula and the five-power statement of interpretation related primarily to the exercise of the Council's powers under Chapters VI, VII, VIII, and XII of the Charter, it was also decided at San Francisco that decisions of the Council in connection with membership and the appointment of the secretary-general should also require permanent member agreement. Only in the case of the election of judges to the International Court of Justice was it expressly provided that a different voting procedure should be followed. In this case the Statute of the Court specifies that an absolute majority is sufficient, "without any distinction between permanent and non-permanent members." [48]

As indicated above, one of the lessons which the authors of the Charter professed to have learned from the experience of the League was the desirability of distinguishing more clearly than had been done under the Covenant between the functions and powers of various organs. Under the Charter, quasi-executive functions and powers of the kind normally considered appropriate for organs of limited membership were divided between three councils—namely, the Security Council, the Economic and Social Council, and the Trusteeship Council. In the case of the Economic and Social Council and the Trusteeship Council, the significance of the attempted differentiation of their powers and functions from those of the General Assembly was reduced by the provision that the powers of the two councils were to be exercised under the authority of the General Assembly.[49]

In the case of the Security Council, however, any such subordination to the General Assembly was strongly and successfully resisted by the Sponsoring Governments and France. Furthermore, these governments emphasized the need to distinguish by specific provisions between the responsibilities and powers of the Security Council and the General Assembly in the maintenance of international peace and security. This process was carried quite far in the proposals submitted by the United States to the Dumbarton Oaks conferees and in the Dumbarton Oaks Proposals. At San Francisco, however, there was some blurring of the lines of differentiation as a result of demands made by the smaller states and the willingness of certain major powers, especially the United States and the United Kingdom, to accede in some degree to these demands.[50] As a result, the language of the Charter is not in all respects clear and has provided the basis for later efforts on the part of some members to expand the role of the General Assembly at the expense of the Security Council and, in effect, to use the General Assembly as a means of circumventing the consequences of the failure of the permanent members to reach agreement in the Council.

While the responsibilities of the Security Council appear to be quite clearly defined by the Charter, and in great detail, the General Assembly is also given powers that are quite broad and comprehensive in scope. Thus, under Article 11, the Assembly may consider the general principles of cooperation in the maintenance of international peace and security and may make recommendations with regard to such principles to member states or to the Security Council, or to both. Furthermore, under the same article, the Assembly may discuss any questions relative to the maintenance of international peace and security brought before it by any member or nonmember or by the Security Council, and may make recommendations with regard to such questions to the state or states concerned, to the Security Council, or to both. Also, the Assembly may call to the attention of the Security Council any situation which it deems likely to endanger international peace and security. Under Article 14 the Assembly may recommend measures for the peaceful adjustment of any situation, regardless of origin, which it deems likely to impair the general welfare or friendly relations among nations and under Article 10 it may discuss "any questions or any matters within the scope of the present Charter or relating to the powers and functions of any organs provided for in the present Charter," and may make recommendations to members, to the Security Council, or to both.

These broad powers, however, are subject to one implied limitation and two specific limitations. The implied limitation results from the specific conferring of primary responsibility for the maintenance of international peace and security on the Security Council.[51] This is further refined by the provisions of Chapters VI, VII, and VIII of the Charter directed explicitly to the Security Council. The specific limitations are that the General Assembly may not make any recommendations with respect to any dispute or situation while the Security Council is exercising its functions under the Charter,[52] and must refer to the Security Council any question on which "action is necessary," either before or after discussion.[53] However, these limitations leave certain important questions unanswered. For example, when does a dispute or situation cease to be before the Security Council for the performance of its functions, what constitutes "action," and, more basically, does the granting of "primary responsibility" to the Security Council permit the exercise by the General Assembly of a residual responsibility, or is it to be understood as exclusive in nature? These uncertainties provided the opportunity for subsequent major disagreements among members and provided an opening by which the role of the General Assembly was developed at the expense of the Security Council in later years.

DEVELOPMENT OF THE SECURITY COUNCIL'S ROLE

The Charter provisions on the role of the Security Council—its composition, responsibilities, and powers—were based on the experience of the past. As so often happens in planning for the future, the Charter system was conceived to deal with the problems of peace and war which the world had faced during the preceding couple of decades, and the methods proposed were those which the experience of those years seemed to indicate as most effective. The Charter implied no prophesy that the conditions necessary to the effectiveness of its peace and security provisions would actually come to pass; rather, it was a blueprint of an organization which at one and the same time was generally acceptable and gave promise of being effective. Given the war experience and assuming the common interest of all Allied governments in avoiding another major world conflict, there was, perhaps, some reason to believe that the conditions necessary to the effectiveness of the proposed organization would materialize. However, the representatives of governments who met at San Francisco were aware of the fact that in the past great powers had tended to pull apart once victory had been achieved by their common efforts. Many at the Conference were deeply troubled by the fear that history would repeat itself and that the best laid plans would fall apart.

Factors Influencing Development of Council's Role

Like all constitutions written by people without the gift of detailed prophesy and acting to meet the pressing needs of the day, the Charter of the United Nations was destined to become with the passing of time an increasingly inadequate description of the organization that developed in response to the changing needs, the changing interests of members, and the many pressures exercised within and upon it. The conditions which influenced the development of the organization, and the Security Council in particular, have been varied in nature. First of all, the Council, as the responsible organ for dealing with questions of peace and security, has inevitably been responsive to the state of international relations at any given time. More particularly, tensions and disagreements among nations have not only created the atmosphere in which the Council has functioned but have also provided it with the problems with which it has had to deal.

At San Francisco it was emphasized that the United Nations was not an organization to make the peace, but rather an organization to keep the peace once peace had been made by those powers primarily responsible for winning the war. It was also understood, and made clear in the Charter, that the responsibility for dealing with the defeated enemy powers until the time of their acceptance into the family of nations rested with the victors and not with the United Nations itself.[54] Consequently, the Security Council was not called upon to deal with the problems relating to the establishment of peace after the war, such as the disposition of territories belonging to the defeated Axis powers. Notwithstanding, the Security Council has not escaped the consequences of an unsettled world following the war and, more particularly, the failure of the major victors to agree upon the terms of peace settlements with the major enemy nations—especially Germany. Probably no one aspect of the postwar international situation has had a more restrictive effect on the work of the United Nations and the role of the Security Council in particular than the failure of the Allied powers to reach any agreement on the resolution of the German problem.

It has commonly been stated that the ineffectiveness of the Security Council has been primarily due to the failure of the permanent members to agree. There is no question that this failure of the permanent members to cooperate more closely was an important and decisive factor in limiting the range of effective action of that organ and in crippling it in the discharge of some of its major responsibilities. This lack of cooperation found its principal expression in the "cold war" which brought the Soviet Union and the Western powers into deep conflict. Though given a highly ideological caste, this conflict was fundamentally due to the rivalry of great military powers, with their own particular national goals and security interests, and though possessing a common interest in peace and security, not having sufficient confidence in each other's motives and good faith to make working cooperation possible.[55]

At San Francisco there had been some ground for hope that such confidence and mutual trust would develop. Nevertheless, there were plenty of indications during the conference that the limited cooperation of the war period was very fragile. Even before the conference was over, but above all during the months following the conference, misunderstandings arose which served to revive and deepen the distrust and hostility which had previously existed. From the first meeting of the Security Council in January 1946 when the question of Soviet military presence in Iran was brought up for discussion, the complete failure of East and West to have any confidence in the good faith and good intentions of each other was clearly manifested. The Iranian move was viewed by the Soviet Union as a Western attack upon it and the subsequent Soviet initiatives in bringing to the attention of the Security Council the British military presence in Greece and Indonesia only added fuel to the flame of misunderstanding and distrust. By 1947 the cold war was well in progress, to reach its maximum intensity in the late forties and early fifties. The by-product of this was the use of the veto by the Soviet Union to defeat those Western initiatives which it considered a threat to its national interests and to gain propaganda advantages wherever possible. The role of the Security Council, as defined in the Charter, was bound to suffer as a result of this use of it as a forum for conducting the cold war instead of for purposes of cooperation.

Another factor influencing the development of the Security Council's role has been the expansion that has taken place in the United Nations membership, including changes in the geographical distribution of membership and the nature of the interests and attitudes of the new members. The organization started with a membership of fifty-one, predominantly Western and primarily concerned with issues of war and peace, particularly problems resulting from the dislocations of the war. During this early period, while the cold war had the effect of seriously limiting the possibilities of using the Security Council and of creating strong pressures to transfer questions from the Security Council to the General Assembly, it did, nevertheless, focus attention on the importance of the responsibilities of the Security Council and provided a constant reminder that the primary purpose of the organization was the maintenance of peace and security.

Once the membership deadlock was broken in 1955,[56] a major influx of new members occurred, mostly from Asia and Africa. Increasingly, the membership came to be dominated by new states with different backgrounds and concerns than those of the original members. Under the impact of the membership explosion, questions of decolonization, economic development of underdeveloped territories, and elimination of racial discrimination came to be the principal concerns of the organization.[57] Since these questions come within areas for which the Security Council does not have the primary responsibility, the effect has been to reduce the relative importance of its role in the organization.

On the other hand, this membership expansion, accompanied as it has been by a great increase in the number of uncommitted members, not allied to either party to the cold war, has made the General Assembly a somewhat less attractive forum for cold war propaganda and has produced an Assembly which is less easy for a major power to influence and control. As a consequence, permanent members themselves, and particularly the United States and the Soviet Union, have shown less interest of late in having questions of peace and security come before the General Assembly for discussion and have used their influence to bring about greater use of the Security Council.

The role of the Security Council in the work of the organization has been largely determined by the attitudes of member states. To a large extent, these attitudes reflect what the members have to gain or lose from having particular questions in which they are interested brought before that organ. The government of a member state, if it decides that a question should be brought before the United Nations, must also decide whether the Security Council is to be preferred to the General Assembly or vice versa as an organ of United Nations action. We have already noted that the major victors in the last war agreed at San Francisco that questions relating to the terms of settlement to be imposed on the defeated enemy states should be handled by them alone, and with few exceptions they have adhered to this position. In other words, the permanent members by and large have not felt free, or that it was in their interest, to bring such questions as aspects of the German problem to the attention of the Security Council. The Berlin blockade was an exception but it was an exception that proves the rule. Furthermore, there has been a reluctance on the part of states to bring to the Security Council questions where there seems to be no likelihood of any useful result. Thus in 1947 the Korean question was brought to the General Assembly by the United States, partly because the administration was convinced there was a possibility of getting the necessary majority support for its program in that body, but also because the discussions that had previously taken place between the United States and the Soviet Union had convinced it that the Security Council would not be able to take any decision acceptable to it. In the case of other members of the organization similar considerations have applied. Thus the members that have been particularly interested in bringing about the independence of non-self-governing territories have usually brought questions of this

kind to the General Assembly. Only exceptionally, as in the case of Indonesia in 1946 and Tunis and Morocco at a later time, have such questions
been brought to the Security Council. It has been done when the General
Assembly is not in session and the time element is considered important
or because, as in the case of Southern Rhodesia, the Security Council is
the only organ in the position to take the kind of action desired.

Finally, the development of the Security Council's role has been
influenced by the nature of the international problems with which governments have been concerned. During the past decade and a half, governments have come to be particularly concerned with the problems of economic development, with the elimination of social injustices, and with
problems of a highly technical nature resulting from the development of
modern technology. These questions, by and large, lay outside the proper
scope of the Security Council's competence. In terms of meetings held,
memoranda prepared, reports produced, and money spent, they have
come to occupy a much larger place in the total work of the organization
than problems of peace and security. This is not to suggest that, even in
a world concerned with these problems, so long as serious conflicts such
as that in the Middle East continue, the work of the Security Council is
not important. And the frequent meetings of the Council to consider aspects of the Middle East situation as well as other areas of tension testify
to the continued importance of its work. Nevertheless, it is of some significance that, from the point of view of the majority of member governments,
it is not the Security Council that is the center of their attention but, rather,
the General Assembly and the multitude of subsidiary organs and agencies
it has spawned.

Membership of the Council

Since the names of the permanent members of the Council are listed in
Article 23 of the Charter, no change has been possible without formal
amendment of the Charter. This has not been attempted though the question has arisen in the minds of many interested observers as to whether
some modification of the permanent membership will not become necessary when Japan assumes more fully the responsibilities of power which
are implicit in its remarkable economic recovery since the war, and when
Germany finally becomes a member of the organization.

While legally not entailing any change in the membership of the
organization or the permanent membership of the Security Council, the
decision of the General Assembly on October 25, 1971, to restore the
"rights" of the People's Republic of China had political significance comparable to a membership decision. By its resolution the Assembly recognized the representatives of the Government of the People's Republic "as
the only legitimate representatives of China to the United Nations." [58]

The question of Chinese representation was first raised in the Security Council in December 1949 and, in the years following, was a perennial item on the agenda of the General Assembly.[59] By its 1950 resolution, the General Assembly recommended that its attitude on the question of representation should be taken into account by other organs.[60] However, as an independent organ, not under the authority of the General Assembly, the Security Council enjoyed the right under the Charter to reach its own independent decision on the question of representation. This would have made it possible for the Chinese Nationalist representative on the Security Council to claim the right of veto in that organ if it had so wished, though the "double-veto" could have been circumvented by a presidential ruling, upheld by the majority required for procedural questions, as had been done in previous cases.[61] It was not necessary, however, to resort to such tactics, because the General Assembly's decision was accepted by the Security Council without a legal challenge. As a consequence, the Security Council has become more representative of world power relations than it was in the earlier years when the Republic of China was represented by a government whose effective authority was limited to Taiwan and several small off-shore islands.

While the original Charter indicated the number of nonpermanent members, the possibility of amending this provision has always existed since a permanent member of the Council would not have the same interest in preventing a change in the nonpermanent membership as in preventing itself from being removed as a permanent member. As a matter of fact, a proposal was made to increase the number of nonpermanent members of the Council as early as the 1956 session of the General Assembly when a group of Latin American states introduced a proposed amendment to that effect. It called for raising the number of nonpermanent members from six to eight. With the rapid increase in membership of the United Nations after 1955, pressure mounted to increase the size of the Council, primarily in order to achieve more equitable geographical distribution. The Soviet Union was opposed on the ground that the Charter could not be amended so long as the Republic of China was not represented by the Peking regime. When the proposal to increase the number of nonpermanent members came to a vote in the General Assembly in 1960, it was defeated in large part because of the insistence by a group of Asian and African states that approval of the amendment be linked to a redistribution of Council seats. In 1963 agreement was finally reached to increase the number of elected members from six to ten,[62] and this amendment came into force in September 1965. The increase in the size of the Council made necessary the modification of the majority vote requirement for Council decisions. The amendment provided that the number of affirmative votes required should be increased from seven to nine. One consequence of this increase of the number of nonpermanent members and of the number of affirmative votes required for a decision was that it now became possible for a procedural decision of the Council to be taken by nine affirmative votes, not including any one permanent member, whereas formerly the affirmative vote of at least one permanent member had been necessary.

According to the Charter, the Assembly, when electing nonpermanent members, is required to take into account contributions of the members to "the maintenance of international peace and security and to the other purposes of the Organization," and also equitable geographical distribution. In the first elections the two criteria were neatly balanced, but over the years geographical distribution has come to be the predominant factor.[63] In practice, geographical distribution has been defined in terms of political groups with the consequence that certain states, though they may fall within recognized geographical areas, are not seriously considered for membership in the Security Council if they do not belong to the predominant political grouping in their areas.[64]

The pattern established at the first session of the General Assembly for the distribution of nonpermanent seats was the following: two for Latin America and one each for the Commonwealth, Western Europe, the Middle East, and Eastern Europe. This distribution was in part the result of a "gentleman's agreement," the exact nature of which has been the subject of controversy.[65] Despite some bitterly contested elections, the general pattern established at the first session prevailed through the first decade. Eventually, it broke down under pressure of the increasingly numerous Asian and African members for greater representation. In its resolution approving an amendment to the Charter increasing the number of nonpermanent members from six to ten, the General Assembly decided that the seats should be allocated in the following manner: five for Africa and Asia, one for Eastern Europe, two for Latin America, and two for Western Europe and "other states." [66]

The states elected to the Council are generally those whose candidacies have been backed by other states in the groups with which they are associated. There have been few contests in the election of states from Latin America, Western Europe, and the Middle East. During the period from 1949 to 1960, however, a contest frequently developed over the election of the representative of Eastern Europe, due to the Soviet insistence that the "gentleman's agreement" permitted the Soviet bloc to designate the Eastern European member of the Council, which the Western powers were not prepared to admit. This controversy often resulted in a compromise agreement in which the two candidates divided the two-year term between them, a solution obviously not consistent with the explicit language of the Charter. Election by groups, combined with the prescription by General Assembly resolution of a pattern of geographical distribution to be followed, has resulted in a nonpermanent membership that satisfies the criteria of the Charter much less than the requirements of regional group politics. The result has been a Security Council which at times has fallen considerably short of meeting the original Charter requirement that responsibility be associated with power. See Table 1 for nonpermanent membership, 1946–1971.

The Process of Decision Making

Probably the most controversial provision of the Charter, at least so far as the Security Council is concerned, is that which accords to each of the permanent members the right by its single negative vote to prevent the taking of a decision on a nonprocedural question. The "veto" was justified at San Francisco by the Sponsoring Governments and France on two major grounds: first, that the interests of the permanent members in the maintenance of international peace and security and their contributions to the work of the organization justified the requirement of their consent in any decisions of a substantive nature; and, second, that the requirement of unanimity would provide assurance that the major powers would cooperate and would not fall into open conflict with each other with fatal consequences to the organization. In fact, in the statement by the delegations of the four Sponsoring Governments,[67] it was announced by way of assurance to those who might be fearful of the obstructive consequences of the proposed voting procedure that it was far from the purpose of the permanent members to "use their 'veto' power willfully to obstruct the operation of the Council." The arguments advanced at San Francisco and assurances given by the major powers, all in the name of greater effectiveness of the organization, were soon being recalled in the early years of the United Nations when the absence of major power agreement again and again stood in the way of a substantive decision by the Council.

Down to the end of 1966, the veto was used 109 times, and in all but 5 instances by the Soviet Union. Three-fourths of these were cast during the first decade and the great majority of these were on membership applications. In the state of international affairs that prevailed during the years 1946–1955 when the cold war was developing and at its height, the great majority of members were prepared to follow the lead of the United States. The Soviet Union saw the veto as the only means of preventing decisions from being taken which it considered contrary to its interests. The repeated exercise of the veto by the Soviet representative led to the claim that the Soviet Union was obstructing the work of the organization by preventing the Security Council from taking decisions supported by the required majority of the members and, consequently, was guilty of preventing the Security Council from discharging its responsibilities. This line of argument, of course, overlooked the fact that none of the major powers were prepared to accept the majority principle as governing the Security Council's decisions and deliberately included the requirement of unanimity to enable each to protect its vital interests.

The question can be fairly raised, however, as to whether the veto

TABLE 1 Geographical Distribution of Nonpermanent Council Members

MEMBERS BY GEOGRAPHICAL AREA

Year	Latin America	Western Europe	Eastern Europe	Africa	Asia	Other (White Commonwealth)
1946	Mexico Brazil	Netherlands	Poland	Egypt (ME)		Australia (WC)
1947	Brazil Colombia	Belgium	Poland		Syria (ME)	Australia (WC)
1948	Colombia Argentina	Belgium	Ukrainian SSR		Syria (ME)	Canada (WC)
1949	Argentina Cuba	Norway	Ukrainian SSR	Egypt (ME)		Canada (WC)
1950	Cuba Ecuador	Norway	Yugoslavia	Egypt (ME)	India (C)	
1951	Ecuador Brazil	Netherlands	Yugoslavia		India (C) Turkey (ME)	
1952	Brazil Chile	Netherlands	Greece		Turkey (ME) Pakistan (C)	
1953	Chile Colombia	Denmark	Greece		Pakistan (C) Lebanon (ME)	
1954	Colombia Brazil	Denmark			Lebanon (ME) Turkey (E. Europe)	New Zealand (WC)

Year						
1955	Brazil Peru	Belgium			Turkey (E. Europe) Iran (ME)	New Zealand (WC)
1956	Peru Cuba	Belgium	Yugoslavia		Iran (ME)	Australia (WC)
1957	Cuba Colombia	Sweden			Philippines Iraq (ME)	Australia (WC)
1958	Colombia Panama	Sweden			Iraq (ME) Japan	Canada (WC)
1959	Panama Argentina	Italy		Tunisia (ME)	Japan	Canada (WC)
1960	Argentina Ecuador	Italy	Poland	Tunisia (ME)	Ceylon (C)	
1961	Ecuador Chile			United Arab Republic (ME) Liberia	Ceylon (C) Turkey (E. Europe)	
1962	Chile Venezuela	Ireland	Romania	United Arab Republic (ME) Ghana (C)	Japan	
1963	Venezuela Brazil	Norway		Ghana (C) Morocco (ME)	Philippines	
1964	Brazil Bolivia	Norway	Czechoslovakia	Morocco (ME) Ivory Coast		

TABLE 1 (Continued)

MEMBERS BY GEOGRAPHICAL AREA

Year	Latin America	Western Europe	Eastern Europe	Africa	Asia	Other (White Commonwealth)
1965	Bolivia Uruguay	Netherlands		Ivory Coast	Malaysia (C) Jordan (ME)	
1966	Uruguay Argentina	Netherlands	Bulgaria	Mali Nigeria (C) Uganda (C)	Japan Jordan (ME)	New Zealand (WC)
1967	Argentina Brazil	Denmark	Bulgaria	Ethiopia Mali Nigeria (C)	India (C) Japan	Canada (WC)
1968	Brazil Paraguay	Denmark	Hungary	Ethiopia Algeria Senegal	India (C) Pakistan (C)	Canada (WC)
1969	Colombia Paraguay	Finland Spain	Hungary	Algeria (ME) Senegal Zambia (C)	Nepal (C) Pakistan (C)	
1970	Colombia Nicaragua	Finland Spain	Poland	Burundi Sierra Leone (C) Zambia (C)	Nepal (C) Syria (ME)	
1971	Argentina Nicaragua	Belgium Italy	Poland	Burundi Sierra Leone (C) Somalia	Japan Syria (ME)	
1972	Argentina Panama	Belgium Italy	Yugoslavia	Somalia Guinea Sudan	Japan India (C)	

NOTE: white dominions indicated by (WC); for Asia and Africa, (ME) after country indicates Middle East; members of Commonwealth other than Australia, Canada, and New Zealand indicated by (C).

36

was always used under circumstances which justified the claim that serious national interests were involved. In other words, was the veto being used for purely obstructive reasons without any attention being given to the consequences it might have for the effectiveness of the Security Council in discharging its responsibilities? Any objective answer to this question would be difficult to give. It should be noted, however, on the one hand, that the number of vetoes cast during the early period gave an exaggerated impression of the Soviet negative attitude since the great majority were on membership questions and many were repeated vetoes of the same applications. On the other hand, instances can be cited—for example, the Soviet veto of a proposal on the Syrian-Lebanese question in 1946—where it is difficult to find any serious basis for its exercise other than the desire to make a propaganda point in the cold war.[68]

Within the membership of the organization a great deal of opposition developed during the early years to what was regarded as the excessive use of the veto. This opposition to and criticism of the "abuse of the veto" led to numerous efforts to reduce the scope and frequency of the veto's use. These took a variety of forms.[69] In the General Assembly, for example, there were frequent debates and resolutions passed on the excessive use of the veto, particularly its use to prevent qualified states from becoming members of the organization. These efforts to influence the Soviet Union by mobilizing wide condemnation of its action in the representative organ of the United Nations had little effect. Another approach was an effort to cut down the permissible use of the veto, particularly on membership questions, by authoritative Charter interpretation. Two requests were made by the General Assembly to the International Court of Justice for advisory opinions on membership questions involving the use of the veto. In one case the Court was asked to give an opinion on whether a member was justified in basing its vote against the admission of a new member on any grounds other than those expressly enumerated in Article 4 of the Charter. The Soviet Union had admitted the qualifications of Italy and Finland under Article 4 of the Charter but had voted against their admission on the grounds that the United States and other Western powers had refused to support membership applications from members of the Communist bloc. The Court, in its majority opinion, supported the Western contention that the Soviet Union had based its veto on grounds not justified under the Charter.[70] The opinion, though accepted by the General Assembly, had no influence upon subsequent Soviet conduct. The second request to the Court related to the power of the General Assembly to admit a new member in the absence of a favorable Security Council recommendation. That the General Assembly did not have this power seemed clear to most members of the organization, but on the insistence of Argentina the Assembly voted to ask the Court for an opinion. The Court advised that a favorable Security Council recommendation was indeed necessary, thus eliminating the possibility of circumventing the requirement of Security Council approval in membership cases.[71]

In one respect, Charter interpretation did introduce some flexibility into the requirement of concurrence of the permanent members. Though Article 27, paragraph 3, is quite specific in saying that nonprocedural decisions require the "concurring votes of the permanent members," it was early accepted in practice that an abstention was not to be treated as a negative vote or as preventing the requirement of "concurrence of the permanent members" from being satisfied. During the Council's consideration of the Spanish question, the Soviet representative explicitly accepted this interpretation of the Charter requirement and the practice has been followed ever since.[72] The position taken by the majority of members that an absence is to be treated in the same way has not been accepted by the Soviet Union, although the conduct of the Soviet Union and other members of the Communist bloc leaves some ambiguity as to what their position is on the legal consequences of decisions taken with a permanent member absent.

Another approach to the veto problem has been in efforts to exclude from the operation of the veto certain areas of Security Council activity. At San Francisco, for example, there was wide insistence on the part of the smaller states that the requirement of unanimity should not apply when the Security Council was performing its function of peaceful settlement and adjustment.[73] We have seen, however, that the Sponsoring Governments and France took the position that decisions in this area were part of a chain of events which might eventually lead to enforcement action. During the early years of the United Nations, the effort was renewed to exclude the veto from decisions of the Council under Chapter VI. One of the recommendations of the Interim Committee established by the Assembly in 1947 was to the effect that permanent members of the Security Council should voluntarily abstain from insisting on the right of veto when the Council was dealing with disputes and situations with a view to peaceful settlement under Chapter VI.[74] Informal proposals to amend the Charter have usually included the proposal that the veto be eliminated in this manner. Up to the present these efforts have produced no positive results.

While during the early years of the United Nations there was a great deal of sentiment within the organization to restrict the use of the veto, in recent years there has been increasing recognition, particularly on the part of the major powers, that the thinking that went into the adoption of the original Charter provisions had a sound basis in the realities of international politics. Though at one time the United States took the lead in attacking the Soviet Union for its abuse of the veto, and though there was within certain official circles some sentiment for limiting the use of the veto, it has been clear all along that even the United States is not willing to completely forgo its veto power and probably at the present time is not seriously interested in limiting it. There appears, too, to be less interest in limiting the special voting rights of permanent members on the part of the smaller states who have been forced to recognize, particularly since the ill-fated nineteenth session of the General Assembly, that the so-called veto power of the permanent members, particularly of the two superpowers, simply reflects the dominant influence in the organization and in world affairs that these states enjoy. Apart from the membership deadlock in the first decade and some slowing up of the United Nations machinery in its operation, the veto has not been a serious obstruction to what might have been achieved in its absence.[75] In other words, the requirement that the permanent members be in agreement on substantive matters within the Council's competence is simply a reflection of the influence which these states exert in the life of the international community.

Relationship to the General Assembly

The relationship of the Security Council to the General Assembly, as envisaged by the architects of the Charter and defined in its provisions, has undergone substantial change during the course of the past twenty-five years. Roughly, this development has fallen into three periods. During the first period from 1946 down to 1949 members sought to use the Security Council substantially as had been envisaged in the Charter. When these efforts were blocked, initiatives were taken to utilize the General Assembly to achieve results which could not be obtained in the Security Council itself. This development reached its height in 1950 with the adoption of the "Uniting for Peace" Resolution[76] which authorized the use of the General Assembly for performing functions which had been specifically vested by the Charter in the Security Council. From 1950 to 1956, under the influence of the cold war and the disrepute into which the Security Council had been cast by the events of the preceding years, the General Assembly occupied a position of relative dominance, with the Security Council falling into relative disuse and meeting with alarming infrequency. The rapid expansion of the membership of the General Assembly from 1955 on and the improvement of relations between the United States and the Soviet Union following the death of Stalin led to a reversal of interest on the part of the major Western powers in the use of the Security Council and a recognition by the major powers that in the long run their interests would best be served through greater use of the Council in the handling of peace and security matters. During the past decade and a half there has been a marked improvement in the importance of the Security Council's relative position in the organization. This has not, however, been marked by any corresponding decline in the role of the General Assembly in the work of the organization due to other influences which have tended to bring to the forefront matters for which the General Assembly has responsibility under the Charter, such as economic and social development, the liquidation of colonialism, the elimination of racial discrimination, and emerging problems of modern technology.

Some indication of the changes that have taken place in use of the

Security Council is provided by statistics on the number of meetings of the Council per year. During the period down to 1949, the Council averaged over one hundred meetings a year. From 1949 to 1956 there was a sharp falling off in the number of meetings. Since 1956, while in single years the number of meetings has been low,[77] overall there has been a substantial increase in the use made of the Council. For a graph showing annual meetings of the Security Council, see Table 2. It must, of course, be recognized that decision to use the General Assembly instead of, or after first appealing to, the Security Council, is only one factor that would help to explain these trends. Another would be the state of international relations and, more particularly, the prevalence of conflicts outside or on the periphery of the most vital security interests of the permanent members, especially the United States and the Soviet Union.

The adoption of the Uniting for Peace Resolution in 1950, though it marked the maximum formal assertion by the General Assembly of its peace and security powers under the Charter, was in reality the consummation of a development and not the basis for further effective expansion of the Assembly's role. From the very beginning there had been a tendency on the part of the major powers, particularly the United States, to utilize the General Assembly as an organ of last resort in case desired action could not be obtained in the Security Council. This was a somewhat surprising development in view of the fact that the Sponsoring Governments and France had presented a fairly united front at San Francisco in opposing the efforts of the smaller states to increase the relative role of the General Assembly in matters of peace and security. What happened, however, in the post–San Francisco period was that, as a result of the conflict that developed between the United States and the Western powers on the one hand and the Soviet Union on the other, each state on occasion saw fit to utilize the General Assembly more for exercising political pressure than for getting decisions which might contribute to a generally acceptable solution of the matter under consideration. Since the composition of the United Nations during the early years favored the West, the United States resorted to this device more commonly than the Soviet Union.

The first example, however, of an appeal to the General Assembly in a matter where satisfaction could not be obtained in the Security Council was in connection with the Spanish question. Following the report of the Commission of Inquiry, the majority in the Security Council took the position that the situation in Spain did not constitute an existing threat to the peace and therefore did not warrant enforcement action under Chapter VII of the Charter. On the initiative of Poland, with full Soviet support, the question was brought before the General Assembly which adopted a resolution calling upon member states to withdraw their heads of missions from Spain and to exclude Spain from participating in conferences held under the auspices of the United Nations.[78] In 1947 initiatives were taken by the United States to bring before the General Assembly matters with respect to which the Security Council had been unable to take decisions or with

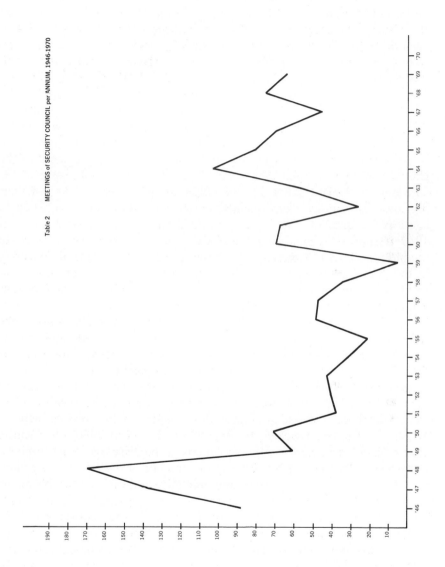

Table 2   MEETINGS of SECURITY COUNCIL per ANNUM, 1946-1970

41

respect to which there was little likelihood that any acceptable decision could be reached. The threat to Greece arising from guerrilla activities supported by Greece's northern neighbors was first brought to the attention of the Security Council. When the Council, following a report of its Commission of Investigation,[79] failed to adopt proposals based upon the report as a result of the negative vote of the Soviet Union, the United States asked that the matter be placed on the agenda of the General Assembly at its second session. It was the General Assembly that continued to deal with this question through to the early fifties and, in the course of this consideration, made recommendations to members that collective measures be used of the nature of those enumerated in Chapter VII of the Charter.[80]

Also, in 1947, the General Assembly was asked by the United States to consider the Korean question. This, too, might properly have been brought before the Security Council but it was clearly the judgment of the United States government that it would be futile to do so because of the failure of the United States and the USSR to agree in the course of their previous negotiations. Consequently, the General Assembly was asked to consider the question and to recommend terms of settlement. Also at its 1947 session, on United States initiative, the resolution was adopted to establish the Interim Committee which was to assist the General Assembly in the discharge of its responsibilities for the maintenance of peace and security by meeting between sessions to perform certain of its functions and to assist generally in preparing its business.[81]

While during the period 1946–1949 a very considerable shift in the respective roles of the Security Council and the General Assembly in the maintenance of peace and security had taken place, it was not until the fifth General Assembly in 1950 that this development was given statutory form in the Uniting for Peace Resolution[82] of that year. The initiative in the adoption of this resolution was taken by the United States with motives similar to those that had prompted that country in its previous actions. When North Korea attacked the Republic of Korea in 1950, the Security Council had been able to adopt resolutions in the discharge of its responsibility under Chapter VII by virtue of the absence of the Soviet representative. When, however, the Soviet representative returned at the beginning of August, it became obvious that the Security Council would no longer be able to take decisions with respect to the collective military operation in Korea. Under these circumstances the United States delegation to the General Assembly introduced a proposal which in modified form was adopted as the Uniting for Peace Resolution. Under its terms, in case the Security Council was prevented by the veto from exercising its "primary responsibility" for the maintenance of international peace in any case where there appeared to be a threat to the peace, breach of the peace, or act of aggression, the General Assembly would consider the matter "immediately" with a view to making appropriate recommendations of collective measures, "including in the case of a breach of the peace or act of aggression the use of armed force where necessary" to maintain or restore international peace and security. If the General Assembly was not in session, it was authorized to meet "in emergency special session within twenty-four hours of the request therefore." Such emergency special session could be called by the Security Council by a procedural vote or by the majority of the members of the organization.

Thus, in effect, the General Assembly asserted its power under the Charter to handle threats to the peace and breaches of the peace in the same manner as the Security Council, except that whereas the Security Council could order collective measures under Articles 41 and 42 the General Assembly could only recommend. This difference did not, however, seem very important at the time, since the failure of members to place military contingents at the disposal of the Security Council by agreements under Article 43 deprived the Council of the effective power to order military measures. The recommendation by the General Assembly, if backed by a significant majority of members, was likely to have as much moral authority as a recommendation of the Security Council, especially if one or more of the permanent members were absent or abstained when the Council took its decision.

The adoption of the Uniting for Peace Resolution was considered a development of great significance at the time since it seemed to involve the assumption by the General Assembly of a responsibility which many had hitherto considered to belong exclusively to the Security Council. Clearly, it was intended by the United States and its principal supporters that a procedure should be available by which the membership of the United Nations could be rallied to take collective measures—including military measures, if necessary—against a permanent member or another state enjoying the support of a permanent member. In effect, what they sought was the revival of something comparable to the League's collective security system with the General Assembly acting as the legitimizing organ. It soon became clear, however, that this development was not to take place in fact. When the General Assembly was asked to consider the military intervention of Communist China in Korea, the efforts of the United States to mobilize United Nations support for collective measures against Peking ran into immediate difficulties.[83] Other members, including close allies of the United States, were unwilling to join even in the initial condemnation of Chinese Communist intervention until efforts had been made to work out a negotiated settlement. Two months were to elapse before members of the General Assembly were ready to formally declare that Chinese Communist intervention constituted aggression and a further period of over three months passed before they were ready to support a resolution recommending economic measures of a comparatively mild nature.[84] Obviously, this did not represent the kind of prompt decisive action that must be taken to defeat a determined aggressor. Furthermore, it was clear from this experience that the majority of members of the

United Nations were not prepared to join in collective measures against a major power when the result might be a major world conflict.

This experience, for all practical purposes, marked the end of any effort to make the General Assembly a substitute for the Security Council in the initiation and direction of coercive military measures. For all practical purposes, also, it meant that members recognized that the General Assembly was not the appropriate organ—or at least the organ best suited —for initiating coercive measures of any kind, even political and economic ones, since the effectiveness of such measures requires the cooperation of the major powers. When, for example, in 1956 the United Kingdom and France vetoed proposals of the Security Council intended to restrain their military intervention in the Middle East and the Uniting for Peace Resolution was invoked for the purpose of bringing the matter before the General Assembly, no proposal for recommending coercive measures by members to defeat the intervention was seriously considered. Rather, the General Assembly called upon the states to withdraw their forces and to accept a plan in which military contingents organized on a voluntary basis and placed under United Nations direction would assist in facilitating the voluntary withdrawal of the British, French, and Israeli forces.[85] While many member states have been unwilling to admit that the General Assembly does not have a role in the initiation and direction of peacekeeping operations of this kind, no one takes seriously any longer the original primary purpose of the Uniting for Peace Resolution of enabling the Assembly to initiate coercive measures. From a realistic point of view, all that remains of the Uniting for Peace Resolution which has present-day utility are those provisions permitting the holding of a special emergency session on twenty-four-hour notice for the consideration of matters referred to it by the Council or at the request of members.

The controversy that developed in the early sixties over the financing of peacekeeping operations contributed greatly to the restoration of the authority of the Security Council, demonstrating the limitations of what could be done through the General Assembly by majority voting. The majority of members in the General Assembly supported the view that the method of financing operations involving military contingents on a voluntary basis could be determined by the General Assembly.[86] Notwithstanding, the Soviet Union and France and certain other members refused to accept this position and the members of the General Assembly were unwilling to apply Charter sanctions to achieve compliance. This experience reinforced the view that in matters of peace and security there is no viable alternative to agreement of the major powers and that consequently the Security Council, as the organ where such agreement could be most easily registered, is normally the appropriate organ for considering disputes and situations, particularly those which require or may call for collective preventive or enforcement measures.

EFFECTIVENESS OF THE COUNCIL

It was commonly argued during the early years of the United Nations that the effectiveness of the Security Council was being destroyed by the excessive use of the veto. In recent years the veto has been used with much less frequency. On many occasions the Council has not been able to take a decision—or, at least, to take a decision which many would consider adequate to the demands of the situation—because of the absence of the necessary consensus among its members. Even when the Council has taken a decision, as in the case of its resolution of November 22, 1967, outlining the terms of settlement of the Middle East situation,[87] it has not found it possible to secure compliance of the parties concerned.

This relative ineffectiveness of the Council in the discharge of its responsibilities has been a source of major concern to member governments and to all people interested in what the United Nations is supposed to achieve. It presents a considerable contrast to claims that were made in the beginning on behalf of the United Nations as the successor to the League of Nations. It was then emphasized that the new organization had "teeth" which the League did not have, and in consequence the means at its disposal to enforce its decisions. This strength was expected to come from the common interests of the major powers and their willingness to act in concert. Without that common purpose and agreement upon means, the Council has frequently been little more than an organ of discussion. And yet, in spite of the disagreements among its permanent members, the Council has discharged its responsibilities with somewhat more success than it has been given credit.

The functions of the Council fall roughly into two categories. First, the constituent functions which have to do with such matters as membership, appointment of the secretary-general, election of judges, and establishment of subsidiary organs; and, second, substantive functions in the maintenance of international peace and security which have to do with the handling of specific disputes and situations and the elaboration of possible schemes for the regulation of armaments. The effectiveness of the Council's work can be considered under these two principal heads.

Constituent Functions

Under the Charter, a state is admitted to membership in the organization by decision of the General Assembly and on the recommendation of the Security Council. The Security Council is associated with the General Assembly in the admission of new members because of its primary responsibility for the maintenance of international peace and security and the importance of peace and security as a purpose of the organization. Since it was decided at San Francisco that membership should not be automatic and that there should be certain qualifications that applicants must satisfy, including willingness and ability to discharge the obligations of membership, it seemed reasonable that the Security Council should have a share in the admission process. Under the Charter its function is to make an initial determination whether an applicant is qualified, leaving to the General Assembly the responsibility for making the final decision.

During the first decade the requirement of initial Security Council approval operated as an obstacle to the admission of the great majority of the states that applied.[88] This was due to the fact that permanent members used the occasion of passing on applications to achieve political advantage in the cold war. Though positions on membership applications were formally developed as a rule on the basis of criteria contained in Article 4 of the Charter, an important consideration influencing votes on applications was the likely voting behavior of the applicant, once a member, on cold war issues. When the membership deadlock was finally broken in 1955, the Security Council's action on membership applications took on a quite different character. Some members appeared extremely anxious to win the favor of applicants by supporting their admission without too close attention to basic qualifications laid down in the Charter. While on a few occasions questions were raised as to whether the applicant state had the capacity for discharging the obligations of membership, objections were rarely carried to the point of negative votes and from 1955 on few applications failed to receive approval. Thus the Security Council passed very suddenly, one might say, from the practice of excessive restraint to that of nearly complete permissiveness. Only in the case of the divided states were objections to admission consistently maintained. Rarely during the period of twenty-five years did the Council perform as a discriminating judge of the qualifications of members by the standards originally laid down under the Charter. On the other hand, except for the first decade and the special case of the divided states, proponents of universality had little cause to complain regarding Council behavior.

The role of the Security Council in the appointment of the secretary-general was also initially justified on grounds of the relevance of peace and security considerations. Since the secretary-general was given important political responsibilities under the Charter[89] in contrast to the role of the secretary-general of the League of Nations, it was argued by the Sponsoring Governments and France that the Security Council should play a part in his appointment. The smaller states had favored appointment by the General Assembly alone. Experience would seem to justify the Charter solution as the secretary-general has been most effective in the discharge of his responsibilities when he has enjoyed the confidence and support of the permanent members. The requirement of a Security Council recommendation has not, except in one instance, resulted in a serious deadlock. In 1950 such a deadlock did develop which was not satisfactorily resolved until Trygve Lie, who had been given a three-year extension of his term by the

General Assembly,[90] voluntarily decided to retire and agreement was reached in the Security Council on the choice of Dag Hammarskjöld as his successor. There was threat of a similar deadlock following Hammarskjöld's death in 1961. This time, initially at least, the problem was not so much that of finding a new secretary-general as of determining the organization of the office. The Soviet Union was in the position, however, where by withholding its approval of a candidate it could bring strong pressure to bear to get the office restructured to meet its desires. When the Soviet Union retreated from its insistence on a "troika" arrangement, agreement was reached on U Thant as acting and then regular secretary-general. The requirement that the secretary-general should be appointed by the General Assembly on the basis of a favorable recommendation by the Security Council has without doubt served to limit the possibilities of choice, both as to country of origin and the qualities of the particular individual. It has definitely placed restraints upon the initiatives which the secretary-general can take but, on the other hand, it gives some assurance to the secretary-general that he has the confidence and support of the major powers which are necessary to effective action on his part.

The election of judges of the International Court of Justice is a function which the Statute of the Court confers upon the Security Council acting concurrently with the General Assembly. What is significant in connection with the performance of this function is that the Council is not governed by Article 27 of the Charter in its voting procedure. All that is required for the election of a judge is an absolute majority in both organs and, consequently, the permanent members of the Security Council do not have a veto. However, it has been customary in the case of the International Court of Justice, as of its predecessor, that there should regularly be a judge of the nationality of a permanent member. The participation of the Security Council in the election process may have contributed to this result. The only exception has been the absence of a Chinese judge of late, due principally to the controversy over Chinese representation in the United Nations.

Capacity for Discharging Peace and Security Functions

The full discharge by the Council of its responsibilities in dealing with disputes and situations was recognized from the beginning as depending upon the completion of certain arrangements envisaged in the Charter which were left for subsequent action by the Council itself. For one thing, the Charter by implication provided, and this was clearly understood at San Francisco, that the power of the Council to take decisions binding upon members with respect to the use of military forces would depend upon the conclusion of special arrangements by which members would undertake to place forces and facilities at the Council's disposal. Article 43 of the Charter provides for the conclusion of such agreements between the Council and individual members or groups of members. One of the first actions of the Security Council was to direct the Military Staff Committee to undertake a study of the principles which should govern the conclusion of such agreements.[91] When the Military Staff Committee undertook the consideration of these principles, it was soon discovered that agreement among the permanent members did not extend much beyond the specific Charter provisions and did not cover important principles essential to the conclusion of the agreements in question. As a result of this basic disagreement the committee's report consisted of forty-one draft articles, only twenty-five of which had been accepted unanimously.[92] Most of the important areas of disagreement were between the Soviet Union, on the one hand, and the other permanent members of the Security Council, on the other. The major point of disagreement between the Soviet Union and the other members concerned the strength and composition of the contributions to be made by the permanent members. China, France, the United Kingdom, and the United States took the position that initial contributions of all permanent members should be comparable but that, in view of differences in the size and composition of their national forces, members might make contributions differing widely as to the strength of the separate components of land, sea, and air forces. The Soviet Union, however, insisted that the contributions of permanent members should be equal both in overall strength and composition. Other major areas upon which the Soviet Union and other permanent members disagreed concerned the provision of bases, the location of forces, and their withdrawal following completion of their assignment. The disagreements in the Military Staff Committee were repeated in the Security Council when the committee's report came before that organ for consideration. As pointed out by the Soviet representative, the problem was primarily political rather than technical;[93] consequently, disagreement reflected not so much the inability of the military experts to agree on technical problems as the failure of their respective governments to agree on basic issues of security and prestige.

The Charter also provides that the Security Council "shall be so organized as to be able to function continuously" and that each member of the Security Council shall for this purpose be represented at all times at the seat of the organization.[94] This requirement has been fully satisfied insofar as the representation of members of the Council at headquarters is concerned. There has been a seeming lack of continuity of the Council at times which has been due to the fact that the business of the Council has not been sufficiently urgent to make frequent meetings necessary. Rule 1 of the Provisional Rules of Procedure, providing that the interval between meetings shall not exceed fourteen days, has frequently not been observed, particularly during the period 1950–1960.

The Charter also provides that the Security Council shall hold periodic meetings at which each of its members may be represented by a member of the government or some other specially designated representative.[95] The clear purpose of this provision was to have periodic meetings of the Council at which members would be represented by officials at the foreign minister level, as had been the frequent practice of the Council of the League of Nations with useful results. It was recognized that the foreign ministers could not regularly represent their countries at meetings of the Council if the Security Council was to be so organized as to be continually in session. However, it was not felt that the requirement of continuity excluded the possibility of periodic meetings with a higher level of representation than the permanent representatives. Though the proposal that this particular provision of the Charter should be implemented has been advanced many times by the secretary-general [96] and by individual governments, the Council, while recognizing that such meetings "could enhance [its] authority," [97] had not held such a meeting up to 1970. The first periodic meeting took place on October 21, 1970, with eleven of the members represented by their foreign ministers and with "Review of the International Situation" as the single agenda item.[98] Until then the occasion for meetings of foreign ministers had commonly been the annual session of the General Assembly when they frequently headed their delegations and took advantage of their presence in New York for discussions. These discussions, however, have not been within the Security Council framework, but have usually been conducted on an informal basis, participation being determined by the nature of the question and the interest and possible contribution of members.

Handling of Disputes and Situations

The Charter goes into great detail in Chapters VI and VII in defining the powers to be exercised by the Security Council and the particular steps to be taken in dealing with disputes and situations submitted to it. For instance, Article 34 provides that the Security Council may carry out an inquiry for the purpose of determining whether a dispute or situation is sufficiently serious to warrant its further consideration. In Articles 36 and 37 the distinction is made between the power of the Security Council to recommend appropriate procedures or methods of adjustment and its power to recommend terms of settlement. In Article 39 the Security Council is directed to determine the existence of any threat to the peace, breach of the peace, or act of aggression as a precondition to deciding what measures are to be taken under subsequent articles of Chapter VII. Article 40 authorizes the Council to "call upon" the parties to adopt provisional measures, and under Articles 41 and 42 the Council may order a whole range of collective measures. In practice, the Security Council has not taken too seriously these specific directives and authorizations of the Charter and has adopted a more flexible attitude in determining the course that it is to follow in dealing with a particular dispute or situation.[99] This flexibility has been due primarily to the fact that the Security Council, as a political organ, in reaching its decisions is guided by its estimate of what is acceptable to the parties as well as by the specific provisions of the Charter.

Thus, in its consideration of the Indonesian question in 1947, the Security Council was prepared to drop any specific references to Charter articles in order to get the needed agreement upon a particular proposal which promised to bring an end to fighting.[100]

As a general rule, the Council has been willing to give consideration to any matter brought to its attention. It has not made it a condition of such consideration that the Council make a preliminary determination with respect to its seriousness.[101] Furthermore, in considering any dispute or situation brought to its attention, the Council has not considered it necessary to indicate whether it is taking action under Chapter VI or Chapter VII. In dealing with the Congo situation, for example, the Council never made it clear whether it was making recommendations for the peaceful adjustment of the situation or taking decisions for the purpose of restoring international peace and security under Chapter VII. While the secretary-general suggested that Council decisions were taken under Article 40,[102] which presupposes a finding under Article 39, others have argued that the Council's action came under Chapter VI or have suggested that perhaps it was necessary to bring them under a mythical Chapter VI and a half. This flexibility of the Council's action in dealing with disputes or situations gives some justification to the view that much of Chapters VI and VII and even VIII are superfluous, and that the course of development of the organization would not have been very different if the Charter provisions had been limited to a simple grant of authority such as is provided under Article 24, paragraph 1, along with the statement of purposes and principles set forth in Articles 1 and 2.

Certain matters relating to the restoration of peace following World War II have by Charter provision[103] and agreement of the permanent members been excluded from consideration by the Security Council. With the exception of the Berlin blockade and the question whether free elections could be held throughout Germany, no aspect of the German problem has come before the Security Council for consideration. Even in these cases, the Soviet Union objected strongly to the Council's competence. Aspects of the German problem have been discussed by the four governments involved: the United States, the Soviet Union, France, and the United Kingdom. Furthermore, questions relating to the Italian, Hungarian, Bulgarian, and Romanian peace settlements were all decided by the major victor nations. The question of the disposition of Italian colonies came before the General Assembly for final decision only because the four powers were unable to agree on the terms of disposition and undertook to submit the question to the final decision of the General Assembly. While the question of Korea was brought before the General Assembly by the United States, the Soviet Union consistently maintained that this was a question relating to the final disposition of Japanese territories and was outside the competence of the United Nations. Other questions relating to the Japanese peace settlement have been settled outside the United Nations. The North Korean attack upon the Republic of Korea came before the Security Council as an alleged breach of the peace or aggressive action under Article 39 with the Soviet representative boycotting meetings of the Council at the time. The Soviet Union has never admitted the validity of Council decisions, though for reasons other than relationship to the peace settlement.

The disputes and situations that have been handled by the Security Council have, generally speaking, fallen within two broad categories. On the one hand, there have been those disputes and situations, commonly arising from the liquidation of colonialism and the establishment of new boundaries between newly created states, in which permanent members of the Security Council have had important interests but in which these interests have not been regarded as of such a vital nature as to exclude some possibility of compromise and third-party decision. On the other hand, other disputes and situations have involved such direct and vital interests of the permanent members, particularly the United States and the Soviet Union, as to exclude the possibility of Security Council consideration and a decision by that organ representing an accommodation of conflicting interests. When it has been asked to deal with disputes and situations in this second category, the Council has found it impossible or inexpedient to take a decision or even, in most instances, to undertake a serious discussion of the matter in question.

The successes of the Council, moderate or limited as they have been in many instances, have been achieved in dealing with disputes and situations falling in the first category. Here the degree of success has been quite uneven, in most instances not going beyond the achievement of a temporary cease-fire or a truce. Rarely has the Council been able to achieve a definitive settlement or accommodation although it has been successful in keeping discussions alive and in creating an atmosphere where there is at least the possibility of an agreement being reached through negotiations between the parties. The methods used by the Security Council have varied greatly, depending in each case upon the Council's evaluation of the particular situation and the conclusions reached by members as to the maximum area of agreement. While there was initially a tendency on the part of some members of the Council to push matters to a vote in order to establish a majority position and, by inference at least, to place the blame for the Council's failure to take a decision on the dissenting permanent member, the more common practice in recent years has been to seek by informal discussions to achieve a consensus which may be registered by a formal vote or often by a statement by the president.[104]

In those cases where an actual armed conflict has taken place or where there has been a movement of military forces across national boundaries, the Council has commonly, as its first step, called upon the parties to withdraw their forces and to cease hostilities where they have occurred. Following on this initial appeal, the Council may establish a commission of inquiry with powers of good offices or mediation to proceed to the spot to inform the Council regarding the facts of the situation and on its own responsibility to undertake discussions with a view to achieving agreement on the terms of a cease-fire or a truce. In dealing with the Palestine situation in 1948, the Council called upon the parties to seek armistice agreements "by negotiations conducted either directly or through the Acting Mediator on Palestine." [105] To assist in the implementation of truce or cease-fire agreements, the Council may decide to have United Nations observers sent to report on violations and to undertake discussions with local authorities for a settlement of minor violations. In the case of the Middle East armistice agreements, the Council authorized personnel of the Truce Supervision Organization to assist the parties in achieving compliance and requested the chief of staff to report to it on observance of the cease-fire.[106] In the Congo and again in Cyprus, the Council authorized peacekeeping forces consisting of contingents contributed by member states and functioning under the general direction of the secretary-general to assist in creating conditions of local order.[107]

In all cases where the Council has been called upon to deal with disputes and situations involving violence or a threat of violence and where it has undertaken with considerable success to put an end to the fighting and create conditions under which peaceful settlement might be achieved, it has also given attention to the final and most important aspect of the process, namely, that of working out some basis of peaceful settlement or accommodation between the parties directly involved. In this area, however, the Council has met with little success. In dealing with the Indonesian question in 1947–1948, the Council, through its Good Offices Committee and the United Nations Commission on Indonesia, was able to assist the parties in reaching agreement upon the basic principles of a political settlement and later, in the second phase of the dispute, played an important role in bringing the parties to final agreement at the Round Table Conference in The Hague.[108] This was, perhaps, the Council's major success in achieving a final peaceful accommodation of a dispute. In dealing with the Palestine situation, the Council initially refused to implement by force the recommendations contained in the General Assembly's resolution of November 1947. Subsequently, efforts to achieve a settlement were pursued primarily through the Conciliation Commission established by the General Assembly. When fighting broke out on a major scale in 1956, the Council was prevented from taking any decision by British and French vetoes and, when major fighting again broke out in 1967, the Council, though able to reach a decision on the principles underlying a peace settlement,[109] was unable to persuade the parties to agree upon the implementation of these terms. The mediator appointed under the terms of the Council's resolution found his efforts blocked by the failure of Israel and the Arab states to agree on the preconditions of negotiations, and the permanent members of the Security Council have not been able to agree among themselves upon any plan for the implementation of its principles which they would be willing to persuade the parties to accept. Likewise, in Cyprus, though a resolution of the Council provided for a United Nations peacekeeping force and also envisaged a parallel effort to achieve agreement between the parties, this effort has up to the present time been unsuccessful.

While the Security Council has achieved considerable success in containing and putting an end to armed conflict in situations where the vital security interests of the permanent members are not directly involved, it has never ordered the use of military measures for that purpose. The nearest the Council has come to doing this was during the Congo crisis when it authorized the use of force, if necessary, to prevent the occurrence of civil war and to secure the removal of foreign military, paramilitary, and political advisory personnel.[110] In these instances, the measures were presumably adopted under Article 40 and the coercion was not to be directed against a member or another state. Also, the Council authorized and did not order the action in question, and the decisions were clearly not taken under Article 42. Not only is the ordering of collective military measures precluded by the absence of special agreements under Article 43, but joint action by the permanent members, as authorized in Article 106, has been practically out of the question because of mutual distrust.[111]

Though the Security Council has not made use of its powers under Articles 41 and 42 to restore international peace and security in a situation of armed conflict, the Council has of late called upon or requested states to take measures of the kind listed in Article 41, such as ceasing the shipment of arms, munitions, and war materials, and the breaking off of diplomatic relations, to induce compliance with the United Nations principles of self-determination and racial equality.[112] In the case of the Smith regime in Southern Rhodesia, it even made a formal determination that the situation there constituted a threat to the peace and ordered political and economic measures under Article 41.[113] It is significant, however, that the Council has been unwilling—even in a situation of this nature in which members are under strong pressure from the Asian and African countries —to authorize military measures, nor has there been any evidence thus far that the permanent members are prepared to take joint military measures on behalf of the organization.

In dealing with those disputes and situations in which permanent members have what they consider to be vital non-negotiable interests, the Council has been unable to take any decisive action. When in December 1946 Greece brought her complaint of intervention in her internal affairs by her northern neighbors, the Council was initially able to set up a Commission of Investigation to inquire into the circumstances and report to the Council.[114] After the commission made its report, the Council was prevented from taking decisions on proposals based on the conclusions of the majority of the commission by Soviet vetoes. The matter was then placed on the agenda of the General Assembly which dealt with the situation until finally, largely as the result of Yugoslavia's defection from the Communist front, the threat to Greece largely disappeared. When in 1948 it was alleged that the Soviet Union had intervened in Czechoslovakia to overthrow the Western-oriented government and establish a Communist regime, the

Soviet Union was able, through its exercise of the double veto, to prevent
any serious consideration of the issue by the Council. In 1950 though the
Council was able to deal with the North Korean military attack for a time,
due to the absence of the Soviet representative, once he resumed attendance at Council meetings it became impossible to get any Council decisions
and the General Assembly took over the responsibility of guidance of the
United Nations military operation. In 1954, when the Arbenz government
in Guatemala requested Council consideration of its claim of outside intervention, the United States was able to prevent any substantial consideration of the matter by the Council on the ground that the Organization of
American States had the question under advisement. Likewise, in 1965 the
United States was largely successful in preventing any decisive consideration by the Council of its military intervention in the Dominican Republic.
When Soviet troops entered Hungary in 1956 to prevent Hungary from
moving out of the Soviet orbit, any consideration by the Council was effectively prevented by the Soviet veto.

On the basis of experience to date, one can conclude that the Security
Also, on a number of occasions the Council has refrained from dealing with a situation on the ground that it was already under consideration
by a regional organization or that it was appropriate for consideration by
such a regional body. Mention has already been made of the case of
Guatemala. Council consideration of American intervention in the Dominican Republic, the economic blockade of Cuba, and American military
threats to Cuba has been objected to on these grounds. Also, following the
Belgian and American rescue operation at Stanleyville in 1964 it was made
clear in the Security Council's discussions that "problems and disputes
affecting peace and security in the continent of Africa" should be handled
by the Organization of African Unity.[115] When Nigeria was torn by internal violence as a result of the Ebos' attempt to set up an independent
state of Biafra, no Security Council consideration took place in deference
to the views of the African republics that this was a matter of purely
African concern.

On the basis of experience to date, one can conclude that the Security
Council has been in some respects a much less effective organ for the maintenance of international peace and security than was originally hoped.
Primarily, this has been due to the divisions that have existed between the
permanent members and the absence of a sufficiently strong overriding interest in the prevention and termination of local conflicts to enable them
to accommodate their divergent national policies and attitudes. It is a
mistake, however, to write off the role of the Security Council as one of
complete failure. It has been successful in a number of cases in putting an
end to fighting and in preserving an uneasy peace, if peace is identified with
the absence of armed hostilities. It has not, except in Korea under very
unusual circumstances, shown the muscle that was expected of it in enforcing peace. In fact, one can say that enforcement action as envisaged
under the terms of Chapter VII has largely become a dead letter. Instead,
it has utilized, under the name of peacekeeping operations, methods more

akin to those which are envisaged in Article 40 of the Charter, namely, provisional measures intended to prevent further deterioration of the situation and create conditions that permit further efforts at peaceful settlement or accommodation.

The failure of the Council to be more effective as an organ of peaceful settlement and accommodation is no doubt due primarily to the fact that while in particular situations the permanent members have seen a common interest in putting an end to fighting, they have not found a like common interest in agreeing upon the terms of settlement which they are prepared to persuade the parties to accept. Left to their own devices, the interested parties have been able to play the major powers against each other and to exploit their conflicting interests to their own particular national advantage. Though they have been largely deterred by their commitments under the Charter and pressures brought to bear upon them through the responsible organs of the United Nations from prosecuting their claims by armed force, they have not been induced to anything like the same degree to accommodate their respective claims in the interest of permanent settlements.

The limited achievement of the Council does not indicate any defect in the basic premise of the Charter that power should be related to responsibility and that substantial decisions of the Council should require agreement of the major powers. It is difficult to see how the Council could have been any more effective if it had been able to take its decisions by simple or majority votes without the requirement of permanent member concurrence. It is the state of international relations in the postwar period that has been responsible for the limited achievements of the Security Council and not the particular structure and voting procedure of the Council which, on the whole, apart from the absence of Communist China, have realistically reflected the state of world affairs.[116]

The Regulation of Armaments

As we have already seen, one of the responsibilities placed upon the Council by the Charter was that of formulating, with the assistance of the Military Staff Committee, plans for establishing a system for the regulation of armaments to be submitted to members for their consideration. Disarmament had been viewed by the framers of the Charter as one of the subsidiary approaches to the maintenance of international peace. In the light of League experience and the experience of the prewar and war periods, the accepted view was that reduction of armaments without guaranteed security might well be an inducement to aggressive action. Consequently, the role of the Security Council in proposing a plan for the regulation of armaments was viewed as following in time the fuller development of the United Nations security system. The explosion of the atomic bomb changed all this. Major powers became concerned from the very beginning with the problem of controlling atomic energy. In its first session, the General Assembly adopted a resolution establishing a United Nations Atomic Energy Commission to make recommendations for the regulation of atomic energy.[117] Though the Soviet Union had favored having this commission established by the Security Council, it agreed to a compromise proposal under which the commission, though established by the Assembly, should report and be accountable to the Security Council in all matters affecting security. The responsibilities of the Security Council were fully recognized in the Assembly's subsequent resolution on principles governing the general regulation and reduction of armaments.[118]

In accordance with the Assembly's recommendations, the Council established a Commission for Conventional Armaments. During the next few years major discussions on plans for the regulation of armaments took place in these two commissions. The Military Staff Committee took no part in these discussions. Efforts to obtain Security Council approval of the recommendations of the Atomic Energy Commission were defeated by the Soviet veto and in the Commission for Conventional Armaments the gap between the positions of the Soviet Union and the Western powers was so great it soon became apparent that no agreement could be reached. From 1950 on the Security Council ceased to play any role in efforts to work out agreements for the regulation of armaments. All discussions within the United Nations took place in the General Assembly and the more significant and meaningful discussions took place between the major powers under arrangements of their own making. However, proposals later made for general and complete disarmament recognized the responsibility of the Security Council in the field by making it responsible for dealing with infringements of the treaty. This responsibility, however, would not be in application of Article 26 but, rather, of the Council's general powers under other articles of the Charter. Also, under the terms of the Treaty for the Non-Proliferation of Atomic Weapons, the responsibility of the Security Council, and, more particularly, the permanent members, is explicitly recognized.

FUTURE PROSPECTS

The future of the Security Council very largely depends upon the course of international relations and more particularly the attitudes of the major powers with respect to the role which the United Nations is to play. It is, of course, impossible to predict with any certainty. One can indicate present trends and assume that the developments of the decade or so ahead will be substantially in line with current trends but there is always the possibility of some unforeseen development.[119] One unforeseeable uncertainty is the impact which the bringing of Communist China into active participation in the United Nations is going to have upon the work of the organization, and upon the role of the Security Council in particular.

If we project the trends of recent years, we would have reason to expect that as the result of the expansion of the United Nations and the presence in the organization of a majority of members whose primary interests are in economic development and in the elimination of colonialism and of racial discrimination, the General Assembly will continue to occupy the center of the stage. The Security Council, however, will be called upon to play an important but somewhat subsidiary role as the organ responsible for keeping violence to an acceptable minimum in those areas where the major powers have an interest in achieving some degree of peace and stability by a process of accommodation, and available to bring additional pressures to bear on states unwilling to accept standards of conduct developed and asserted by the Assembly.

There is, however, another possible consequence of the enlargement of membership and the increase in the number of new states—namely, that the internal instability and boundary conflicts to which these new states may be prone will create a rash of new disputes and situations in which the Security Council will be called upon to discharge its Charter responsibilities. If the permanent members, particularly the United States and the Soviet Union, see a common interest in keeping their rivalry from entering these areas, the Security Council may find here an important field of activity. This suggests the possibility that, with agreement between the permanent members of the Security Council on conditions under which peacekeeping operations will be initiated and carried out, this particular function of the United Nations may come to have a revived and important role in the work of the organization.

It is difficult to foresee that agreement will be reached on conditions of initiating and conducting peacekeeping operations, except generally on those terms which are being insisted upon by the Soviet Union and which seem to be increasingly acceptable to the United States and the other Western powers. On the other hand, there is the possibility that, with Communist China occupying the permanent seat in the Security Council and engaging in what the Soviets may regard as obstructive activity, the Soviet Union may see some advantage in accepting a limited role for the General Assembly in the initiation and conduct of peacekeeping operations. This would not have the consequence of reducing substantially the relative importance of the Security Council's role since its primary responsibility would certainly be generally accepted.

One definite consequence of the expansion of membership and the particular attitudes that the new members have come to adopt with regard to the priorities of the organization and matters of particular concern to themselves is that even the United States, which in the past has tended to look upon the General Assembly as providing a forum where supporting majorities could be mobilized, will look with less favor upon the use of that organ for peace and security purposes. In the last decade or so, on the other hand, the Soviet Union has shown an increasing inclination to use the General Assembly for promoting proposals which tend to have divisive and weakening effects so far as the West is concerned and to attract the support of the new members of the organization. This, however, is not likely to mean a change in the Soviet Union's attitude with regard to the primary responsibility of the Security Council for dealing with disputes and situations affecting the maintenance of international peace and security. Consequently, the major powers are likely to find themselves in greater agreement than in the past that the Security Council provides the forum where their special interests in international peace and security can best be safeguarded.

It seems to be generally agreed that particularly since the middle fifties tensions of the cold war have tended to lessen. While there is as yet no complete agreement between East and West and no likelihood that in the immediate future important differences will not continue, there are some indications, though not fully conclusive, that the relations of the Soviet Union and the principal Western powers will continue to improve. It is interesting to speculate on what the effect of such a development upon the role of the Security Council will be. If the major powers find it easier to reach agreement on issues of great concern to them, such as questions relating to the future of Germany and the limitation, if not reduction, of armaments, this may result in the United Nations becoming a more active and effective organization with the Security Council discharging more effectively the functions which it was originally intended to carry out.

On the other hand, the result of such improvement in relations may be quite the opposite. The final outcome will largely depend upon whether the major powers find it in their interest to work through the organization or outside it. As a matter of fact, such an improvement could conceivably reduce the work of the organization in the peace and security field to a still lower level, leaving as its principal concern the economic, social, and technical problems that are increasingly occupying its attention today and in the handling of which the Security Council would have little concern. The responsibility for these matters would fall on the General Assembly and its subsidiary organs along with the specialized agencies.

If tensions between East and West continue to be fairly high, then we could reasonably expect the continuation of the present situation with the Security Council performing an important function but being far less effective as an instrument for preserving the peace and security than the framers of the Charter had originally hoped. If we have mounting internal violence and border conflicts between the more newly established states, the major powers, even with tensions continuing between East and West, may, as we have seen, find it to their common interest to avoid involvement in these difficulties, fearing they may trigger a world holocaust which all seek to avoid. Consequently, even with the continuing level of tension between East and West, the importance of the organization and particularly of the Security Council may still remain. The very existence of this tension may make it seem to their interest and, in fact, necessary for them to make greater use of the United Nations, and the Security Council in particular, than they would find it necessary to do if their relations were more fully harmonious.

On the assumption of this kind of development, it becames especially important for the future role of the Security Council that agreement should be reached among the permanent members on the role that the Security Council is to play in the initiating and conduct of peacekeeping operations. There seems to be little possibility that military forces will be used under United Nations auspices and Security Council direction for enforcement purposes. Consequently, those provisions of the Charter relating to enforcement in the military sense are likely to continue a dead letter. On the other hand, there is the possibility that agreements envisaged under Article 43 can be used for the purpose of making available to the Security Council forces and facilities to be used in connection with military operations which have as their purpose not coercion, but pacification on the basis of general consent.

In the final analysis, the future of the Security Council will largely depend upon the attitude of the principal member governments. The attitudes of the permanent members will be the most decisive influence because they alone have it within their power to determine whether the Security Council plays an important and effective role or not. Their interest in the Security Council may well be decisively influenced by the extent to which the Security Council, by its composition and operating procedures, provides a forum where the representatives of the major powers can exercise the influence to which they feel entitled over the course of international affairs. Any attempt to further enlarge the Council to increase the number of nonpermanent representatives and permit more extensive participation and wider representation may be highly detrimental to the organ's future. Any attempt by the smaller states to use their voting power in the Council to serve their particular purposes, even to the detriment of major power interests, is likely to be self-defeating. The basic concept which the authors of the Charter had in mind in the establishment of the Security Council corresponds to the realities of international politics, and any attempt to circumvent it in the name of "sovereign equality" is likely to have serious consequences not only for the Security Council but also for the United Nations itself.

NOTES

1. See *Report to the President on the Results of the San Francisco Conference by the Chairman of the United States Delegation, the Secretary of State* (Department of State Publication 2349), pp. 66–80.
2. See League of Nations Covenant, Articles 12, 13, and 15.
3. *Ibid.,* Article 4.
4. *Ibid.,* Article 16.
5. *Ibid.,* Article 10.
6. *Ibid.,* Article 5, paragraph 1.

7. On early U.S. Department of State thinking, see Ruth B. Russell and Jeannette Muther, *A History of the United Nations Charter* (Washington, D.C.: Brookings Institution, 1958), pp. 208–212.

8. In the report of the International Blockade Committee and in the practice followed in the application of sanctions against Italy in 1935–1936.

9. See Royal Institute of International Affairs, *International Sanctions* (London, 1938).

10. League of Nations Covenant, Article 8.

11. William E. Rappard, *The Quest for Peace* (Cambridge: Harvard University Press, 1940), chap. V.

12. See Russell and Muther, *United Nations Charter*, Part II; and *Post-War Foreign Policy Preparation* (Department of State Publication 3580).

13. See Russell and Muther, *United Nations Charter*, Part III.

14. *Ibid.*, pp. 1019–1028.

15. See *Ibid.*, Part V; and Goodrich and Hambro, *Charter of the United Nations: Commentary and Documents*, rev. ed. (Boston: World Peace Foundation, 1949), Introduction.

16. UN Charter, Article 1.

17. *Ibid.*, Article 26.

18. *Ibid.*, Article 24, paragraph 1.

19. *Ibid.*, Article 23.

20. Article 4, paragraph 2 of the Covenant provided that the Council, with the approval of the Assembly, might name additional permanent members of the Council, and Germany and the USSR were so added.

21. See *Report to the President on the Results of the San Francisco Conference*, p. 68. On the desirability of associating responsibility with power in the organization of peace, see William W. Kaufmann, "The Organization of Responsibility," *World Politics*, I (1949), 511–541.

22. President Roosevelt and Secretary of State Hull insisted that the Republic of China be accepted as a major power in line with U.S. policy of seeking a united, democratic, and friendly China as a counterweight to Japan in the Far East. See Russell and Muther, *United Nations Charter*, pp. 54–55.

23. France, Great Britain, Italy, Japan, and the United States.

24. League of Nations Covenant, Article 4, paragraph 1.

25. UN Charter, Article 23, paragraph 1.

26. See Goodrich, Hambro, and Simons, *Charter of the United Nations: Commentary and Documents*, 3rd rev. ed. (New York: Columbia University Press, 1969), pp. 202–207.

27. League of Nations Covenant, Article 1, paragraph 2.

28. UN Charter, Article 5.

29. *Ibid.*, Article 6.

30. *Ibid.*, Article 97.

31. League of Nations Covenant, Article 6, paragraph 2.

32. Article 4 of the Statute.

33. Though Article 24 refers to chaps. VIII and XII in addition to VI and VII, neither of these chapters adds importantly to the powers of the Council. Chap. VIII emphasizes the importance of using regional arrangements where appropriate, and chap. XII gives the Council certain powers with respect to "strategic areas" under the trusteeship system.

34. UN Charter, Article 34.

35. *Ibid.*, Article 36.

36. *Ibid.*, Article 37.

37. *Ibid.*, Article 52.

38. *Ibid.*, Article 39.

39. See Goodrich, Hambro, and Simons, *Charter of United Nations,* pp. 293–302.

40. UN Charter, Article 40.

41. *Ibid.* Especially Articles 25, 39, and 42.

42. Goodrich, Hambro, and Simons, *Charter of United Nations,* pp. 314–317.

43. UN Charter, Article 26.

44. *Ibid.,* Article 11, paragraph 1.

45. *Ibid.,* Article 27, paragraph 3. See Dwight E. Lee, "The Genesis of the Veto," *International Organization,* I (1947), 33–42.

46. UN Charter, Article 27, paragraph 2.

47. United Nations Conference on International Organization, *Documents,* XI, 710–714; Goodrich, Hambro, and Simons, *Charter of United Nations,* pp. 217–220.

48. ICJ Statute, Article 10, paragraph 2.

49. UN Charter, Articles 60 and 85.

50. See Russell and Muther, *United Nations Charter,* pp. 754–775.

51. UN Charter, Article 24.

52. *Ibid.,* Article 12, paragraph 1.

53. *Ibid.,* Article 11, paragraph 2.

54. *Ibid.,* Article 107.

55. For accounts of the "cold war" see Louis J. Halle, *The Cold War as History* (New York: Harper & Row, 1967); and Herbert Feis, *From Thrust to Terror: The Onset of the Cold War, 1945–1950* (New York: Norton, 1970).

56. See *Yearbook of the United Nations, 1955,* pp. 22–30.

57. See David Kay, "The Impact of African States on the United Nations," *International Organization,* XXIII (1969), 20–47; and *The New Nations in the United Nations, 1960–1967* (New York: Columbia University Press, 1970).

58. General Assembly Resolution 2758 (XXVI), October 25, 1971.

59. See Herbert W. Briggs, "Chinese Representation in the United Nations," *International Organization,* VI (1952), 192–209; and Sydney D. Bailey, "Chinese Representation in the Security Council and the General Assembly of the United Nations," *ISIO Monographs,* 1st series, No. 1.

60. General Assembly Resolution 396 (V), December 14, 1950.

61. See Sydney D. Bailey, *Voting in the Security Council* (Bloomington: Indiana University Press, 1969), pp. 23–24.

62. General Assembly Resolution 1991 (XVII), December 17, 1963.

63. See Goodrich, Hambro, and Simons, *Charter of United Nations,* pp. 196–199.

64. An obvious example is Israel which has never been elected to the Security Council though geographically located in the Middle East.

65. See Geoffrey L. Goodwin, *Britain and the United Nations* (New York: Carnegie Endowment for International Peace, 1958), pp. 240–241.

66. "Other states" include notably the white dominions—Australia, Canada, and New Zealand.

67. UNCIO, *Documents,* XI, 710–714; Goodrich, Hambro, and Simons, *Charter of United Nations,* pp. 217–220.

68. For an analysis of the use of the veto, see Bailey, *Voting in the Security Council,* cited above, pp. 26–74; and John G. Stoessinger, *The United Nations and the Super Powers* (New York: Random House, 1965), pp. 3–19.

69. See Bailey, *Voting in the Security Council,* pp. 48–54.

70. ICJ *Reports* (1948), p. 65.

71. ICJ *Reports* (1950), p. 10.

72. See Goodrich, Hambro, and Simons, *Charter of United Nations,* pp. 230–231 and footnote 127.

73. See Russell and Muther, *United Nations Charter,* pp. 713–749.

74. For text of report see General Assembly, *Official Records,* 3rd sess., Suppl. 10 (A/578).

75. See Stoessinger, *Super Powers,* pp. 3–19.

76. General Assembly Resolution 377 (V), November 3, 1950.

77. In 1959, for example, only five meetings were held.

78. General Assembly Resolution 39 (I), December 12, 1946.

79. Security Council, *Official Records,* 2nd yr., Sp. Suppl. 2 (S/360, Rev. 1).

80. General Assembly Resolutions 193 (III), November 27, 1948, and 288 (IV), November 18, 1949.

81. General Assembly Resolution 111 (II), November 13, 1947.

82. General Assembly Resolution 377 (V), November 3, 1950.

83. See Leland M. Goodrich, *Korea: A Study of U.S. Policy in the United Nations* (New York: Council on Foreign Relations, 1956), pp. 149–177.

84. General Assembly Resolutions 498 (V), February 1, 1951, and 500 (V), May 18, 1951.

85. See Gabriella Rosner, *The United Nations Emergency Force* (New York: Columbia University Press, 1963).

86. General Assembly Resolution 1854A (XVII), December 19, 1962.

87. Security Council Resolution 242 (1967). On Security Council handling of the 1967 Middle East crisis, see Arthur Lall, *The U.N. and the Middle East Crisis, 1967* (New York: Columbia University Press, 1968).

88. See Goodrich, Hambro, and Simons, *Charter of United Nations,* pp. 85–96.

89. Article 99, in particular, which confers what the Preparatory Commission characterized as the secretary-general's "special right." *Report of the Preparatory Commission of the United Nations* (PC/20, December 23, 1945), p. 87.

90. General Assembly Resolution 492 (V), November 1, 1950.

91. Security Council, *Official Records,* 1st yr., 1st series, No. 2, 23rd meeting (February 16, 1946), p. 369.

92. On report see Security Council, *Official Records,* 2nd yr., Sp. Suppl. 1; and Goodrich, Hambro, and Simons, *Charter of United Nations,* pp. 319–324.

93. Security Council, *Official Records,* 2nd yr., 146th meeting (June 25, 1947), p. 1099.

94. UN Charter, Article 23, paragraph 1.

95. *Ibid.,* Article 28, paragraph 2.

96. See, for example, Secretary-General Thant's "Introduction to the Annual Report of the Secretary-General . . ." for the years 1967–1968 and 1970. Trygve Lie and Dag Hammarskjöld had earlier urged the implementation of the article.

97. Resolution of June 12, 1970. The Provisional Rules of Procedure have from the beginning provided that "periodic meetings" as called for in Article 28, paragraph 2, of the Charter "shall be held twice a year" (Rule 4).

98. *UN Monthly Chronicle,* November 1970, pp. 124–125.

99. See Leland M. Goodrich and Anne P. Simons, *The United Nations and the Maintenance of International Peace and Security* (Washington, D.C.: Brookings Institution, 1956), Part III.

100. See Goodrich, Hambro, and Simons, *Charter of United Nations,* pp. 279–280.

101. *Ibid.,* pp. 265–270.

102. Security Council, *Official Records,* 15th yr., 920th meeting (December 13–14, 1960), pp. 14–15.

103. UN Charter, Article 107.

104. See, for example, account of discussions leading to the adoption of the Council's resolution of November 22, 1967, on the Middle East situation in Lall, *Middle East Crisis,* pp. 230–270.

105. Security Council Resolution of November 16, 1948.

106. Security Council Resolution of August 11, 1949.

107. See Ernest W. Lefever, *Crisis in the Congo* (Washington, D.C.: Brookings Institution, 1956); James A. Stegenga, *The United Nations Force in Cyprus* (Columbus: Ohio State University Press, 1968); and Alan James, *The Politics of Peace-Keeping* (New York: Praeger, 1969).

108. See Alastair M. Taylor, *Indonesian Independence and the United Nations* (Ithaca, N.Y.: Cornell University Press, 1960).

109. Security Council Resolution of November 22, 1967.

110. UN Documents S/4741, February 20–21, 1961, and S/5002, November 24, 1961.

111. In 1948, for example, joint military action by the permanent members to restore peace in Palestine, though considered, was not possible because neither the United States nor the Soviet Union wanted to see the forces of the other introduced into the area.

112. See Leland M. Goodrich, "Peace Enforcement in Perspective," *International Journal,* XXIV (August 1969), 663–666.

113. Security Council Resolution 232, December 16, 1966.

114. Security Council, *Official Records,* 1st yr., 2nd series, 87th meeting (December 19, 1946), p. 701.

115. UN Document S/6128, December 30, 1964.

116. For analysis of effect of the use of the veto on the ultimate resolution of international issues, see Stoessinger, *Super Powers,* pp. 3–19.

117. General Assembly Resolution 1 (I), January 24, 1946.

118. General Assembly Resolution 41 (I), December 14, 1946.

119. For one thoughtful attempt to foresee the world of the seventies, see Lincoln P. Bloomfield, "Is the U.N. Relevant to the 1970's?", *Vista,* May–June 1970, p. 106.

Stephen G. Xydis

THE GENERAL ASSEMBLY

Among the principal organs of the United Nations, the General Assembly functions as the plenary body for the United Nations system as a whole. Its competence is general, not special. With regard to the internal setting of the United Nations, it constitutes the core of the organization and performs diverse functions in relation to the other principal UN organs and, of course, in relation to its own setup, procedure, and mode of operations.

With regard to its external setting, it performs functions in the political, economic, social, humanitarian, and cultural fields. It constitutes a regular diplomatic conference for all UN members. It has the right to request the International Court of Justice for advisory opinions and to authorize other principal organs of the United Nations to do likewise.[1] However, the Assembly is no legislature. It produces no statutes but only resolutions,[2] of which only some are legally binding and most are recommendations. Nor is the Assembly a parliament. For it has no power to unseat the Security Council, which resembles the executive branch in the American system rather than the cabinet in a parliamentary system.

Viewed in broad historical perspective, the Charter provisions on the Assembly represent, despite a few differences, the formalization of practices introduced and developed by its predecessor, the Assembly of the League of Nations, as it determined the performance of its functions under the Covenant of the League. Thus the Charter formalized the practice of the annual sessions of the Assembly, as the League itself had decided at its first session in 1920, despite views of British and French statesmen that it should meet quadrennially only and constitute a "temporary body" or a "recurrent ambassadorial conference," [3] in contrast to the League's Council. The Charter also formalized the Assembly's role as a supervisory organ over the whole organization—a role that derived partly from the decision of the League Assembly to meet annually and partly from its decision, likewise reached at its first session, to include on its agenda every year a report on the Secretariat's work. Moreover, the Charter also formally proclaimed the Assembly's "power of the purse." This power, which was not mentioned in the Covenant of the League, was assumed by the League Assembly, again at its first session, when its members insisted that the financial authority should reside in the organ of the League in which all member states were represented.[4] Finally, the broadening of the set of exceptions to the basic rule of unanimity proclaimed in the League Covenant through practices introduced in the Assembly's rules of procedure and by other means[5] which will soon be noted, was formally reflected in several provisions of the Charter, where majority voting is the rule and unanimity an exception limited to the permanent members of the Security Council when dealing with substantive resolutions.

The structure and methods of operation of the UN General Assembly will first be described; then its internal and external functions and its resolutionary process will be analyzed; finally, the scope, nature, and effects of its resolutions will be explained.

STRUCTURE AND METHODS OF OPERATION

The General Assembly consists of all the member states of the United Nations.[6] Some nonmember states which have observers with the United Nations attend its sessions only as distinguished guests.[7] It meets once a year in regular session, commencing on the third Tuesday in September. It normally holds its sessions at UN headquarters in New York, unless a majority of members agree on another site 120 days before the session. It adopted its rules of procedure in 1947 and has repeatedly amended them since then.[8]

At the request of the Security Council, of a majority of UN members, or of one member with the concurrence of the majority, the Assembly may meet in special session. Under the "Uniting for Peace" Resolution of November 3, 1950, however, it may also meet in emergency special session at the request of any ten members of the Security Council or by a majority of UN members, within twenty-four hours, not within thirty days as in the case of special sessions. The special and special emergency sessions of the Assembly operate under progressively simpler rules of procedure than the Assembly's regular sessions. They deal only with the matter that prompted the calling of these sessions, unless a two-thirds majority of the Assembly decides to deal also with connected matters. In special emergency sessions the Assembly deliberates in plenary session only. During the quarter century of its existence, the Assembly has met five times in special sessions (1947, 1948, 1961, 1963, and 1967) and six times in special emergency sessions (twice in 1956, and once in 1958, 1960, 1967, and 1971).

No member can send more than five representatives to Assembly sessions.[9] This provision was adopted at the San Francisco Conference (April 25–June 26, 1945) in order to protect the interests of the lesser state members. Under the Assembly's rules of procedure, however, members may send five alternate representatives to its sessions. Each delegation, of course, may have quite a number of advisers on its staff to carry out its work and cover the various Assembly committees. The credentials of these government representatives must be sent to the secretary-general by the head of state or government or the foreign minister not less than a week before the date of the opening of the session. From 1950 to 1971, because of the controversy over the representation of China in the United Nations, the Assembly's approval of the Credential Committee's report, instead of being among the first items of business, was one of the last.

The Assembly operates through (1) plenary meetings; (2) seven main committees; (3) two organizational committees; and (4) occasional ad hoc committees established to speed up the session's work.

The nine-member Credentials Committee is one of the two organization committees; the other is the twenty-five-member General Committee. Both are of limited membership, in contrast to the seven main committees, on which all members are represented.

These seven main committees, which prepare recommendations for approval of the Assembly in plenary meetings, are:

1 First Committee (Political and Security, including the regulation of armaments; also admission, suspension, and expulsion of UN members)
2 Special Political Committee, which shares the work of the First Committee
3 Second Committee (Economic and Financial)
4 Third Committee (Social, Humanitarian, and Cultural)
5 Fourth Committee (Trusteeship and Non-Self-Governing Territories)
6 Fifth Committee (Administrative and Budgetary)
7 Sixth Committee (Legal)

Originally, the Special Political Committee was an ad hoc body set up because of the plethora of political questions on the Assembly's agenda. It was established on a permanent basis, however, since 1956.

Among the first items of business on the Assembly's agenda is the election of the session's president by secret ballot and without nominations. This ban discourages nomination speeches, and the nomination process takes place backstage, with public withdrawals, when they occur, being the equivalent of nominations.[10] Until this election, the chairman of the delegation from which the president of the previous Assembly session has been elected presides. The practice has been followed of excluding from the presidency representatives of the Security Council's permanent members. The office rotates among the major groups of states in the United Nations —the African and Asian, Eastern European, Latin American, Western European, and other states. The president, who is elected in his personal capacity, is considered an officer of the United Nations and has no vote. He presides over all plenary meetings of the Assembly, directs the debate, recognizes speakers, ensures observation of the rules, puts questions, rules on points of order. He may propose a time limit on speakers, closure of the list of speakers or of the debate, suspension or adjournment of a meeting or adjournment of the debate of an item under discussion.

The rules of procedure, not the Charter, mention the offices of vice-presidents of the Assembly. As the number of UN members increased, the Assembly decided to have 17 vice-presidents and to elect them as follows, on the basis of ensuring the representative character of the General Committee:[11]

7 from Asian and African states
3 from Latin American states
2 from Western European and other states
1 from Eastern European states

The five permanent members of the Security Council also have a right to have vice-presidents of their own, and the region from which the president is elected has one vice-president less than indicated by the above allocation of vice-presidents.[12] The election of the vice-presidents on the above geographic basis, like the election of nonpermanent members of the Security Council, fosters the regional group activities of UN members. The vice-presidents preside in rotation over the Assembly in the absence of the president. If the president resigns or is unable to continue performing his duties, the Assembly elects a new president to complete his unexpired term. As yet this has never happened even though once, at the Assembly's twenty-third session, its Guatemalan president, Emilio Arenales Catalan, was gravely ill most of the time.

Together with the president and the chairmen of the seven main committees, the vice-presidents form the General Committee, which organizes the work of the Assembly throughout its session. The General Committee recommends to the Assembly the inclusion, exclusion, or postponement of items on the agenda; the rewording of items and the grouping or amalgamation of related items; the allocation of items to the plenary Assembly itself or to the main committees; and the closing date of the session. The Assembly also appoints the members of the Credentials Committee on the acting president's proposal. The Assembly president, at weekly working luncheons with the committee chairmen and the competent members of the Secretariat, actually deals with the organizational details of the Assembly throughout its session.

For preparing matters for the Assembly's further consideration or for implementing Assembly resolutions, the Assembly has the right to set up various subsidiary bodies. Thus, during the quarter century of its existence, it has appointed more than two hundred subsidiary bodies, committees, commissions, panels, boards, agencies, or special representatives which assist it in carrying out its diverse internal and external tasks and operate independently of its sessions. For fulfilling its internal functions, it established the Advisory Committee on Administrative and Budgetary

Questions, the Committee on Contributions, and the Board of Auditors. And, for fulfilling its functions in its external setting, it has set up subsidiary bodies for dealing with problems in the Balkans,[13] Palestine and the Middle East,[14] South Africa,[15] Libya,[16] West Irian,[17] or for considering general problems such as disarmament,[18] peace observation, peacekeeping, and collective measures,[19] and for developing and codifying international law,[20] for technical assistance and training and research,[21] for trade and development,[22] for dealing with problems of non-self-governing territories,[23] refugees,[24] children,[25] or narcotic drugs.[26]

The membership of these various subsidiary organs of the General Assembly ranges from participation of all UN members to a single individual. The Assembly itself usually decides on the membership of these subsidiary organs. Occasionally, however, it leaves the matter of nomination up to the president of the Assembly or the secretary-general. These subsidiary bodies consist mostly of government representatives, though in some cases they consist of experts. Some of the bodies are involved in the administrative and budgetary field or in continuous operations and are therefore permanent; others are terminated once their specific task is completed. In all cases the Assembly is free to modify their functions.

ASSEMBLY DECISION MAKING— THE FORMAL RULES

For Assembly decision making, each member has one vote.[27] This is both consistent with past international practice and with the Charter's recognition that the organization is based on the principle of sovereign equality of the member states. No system of weighted voting was considered at San Francisco.[28] This is not surprising. The lesser states, despite their often limited resources in territory, population, and wealth, would have resented any effort to do away with this traditional principle of international law. Weighted voting exists only in the UN Security Council, because of the veto power of its five permanent members. It also appears in some of the specialized agencies which are part of the entire UN system, and specifically in the International Bank for Reconstruction and Development and the International Monetary Fund.

Assembly decisions are in the form of resolutions. These consist of one or more preambular or declarative clauses and of one or more operative clauses. The former explain the reasons for the adoption of the latter. The Assembly adopts these resolutions by two types of majority vote. As compared with the earlier practice of international conferences, majority voting constitutes an innovation. Under the Covenant of the League of Nations, unanimity was the rule except where otherwise expressly provided in the Covenant and in matters of Assembly or Council procedure.[29] This voting innovation in the UN General Assembly, however, is somewhat less startling than it appears at first glance. For its predecessor, the League

Assembly, had developed the practice of adopting by simple majority vote the type of resolutions called *"voeux"* which expressed a sort of general wish of the majority of its members addressed to an actor in its external setting, and these were not binding on their addressee, as in the case of the UN Assembly's "recommendations." Perhaps the latter may have greater weight than mere *"voeux"* [30] but they have less weight than legally binding decisions such as those which the Security Council may take in certain circumstances, under Chapter VII of the Charter.[31] The force of Assembly resolutions, however, will be discussed at greater length below.

Elections for both the Assembly and committee officers are by secret vote. Other votes are usually taken by a show of hands. Voting by standing is permissible but has not been used. At the request of any member, a roll call vote may be applied. The roll is taken in the English alphabetical order of the names of members, beginning with the member whose name has been drawn by lot by the presiding officer. Since 1967 voting by mechanical means has been used. Occasionally, no formal voting takes place when a consensus clearly exists, in which case it is announced by the president of the Assembly. Thus time is gained and explanations of vote may be avoided. New members recommended by the Security Council have at times been welcomed by acclamation. On a particular occasion, at the Assembly's nineteenth session of 1964, because of the crisis over the refusal of the USSR, its allies, and France to contribute to the expenditures of the United Nations Emergency Force (UNEF) and the United Nations Operation in the Congo (ONUC) and the possibility of their being deprived of vote in the Assembly because of being in arrears on their financial obligations to the United Nations,[32] a "no-objection" procedure was devised to allow the stymied Assembly to take certain urgent decisions. Under this procedure, the Assembly president or the secretary-general consulted individually the UN members and, if unanimity was ascertained, this was announced by the president. In case of disagreement, on the other hand, the decision was reached by vote taken informally and outside the Assembly hall.[33]

Except in the case of important matters, the Assembly adopts resolutions by a simple majority of members present and voting. In the case of important matters a two-thirds majority vote is required. In either case abstainers are considered nonparticipants in the vote. Hence at times the Assembly adopts resolutions by a vote of the minority of its total membership.

The Charter specifically mentions a number of important matters in which the Assembly has to apply the principle of a two-thirds majority vote. However, the Assembly itself, by a simple majority vote, may decide whether a question under consideration should be resolved by a two-thirds vote. Important matters specifically mentioned in the Charter pertain to the Assembly's performance of its constituent and elective functions (to be described below), its functions that are related to the operation of the trusteeship system and to the maintenance of international peace and security.[34] The Assembly resorts to the same two-thirds majority vote in placing additional items on its agenda,[35] as well as for adopting amendments to the UN Charter.[36] In the latter case, however, a two-thirds majority vote of the total UN membership is required, the concurrence of the five permanent members of the Security Council included.

In practice, the vast majority of Assembly resolutions have been adopted unanimously or by a two-thirds majority. At times the Assembly adopted resolutions which maintained that the two-thirds majority requirement did not apply to a particular question the Assembly was considering. In a few instances, on the other hand, it adopted resolutions which maintained that the two-thirds majority did apply to the matter under consideration. This has been the case since 1961, when dealing with the question of the representation of China in the United Nations, or in a 1954 resolution concerning special rules for considering reports of the Committee on South-West Africa.

THE ASSEMBLY'S FUNCTIONS

And now first the internal and second the external functions of the Assembly will be analyzed.

Internal Functions of the Assembly

The Assembly's internal functions are constituent, elective, financial and administrative, and supervisory over other UN organs.

The Assembly performs constituent functions when it votes on Security Council recommendations with regard to the admission of new UN members, the suspension of a member against which the Security Council has taken enforcement action under Chapter VII of the Charter,[37] or its expulsion because it has been found to violate persistently the principles of the Charter.[38]

In its elective functions, the Assembly elects the ten nonpermanent members of the UN Security Council who serve on it for a two-year term and are not eligible for immediate reelection. In doing so, it has to pay due regard to the contribution of UN members to the maintenance of international peace and security, to the other purposes of the organization, and also to equitable geographical distribution.[39] In 1965, when the Assembly approved of the Charter amendment under which the number of non-permanent members of the Security Council was raised from six to ten, it resolved that the seats of nonpermanent members should be allocated to various geographic regions as follows: five seats to African and Asian members; two seats to Latin American members; two seats to Western European members and "other states" (Western though not European, such as Australia, New Zealand, or Canada); and one seat to an Eastern

European state. This resolution superseded the earlier "gentlemen's agreement" on geographic representation on the Security Council. As far as the Assembly was concerned, it strengthened the role of geographic groups in dealing with such issues, to the detriment of states which belonged to no regional group though geographically part of one.

The Assembly also elects the twenty-seven members of the Economic and Social Council who serve on it for a term of three years and are reeligible for immediate election.[40] Under the same above-mentioned resolution of 1965, the Assembly decided that without prejudice to the current distribution of seats in that council the nine additional seats should be allocated to various geographic regions as follows: seven seats to African and Asian states; one to Latin America; and one to Western European and other states. This provision, too, enhances the role of geographic groups in the Assembly. The Assembly also elects the category of members of the Trusteeship Council who serve for three-year terms and whose number depends on the requirement of ensuring that the total membership of the Trusteeship Council is equally divided between those UN members who administer trust territories and those who do not.[41]

Finally, the Assembly appoints, on the Security Council's recommendation, the secretary-general and, voting separately from the Security Council, it elects the fifteen members of the International Court of Justice.[42]

In performing its financial and administrative functions, the Assembly considers and approves the UN's budget; apportions among UN members the expenses of the organization and supervises the entire organization's financial and administrative affairs. It also examines the financial and budgetary arrangements of the specialized agencies, with the right of making recommendations to them.[43]

The budgetary procedure passes through the following four phases:

First, the secretary-general prepares the budgetary estimate and, at least twelve weeks before the opening of the Assembly's regular session, submits it to its Advisory Committee on Administrative and Budgetary Questions.

Second, the above committee, composed of twelve experts, studies this estimate and then transmits it to all UN members for their perusal at least five weeks before the opening of the Assembly's regular session.

Third, during the Assembly's session, its Fifth Committee goes over the proposed budget and sends it to the Assembly with a relevant resolution, adopted by majority vote.

Fourth, the Assembly in plenary session decides on the committee's draft resolution by a two-thirds vote.

Under certain conditions, the Assembly also authorizes the secretary-general to deal with unforeseen and extraordinary expenses—the former for covering additional expenditures needed for implementing programs approved of in the budget; the latter for covering expenditures of projects which were not originally envisaged when the budget was adopted.

The latter occurred, for instance, in the case of expenditures for the UN Emergency Force or the United Nations Operation in the Congo, the peacekeeping forces of the Assembly and the Security Council, respectively, for the Middle East and the Congo (Zaire).

In apportioning among UN members the regular expenses of the organization, the Assembly is assisted by the Committee on Contributions, staffed by ten experts. In estimating the financial capacity of UN members, the committee is guided by the comparative estimates of their national income. For several years, this committee took into account the economic dislocation suffered by several UN members during World War II as well as their ability to get foreign exchange. Thus, in 1946, the United States paid 39.89 percent of the UN budget. In 1957, however, the Assembly decided that in principle no members should contribute more than 30 percent of the UN's regular budget. Because of the inequality of members' national incomes, contributions in 1965–1967 ranged from a high of 31.91 percent for the United States to a minimum of 0.04 percent for many lesser members. During those two years eighteen members contributed 86.21 percent; the five permanent members of the UN Security Council contributed 64.38 percent. Over the years UN budgets have progressively increased because of increased membership and needs and higher price levels. In 1946 the figure was close to $20 million; two decades later it had passed the $121 million mark. For 1970 the requested budget amounted to $168,420,000.

The scope of the Assembly's role with regard to the budgets of the specialized agencies falls far short of the principle of budgetary consolidation recommended by the Negotiating Committee of the Economic and Social Council at the time the agreements between the United Nations and these agencies were being negotiated as required under Articles 57 and 63 of the Charter. In this supervisory task the Assembly is assisted by the Administrative Committee on Coordination, which helps in coordinating administrative and budgetary practices. Although most of the agreements between the United Nations and the specialized agencies recognize the need of setting up close budgetary and financial ties, to avoid duplication and ensure coordination, the specialized agencies enjoy considerable autonomy in their choice of programs and the means of carrying them out. On occasion they have ignored Assembly resolutions addressed to them. For example, the International Bank for Reconstruction and Development did not comply with an Assembly resolution of 1965 which called on specialized agencies to furnish no kind of aid to the Portuguese and South African governments. Prior to the resolution, the bank had already approved loan applications from those two governments.

The Assembly is also authorized to review the work of other UN organs which transmit to it annual or special reports on their work. However, it hardly ever discusses the annual report it receives from the Security Council and merely takes note of it in plenary session. The Assembly, on the other hand, has discussed in the past certain special Security

Council reports, such as those on the deadlock over the admission of new members between 1946 and 1955, and it adopted relevant resolutions addressed to the Security Council. As for the secretary-general's annual report to the Assembly,[44] this is usually the focus of the general debate which takes place in the Assembly's opening plenary meetings at its regular session. The Assembly, however, does not even take note of this report.

The annual reports submitted to the Assembly by the Economic and Social Council and the Trusteeship Council, both of which operate under the Assembly's authority, receive greater Assembly attention. Its competent main committees—the second, third, or fourth—consider them. In practice, the Assembly has exercised to the full its supervisory authority over those two principal UN organs so that they have come to resemble permanent subsidiary organs of the Assembly.

External Functions of the Assembly

The Assembly has the right to discuss and adopt resolutions not only on matters relating to the powers and functions of any UN organ and other internal matters already noted, but also on any matters within the scope of the Charter—that is, on any question arising out of the external setting of the United Nations, regardless of whether it is political, economic, social, cultural, or other, or involves human rights and fundamental freedoms, as long as these are within the Charter's purview. This general authorization is of major importance. It is proclaimed in Article 10 of the Charter and particularized in the Charter's next four articles.[45] For it empowers the Assembly to discuss matters which, under the Charter, are the "primary responsibility" of the Security Council: the maintenance of international peace and security.[46] This particular right is expressly mentioned in Article 11 of the Charter. The Assembly's right to adopt resolutions on such matters is limited only whenever the Security Council happens to be considering the same issue.[47] The rationale of this limitation is that otherwise the Assembly and Security Council, when concurrently dealing with the same issue, might adopt divergent if not incompatible and conflicting resolutions. This limitation, on the other hand, does not prevent the Assembly from adopting resolutions that are supportive of, or complementary to, resolutions already adopted by the Security Council on a particular conflict and some of its special aspects. Thus, at its emergency special session of June 1967, the Assembly adopted a resolution on the Middle Eastern crisis (the status of Jerusalem) while the Security Council was considering the same international conflict.[48]

Article 10 of the Charter represented a success of the lesser states at the San Francisco Conference. These states did not wish to permit issues of international peace and security to become the monopoly of the Security Council, where the five permanent members play a predominant role. The U.S. delegation at that conference supported the lesser states in their demand and a U.S.-Soviet crisis ensued, with the USSR eventually giving in. Five years later, during the Korean war, the United States was to reap the benefits of its insistence. As for the lesser states, they found this provision particularly valuable whenever they wished to raise issues of self-determination before the United Nations. For they could resort to the Assembly on such issues and avoid the Security Council, in which two of the veto-wielding members were colonial powers. Besides, since the right of the Assembly to deliberate on any matter is not limited, even if the Security Council is considering it concurrently, they always had the possibility of using the forum of the Assembly for airing their viewpoints on an issue and engaging in propaganda on it.

As originally envisaged, the principal role of the Assembly in the maintenance of international peace and security was to help promote the political, economic, social, and other conditions for peace and general international cooperation. By contrast, the Security Council was to serve as an organ of crisis decision making and action whenever international peace was imminently threatened or had been broken. However, thanks to Articles 10 and 11 of the Charter, the Assembly has been able to enlarge its peace-shaping role and to engage also in crisis decision making and management when the Security Council was unable to fulfill its primary function. Any UN member and even a nonmember state (as long as it declares its willingness to accept in advance the obligation of UN members under the Charter to seek peaceful settlement in the particular issue it wishes to raise before the Assembly) or the Security Council (but not the secretary-general)[49] may resort to the Assembly to get it to discuss and pass a resolution that involves matters of international peace and security. The Assembly, in turn, may draw the Security Council's attention to such a matter by a relevant resolution.[50]

An early step toward the shift of Security Council responsibilities on the Assembly was made in 1947 when a Soviet veto-paralyzed Council decided in September to take off its agenda the "Greek question" which the USSR had first raised before the Council in January 1946, and the Assembly then took up the question and set up an eleven-member special committee, the UN Special Committee on the Balkans (UNSCOB), to conciliate Greece with Albania, Bulgaria, and Yugoslavia, which since mid-1946 had been providing moral and material support to the Communist-led Greek guerrillas fighting in northern Greece.

That same year, despite Soviet opposition, the Assembly also set up the Interim Committee, composed of the entire UN membership, as a subsidiary organ that might be able to function between regular Assembly sessions.

Three years later, during the Korean war, a further step was made in the same direction. The Uniting for Peace Resolution of 1950 provided for the possibility of convoking the Assembly within twenty-four hours in special emergency session, as mentioned earlier, for crisis management purposes whenever Security Council action was precluded because of the lack of unanimity among its permanent members. Under this same resolution, the Assembly was specifically empowered to make recommendations to members for collective measures to deal with threats to the peace, breaches of the peace, or acts of aggression, all of which are normally the primary responsibility of the Security Council, particularly under Chapter VII of the Charter. Also set up under this resolution were two fourteen-member subsidiary bodies of the Assembly, a Peace Observation Commission and a Collective Measures Committee. The task of the former was to observe and report on the situation in areas where peace was threatened; the task of the latter was to report on methods that might be collectively used for maintaining peace.

This epoch-making resolution, which the USSR and its supporters denounced as a violation of the Charter, was a high point in the constitutional shift of UN peacekeeping responsibilities from the Security Council to the Assembly. It proved invaluable in several other crises, some of which were not caused by an East-West conflict. For example, during the Suez affair of 1956, the Assembly met in special emergency session after Britain and France cast vetoes in the Security Council, and it authorized the UN secretary-general to set up UNEF for the Middle East. Thus the secretary-general's peacekeeping role was enhanced through Assembly resolution making. His role was strengthened four years later by the Security Council, during the Congo crisis of 1960.

The shift in relative roles of the Assembly and Security Council in dealing with international political disputes and conflicts was also reflected in the fact that since 1948 the annual number of Security Council meetings decreased while the Assembly was called upon to consider an increasingly greater number of political questions. This was not merely the consequence of the "cold war" and the Council's inability to act because of the lack of unanimity among the Council's permanent members. It was also due to the fact that since 1951, when the Arab members raised the question of Morocco before the Assembly, several of the lesser member states increasingly began to resort to it in matters of self-determination and found it a more useful organ than the Security Council for promoting such issues, even though until 1960 it failed to adopt resolutions that satisfied the champions of self-determination. In this respect, 1960 marked a turning point for two reasons: first, when dealing with the Algerian question that year, the Assembly for the first time adopted a resolution that referred to the right of self-determination[51]; second, it also adopted Resolution 1514 (XV), the Declaration on the Granting of Independence to Colonial Countries and Peoples.[52] This cast the Assembly in an almost revolutionary role in the sphere of state-building or decolonization in world politics. As a large number of new states from Asia and Africa joined the United Nations in the 1960s,[53] the attractiveness of the Assembly as a forum for considering political issues directly or indirectly connected with self-determination increased.

But the Assembly deals not only with political disputes and engages in crisis decision making and management. It is also empowered to consider "the general principles of cooperation" in maintaining international peace and security, as well as disarmament and the "regulation" of armaments.[54]

With regard to the first of these questions, the Assembly adopted several resolutions that reflected the East-West conflict and the efforts of the USSR and the United States and their respective supporters to exploit the Assembly in getting it to adopt resolutions favorable to their propaganda viewpoints. Thus in 1947, as a result of a Soviet-sponsored agenda item, it adopted a resolution that condemned "all forms of propaganda, in whatever country conducted, designed to provoke or encourage any threat to the peace, breach of the peace, or act of aggression." It also requested each member state to take "appropriate steps within its constitutional limits" to promote "by all means of publicity and propaganda available . . . friendly relations among nations." During the debate that preceded this resolution's adoption, representatives of the West argued that under the principle of freedom of the press, newspapers often took views that were diametrically opposed to the government's and that a free press was likely to secure a balance of good sense that might be the chief defense of a free country against the hysteria or madness of war. If one newspaper published incorrect news, another newspaper would put it right. A government-controlled press, on the other hand, could be used for any purpose. Hence its hostile views were far more disturbing than those published in free-press countries.[55]

At the same session, the Assembly also adopted another resolution, this one directed mainly against the USSR and its Communist-controlled neighbors who raised barriers against the gathering and transmission of news for press publication. "Freedom of information," according to this resolution, was "a fundamental human right . . . and the touchstone of all the freedoms to which the United Nations is consecrated." The following year the Assembly adopted another resolution about the press. It urged member states to "combat, within the limits of their constitutional procedures, the diffusion of false or distorted reports likely to injure friendly relations between states."

In 1950, likewise, the Assembly adopted a resolution on warlike propaganda and in 1954, recalling the two earlier resolutions, it called on all states to remove the barriers to the free exchange of information and ideas.

On the other hand, as a result of West-sponsored agenda items, the Assembly adopted resolutions on the "essentials of peace" and "peace by deeds," in 1949 and 1950, respectively.

Then, as the cold war somewhat abated and the USSR launched its campaign for "peaceful coexistence," the Assembly, in 1957, 1958, 1965, and 1970, adopted resolutions for promoting peaceful and neighborly relations among states. The latest, Resolution 2625 (XXV), adopted on

October 24, 1970, the twenty-fifth anniversary of the United Nations, is the Declaration on Principles of International Law concerning Friendly Relations and Cooperation among States in Accordance with the Charter of the United Nations.

The Assembly's role in the problem of disarmament reflected the same East-West conflicts that colored its various resolutions concerning the need for international cooperation in the maintenance of international peace and security. Until 1959, when the Big Four—the United States, the USSR, Britain, and France—announced their agreement to set up a ten-state disarmament committee outside the framework of the United Nations (since 1961, the so-called Eighteen-Nation Disarmament Committee), the disarmament efforts of the Assembly may be summed up as follows:

In 1946 and 1947, respectively, the Assembly set up the Atomic Energy Commission and the Commission of Conventional Armaments, both consisting of the representatives of Security Council members, with Canada as an additional member of the Atomic Energy Commission. In 1952 the Assembly dissolved both these subsidiary organs and replaced them with a single Disarmament Commission with the same membership as that of the defunct Atomic Energy Commission. In 1957, to satisfy the desires of the USSR, this commission's membership was enlarged to twenty-five. However, the USSR continued to be dissatisfied. Then the Big Four decided to deal with the problem outside the United Nations.

This did not mean that since 1959 the Assembly ceased altogether playing a role in the matter of disarmament and the regulation of armaments. Thus, by appealing in 1961 for the suspension of nuclear tests and vainly urging the USSR to refrain from testing its fifty-megaton bomb, it contributed to the conclusion of the limited Test-Ban Treaty of 1963. And in 1964 it adopted a resolution sponsored by Ireland which called for prohibition of the dissemination of nuclear weapons to states that did not produce them. This resolution was a forerunner of the Non-Proliferation Treaty of 1968. As for the treaty of 1966 on the activities of states in the exploration and use of outer space, this followed recommendations adopted by the Assembly in 1963, after the U.S. and Soviet proposals to the Assembly in 1958 for the peaceful use of outer space.[56] Likewise, the germs of the Treaty of Tlatelolco of 1967, which provides for a denuclearized Latin America, are to be found in a proposal made in 1961 for the establishment of such a denuclearized zone in that part of the world. More recently (1969–1970), the Assembly also played an important role as a collective instrument of statecraft for approving the treaty which prohibits the emplacement of weapons of mass destruction on the seabed beyond a twelve-mile zone of territorial waters.

In 1953 and 1955, respectively, the Assembly also dealt with the problems of the peaceful use of atomic energy and the effects of radiation on man's environment. Thus it contributed to the establishment of the International Atomic Energy Agency, which came into being in 1957 following President Eisenhower's "atoms for peace" proposal of 1953 before the Assembly,[57] as well as to the decision to conclude the afore-mentioned limited Test-Ban Treaty.

Several of the above resolutions adopted by the Assembly either in crisis management or disarmament and arms regulation also involved studies initiated by the Assembly for promoting international cooperation in the political field, as it is authorized to do under Article 13 of the Charter. Thus, in the Uniting for Peace Resolution of 1950, the Assembly set up the already mentioned Collective Measures Committee to report on methods that might be used for collectively maintaining peace. In 1958 it established the twenty-four-member committee for studying the peace-ful uses of outer space[58] as well as the legal problems that might arise from the use and exploration of outer space. And in 1965 it set up a Special Committee on Peace-Keeping Operations under the chairmanship of the Assembly's president to undertake a comprehensive review of UN peacekeeping operations, including ways for overcoming the UN's financial difficulties which were caused by the refusal of the USSR and its satellites as well as of France to pay their share in the expenses of UNEF and ONUC.

Likewise, under the provisions of Article 13, the Assembly has en-couraged the progressive development and codification of international law; promoted international cooperation in the economic, social, cultural, educational, and health fields; and assisted in the realization of human rights and freedoms.

In the area of international law and its progressive development, the Assembly has helped in the preparation of conventions on subjects not previously regulated by international law—such as outer space—or in which the law had not yet been sufficiently developed. And, in the codifi-cation of international law, it has helped in the preparation of conventions which formulated with greater precision and more systematically than heretofore customary or conventional rules of international law in areas of extensive state practice and precedent.

In encouraging the development and codification of this law the Assembly resorted to various techniques of action. At times it used for this purpose the Sixth Committee which, for instance drafted at the As-sembly's request, the Genocide Convention of 1948. At other times it asked the secretary-general to prepare a report on a particular problem of international law. It did so in the case of the eight-point declaration of 1962 about the permanent sovereignty of peoples and nations over their natural resources. Or the Assembly may set up special committees for studying and making recommendations on particular legal problems, as it did with regard to the statement of 1962 about the seven principles of international law that deserved study.[59] Finally, it may rely on the Inter-national Law Commission it set up in 1947. This is composed of twenty-five legal experts (originally fifteen) who are elected by the Assembly for five-year terms. Normally, the commission meets for one session a year in Geneva. After consideration by the International Law Commission, states have adopted several multilateral conventions of major importance —for instance, on the Law of the Sea (the territorial sea, the continental shelf, the high seas, fishing, and the conservation of the sea's living resources), on diplomatic intercourse and immunities, on consular relations, and on the law of treaties.

The Assembly's work in promoting international cooperation in the economic, social, cultural, and educational fields will be dealt with elsewhere.[60] In the field of human rights and fundamental freedoms, the Universal Declaration of Human Rights adopted by the Assembly in 1948 and the two Covenants on Human Rights endorsed by the Assembly in 1966 are major highlights.

The Universal Declaration of Human Rights, in thirty articles, set forth the basic rights and freedoms to which all men and women everywhere in the world are entitled without any discrimination. These rights and freedoms include the right to life, liberty, and security of person; freedom from slavery and servitude; freedom from arbitrary arrest and detention; the right to a fair trial by an independent and impartial tribunal; the right to be presumed innocent until proven guilty; inviolability of the home and secrecy of correspondence; freedom of movement and residence; the right to a nationality; the right to marry and to found a family; the right to own property; freedom of thought, conscience, and religion; freedom of opinion and expression; freedom of peaceful assembly and association; the right to vote and take part in government; the right to social security; the right to work; the right to an adequate standard of living; the right to education; and the right to take part in the cultural life of the community.

The two international covenants, unlike the Universal Declaration of Human Rights, would be legally binding once they came into force through ratification by the required number of governments.[61] One of these covenants deals with economic, social, and cultural rights; the other with civil and political rights. Both, unlike the Universal Declaration of Human Rights, regulate the right of people to self-determination and the right of people to freely dispose of their natural wealth and resources. These innovations reflect the growing influence of the anticolonialist group of states in the United Nations.[62]

The Assembly is also authorized under a provision adopted at the San Francisco Conference to recommend measures for the peaceful adjustment of any situation, "regardless of origin," which, in its view, is likely to impair the general welfare or friendly relations among states, "including situations resulting from a violation of the Charter's provisions." [63] Representing a compromise between those at San Francisco who wished to see the Charter include a provision that would empower it to play a role in treaty revision, on the analogy of the relevant provision of the Covenant of the League of Nations,[64] and those who attached primary importance to the principle of the sanctity of treaties, at a time when the foundations for a new world order were being laid, this provision allows the Assembly to consider situations not necessarily covered by Article 11 of the Charter.

Until now, governments of member states have not called on the Assembly to assist them in matters of treaty revision. However, they have often invoked this Charter provision to justify their resort to the Assembly in order to promote "the principle of equal rights and self-determination" (Article 1, paragraph 2 of the Charter) and bring about a change in the status of a people living under a colonial regime or to get the government of South Africa to drop its policies of discrimination and apartheid toward Indians and black South Africans—all matters which lay essentially in the sphere of the domestic jurisdiction of the colonial states concerned but impaired friendly relations among states. In 1951, for dealing with the question of Germany's reunification through free elections, the Western powers invoked this particular provision of the Charter, despite Soviet counterarguments that Article 107 of the Charter precluded General Assembly consideration of the matter because it had reserved the right of the victorious powers of World War II to deal with former enemy states without taking account of Charter provisions.

Now, after the discussion of the Assembly's structure, formal mode of operations, and internal and external functions, the dynamics of the political process that occurs in the Assembly when it deals with a particular issue—an input—will be described, as well as pressure groups in the Assembly. The value and weight of its resolutions—its outputs—will then be discussed.

"PARLIAMENTARY DIPLOMACY" IN THE ASSEMBLY[65]

When a government wishes to have a particular issue considered by the General Assembly, the process goes through eight phases, the last of which is the Assembly's adoption (or nonadoption) of a resolution on this issue.

First, the initiating government declares its intention to induce the Assembly to consider a particular question. Accordingly, it requests the secretary-general to place the question on the Assembly's provisional agenda as a supplementary or additional item, depending on whether it sends in this request at least thirty days before the date set for the opening of the Assembly's regular session or sooner than that. At this phase the initiating government is also supposed to transmit an explanatory memorandum which sets forth the basic reasons for its recourse as well as its views about the particular question it wishes to raise in it. If possible, basic documents and a draft resolution should accompany this memorandum.[66]

In the second phase, the Assembly's General Committee considers the provisional agenda submitted to it by the secretary-general and decides to recommend or not to recommend to the Assembly the inclusion of the provisional agenda's items on the Assembly agenda.

In the third phase, the Assembly decides to accept or reject the General Committee's recommendations on items for inclusion in its agenda. This phase is of crucial importance. On its outcome depends whether a particular item will go through the remaining five phases of "parliamentary diplomacy" and be considered by the Assembly.

The fourth phase occurs in the general debate which takes place during the first plenary meetings of the Assembly and gives representatives of member states the opportunity briefly to comment on the substance of various items on the Assembly's agenda and suggest publicly the attitudes they will take toward it. The rules of procedure do not provide for the general debate. However, in 1963 the Committee on Procedure described it as a series of statements which chairmen of most delegations make on world problems and the role of the United Nations, on the basis of the secretary-general's annual report and the reports of other UN organs. The general debate is an important diplomatic occasion and is a sort of barometer of the international atmosphere because many chiefs of state, heads of government, foreign ministers, and high cabinet officials take part in it and engage backstage in various personal contacts, exchanges, soundings, and informal proposals.[67]

In the fifth phase, the committee of the Assembly to which the particular item has been assigned for consideration decides the relative order in which it will consider this item.

In the sixth phase, debate on the substance of the question takes place in the committee.

In the seventh phase, the committee debate focuses on the draft resolution or resolutions which member states have tabled for dealing with the particular item under consideration, and the committee decides to endorse for the Assembly's adoption a particular draft resolution.

In the eighth and final phase, the Assembly in plenary session decides whether it will adopt the particular resolution which the committee has endorsed.

When the question is a political dispute involving East versus West, North versus South, self-determination, human rights, or economic, social, and other issues in which a "spillover" of politics has occurred, the process of parliamentary diplomacy resembles the legislative struggle in domestic politics of a multiparty political system which, with regard to the U.S. Congress, has been called "a drama played behind closed curtains." [68] It takes place on two levels: one is formal, public, and "upstage"; the other is informal, secret, and "backstage." On the public level, the members of the various delegations tend to assume legalistic-moralistic attitudes; on the secret one, they get down to naked politics. The secret exchanges or quiet diplomacy may take place in exchanges between permanent missions to the United Nations or delegations to the Assembly, or both. They may also involve Assembly officials, the secretary-general, and Secretariat members in what has been termed "corridor" or "office diplomacy." [69] However, these exchanges may also be conducted through the diplomatic channel in forms of probes and *démarches* with the foreign ministries of other states or the diplomatic representatives stationed in the national capital.

In controversial questions the political process becomes particularly intense during those phases of parliamentary diplomacy that involve collective decision making. Thus at the second phase—of General Committee consideration—a government requesting the inclusion of an item on the Assembly's agenda, if not represented on the committee, is entitled to send a representative to attend any committee meeting at which its request will be considered.[70] This representative may take part in the relevant discussion without right to vote. And, under a liberal interpretation of the rules of procedure by the committee,[71] another state that is interested in the same item may be allowed to take part in the committee's relevant deliberations. If that other government, for one reason or another, opposes Assembly consideration of this particular item, its representative thus has the opportunity to express its views before the committee in efforts to influence it against recommending the item's inclusion in the Assembly's agenda. Although at this point the parties concerned are merely supposed to put forward their arguments for or against the item's inclusion in the agenda and not to debate the substance and merits of the issue, this is seldom feasible.[72] In case of debate, the committee's chairman strives to ensure compliance with this rule. Occasionally, controversy occurs over the wording in which the issue will be placed on the Assembly's agenda. As in all cases where voting takes place in a controversial issue, backstage exchanges and negotiations may occur between the parties concerned and committee members.

At the third phase of the process—of the Assembly's decision to include or exclude an item from its agenda—backstage exchanges and negotiations may again take place in order to achieve the desired result in the Assembly's voting. At this phase, if debate occurs, it must be limited to three speakers for and three speakers against the committee's recommendation to the Assembly. The Assembly president may limit the time allowed speakers under this rule.[73] And a majority of members present and voting may amend or delete an item on the agenda.[74]

During the fifth phase of the process—of the committee's decision on the order in which it will consider the various items on its agenda— resort to a vote may again be needed if the initiating government wants an early consideration of its item, while another government prefers to have it considered among the last items on the committee's agenda when members are weary because of months of debate and are in a hurry to see the Assembly's session come to a close.

Political debate reaches its climax during the sixth and seventh phases of the process of parliamentary diplomacy when the disputants seek to exploit the value of the Assembly as a forum for propaganda to its full. During the sixth phase, the representative of the initiating government, in a set statement, presents to the committee his government's views on the issue and the representatives of other states that are parties to the dispute present their viewpoint on the issue, likewise in set statements. In the verbal combat that ensues, the disputants hurl charges against each other, making use of connotational terms. They try to shield themselves by denials and hurl back countercharges, using their right of reply, often improvising their lines. They utter predictions, warnings, even veiled threats. They appeal to third parties, even to each other, or to the United Nations as a corporate body. In their arguments, they strive to show off their rectitude and enhance their prestige. Or they aim at impressing each other and third parties with the firmness of their position and the steadfastness of their adherence to their commitments and proposals, or with their conciliatory intentions and their lack of intransigence. They may also try to win small victories in a debating point. Intentionally or unintentionally, in the heat of the debate representatives speaking without prepared texts may misunderstand another representative's words or resort to fallacious arguments which they will afterward strike off the official record. They may also become quite vague and rambling, perhaps to gain time while desperately groping for an appropriate argument.

Meanwhile, third parties may express their views on the issue and either take sides or try to play various types of mediatory and conciliatory roles onstage or backstage or both. Some might prefer to remain publicly silent. This does not necessarily mean lack of interest, nonalignment, neutrality, and eventual abstention from voting or from backstage efforts to mediate and conciliate. Silence may also signify a desire to avoid statements that might offend both disputants. Verbal alignment, on the other hand, does not necessarily mean voting alignment. It is incompatible neither with abstention on a particular resolution nor even a negative vote on it. Generally, the gathering of third parties in the Assembly that surrounds the disputants hardly fulfills the presupposition of rhetoric: a public that can be swayed.[75] For the representatives of third-party states assume attitudes that are usually based on instructions received from their governments in advance of the debate. These instructions are founded not merely on consideration of the merits of the case being discussed, but on the overall policy of governments individually or as members of groups in international politics both inside and outside the Assembly. Thus the drama has somewhat the character of the theater of the absurd. The debate may change opinions but not votes.

During the seventh phase of the process of parliamentary diplomacy which centers on the draft resolution or resolutions tabled by various representatives, bilateral and multilateral negotiations and bargaining may take place onstage and backstage. Representatives may offer various amendments and subamendments, and third-party members may strive to produce a resolution acceptable to all rather than a solution of the particular issue. As a result, the Assembly is transformed into a center for at least verbal accommodation and harmonization and resolutions adopted may be highly ambiguous. The parties concerned in getting their draft resolutions adopted tend to emphasize at this phase their roles as members of the society of nations rather than as representatives of sovereign states pursuing particular national goals. Just as in domestic politics pressure groups and their spokesmen proclaim that the bill they back is in the "public interest," they present their national interests as UN interests. Invoking the UN spirit, they mask their ethnocentric viewpoints in cosmocentric terminology.

Backstage, members try to ensure votes for the draft resolution they favor, by log rolling, vote swapping, horse trading, arm twisting, buttonholing. The parties concerned try to make sure that their friends are present and voting or at least abstaining. One way of checking if indeed they are is to request a roll call vote when the time of decision arrives.

At the eighth phase of the process of parliamentary diplomacy, the outcome is normally clear in advance because the committee vote has already revealed whether a draft resolution enjoys the backing of two thirds of the members present and voting that is usually required for Assembly adoption of resolutions concerning political matters. Nonetheless, if the committee vote has fallen only slightly short of the required two-thirds majority, the concerned delegations may continue backstage efforts to influence the outcome, by trying to persuade other representatives to change their votes in the Assembly. And there have been cases of the Assembly adopting a resolution not even discussed in the committee, because during the interval between the seventh and eighth phase of parliamentary diplomacy the parties concerned together with third parties negotiated backstage among themselves a new, mutually acceptable resolution.

Generally, resort to parliamentary rather than to conventional diplomacy for dealing with international disputes transforms a basically dyadic relationship into a triadic one. For the international organization represents a collective third party which is invited to undertake a process of implicit mediation, in the nontechnical and broadest sense of the latter word. As this collective third party interposes itself between the two disputant parties, the conflict becomes like a lawsuit: each disputant tries to persuade this third party about the rightness of his own position and the wrongness of his opponent's. Because this collective third party is composed of representatives of quite a number of individual states, draft resolutions put forward by the disputants, like bills in legislatures of multiparty national political systems, are seldom adopted in the exact form and content which they had when introduced, unless an overwhelming majority of members favors a strongly phrased draft resolution. Third parties striving to achieve an accommodation between the disputants, at least on paper, table draft resolutions of their own which may replace those of the disputants or of their proxies. Thus the output of the whole resolutionary process of parliamentary diplomacy is likely to consist of procedural and

colorless resolutions that are deliberately ambiguous and therefore acceptable to the parties to the dispute. That the resolutions put forward represent the wishes of a collectivity of third parties in a community spirit may
facilitate their acceptance by the parties directly concerned, which may
make concessions not as a result of the superiority of the opponent in
mobilizing support for his viewpoint, but for the sake of this community
spirit.

But, regardless of result, the publicity of parliamentary diplomacy
permits the simultaneous exercise of relationships of manipulation and
propaganda directed to the constituencies of other governments as well
as to one's own, the opposition parties included in both cases. Occasionally, indeed, governments resort to the Assembly not because they estimate
they will be able to induce member states to adopt a resolution that will
justify their viewpoint in a dispute but because they wish to engage in
propaganda against another member state. And they may be satisfied if
the Assembly ends up adopting no resolution at all—which ostensibly
represents a defeat for the initiating member. Thus in December 1956 the
USSR complained to the Assembly about U.S. intervention in the domestic affairs of its East European satellites. In the debate that ensued,
the Soviet and East European representatives emphasized various aspects
of U.S. "gray" and "black" propaganda and other activities through broad-
casts, the dropping of subversive literature from aircraft or balloons, and
the training and introduction of saboteurs and political agitators. The U.S.
representative rejected these allegations and countercharged that the USSR
was merely trying to divert world attention from its own subversive activities in free countries all over the world, and particularly from its coercive intervention in Hungary. The primary goal of these Soviet moves was
to produce a worldwide image of a peace-loving USSR as against a
"warmongering" and subversion-fomenting United States. In countering
these moves, the U.S. government denied entertaining any warlike intentions; emphasized that the deeds of the Soviet government were primarily to blame for the high international tension and the recurring crises
between West and East in the cold war; drew attention to the vituperative
tone of Soviet propaganda to other countries; and underlined Soviet efforts
to obstruct the free flow of information over state borders. In February
1957 the General Assembly rejected the relevant Soviet draft resolution.

PRESSURE GROUPS IN THE ASSEMBLY

Because the Assembly, in performing its internal elective functions, has
established the principle of geographic distribution of seats in the Security
Council, the Economic and Social Council, and several of its committees,
geographic-distribution voting blocs emerge—the African and Asian, the
Latin American, the West European "and other," and the East European
—for deciding on their candidates and getting them elected when the

relevant elections come up.[76] Tables 1–4 reveal the membership of these groups.

Moreover, as the Assembly performs its external functions, other voting or pressure groups emerge in it because in the entire multistate

TABLE 1 African and Asian Member States

A. *Africa South of the Sahara*

1. Botswana—9/20/66
2. Burundi—9/19/62
3. Cameroon—9/20/60
4. Central African Republic
   —9/20/60
5. Chad—9/20/60
6. Congo (Brazzaville)—9/20/60
7. Congo (Kinshasa)—9/20/60
8. Dahomey—9/20/60
9. Ethiopia*
10. Equatorial Guinea—11/12/68
11. Gabon—9/20/60
12. Gambia—9/21/65
13. Ghana—3/8/57
14. Guinea—12/12/58
15. Ivory Coast—9/20/60
16. Kenya—12/16/63
17. Lesotho—10/17/66

18. Liberia*
19. Madagascar—9/20/60
20. Malawi—12/1/63
21. Mali—9/28/60
22. Mauritania—10/21/61
23. Mauritius—9/24/68
24. Niger—9/20/60
25. Nigeria—10/7/60
26. Ruanda—9/18/60
27. Senegal—9/28/60
28. Sierra Leone—9/21/61
29. Somalia—9/20/60
30. Swaziland—9/24/68
31. Tanzania—12/14/61
32. Togo—9/20/60
33. Uganda—10/25/62
34. Upper Volta—9/20/60
34A. Zaire—see Congo (Kinshasa)
35. Zambia—12/1/64

B. *Arab States*

36. Algeria—10/8/62
36A. Bahrain—9/21/71
37. Iraq*
38. Jordan—12/14/55
39. Kuwait—5/14/63
40. Lebanon*
41. Libya—12/14/55
42. Morocco—11/12/56
42A. Oman—10/7/71
42B. Qatar—9/21/71
43. Saudi Arabia*
44. South Yemen—12/14/67
45. Sudan—11/12/56
46. Syria*
47. Tunisia—11/12/56
47A. Union of Arab Emirates—12/8/71
48. United Arab Republic (UAR)*
49. Yemen—9/30/47

C. *Asian States*

50. Afghanistan—11/9/46
50A. Bhutan—9/21/71
51. Burma—4/19/48
52. Cambodia—12/14/55
53. Ceylon—12/14/55
54. Cyprus†—9/20/60
55. India*
56. Indonesia—9/28/50
57. Iran*
58. Japan—12/18/66
59. Laos—12/14/55
60. Malaysia—9/17/57
61. Maldive Islands—9/21/65
62. Mongolia‡—9/27/61
63. Nepal—12/14/55
64. Pakistan—9/30/47
65. Philippines*
66. Singapore—9/21/65
67. Thailand—12/16/46

NOTE: Not members of the Afro-Asian group: China, Israel, and South Africa; all African states are members of the Organization of African Unity (OAU); all Arab states are members of the Arab League.
* Charter members.
† Cyprus is also a member of the Council of Europe and a European influence within the Asian and African group.
‡ A Communist party state voting with the Soviet bloc.

TABLE 2 Latin American Member States

(In Alphabetical Order)

1. Argentina	11. Guatemala
2. Bolivia	12. Haiti
3. Brazil	13. Honduras
4. Chile	14. Mexico
5. Colombia	15. Nicaragua
6. Costa Rica	16. Panama
7. Cuba*	17. Paraguay
8. Dominican Republic	18. Peru
9. Ecuador	19. Uruguay
10. El Salvador	20. Venezuela

NOTE: The above states, together with the United States, Jamaica, Trinidad—Tobago, and Barbados, are members of the Organization of American States (OAS).
* Cuba was excluded from the Organization of American States in 1962. Normally, it votes with the Soviet bloc.

TABLE 3 Western European Member States "And Other" *

(In Alphabetical Order)

1. Austria†—12/14/55	10. Luxembourg
2. Belgium	11. Malta†—12/1/64
3. Denmark	12. Netherlands
4. Finland†—12/14/55	13. Norway
5. France	14. Portugal—12/14/55
6. Greece	15. Spain†—12/14/55
7. Iceland—11/19/46	16. Sweden†—11/19/46
8. Ireland†—12/14/55	17. Turkey‡
9. Italy—12/14/55	18. United Kingdom

* "And Other" would include, on the basis of practice, Australia, Canada, New Zealand, South Africa, and Israel, and possibly Jamaica, Trinidad—Tobago, Barbados, Guyana, and Fiji, which are Commonwealth members.
† Nonmembers of NATO or of the Warsaw Treaty Organization.
‡ In some cases, Turkey also takes part in the Asian caucusing group. It represents an Asian influence in the Western European group.

TABLE 4 Eastern European Member States

(In Alphabetical Order)

1. Albania*—12/14/55
2. Byelorussian SSR
3. Bulgaria—12/14/55
4. Czechoslovakia
5. Hungary—12/14/55
6. Poland
7. Romania—12/14/55
8. Ukrainian SSR
9. USSR
10. Yugoslavia*

* Not members of the Soviet bloc.

system of world politics there is the alignment of East versus West, led by the two superpowers respectively, against a background of unaligned states; the alignment of South versus North, which consists of the less developed as against the developed countries of the world; and the various "regional" associations of states set up for satisfying common interests and attaining common goals in the security, political, economic, or social fields. All these alignments and associations may strive to get the Assembly to adopt resolutions favorable—or at least not unfavorable—to their group interests and goals. Then, in a particular issue or category of issues, special common interests and goals of states may be involved, so that for dealing with it the states concerned might decide to act as a group in the Assembly, even though they are not associated outside the United Nations.

In the caucuses of these groups, members may exchange information on all or part of the agenda either in advance or during the Assembly session; or they may develop common general positions on important agenda items with or without definite voting commitments; or they may agree on a common spokesman and on the contents of the statement he is to deliver, or on joint action and strategy for or against a proposal.[77]

Several scholars have carefully examined the voting behavior and voting data in the Assembly, trying to identify the various pressure and voting groups in the Assembly and to measure their cohesiveness.[78] Partly because of the different methods they use, partly because they base their studies on different periods in the life of the Assembly when not only its composition had changed because of the admission of new members but the world political setting had also altered, their research has resulted in no consensus. However, all agree that in addition to the above-mentioned geographic-distribution type of group, several other voting and pressure groups could be distinguished. One of them proposed five additional types of groups: the caucusing bloc, the caucusing group, the regional organization group, the common interest group, and the temporary group.[79]

Four other points should be made in this connection:

First, since some UN members belong to two or three associations outside the United Nations, they may also belong to two or three pressure groups within the Assembly, so that cross-cutting solidarities or loyalty conflicts may appear in debating and voting behavior.

Second, the cohesion of these voting blocs depends on the cohesion of their association in world politics and the lack of cross-cutting solidarities and loyalty conflict. Thus the Soviet bloc or "Commonwealth of Socialist States" shows considerably greater voting cohesion in the Assembly than does the British Commonwealth of Nations, regardless of the issue the Assembly is considering. It is the only real voting bloc in the Assembly. The cohesion of a pressure group is affected by intra-allied disputes, as witness the NATO group voting on issues of self-determination during the Cyprus dispute between 1954 and 1958. It also depends on the community of interests individual members may have in a particular issue under Assembly consideration.

Third, the duration of the pressure group depends on the duration of the association to which individual members belong or on the duration of the issue or type of issue that brought individual members together as a voting group in the first place.

Fourth, not all UN members belong to voting groups, as witness the cases of the United States, Yugoslavia, Israel, China, Greece, Albania, or South Africa, even though some are members of regional associations.

With regard to the impact of economic relations between states and voting behavior, it has been found that economic aid was one of the major factors that determined the political stance of nonaligned or neutralist states toward the USSR when the Assembly was dealing with cold war issues in 1961 and 1962. A careful analysis of the voting record of a number of less developed countries on such issues revealed a strong relationship between a positive index number for economic aid and a pro-Communist voting record. Thus Iraq, Guinea, Afghanistan, Indonesia, Burma, and Ghana—which had received more aid from the Communist party-states than from the West from 1954 to 1962—strongly supported the Communist viewpoints in the Assembly. Without much harm to themselves, they were thus able to express their gratitude for the aid they had received. This study also suggested that economic aid was more closely correlated with UN voting than was the flow of trade.[80]

Generally, higher polarization has been found in the Assembly voting of uncommitted states with Soviet economic links of aid and trade than in those with Western economic links. This phenomenon may be largely due to the fact that aid from and trade with Communist party-states are exclusively intergovernmental affairs. On the other hand, poor, imperfectly Westernized Latin American states, such as Bolivia, even though more closely bound economically to the United States and members of the OAS, were found to vote less with the West than the advanced and thoroughly Europeanized states such as Uruguay.[81] Such voting attitudes in the United Nations may represent the international equivalent of protest voting in the domestic arena and a desire to emphasize political independence, despite economic dependence, in the face of Communist propaganda charges that such states are "lackeys of imperialism." [82]

NATURE, SCOPE, AND LEGAL EFFECTS OF ASSEMBLY RESOLUTIONS

Member states exert great efforts to induce the Assembly to adopt resolutions, regardless of the acrimony of the debate, the intensity of a conflict, and the highly controversial character of the issue with which the Assembly may have been seized. Inclusion of the particular item in its agenda in itself constitutes a sort of collective commitment of member states to exert efforts to adopt a resolution on the issue, if not to recommend a solution of the problem to be considered. Nonetheless, at times the Assembly, despite efforts exerted by members, is unable to adopt a resolution on a particular issue, either because a draft resolution has not been put forward that satisfied the required majority of members or because certain members do not wish to have the Assembly adopt any resolution on the issue, perhaps because they do not regard the Assembly as the appropriate or competent body for dealing with the issue.

With regard to the resolutions adopted by the Assembly, the extremely complex matter of their precise nature, scope, and effects must be examined. In dealing with this, the distinction between the internal and external functions of the Assembly should be kept in mind.

Resolutions on matters relating to the internal setting of the Assembly or of the United Nations, unless they are explicitly termed recommendations, are of a binding character or "nonrecommendatory"—resolutions adopted, for instance, in placing items on the Assembly agenda, or in the performance of the Assembly's constituent, elective, and financial and administrative functions, such as the admission of new members, the appointment of the secretary-general, the election of members to the various UN councils or of the Assembly's president and vice-presidents or of the judges on the International Court of Justice.[83] Thus the resolution of the Assembly to elect a particular state as a member of the Security Council is binding on those members that voted against the appointment of this particular individual. The only thing a member can do if it dissents with this election is either to boycott the work of the United Nations or withdraw from it altogether. Indonesia did the latter when it disapproved of the election of Malaysia as a nonpermanent member of the Security Council in 1960. Or, with regard to budgetary matters, a member may refuse to pay part or the whole of its dues to the organization, at the risk of losing its right to vote in the Assembly under the sanction contained in Article 19 of the Charter or of creating a serious crisis in the United Nations. France, the USSR, and its satellites did so with regard to expenditures for UNEF and ONUC which the International Court of Justice, in an advisory opinion of 1962, considered to be part of the organization's regular expenditures, so that the dissenting members were legally bound to pay them. Or, in case a member maintains that the Assembly should not have included a particular item on its agenda because that item, in its opinion, is essentially within the sphere of its domestic jurisdiction, it may refuse to attend meetings of the Assembly when the relevant committee considers that item. However, it cannot resort to any legal remedy against the Assembly's decision to deal with that item.

Assembly resolutions on matters relating to the external setting of the United Nations, on the other hand, are primarily in the nature of recommendations, as the Charter explicitly provides in several articles.[84] A recommendation may be defined as an invitation which an international organization addresses to a particular actor or set of actors in world politics requesting it to perform or refrain from performing a particular action or set of actions, without implying that the addressee has a legal obligation to behave as it is requested to behave.[85] This form of international political communication is typical in international politics where the voluntary cooperation of political actors is required even for the fulfillment of international obligations, and no actor can be bound to act or refrain from acting without its consent under the principle of sovereignty.[86]

The addressee of the Assembly's recommendations may be all states, some states, a single state, other UN organs, another international organization, or even substate actors, such as organized groups struggling for self-determination. And the contents of these recommendations may be procedural or substantive or both. If they deal with an international dispute and are procedural, they suggest the Assembly's mediatory role; if substantive, its conciliatory role. These recommendations appear as a request or a hope, the consequence of the Assembly's deliberative and decision-making process. They express a collective diplomatic opinion or consensus that ranges from that of the two-thirds majority of members present and voting for the recommendation to that of the virtual unanimity of member states that voted in favor of the recommendation. Their effects are of a moral character. They may serve to bring moral pressure to bear on the addressee or stimulate the morale of the actor favored by this formal expression of Assembly opinion. They may also serve morally to justify the recourse of the initiating government to the United Nations, if they favor its viewpoint in the issue it raised before the Assembly.

Although these recommendations are not legally binding—which facilitates their acceptance even by the parties to an international dispute —some resemble "pseudoagreements." [87] As such, they may not be altogether devoid of political value if the parties concerned read in them certain implications and regard them as a symbol of some sort of tacit bargain—a promise, for instance, to become more accommodating to each other in the future, or a commitment to try to reach agreement. Thus recommendations may be something better than a second-level agreement, which is an agreement to disagree.[88] And, if some sort of agreement is involved, pseudo- or quasi-legal obligations may stem from such recommendations.

Moreover, although in 1945 at San Francisco the founders of the United Nations rejected all attempts to grant the Assembly the right to create international law through its resolutionary process, and although states have refrained from formally recognizing UN resolutions as sources of international law under Article 38 of the Statute of the International Court of Justice,[89] and a study of the 2,247 resolutions adopted by the Assembly between 1946 and 1967 has revealed that the Assembly has never stated that it had adopted in this way a binding principle of international law,[90] nonetheless, some of its resolutions are not merely recommendatory but also have legal effects. Five types of such "nonrecommendatory" and legally binding resolutions have been distinguished in addition to those that deal with matters related to the *interna corporis* of the Assembly or the United Nations.[91]

First, certain resolutions establish the existence of facts and concrete legal situations—that is, the factual and legal reality of certain situations. For instance, in Resolution 1542 (XV) the Assembly established that the Portuguese territories in Africa were non-self-governing territories within the meaning of Chapter XI of the Charter, and not part of Portugal's metropolitan territories. It followed that Portugal had a legal obligation to transmit information on those territories to the United Nations under that particular chapter of the Charter.[92]

Second, certain resolutions, though not *creating* international law, either confirm the existence of customary rules of international law or express general principles of law.[93] The latter constitute a source of international law under Article 38 of the Statute of the International Court of Justice. For example, in Resolution 95 (I), the Assembly confirmed without reservation the Nuremberg principles on war crimes.[94]

Third, certain resolutions on international peace and security have a binding effect.[95] The main example: Resolution 377 (V), the Uniting for Peace Resolution. This, from the strictly legal viewpoint, has been considered (even by some non-Communist jurists) as contrary to the Charter. However, it led to a modification of the law because of political necessity and constituted the Assembly's interpretation of its legal capacity to act in the future.[96]

Fourth, certain resolutions express and register agreement among members of the Assembly.[97] Such resolutions, it has been proposed, might be called "multilateral executive agreements." [98] Resolution 1962 (XVIII) —the Declaration of Legal Principles Governing the Activities of States in the Exploration and Use of Outer Space—is a good example of such binding nonrecommendatory resolutions. It was followed by the conclusion of the treaty of December 8, 1967, on the activities of states in the exploration and use of outer space.

Fifth, certain resolutions derive their binding force from instruments other than the Charter.[99] This was the case of Resolution 289 (IV) on the question of the Italian colonies (Libya, Eritrea, and Somalia) which derived its binding character from the Italian Peace Treaty of 1947 under which the "Powers concerned" agreed to accept the Assembly's recommendations in case of nonagreement among themselves about the future of these colonies.[100]

In the view of the International Court of Justice as expressed on the occasion of its Advisory Opinion of June 21, 1971, on the consequences for states of the continued presence of South Africa in Namibia (formerly South-West Africa), Resolution 2145 (XXI) of 1966 [101] would fall in the first of the above categories of legally binding nonrecommendatory resolutions of the Assembly. Under this resolution, the Assembly decided that South Africa's mandate over Namibia was terminated and that South Africa had no other right to administer that territory. As noted in the relevant press release issued by the Court on that occasion, it was incorrect to assume that, because the Assembly was in principle vested with recommendatory powers, it was debarred from adopting in special cases within its competence binding resolutions that made determinations or had an operative character.

The frequency of the re-citation of certain resolutions, not only their substance, has also been proposed as an indication of the legal significance of Assembly resolutions. For instance, Resolution 1514 (XV) of 1960, the Declaration on Colonialism, was cited ninety-five times in subsequent resolutions until 1967; and Resolution 217 (III) of 1948, the Universal Declaration of Human Rights, was cited seventy-five times in subsequent resolutions, likewise until 1967.[102]

All in all, jurists of both West and East are agreed that certain Assembly resolutions are binding and have contributed to the development of international law.[102a] Controversy, however, has arisen among Western jurists over whether the Assembly's adoption of certain resolutions merely reveals the emergence of rules of customary law, provided major states or groups of states do not reserve their position on them; or whether the Assembly actually exercises in this way certain quasi-legislative functions.[103] Nonetheless, even those who support the latter view do not maintain that, as matters stand, the world political system has any legislative machinery of either an ad hoc or permanent character for legislating in world politics in the same way that domestic legislatures legislate in internal politics and for allowing a majority to adopt measures into law that would also be binding on an outvoted and dissenting minority.

On the whole, the weight of Assembly resolutions in world politics depends greatly on the same factors that account for the binding character of the rules of international law:[104] on a stable, definite core of consent among the major states and of acquiescence on the part of the lesser states.

THE ASSEMBLY IN WORLD POLITICS

Viewed in the entire context of world politics, the Assembly's role as an instrument of statecraft of the two superpowers and the other members of the United Nations may be summed up as follows:

From 1947 to 1955, the United States found in the Assembly a valuable auxiliary instrument of statecraft in dealing with problems of international peace and security that threatened the status quo which had emerged from World War II.[105] Through the Assembly it was able to supplement its policy of containment of the USSR which it was pursuing by other techniques of statecraft as well. Indeed, through the Uniting for Peace Resolution of 1950, it brought about a quasi-constitutional amendment to the Charter provisions concerning the Assembly by getting it to adopt an extremely liberal interpretation of its external functions in the realm of the maintenance of international peace and security under Articles 10 and 11 of the Charter. This resolutionary interpretation allowed the

Assembly to play an important role in subsequent cases of crisis decision making and crisis management, both of which, under the Charter, are the primary responsibility of the Security Council.

The Uniting for Peace Resolution represented the high point of U.S. influence in the United Nations—and in the Assembly, in particular. In Korea, it will be recalled, the United States provided the South Korean government with the bulk of outside military support in military operations that came close to representing "collective security" in action yet fell short of it, because the USSR and its satellites opposed it and, together with China, provided considerable moral and material support to North Korea.

After the *en bloc* admission of fifteen new members to the United Nations in 1955, however, matters changed. For a while the assembly became a valuable auxiliary instrument of Soviet statecraft. Eleven of the fifteen new members admitted then to the United Nations were U.S.-sponsored;[106] four, USSR-sponsored.[107] However, among the former group, four were uncommitted Asian or African states with the anticolonialist and anti-European attitude expressed at the Bandung Conference of 1955.[108] On the other hand, all four USSR-sponsored new members were at the time docile satellites of the USSR and members of the Soviet bloc.[109] Moreover, after Stalin's death, the USSR had dropped the Stalinist policy of viewing the emergent new states of Asia and Africa as mere pawns of their former colonial masters. Through a new program of economic aid begun in 1954, it started to support nonalignment and neutralism among these emergent states and, more vigorously than before, it followed the anti-imperialist line of supporting wars of "national liberation" in Asia, Africa, and Latin America, even if these were in many cases led by "bourgeois nationalists." In the Assembly the USSR now found a valuable forum for promoting these aims and for proclaiming its support for the policy of "peaceful and competitive coexistence" of different social systems and for its new doctrine that wars were no longer inevitable, as Lenin had maintained—although the class struggle had to go on. As a result, the United States now found itself at a disadvantage in the Assembly, despite its anticolonialist origin and tradition. For culturally it was bound to Western Europe, the home of colonialism since the fifteenth century, and politically it was allied, through NATO, with the main colonialist states of the nineteenth century—Britain, France, the Netherlands, Belgium, and Portugal.

In pursuing these policies in the Assembly, the USSR was supported by the anticolonialist group of UN members whose number had risen since 1955 and was to rise even more in the 1960s. It was able to bring about a virtual constitutional amendment of its own to the Charter, ten years after the Uniting for Peace Resolution of 1950. With Khrushchev himself on the Assembly rostrum, the USSR sponsored a draft resolution that led to Assembly adoption of the Declaration on the Granting of Independence to Colonial Countries and Peoples. This declaration was the climax of the gradual assimilation of the Charter's Declaration on Non-Self-Governing Territories to the Trusteeship System. It was based on a very liberal interpretation of Article 14 of the Charter, whose original purpose was to allow the Assembly to play a role in the revision of treaties. It transformed the "principle of equal rights and self-determination" which the Soviet delegation had introduced in Article 1, paragraph 2, of the Charter, at San Francisco, into the "right" of self-determination for people in non-self-governing territories, regardless of their political, economic, social, or educational preparedness for independence.

Since the early 1960s, however, the USSR in turn started encountering difficulties similar to those encountered by the United States since the mid-1950s in using the Assembly as an auxiliary instrument of statecraft. The new Asian and especially African members that joined the United Nations since 1960 were added to the earlier group of such members. Their influx necessitated two formal amendments to the Charter with regard to the composition of the Security Council and the Economic and Social Council. Moreover, as a group, they were unwilling to act as instruments of statecraft for either superpower. Their negative attitude toward Khrushchev's "troika" proposal for the UN secretary-general sealed its fate. In 1960 Dag Hammarskjöld reminded them that it was not the USSR or, indeed, any of the Great Powers who needed the United Nations for their protection, but all others. Together with other less developed countries of the "Third World," they had demands of an economic nature on both superpowers and the whole "North." Hence, for dealing with issues of peace and security and for arms control, the two superpowers reverted to reliance on the Security Council as an auxiliary instrument of statecraft; avoided resorting on their own to the United Nations on such matters; or negotiated between themselves outside the United Nations through the diplomatic channel or special conferences that included a limited number of other states. They also became conscious of the problem created by the strict application of the principle of universality to UN membership, which led to the great increase in the number of UN members and to the admission into the organization of twenty-one states with populations of less than one million inhabitants. As a result of the influx of new members the Assembly became unwieldly. States with only 10 percent of the world's population and contributing all together only 5 percent of the assessed UN budget could theoretically muster a two-thirds majority in the Assembly in favor of a resolution they had tabled.

For dealing with this problem, agreement will have to be reached on defining a microstate and its status in relation to the United Nations, if such states are not to be altogether excluded from the organization. Because of population growth, the criterion of, say, a population of less than one million people would not in itself be sufficient. Suggestions have been made that such states, because of their lack of material capability to carry out all the obligations of UN members, should be granted the status of associate members, with the right to take part in economic, technical, social, educational, and other UN programs.[110] This would require an amendment to the UN Charter. The gravity of the problem becomes evident when one contemplates the possibility of all non-self-governing territories achieving statehood and seeking to become members of the United Nations. At present, the United Nations recognizes the existence of fifty such territories with populations of less than one milion. Two thirds of these—mainly islands—have populations of less than one hundred thousand inhabitants! [111] Not that microstates have at times played insignificant roles as subjects or objects of international politics in the Assembly. It was Malta which raised the question of dealing multilaterally with the important question of the seabed and its resources. And Cyprus became the stimulus for not inconsiderable debate over its right to self-determination and to free and unfettered independence, in 1954–1958 and 1966, respectively.

For the European states with colonies—Britain, France, the Netherlands, Belgium, or Portugal—the Assembly has been a forum in which they have had to fight losing battles in the long run. At times they tried to prevent the placing of decolonization items on the Assembly's agenda by invoking Article 2, paragraph 7, of the Charter which prohibits the United Nations from dealing with matters which are essentially within the domestic jurisdiction of states. When the Assembly, despite these arguments, decided to consider such issues, they sought to prevent it from adopting any resolution that would justify the viewpoint of these items' sponsors. At times they also walked out of committee meetings dealing with such items. These states also opposed the transformation of the principle of self-determination into a right.[112] Nonetheless, one of the two Covenants on Human Rights endorsed by the Assembly in 1966 proclaims self-determination as a right, in contrast to the Universal Declaration of Human Rights of 1948. For these states the Assembly was hardly a useful instrument of statecraft.

This is not true for the states of the "Third World," whether they are aligned or nonaligned. Through the Assembly, their governments have been able to present their viewpoints and air their grievances not only over issues of decolonization but over their rising frustrations in economic growth and development. The Assembly educates their representatives to the intricacies of parliamentary diplomacy. For them it functions as an important and relatively inexpensive auxiliary of their often rudimentary national instruments of diplomacy and propaganda and serves as a mechanism (established and maintained mainly by the major states) for expressing, in resolutions of a recommendatory nature, at times without the backing of any major states, their hopes and desires for the future.

Generally, in the seventies and eighties of our century, for East and West and North and South, the Assembly (barring a nuclear war or any worldwide economic crisis) is likely to serve as a valuable forum for discussing and reaching consensus on principles for dealing with worldwide issues that involve man and his physical milieu, such as the demographic revolution and the nondeliberate and deliberate modification of this milieu through environmental pollution and large-scale projects of weather con-

TABLE 5 General Assembly: Regular Sessions: Certain Statistical Data 1946–1970

Sessions	Number of Members	Number of Agenda Items	Items per Member	Duration (Approx. No. of Weeks)
1946 First, First Part	51	33	0.6	5
First, Second Part	55	65	1.1	8
1947 Second	57	65	1.1	10½
1948 Third	59	73	1.2	18
1949 Fourth	59	68	1.1	11
1950 Fifth	60	76	1.2	13
1951 Sixth	60	70	1.1	13
1952 Seventh	60	77	1.2	19½
1953 Eighth	60	76	1.2	12
1954 Ninth	60	73	0.9	12½
1955 Tenth	76	66	0.8	13
1956 Eleventh	81	71	0.8	17
1957 Twelfth	82	69	0.8	12½
1958 Thirteenth	82	73	0.8	15½
1959 Fourteenth	82	72	0.7	13
1960 Fifteenth	99	92	0.9	19½
1961 Sixteenth	104	97	0.9	22
1962 Seventeenth	110	94	0.8	13
1963 Eighteenth	113	82	0.7	13
1964 Nineteenth	115	92*	0.8	8
1965 Twentieth	117	108	0.8	13
1966 Twenty-first	122	98	0.7	13
1967 Twenty-second	124	99	0.7	20
1968 Twenty-third	126	98	0.7	13
1969 Twenty-fourth	126	107	0.8	13
1970 Twenty-fifth	127	101	0.7	13

* Number of items on the draft agenda. That session adopted no final agenda.

trol and climate modification, all of which transcend political boundaries and call for close international cooperation and regulation.[113]

As Table 5 shows, despite the steep rise in UN membership from 51 in 1946 to 127 in 1970, and the increase in the number of items on the agenda of the Assembly's regular sessions, which ranged from a low of 33 items at the first part of the Assembly's first session to a high of 108 items at its twentieth, the percentage of agenda items per member fell from 1954 on to 0.7–0.9 as compared with 1.1–1.2 during the period 1946–1953. Since it was possible to maintain the duration of several sessions during the period 1955–1970 to thirteen weeks, which was the average duration of sessions during the period 1946–1954, one must conclude that the average time devoted to each item must likewise have declined. Would this phenomenon be the consequence of more rational procedures in the conduct of the Assembly's regular sessions? Would it reflect a decline in the interest of member states in the Assembly as an instrument of international policy? Or might it be the result of both? This is a matter that deserves further research.

But, whatever the reason for this phenomenon, the fact remains that of all six principal organs of the United Nations the Assembly best reflects the state of affairs in the world multistate system and the aspirations of all governments to peaceful symbiosis, despite political, ideological, economic, social, and cultural differences and conflicts. It is therefore quite fitting that it should meet in the only building in the UN complex at Turtle Bay which is domed, albeit far more modestly than are the Pantheon, Hagia Sophia, St. Peter's, St. Basil's, St. Paul's, or the U.S. Capitol. Since ancient times, the dome is a symbol of religious or secular authority with universal if not utopian aspirations.

NOTES

1. UN Charter, Article 96.
2. The UN Charter itself nowhere uses the term *resolution*. It refers to recommendations or decisions. However, in UN practice, these recommendations or decisions are titled "resolutions." UN documents assign to each an Arabic numeral in the order of its adoption, with the number of the Assembly session in parentheses, in Roman numerals, e.g., Resolution 1013 (XI).
3. M. E. Burton, *The Assembly of the League of Nations* (Chicago: University of Chicago Press, 1943), p. 94 (views of Arthur J. Balfour and René Viviani, respectively). It has also been said that Woodrow Wilson envisaged the Assembly as a mere rubber stamp. F. Morley, *The Society of Nations* (Washington, D.C.: Brookings Institution, 1932), p. 39.
4. Burton, *Assembly of League of Nations*, pp. 73–75, 376–377.
5. *Ibid.*, pp. 174–175, 377–378. The Covenant exceptions to the unanimity rule are found in Article 1, paragraph 2, of the Covenant, on the admission of new members (two-thirds majority); Article 4, paragraph 2, on the increase of permanent or nonpermanent members of the Council (simple majority vote); Article 6, paragraph 2, appointment of the secretary-general (simple majority vote); Article 15, paragraph 2, on making and publishing reports with recommendations after the Council's failure to settle a dispute (simple majority vote); Article 15, paragraph 10, on adopting reports on a dispute referred to it by the Council and accepted by the Council (simple majority vote); Article 26, paragraph 1, on amendments to the Covenant, which had to be ratified by the Council members and a simple majority of Assembly members. The unanimity rule was also bypassed by the practice of considering abstentions as an absence and by making a distinction between decisions and *voeux*. The latter could be adopted by a simple majority vote. Only five Assembly resolutions failed to be adopted because of a member's negative vote. *Ibid.*, p. 191.
6. UN Charter, Article 9, paragraph 1.
7. A. G. Mower, "Observer Countries: Quasi-Members of the United Nations," *International Organization*, XX, No. 2 (Spring 1966), 266–283. The following six states hold an observer status: West Germany, the Holy See, South Korea, Monaco, Switzerland, and South Vietnam. The UN Charter has no provisions for observers of nonmember states, nor has it taken any action for creating this relationship. The status is regarded as being directly the result of the example set by Switzerland, the establishment of permanent missions to the UN, and the beginning of the cold war with the deadlock in the admission of many new applicants for membership between 1946 and 1955.
8. The latest text is A/520/Rev. 10, which embodies amendments and

additions adopted by the Assembly up to December 31, 1969. Its introduction (pp. xi–xiv) sums up the story of these rules. For successive texts of the rules of procedure until 1964, see S. D. Bailey, *The General Assembly of the United Nations,* rev. ed., (New York: Praeger, 1964), pp. 269–270.

9. UN Charter, Article 9, paragraph 2.

10. Bailey, *General Assembly,* pp. 53–54.

11. Rule 31 of the rules of procedure.

12. *Ibid.,* p. 38 (Resolution 1990 [XVIII]). For the Assembly officers, see S. E. Werners, *The Presiding Officers in the United Nations* (Haarlem: F. Bohn, 1967).

13. The UN Special Committee on the Balkans (UNSCOB) (1947–1951), and the Balkan Subcommission of the Assembly's Peace Observation Commission (1951–1954).

14. The Mediator for Palestine, the Palestine Conciliation Commission, the UN Relief for Refugees, all of 1948; the UN Relief and Works Agency (UNRWA) (1949); the UN Emergency Force (UNEF) (1956–1967); the Mediator (1967).

15. The UN Good Offices Commission with regard to the Treatment of Indians and Pakistanis in South Africa (1952–1953).

16. The UN Commission for Libya (1949–1951).

17. The UN Temporary Authority (1962–1963).

18. See p. 77.

19. The Peace Observation Commission and Collective Measures Committee, both of 1950, and the Special Committee on Peace-Keeping Operations (1965).

20. The International Law Commission, set up in 1947. For this commission see H. W. Briggs, *The International Law Commission* (Ithaca, N.Y.: Cornell University Press, 1965). See also Mr. Gross's essay, pp. 172–217.

21. The Expanded Program of Technical Assistance (1950–1965); the Special Fund (1959–1965); and the UN Development Program (1965).

22. The UN Conference on Trade and Development (UNCTAD) of 1964, which became a permanent UN agency.

23. The Special Committee on Information on Non-Self-Governing Territories (1949) and the Special Committee on the Granting of Independence to Colonial Countries and People (1961).

24. The Office of the UN High Commissioner on Refugees, set up in 1950.

25. The UN International Children's Emergency Fund, set up in 1946, to continue the work carried out by the UN Relief and Rehabilitation Administration (UNRRA), a wartime, pre-UN agency.

26. The Commission on Narcotic Drugs (1946) which continued international work begun in 1912.

27. UN Charter, Article 18, paragraph 1.

28. The membership of the Byelorussian and Ukrainian SSRs in the UN constitutes a sort of weighted voting for the USSR, which has also a vote of its own in the Assembly. This, however, is a special case, since the United States and other major states do not enjoy any similar weighted voting in the Assembly. For the exchange of letters between Roosevelt and Stalin on the three votes for the USSR in the Assembly and Stalin's assent for the same number of votes for the United States, see *Foreign Relations of the United States. The Conferences at Malta and Yalta 1945* (Washington, D.C.: Government Printing Office, 1955), pp. 966–968. Incidentally, during the Russian revolution and civil war, the Ukraine proclaimed its independence and applied for membership in the League of Nations. So did Georgia, Armenia, and Azerbaijan. However, the relevant League Committee advised rejection of

these applications for admission, as well as the applications of Albania and
Liechtenstein. The Assembly followed these recommendations, except in the
case of Albania's application for League membership. Burton, *Assembly of
League of Nations,* p. 88.

29. League of Nations Covenant, Article 5, paragraphs 1 and 2.

30. The French text of the UN Charter translates "recommendations"
as *"recommandations,"* not as *"voeux,"* although Paul Hymans, the Belgian
president of the first League Assembly, considered that a *"voeu"* in English
was a recommendation. Burton, *Assembly of League of Nations,* p. 183. On
the other hand, according to a British jurist, the French word was almost un-
translatable. Its English equivalents could be a "wish," a "hope," a "view,"
an "opinion," a "recommendation." It resulted in no obligation for its addressee outside the League of Nations. J. F. Williams, "The League of Nations
and Unanimity," *American Journal of International Law,* XIX, No. 3 (1925),
479–480. The Council's recommendations, on the other hand, when these
were made under Article 15 of the Covenant, had to be adopted by unanimity
(except for the disputants' votes).

31. UN Charter, Articles 40 and 41.

32. *Ibid.,* Article 19. For this issue see J. G. Stoessinger and Associates,
Financing the United Nations System (Washington, D.C.: Brookings Institution, 1964).

33. L. M. Goodrich, E. Hambro, and A. Simons, *Charter of the United
Nations,* 3rd rev. ed. (New York: Columbia University Press, 1969), p. 170.

34. UN Charter, Article 18, paragraph 2. For the ambiguities of this
article, see E. L. Kerley, "Voting in the United Nations General Assembly,"
American Journal of International Law, LIII, No. 2 (April 1959), 324–340.

36. UN Charter, Article 108.

37. *Ibid.,* Article 5.

38. *Ibid.,* Article 6.

39. *Ibid.,* Article 23.

40. *Ibid.,* Article 61.

41. *Ibid.,* Article 84, paragraph c.

42. *Ibid.,* Article 97. Article 8 of the Statute of the International Court
of Justice.

43. UN Charter, Article 17.

44. *Ibid.,* Article 98.

45. *Ibid.,* Articles 11–14.

46. *Ibid.,* Article 24.

47. *Ibid.,* Article 12.

48. A. Lall, *The UN and the Middle East Conflict* (New York: Columbia University Press, 1968), pp. 119–120, considers this as a deviation in
practice from UN Charter rules and refers to these resolutions and to their
precedents.

49. Under Article 99 of the UN Charter, the secretary-general, however, may draw the Security Council's attention to any matter which in his
opinion threatens international peace and security.

50. UN Charter, Article 11, paragraph 2, and Article 35.

51. General Assembly Resolution 1573 (XV).

52. See Mr. Kay's essay, pp. 143–170.

53. The high tide of the influx of new African members in the UN
occurred in 1960 when nineteen African states were admitted into the organization.

54. The Covenant of the League referred to the "reduction" of armaments (Article 8, paragraphs 1 and 2).

55. See S. G. Xydis, "The Press in World Politics and in the Conduct

of Foreign Policy," *Journal of International Affairs,* X, No. 2 (1956), 208–210.

56. This treaty includes a commitment to refrain from placing in orbit around the earth any objects carrying nuclear weapons or any other kinds of weapons of mass destruction; from installing such weapons on celestial bodies, such as the moon, or from stationing such weapons in outer space in any other manner. However, it does not ban fractional orbital bombs (FOBs).

57. For an interesting inside account of the genesis of the International Atomic Energy Agency, see J. J. Wadsworth, "Atoms for Peace," in J. G. Stoessinger and A. F. Westin (eds.), *Power and Order* (New York: Harcourt, Brace & World, 1964), pp. 33–65.

58. Its membership was later increased to twenty-eight.

59. These seven principles were: abstention from threats or use of force, peaceful settlement of disputes, noninterference in matters of domestic jurisdiction, sovereign equality, equal rights and self-determination, duty of states to cooperate with each other, and good faith in the fulfillment of obligations.

60. See Mr. Gregg's essay, pp. 172–217.

61. Until October 1970 the governments of forty-eight UN members had signed the two covenants and seven governments had ratified them (Costa Rica, Ecuador, Tunisia, Cyprus, Colombia, Uruguay, and Bulgaria). Among the seventy-eight remaining UN members who had not even signed the covenants were the United States, France, Japan, and India.

62. For the UN work on human rights see E. Schwelb, "The International Protection of Human Rights," *International Organization,* XXIV, No. 1 (Winter 1970), 74–92. Also V. Van Dyke, *Human Rights, the United States, and the World Community* (New York: Oxford University Press, 1970), and A. E. Luard (ed.), *The International Protection of Human Rights* (New York: Praeger, 1967).

63. UN Charter, Article 14.

64. League of Nations Covenant, Article 19.

65. Much of this section is based on conclusions reached about "parliamentary diplomacy" based on a case study in depth, S. G. Xydis, *Cyprus: Conflict and Conciliation 1954–1958* (Columbus: Ohio State University Press, 1967), pp. 529–563. (Cited hereafter as Xydis, *Cyprus.*) See also G. Hadwen and J. Kaufman, *How UN Decisions Are Made* (Leyden: Sijthoff, 1960); and R. O. Keohane, "The Study of Political Influence in the General Assembly," *International Organization,* XXI, No. 2 (1967), 221–237.

66. Rule 20 of the Assembly's rules of procedure.

67. Bailey, *General Assembly,* p. 70.

68. S. D. Bailey, *Congress Makes a Law* (New York: Columbia University Press, 1950), p. vii.

69. A. W. Cordier, "Diplomacy Today," *Journal of International Affairs,* XVII, No. 1 (1963), 6.

70. Rule 43 of the Assembly's rules of procedure.

71. L. M. Goodrich and A. P. Simons, *The United Nations and the Maintenance of International Peace and Security* (Washington, D.C.: Brookings Institution, 1955), p. 103.

72. *Ibid.,* p. 105. These authors observe that it is difficult to see how the General Committee can perform any useful function unless it is given considerable latitude in the range of its discussions and recommendations.

73. Rule 23 of the Assembly's rules of procedure.

74. Rule 22 of the Assembly's rules of procedure.

75. K. Burke, *A Rhetoric of Motives* (New York: Prentice-Hall, 1950), p. 50.

76. N. J. Padelford, *Elections in the United Nations General Assembly, A Study of Political Behavior* (Cambridge: Center for International Studies, M.I.T., 1959).

77. J. Kaufman, *Conference Diplomacy* (Leyden: Sijthoff, 1968), pp. 145–148.

78. A. Lijphart, "The Analysis of Bloc Voting in the General Assembly: A Critique and a Proposal," *American Political Science Review*, LVII, No. 4 (December 1963), 902–917. For useful bibliography, see pp. 902–903. Also B. M. Russett, "Discovering Voting Groups in the United Nations," *American Political Science Review*, LX, No. 2 (June 1966), 327–339. J. E. Mueller, "Some Comments on Russett's 'Discovering' Voting Groups in the United Nations," *American Political Science Review*, LXI, No. 1 (March 1967), 146–148. Also D. Kay, "Instruments of Influence in the United Nations Political Process," in D. Kay (ed.), *The United Nations Political System* (New York: Wiley, 1967), pp. 98–102.

79. T. Hovet, *Bloc Politics in the United Nations* (Cambridge: Harvard University Press, 1960), pp. 29–101, describes these different voting groups at length.

80. J. F. Triska and D. D. Finley, *Soviet Foreign Policy* (New York: The Macmillan Company, 1968), pp. 273–280, for the effects of Soviet economic aid on voting in the UN.

81. H. R. Alker and B. M. Russett, *World Politics in the General Assembly* (New Haven: Yale University Press, 1965), pp. 227, note 12, and 264.

82. Xydis, *Cyprus*, p. 546.

83. J. Castañeda, *Legal Effects of United Nations Resolutions* (New York: Columbia University Press, 1969), deals with these resolutions pertaining to the structure and operations of the UN in pp. 22–69. International lawyers are not in agreement as to whether the rules of internal law of international organizations constitute an autonomous legal system that differs from both international law and state law or whether they are actually part of international law and of conventional origin. However, this lack of consensus does not effect the binding character of these rules, over which all jurists are agreed. *Ibid.*, pp. 22–23.

84. UN Charter, Articles 10, 11, 12 (*a negativo*), 13, 14, and 18.

85. This definition is based on Castañeda, *Legal Effects*, p. 7.

86. Castañeda, *Legal Effects*, p. 9.

87. F. C. Iklé, *How Nations Negotiate* (New York: Harper & Row, 1964), p. 21. For the compliance of the parties concerned with 29 important Assembly resolutions between 1946–1962, see Gabriella Rosner Lande, "An Inquiry into the Successes and Failures of United Nations General Assembly Resolutions," in Leon Gordenker (ed.), *The United Nations in International Politics* (Princeton: Princeton University Press, 1971), pp. 106–129.

88. Xydis, *Cyprus*, p. 532. In legal terms, to be analyzed below, Resolution 1287 (XIII) on the Cyprus question could be regarded as a bilateral executive agreement between the Greek and Turkish foreign ministers to exchange views and negotiate on the Cyprus question. The day after that resolution was adopted, the two foreign ministers met in the delegates' lounge at UN headquarters on December 6, 1958, and this exchange led to further negotiations that culminated in the Zürich summit conference of the Greek and Turkish premiers (February 5–11, 1959) under which the Greek and Turkish governments agreed to the setting up of Cyprus as an independent republic. Xydis, *Cyprus*, p. 525.

89. Castañeda, *Legal Effects*, pp. 2–3.

90. S. A. Bleicher, "The Legal Significance of General Assembly Resolutions," *American Journal of International Law*, LXIII, No. 3 (1969), 478. Until the end of 1969 the Assembly had adopted 2,619 resolutions.

91. Castañeda, *Legal Effects,* pp. 18–20.

92. *Ibid.,* pp. 117–138.

93. *Ibid.,* pp. 165–196.

94. *Ibid.,* p. 173.

95. *Ibid.,* pp. 81–116.

96. *Ibid.,* pp. 85–86.

97. *Ibid.,* pp. 150–164.

98. *Ibid.,* p. 152.

99. *Ibid.,* pp. 139–149.

100. *Ibid.,* p. 141.

101. This advisory opinion of the ICJ was a response to a question put to it by the UN Security Council: "What are the legal consequences for states of the continued presence of South Africa in Namibia notwithstanding Security Council Resolution 276 (1970)?" The Security Council's Resolution had been based on the Assembly's Resolution 2145 (XXI). Advisory opinions of the ICJ, it should be noted, are not legally binding.

102. Bleicher, "General Assembly Resolution," p. 456.

102A. Such a consensus is of importance because under Article 38 of the Statute of the ICJ the teachings of the most qualified jurists of various states constitute a subsidiary means for determining rules of law.

103. N.G. Onuf, "Professor Falk on the Quasi-Legislative Competence of the General Assembly," *American Journal of International Law,* LXIV, No. 2 (1970), 349–355. This article refers to the extensive bibliography on the question of the legal nature of General Assembly resolutions.

104. G. De Visscher, *Theory and Reality in Public International Law,* rev. ed. (Princeton: Princeton University Press, 1968), pp. 153–163.

105. For U.S. influence in the Assembly, see R. S. Riggs, *Politics in the United Nations: A Study of U.S. Influence in the General Assembly* (Urbana: Illinois University Press, 1959).

106. Austria, Italy, Finland, Spain, Ireland, Portugal, Jordan, Libya, Laos, Cambodia, and Ceylon.

107. Albania, Bulgaria, Hungary, and Romania.

108. Jordan, Laos, Cambodia, and Ceylon. Until 1956 Jordan was tied to Britain by treaty but denounced it during the Suez affair of that year.

109. By 1960 Albania was excluded from the Soviet bloc which, however, had been joined by Cuba.

110. W. L. Tung, *International Organization under the United Nations System* (New York: Crowell, 1968), pp. 53–54. For microstates and dependencies, see UNITAR's study by J. Rapaport, E. Muteba, and J. J. Therattil, *Small States and Territories* (New York: Arno Press, 1971).

111. J. G. Rapoport, "The Participation of Ministates in International Affairs," *Proceedings of the American Society of International Law,* 62nd Annual Meeting, Washington, D.C., April 25–27, 1967, p. 159.

112. Under Resolution 637A (VII), the Assembly in 1952 recommended that UN members should uphold the principle of self-determination of all peoples and nations and recognize and promote the realization of the "right of self-determination" of peoples of non-self-governing and trust territories with the wishes of the people being ascertained by plebiscites or other recognized democratic means, preferably under UN auspices. The United States voted against this resolution.

113. R. F. Taubenfeld and H. J. Taubenfeld, "Some International Implications of Weather Modification Activities," *International Organization,* XXIII, No. 4 (Autumn 1969), 803–833.

Leon Gordenker

THE SECRETARY-GENERAL

If the relations among the countries of the world followed laws engraved ineffaceably on immortal rock, to study the office and work of the secretary-general of the United Nations would be an unrewardingly static exercise. But international relations change and, if the actions of statesmen are read accurately, can be changed by the use of ideas, persuasion, pressure, and force. The United Nations and other international organizations rest solidly on a fundamental assumption that the international environment can be altered and the patterns of politics affected by deliberate actions.[1] The office of secretary-general constitutes an outcome of making that assumption.

This view of the universe of international institutions as having malleable qualities ultimately turns the attention of an observer away from the larger system to the people involved. It is the persons who act in the institutional frameworks and outside them who initiate action and set policies. It is they who carry out the policies and make the choices to adapt the general statements of strategy to the unexpected tactical specifics of administration. It is they who suggest the revisions of policies and structures that take advantage of experience.

At any one time, the work of the United Nations involves many thousands of people—governmental representatives, international civil servants, national civil servants, and ultimately even individual citizens whose lives are affected. Of all of these people, who come and go at the direction of governments and their organs, one man has a certain permanency and preeminence. His office provides him with a role that makes him outstanding in the institutional setting of the United Nations. His title is secretary-general of the United Nations, but it bears remembering that he remains a human being who can make choices and, by virtue of his position, must do so, whether for good or evil.

The position of the secretary-general implies a certain paradox. He is elected to his office as an individual, not as representative of a government.[2] He bears personal responsibility for his actions. He is also responsible for the work of his subordinates. He has a certain latitude within which he may take policy positions and make decisions. He is the only individual, acting on personal responsibility, who has the explicit charge to concern himself with the maintenance of peace and security among states.

But the United Nations is not an organization of individuals or of citizens. It is an organization of states, represented by governments.[3] The persons who speak for governments in the United Nations setting formally are considered to have instructions. Their very representative role tends to minimize their individual discretion. The United Nations makes recommendations and takes limited mandatory actions that are addressed to governments, not to individuals. In theoretical terms, the United Nations operates at the level of the international system in which states are the actors. In political terms, governments serve as organizations of individuals and influence each other by the products of their organizations. They have administrative arrangements, such as a civil service; means of organizing, such as ability to tax and police; and military arms with which to beat off and destroy outside threats and to threaten on their own.

Thus the existence of the office and function of the secretary-general immediately raises the question of the role of an individual in an international environment where states are the actors. Is the secretary-general equivalent to a state? What does he in fact represent? What means of action does he, a pygmy among the governmental giants, possess? Is he comparable to national statesmen in his role? Is his role analogous to that of the American president or of the secretary of the Communist party of the USSR? Is he primarily a symbol or is he an influential factor in the international environment?

CONSTITUTIONAL FOUNDATIONS

Whatever the character and predilections of the individual who has the title of secretary-general, the office has, as could be expected in an organization deliberately created by governments, a set of legal foundations. From these foundations the incumbents in the office have built up their policies and their influence, their responsibilities and their initiatives. An examination of the constitutional bases of the office can indicate expectations of and limitations on the secretary-general and his formal position.

The United Nations Charter established a Secretariat as a main organ of the organization.[4] Apparently, the implication is that the Secretariat in some fashion ranks with the Security Council, the General Assembly, the Economic and Social Council, the Trusteeship Council, and the International Court of Justice in prestige and importance, if not in legal powers.

The head of the Secretariat is the secretary-general. He is the chief administrative officer of the organization and has full responsibility for the work of the Secretariat. The Secretariat includes the secretary-general and such staff as he may require.[5] The secretary-general reports each year to the General Assembly on the work of the organization.[6]

These legal provisions come close to saying that the secretary-general is a main organ of the United Nations, for he both represents and directs the organ he heads. Furthermore, it is he who serves as secretary-general of all the other organs. This gives him a place at the council tables and the right, as provided by the rules of procedure of the organs, to address them, to intervene in debates, and to put reports before them.[7] In addition, the secretary-general performs such other functions as he is directed to carry out by the organs.[8] It is the secretary-general who has the responsibility, not a generalized and abstract entity called the Secretariat.

It would be pedantic to emphasize on the basis of a Charter provision the equality of the secretary-general and, say, the Security Council. But the fact that the Secretariat is a main organ and that the secretary-general acts on behalf of and at the head of the Secretariat once again calls attention to his role as an individual in an environment peopled by states.

This role received even stronger emphasis from the renowned political provisions of Article 99 of the Charter.[9] It empowers the secretary-general to bring to the attention of the Security Council any matter which in his opinion may threaten the maintenance of peace and security. Calling matters to the attention of an international organ is usually a prerogative of a government or, if given to an international official, is hedged in with explicit restrictions. Governments tend to exhibit jealousy about their prerogatives, especially those which may involve questions of war and peace. And yet, in the United Nations Charter, an international official receives a power usually reserved to governments and is told that he may exercise it on the basis of his opinion, for which he is personally responsible.

The intention of Article 99, narrowly interpreted, certainly was not that of creating a paradoxical position for an individual in an international environment of states. Rather, it related to the function of the Security Council in maintaining peace. If a member government found it embarrassing to call attention to a matter of peace and security, in the Security Council, the secretary-general could do so. But in order to so act, the secretary-general had to have a basis, an opinion. Unavoidably, the position of the secretary-general in this arrangement involves political judgment, not merely technical reckoning. The implications, therefore, of even a narrow interpretation of Article 99 tend toward a broad political role for the secretary-general.

Although the secretary-general must bear much individual responsibility in an environment formally occupied by states, he receives some legal protection from the formal provisions of the Charter. Most importantly, these treat the Secretariat as an international body whose members may receive instructions only from its head. No government may give instructions to the secretary-general or his subordinates; nor may members of the international Secretariat seek such instructions. The Charter uses the phrase ". . . international officials responsible only to the Organization." Also, Article 100 of the Charter clearly means that members of the Secretariat serve only the secretary-general, not a politician or civil servant of a member government. For their part, the member governments undertake not to try to influence the Secretariat members in the discharge of their responsibilities. As for the secretary-general, his responsibilities are supposed to have an "exclusively international character." All members of the organization undertake to respect this status.

The emphasis on the non-national character of the international civil service continues in the Charter provisions for appointment of the staff. This is the responsibility of the secretary-general. Thus the international staff, according to the Charter, is organized by actions beyond the influence of any single government by a chief administrative officer who can receive instructions only from international bodies. The basis of appointment conforms, in part, to the pattern of international status for the Secretariat, for officials are to be selected on the basis of the highest standards of efficiency, competence, and integrity. These tests, the Charter declares, are paramount. Yet, in a succeeding sentence, the Charter introduces another test which neither necessarily underlies an international staff nor implies the perfect impartiality sought in other provisions. This sentence enjoins the secretary-general to pay due regard to the importance of recruiting his staff on "as wide a geographical basis as possible." In fact, the representational camel nose intrudes into the exclusively international tent.[10]

Although the emphasis on an independent international stance for the secretary-general cannot be mistaken, the provisions for his selection imply that some members of the international community have a greater share in his appointment than others.[11] The secretary-general owes his appointment to the General Assembly, which, however, acts only after receiving a positive recommendation from the Security Council. Because the Security Council must in the first instance make up its collective mind, the selection of a secretary-general is subject to the great power unanimity rule. Thus the candidate secretary-general must not have incurred the opposition of the governments of the five permanent members of the Security Council. No legal limitations apply to the standards each of them implicitly applies in making this recommendation. Furthermore, the General Assembly is legally free to reject recommendations from the Security Council on the appointment of a secretary-general, although in fact it has never shown any hesitance in endorsing them.

The General Assembly also has a role in the organization of the Secretariat. It must approve rules under which the staff is appointed. In practice, the secretary-general proposes these rules and an organizational structure. For the most part, the General Assembly has approved them without difficulty. The same applies to alterations of the rules which have been proposed from time to time. Because the General Assembly approves the budget of the organization, which is also proposed by the secretary-general, it has the legal right to set expenditures in such a way as to determine the total number of the staff and how it is employed. Thus the budgeting and financing functions are necessarily shared by the secretary-general and the General Assembly.[12]

For the most part, the General Assembly maintains the exclusive responsibility of the secretary-general for the Secretariat. It has, however, added to the arrangements sketched in the Charter an Administrative Tribunal,[13] a quasi-judicial organ manned by individuals selected for their competence by the General Assembly. The Administrative Tribunal decides cases in which the secretary-general is charged by members of the Secretariat with exceeding his authority or acting unjustly in personnel matters. Secretary-General Trygve Lie opposed the establishment of this tribunal on the grounds that it diluted the responsibility of his office. Furthermore, the General Assembly takes a keen interest in the geographical distribution of appointments to the Secretariat, always pressing for a staff to which each member state sends some employees. Obviously, this pressure must run afoul of the constitutional provisions giving paramountcy to the highest standards of efficiency, competence, and integrity.

LEADER OR CLERK?

The provisions of the United Nations Charter implicitly pose an important question about the scope and content of the role of the secretary-general in the organization but offer no sharp answer. The question is whether the secretary-general is above all the clerk of the organization or whether he can exercise leadership functions. It is this question which has often led observers to compare the secretary-general with the office of president of the United States, for the latter clearly combines both functions.

The argument that the secretary-general has primarily clerkly duties begins with an estimate of his place as an individual in the system of states. Because he has neither the power nor the administrative trappings of a government, he has only a role as an aide to the governments that make up his organization. Even were he to wish to go beyond that role, he has no equipment with which to do so. Furthermore, he is appointed as chief administrative officer of the organization and serves as secretary-general to the other main organs. Main organ or not, his Secretariat exists primarily to prepare the way for decisions, not to make them. The secretary-general is responsible for the work of the Secretariat and the member governments are responsible for the decisions that activate the Secretariat. The powers under Article 99 are intended to aid the member governments, not to provide the secretary-general with an independent role.

The argument that endows the office of secretary-general with leadership functions really assumes that it has clerkly functions and that these will be carried out. But even these functions offer leadership opportunities to the secretary-general. Because he has a right to be present and to speak in all of the principal deliberative organs, he can urge particular courses on the representatives of government. In fact, he does so constantly, especially in the Economic and Social Council, where it is fair to say that the intellectual basis for a great proportion of the resolutions adopted and later repeated in more generalized form by the General Assembly originate.[14] His constitutional duty to put before the General Assembly an annual report on the work of the organization allows him to make an assessment and judgments that no other person can make. It also gives him a ready-made platform from which to project suggestions. His staff can help him inform and persuade delegates of national governments about his suggestions.

Article 99 of the Charter supports, according to this argument, a leading role for the secretary-general. His power to summon the Security Council into session goes beyond anything ever given an international official with duties related to maintaining the peace and security. His use of this power means that he has pointed out a situation involving governments in which their behavior threatens peace and security. To take that action in itself constitutes leadership. It implies, moreover, that the secretary-general has a great responsibility to analyze the international situation constantly so that he can competently exercise his powers under Article 99. Furthermore, if he has a political role of this sort, then it is only a short step to his trying to prevent conflicts that may threaten the peace. He can do this by persuasive means and by the use of his staff and the facilities it offers. He has, moreover, acted in precisely this fashion in numerous incidents and, it is argued, he should be expected to do so in the future. In addition, the secretary-general takes on duties assigned by other organs; he may suggest such duties.

Although the roles of clerk and leader are more strongly opposed here than is usual in the day-to-day politics of the United Nations, it should not be thought that the distinctions are merely academic. They were strongly posed by Dag Hammarskjöld in his report for 1961 on the work of the organization.[15] He was responding to Soviet attacks on him and on the conduct of his office in directing the United Nations force in the Congo. Forthrightly, Hammarskjöld pointed out that the secretary-general could serve a conference organization (where he would act as a clerk) or could serve as an administrator of the needs and wishes of the organization (where he could not fail to exercise some leadership functions). If Hammarskjöld defended his stance in the Congo, he also defended the role of secretary-general as a leader.

HISTORICAL DEVELOPMENT

The office of secretary-general hardly sprang full blown from the ashes of World War II. The ideas underlying it already had a considerable historical background. The development of that background comprises essential material for an understanding of the office.

The function of the secretary-general as provider of conference facilities has roots in the ad hoc diplomatic conferences that were so common in the nineteenth century.[16] In such conferences as that at Berlin in 1878 the host state provided a staff. Where something more than common services was required, such as the drafting of a legal instrument or communiqué, the various delegations attending the conference contributed personnel, often on a basis of numerical equality. Because the conferences met only once, no permanent organization became necessary.

With the creation of permanent international institutions during the second half of the nineteenth century, permanent staffs had to be provided. Periodic meetings required preparation not only in a physical sense but also in an intellectual sense. A permanent record of proceedings had to be kept and questions left over for study from one meeting to another had to be brought up again. Sometimes reports had to be prepared, especially those involving a budget, which were not appropriately left in the hands of any one of the member governments. A typical method of meeting these needs could be found in the Universal Postal Union which in effect hired a staff from the Swiss government. Other institutions, some of them nongovernmental but of transnational scope, began to experiment with independent international staffs.

Secretary-General of the League

The ambitious attempt after World War I to institutionalize a broad segment of international relations in the League of Nations posed requirements for a bigger staff than had been seen at the international level. Moreover, the League was not alone; its sister organization, the International Labour Organisation (ILO) also needed a staff.

The nature of the Secretariat of the League and of ILO got relatively less attention than the overarching need for decisions on how to organize the institutions that were to keep the peace in the future. For such institutions a Secretariat might be a necessary appurtenance but at that stage not a major question. Yet many of the issues that were to prove of continuing importance in the League and other international organizations emerged.

Some of the most active organizers of the League conceived of the post at the head of the Secretariat as one having considerable political importance.[17] By this was apparently meant involvement with the policy-making process, the contribution of substantive policies and a degree of independent prestige sufficient to act persuasively on member governments. Accordingly, an eminent political figure, Eleutherios Venizelos of Greece, received the first bid to become what was termed "Chancellor of the League." After considering the idea, he declined.

A second feeler went out to a British civil servant, Sir Maurice Hankey, who had had extensive wartime experience with the administration of technical cooperation involving the several allies. Hankey dealt with intergovernmental decision-making bodies made up of national civil servants. The new League post was transmuted to that of secretary-general, a literal translation from the French document on the League and fully in accordance with earlier diplomatic practice. Presumably, Hankey would have had a lesser political role than a chancellor while, in view of his war-time experience, he would have had deep involvement in policy making. Moreover, this experience indicated a pattern of organization for the Secretariat, for he had worked with experts representing their own governments and having certain powers of decision. But Hankey also declined the post.

A second British civil servant, Sir Eric Drummond, accepted an offer to become the first secretary-general of the League. He was a product of the British Foreign Office and of association with a skillful group of civil servants who viewed their positions as both influential on policy issues and anonymous so far as the mass of people was concerned. Drummond knew both the diplomatic world and the plans for the League of Nations on which he had worked hard at the Paris Peace Conference and earlier.

Drummond stipulated that the Secretariat he was to head would be a career civil service, not a body of governmental representatives.[18] He also insisted that it should be an *international* civil service, not receiving instructions from any individual government but carrying on despite changes in member governments or in League policies. This all carried strong echoes of the British civil service with its tradition of independence from any particular party, service to any government whatever its party base, and long-term careers for individuals within the civil service framework. It soon developed that Drummond carried another British tradition to his office at the permanent seat of the League at Geneva. He avoided appearances and any sign in public of leadership. Behind the scenes he was busy in consultations, making suggestions and participating in various diplomatic maneuvers intended to further League policy.

Meanwhile, the ILO, also located in Geneva and constitutionally connected with the League, had organized its Secretariat under the leadership of Albert Thomas,[19] a leading French socialist politician and former cabinet minister. Thomas saw his role as rather more like that envisaged for Venizelos than that designed by Drummond. Relying on his parliamentary experience, he constantly joined debates in ILO conferences; as if he were chief minister of a government, he outlined programs to the ILO and sought their acceptance. He toured a great deal and cultivated constituencies, such as the labor unions, outside of official government structures. In a political manner which Drummond never tried, Thomas became a public and explicit leader, a role that Drummond never sought.

Thus, within five years of the founding of the League and ILO, some of the enduring problems of the United Nations Secretariat had been posed. Should the secretary-general be a leader operating openly before the public? Should he, rather, assume a self-effacing public stance and continue policy-influencing activities behind the scenes? Should he try mainly to work on technical lines or should he attempt to develop a broad influence on the international system? Should the Secretariat be organized on the basis of an independent civil service, responsible for its work to political leaders who themselves had responsibility for policies they proposed? Or should it be composed of expert representatives of governments? The answers given by Venizelos, Hankey, Drummond, and Thomas did not permanently end discussion and, indeed, at various periods in the 1920s and 1930s the questions were again posed by member governments and, implicitly, by the League Secretariat.

The patterns laid down by Drummond and Thomas held during the period between the two wars. Drummond established himself as a man in whom governmental representatives at Geneva could confide. He adroitly and quietly interjected his views into the conflicts threatening international peace and security that came to the League.[20] In large part by selecting highly able officials, he created a competent Secretariat that made suggestions leading to the expansion of its task, especially related to economic and social cooperation. The League grew in both expected and unexpected directions, above all in mechanisms to deal with economic and social problems.

Drummond's resignation in 1932 and Thomas' death in 1932 produced no great upheavals, indicating that the patterns had been well established. The director-general of ILO always has had a major influence on policy in the organization. The second secretary-general of the League, Joseph Avenol,[21] a French civil servant, continued Drummond's practice of assiduous consultation and involvement in political affairs, but his rightist political tendencies and his insensitive reaction to the changes taking place in the European order as Hitler and Mussolini destroyed the legacy of Versailles led him to stances that perceptibly weakened the League and its Secretariat. Avenol resisted moving the Secretariat from Geneva to shelter in the United States and Canada and eventually resigned in 1940 while under a cloud of suspicion.

Old Questions Newly Posed

The outbreak of World War II in 1939 shattered most of the remaining links of international cooperation within the already faltering League of Nations. Secretary-General Avenol actively tried to protect what was left and made a series of decisions that at the time were controversial and in retrospect destructive. Whatever he may have done, however, it seems all but certain that the League would have been legally dismantled and replaced, if there was to be a replacement at all, with a new organization. By 1942 it was already clear as a result of commitments and leadership by the United States that a new international organization would be created after the defeat of Germany and Japan.

The League of Nations experiment figured strongly in the comprehensive efforts to sketch a postwar international organization.[22] The resultant plans gave far greater attention to the office of secretary-general than the Paris conferees had in 1919. Inside governments and in private groups, the veteran officials of the League digested their experiences and concluded that the office of secretary-general should have greater political power and broader scope than it had during the League days and that it should have a more public, leading role in the organization.[23] Similar views were projected in the United States Department and President Roosevelt strongly favored a political secretary-generalship.

That did not end the matter, as the San Francisco Conference was to show. The old questions of how broad a scope for action an international official should have, how his staff should be organized, and what influence the members should have on it arose there. The Soviet Union showed some reluctance to accept an independent, international Secretariat and wanted certainty that officials it nominated would have key positions. Some of the smaller states sought assurance that the Secretariat would not be dominated by the Great Powers who would control the appointment of the secretary-general. Much debate centered around whether the secretary-general should be elected by the majority of members or whether he should be appointed only after a recommendation by the Security Council—that is, with Great Power concurrence. Favorable decisions were reached by inserting sparse language in the Charter and giving strong protection to the international position of the Secretariat. Thus the precise role of the secretary-general certainly remained somewhat undefined, but it was beyond doubt that he could call to the attention of the Security Council matters impinging on peace and security and that he would have an international staff. Thus some questions raised in 1919 in Paris and by the experience of the League received partial answers.

The suspicion among some of the leaders of the lesser powers that the post of secretary-general would be filled by a national of a Great Power disappeared with the appointment of the first incumbent. After some discussion, including consideration of candidates from the Great Powers, the five permanent members of the Security Council settled on Trygve Lie, the Norwegian foreign minister, as their candidate.[24] Other members of the Council joined them in making a unanimous recommendation to the General Assembly. Trygve Lie became the first secretary-general of the United Nations early in 1946 and remained in office until 1952. Both his successors, Dag Hammarskjöld of Sweden, who held the office until his death in 1961, and U Thant of Burma, who took over after Hammarskjöld and was elected to a second five-year term in 1967, were nationals of small countries. So is the present Secretary-General, Kurt Waldheim, a former foreign minister of Austria, who took office at the beginning of 1972. The election process, however, insures that no one whose record is objectionable to a permanent member of the Council can become secretary-general. This, in turn, has meant that the candidates most obviously backed for a first appointment by one or another of the Great Powers have been passed over for a less-well-known person.

The mere fact that the secretary-general has so far always come from a small state does not indicate that the Great Powers have deliberately or tacitly abandoned their influence. To begin with, a part of the secretary-general's status, influence, and prestige derives from his election on the basis of positive Great Power approval. This implies that he has some claim, at least, to backing from the Great Powers. The corollary of this proposition is that if he loses Great Power support, his own position becomes weak or untenable. Furthermore, the Great Powers contribute a major proportion of the United Nations budget and have the resources and energy to observe closely the operations and policies of the secretary-general. Of all the United Nations members, they have the most effective means for exerting pressure on the secretary-general.

Thus the formal-legal position of the United Nations secretary-general stands on the experience of the League; the political powers of the new office were enlarged on the basis of the earlier experience. But the political position still contained some of the uncertainties and all of the limitations that were prominent earlier. The questions newly posed in 1945 still had no conclusive answers in 1972.

ACTOR IN WORLD POLITICS

In three main ways the secretary-general becomes an actor in world politics. He serves as an operator in political and security matters by giving early warnings of peril, by carrying out programs designed by other bodies and deliberately initiating action of his own or stimulating other bodies to act. He heads a vast network of institutions, policies, and field programs in economic and social fields. And, finally, he directs a Secretariat of more than five thousand officials and through it influences other international secretariats, probably well over five times the number of the United Nations staff. These three main directions of action, separated here for analytical purposes, in reality overlap, compete with, and reinforce each other at any given moment. Furthermore, they involve individuals, organizations made up of those same individuals, and competing interests of individuals and organizations in complex mixtures. These individuals and organizations connect with analogous actors whose roles look primarily to domestic polities. As a consequence, what may seem simply sketched in the academy can assume formidable complexity to the persons actually involved in the day-to-day work.

Political and Security Activities

Whatever the secretary-general undertakes in connection with peace and security lies within institutional and systemic restrictions. The institutional restrictions begin with his position as one organ among the two or three —the Security Council, the General Assembly, and occasionally the International Court of Justice—that have prescribed positions related to the maintenance of the peace. The Security Council has "primary responsibility" for the maintenance of peace and security.[25] Its role was intended by the framers of the United Nations Charter to overshadow that of the General Assembly, which could discuss general principles but could not intervene in a dispute or situation that had come before the Security Council.[26] The General Assembly could indeed receive a complaint from a member country about some affair that troubled international peace and security, but any member might complain to the Security Council, which was to have the central and, if its members wished, exclusive position in dealing with keeping the peace.

In fact, the Security Council has always reflected the divisions of the world around it. The protagonists of the cold war frequently dramatized their opposition by tying the Security Council into knotted frustration. When the Soviet Union reached its lowest ebb of international influence, immediately after the United Nations (with powerful American support) had intervened in Korea to repel what was defined as aggression by the vast majority of member governments, the General Assembly turned itself into a more flexible and active instrument for dealing with peace and security. This development eventually provided the secretary-general with opportunities to improvise and then make permanent a number of practices which increased his political leverage. To the extent that these practices have become institutionalized and made part of the thinking of international and member government bureaucracies, the scope of activities by the secretary-general to maintain peace has widened.

Nevertheless, the secretary-general can never be regarded as an entirely autonomous actor. He remains the servant of his organization.[27] Indeed, one of his main political defenses can be found in his ability to get formal, if possible, and informal backing for his work from the member governments. Furthermore, he has no coercive capacity whatever and no constituency to create vast popular movements. He remains a prisoner of the uniqueness of his position.

Early warning. Prisoner though he may be, the secretary-general need not remain a silent one. From the instruction in the United Nations Charter to deliver an annual report on the work of the organization, the secretary-general has created for himself a device by which he can put his views on the development of international life before the member governments. Each year he produces an introduction of several thousand words to his much longer and drier accounting of the work accomplished. This introduction has set forth for the member governments and those perhaps rather narrow public groups who take a close interest in international affairs some warnings of future problems. These have, for example, included a notice (as early as 1948) of the growing trend to decolonization and the resulting unrest to be expected in remaining colonial territories;[28] the need for economic development of less developed territories;[29] the widespread resentment of racism;[30] the dangers from nuclear arms races and radioactive fallout growing out of atmospheric testing of new weapons;[31] and the lack of progress toward peaceful settlement of the disputes disturbing the Middle East even while a peacekeeping force was still on duty.[32]

Because the secretary-general's annual report goes before the General Assembly, it tends to attract some comments from national representatives, especially during the long series of statements by governmental leaders that makes up the "general debate." Furthermore, it was clearly the intention of the framers of the Charter to make the annual report the center around which the business of the General Assembly was accomplished. In this hope they were doomed to be disappointed, but there is little question that the views of the most important international civil servant find their way at least into influential governmental channels and into the minds and mouths of pressure group leaders (such as the United Nations Associations in the United States and in Great Britain).

In addition to this published annual report, the secretary-general, who remains much in demand as a speaker even if some publics hold his organization in low esteem, makes several speeches each year in which he gives his views of international problems. In a notable speech in Baltimore in 1962, for example, U Thant strongly chided the United States (whose government was almost within hearing distance of the hall) and the Soviet Union for their obstinate antagonism and foresaw much future danger if it continued.[33] While such comments may contain little novelty, at least they come from a source regarded as by nature less partial than national governmental spokesmen. His arguments can be used by national officials and politicians who accept their wisdom. By doing so, such consumers of the secretary-general's ideas try to associate to their own views the prestige and broad scope of the United Nations.

Another much more solemn early warning device is available to the secretary-general under Article 99 of the United Nations Charter. In its pristine form, Article 99 could have been conceived of merely as an alternative means for summoning the Security Council. But, because it gave so much opportunity for the secretary-general to exercise his own judgment about what would be appropriate to bring before the Council, he could certainly consider it as a means to focus attention on a developing problem before it became an irreversible conflict.

In fact, Article 99 has found little direct use of this sort. When it was used explicitly by Dag Hammarskjöld in 1960 after the faltering government of the Congo (Kinshasa) complained of the intervention of Belgian troops, the conflict had reached full, menacing blossom. Its use did lead to an extraordinary executive role for the secretary-general but not to an early warning of trouble in that specific place. The closest that Hammarskjöld had come to such a warning occurred in statements during the previous year about the turbulence that could result from decolonization and the need for prompt economic aid to the new countries.[34] It was this perception of impending trouble in Africa generally and the rudiments of an economic program that led the secretary-general to dispatch a strong team of development experts and the experienced Undersecretary Ralph Bunche to the Congolese independence ceremonies. If Hammarskjöld had no early warning to give under Article 99, he did at least have reliable reports and a team of representatives fortunately on the trouble spot.

After the outbreak of fighting in Korea in 1950, Trygve Lie intervened in the Security Council debate to make it clear that he regarded the North Korean attack as a violation of the United Nations Charter.[35] But neither the Council nor he then explicitly treated this as a use of Article 99. Furthermore, in this instance, the secretary-general had had available information from a field body, the United Nations Commission on Korea, which might have led to an early warning, but little reaction followed either the public reports or private communications about impending trouble.

In the light of this experience and the delicacy of trying to induce action by possibly reluctant governments, it seems likely that much of the secretary-general's function as an early warning device would probably have to be confined to private consultations. Such consultations constitute a principal operating device available at all times to the secretary-general and are used in connection with any one of his activities that is likely to have a substantial effect on a government. It is consistent both with conventional diplomatic experience and with expectations about the office of secretary-general that go back to the founding of the League of Nations. The General Assembly made it quite plain during the earliest days of the United Nations when it was considering the organization of the Secretariat that the secretary-general should be looked upon as the confidant of governments, a man of trust and impartiality who could aid in communication and in the production of ideas for solving problems.[36]

Each of the four secretaries-general has enthusiastically used consultations to further what he considered the interests of his organization and of the member governments. Dag Hammarskjöld pointed out, moreover, that the presence in the New York headquarters of permanent representatives of almost all the member states created a unique "standing diplomatic conference" which greatly aided the consultative process.[37]

In fact, the secretary-general has several hundred consultations a year. Some of these take place in his office and others during his rather frequent travels to capitals of member governments and to United Nations meetings at distant points or at the United Nations European headquarters in the old League of Nations buildings in Geneva. Still others, consultations, generally of lesser meaning despite the romantic notions of some outside observers, are carried on at official receptions, luncheons, and dinners. On a few occasions, as in connection with United Nations treatment of the policy of apartheid in South Africa or the breakdown of the Middle East armistice in late 1955 and early 1956, the secretary-general has been instructed by the Security Council to undertake consultations.[38]

The consultative atmosphere provides excellent conditions for the secretary-general to call to the notice of member governments the possible emergence of new or unanticipated security problems. This is especially true when public statements could prove embarrassing to a government or controversial for the secretary-general. U Thant, for example, has carried on numerous consultations in which he was able to caution the United States government about the expansion of the war in Vietnam and about the unsettling consequences in several parts of the world of the use of American military power in the Far East. Similar warnings have been used in connection with the recurring Middle East crisis. Consultations, moreover, provide the secretary-general with a basis for broadening discussions and for involving other governments in a problem. This basis has frequently been used.

The secretary-general's staff, especially its higher officials in New York and Geneva and its senior field representatives, also take part in what can be seen as a continuous web of consultations. Some of these have also the preventive implication of early warnings. For example, a resident representative of the UN Development Program may be able to warn a government that its requests for technical aid have less credibility to decision makers in New York than those of other states because of a failure to integrate them closely with an articulated development program. To a limited extent, such officials may also provide highly relevant information to the secretary-general on the development of security crises.[39]

Policy initiation. In principle, from early warning to initiation of policies and programs involves only a short step, although politically it may constitute a long and uncertain one. The secretary-general has often made that step, sometimes in highly controversial situations and sometimes at a considerable cost to his own prestige. The same information required for the early warning function can serve as the basis of policy suggestion. But to suggest a policy to governments which tend to jealously guard their prerogatives risks rebuffs. Furthermore, if such a policy does not succeed in achieving the stated goals or attracts opposition from a major power during the course of its execution, the consequences can sharply limit the effectiveness of the secretary-general in consultations and even drive him from office.

The limitations on the secretary-general's ability to initiate policies that governments will accept and carry out show particularly starkly in peace and security activities.[40] Yet, ironically, it is precisely in such matters that he has the most encouragement from the constitutional arrangements of Article 99 to take the initiative. Moreover, because matters of war and peace tend to have dramatic features and because everyone regards them as his business, initiatives by the secretary-general in this field tend to become well known. As matters of public discussion, they have the disadvantage that rarely are all of the facts disclosed and ideological assumptions tend to reign supreme. It is therefore not surprising that frequently the initiatives of the chief officer of the United Nations barely get beyond the suggestion stage. Some which do often win only partial adoption and, as so much in the international scene, appear fragmentary and frustrated.

It may be taken as a measure of how far the office of secretary-general has been accepted as a normal part of international relations that U Thant permitted himself to try to initiate policy in the Cuban missile crisis and in Vietnam. His intervention in the former sharp crisis and the latter chronic one never led the parties to denounce him as a meddler or to treat him with the cold disdain diplomats sometimes reserve for those who show too much enthusiasm about their own positions. Yet in neither instance did the secretary-general succeed either in having his ideas become the basis of a peace settlement or in giving his organization a commanding position in the search for means to ease the crisis. In both instances, however, the secretary-general acted on his own initiative and without the formal backing of another organ which would presumably have followed at some point had he reached his goals.

In the Cuban missile crisis in 1962, Thant followed a deadlocked session of the Security Council with letters to the American president and the Soviet premier, urging them to halt temporarily all shipments of Soviet missiles to Cuba and movements of American naval forces so that negotiations could resume. The secretary-general claimed to speak on behalf of more than fifty noncommitted countries, implying that his letter resulted from consultations. Both President Kennedy and Premier Khrushchev replied in favorable but qualified terms to the suggestion that negotiations begin; in fact, almost frantic exchanges were taking place through normal diplomatic and other means. The secretary-general's intervention made it easier for both sides to claim that an impartial third party was furnishing the ideas which permitted them to adopt less belligerent policies. Thant's intervention also gave greater significance to an agreement, later rendered useless by Cuban Premier Castro's refusal to go along, to supervise the withdrawal of Soviet missiles from Cuba by using a United Nations observer team.

Probably less than the full story of the secretary-general's role in the missile crisis is known, but it appears that he had a useful part in facilitating communications. He also offered a neutral procedural device for backing away from the hard positions implied by the emplacement of the missiles and the American response to it. A more active administrative role for the United Nations and secretary-general was clearly envisaged in the proposal for international observation.

In the Vietnam case, the secretary-general tried over a period of years to persuade the United States government to enter negotiations with North Vietnam with a view to ending the intensifying struggle. Repeatedly, U Thant urged in public statements that the parties to the conflict come together, but he did not actively urge a United Nations role. Indeed, he appeared to accept without much protest the marked unwillingness of the Security Council to accept even the minimal responsibility of a thorough debate on Vietnam.

In private, however, U Thant succeeded on two occasions in bringing the North Vietnamese government and once the United States as far as an agreement to talk in preparation for full-dress negotiations. But, in both instances, even the talks-before-negotiations failed to take place. On the second occasion, it became known that the United States government had repudiated the efforts of Ambassador Adlai Stevenson which had led to an understanding that his government and the North Vietnamese would be represented at a meeting to be convened by Thant in his native Burma.

Following this disappointment in 1965, Thant spoke often and increasingly in bitter tones about the destructive war in Vietnam. Sharply opposing United States government views, he called the war an attempt to suppress a nationalism and to interfere with self-determination. It was evident that neither the Johnson nor the Nixon administrations made any special point of keeping him informed or of consulting him. But they did not overtly reply to his comments which at an earlier time would have been taken as much too bold for an international civil servant. Certainly, he did not entirely succeed in his initiatives, but he probably contributed something to the atmosphere of growing domestic and foreign opposition to the war which finally led to President Johnson's retiring from office and to a perceptible alteration of his policy by his successor.

Most of the secretary-general's attempts to initiate policy enter neither into quite such dramatic affairs as the Cuban missile crisis nor into open fighting of such magnitude as that in Vietnam. Rather, the secretary-general has been a factor in such affairs as the Berlin blockade of 1948, the internal violence in Laos during 1959, and the dispute between Cambodia and Thailand over the Temple of Preah Vihear from 1958 until 1964. In the latter two affairs his activities were conducted mainly in private.

Another initiative by the secretary-general, not directly connected with a security crisis but of long-range importrance, achieved a good deal of success. This was Dag Hammarskjöld's effort, soon after he took office in 1953, to bring about a better understanding of the effects of nuclear energy on international relations and especially on relations between the United States and the Soviet Union.[41] He did this by suggesting that an international conference on the peaceful uses of atomic energy could have soothing and beneficial effects on international relations. By 1956 such a conference had been prepared with cooperation from both of the nuclear giants. The conference permitted the nuclear powers to exchange a great deal of information and gave the rest of the world a window on what had until then been a rather secret recess of national activity. In addition, it led to a second conference and continuing cooperation through the United Nations and some of its associated agencies in the field of nonmilitary nuclear energy. Over the long-term, such cooperation could have an important contribution to make toward the control of nuclear armaments.

Executive activities. Although the early warning and initiating actions of the secretary-general have a remarkable quality, in quantity they take second place to his executive activities. Such activities are characterized as falling under the direction of another organ and consist of carrying out policies which are the responsibilities of that organ. The secretary-general thus becomes an executive agent of the organization.

Familiar as it is in national governments, this function has anything but routine qualities at the international level. In the United Nations it has developed into a capacity for mounting missions, such as those military bodies that have peacekeeping functions, which operate deep within national territory.[42] No matter how scrupulous the directors of such efforts are about influencing the situation around them, they cannot help producing some reactions. Furthermore, in nonsecurity missions, such as economic surveys and training institutes, personnel directed by the secretary-general under instructions from another organ can be found in the heart of national administrations as advisers and planners.

In addition to these results from the actual tasks assigned to the secretary-general, it is axiomatic in administrative practice that the head of an organization develops important influences on policies. This has consistently been true of the secretary-general, who has used his reports to deliberative organs to suggest changes in policies and practices.

The executive functions, moreover, tend to overlap with initiatives, for in the course of suggesting actions the secretary-general almost necessarily must foresee the executive ramifications. In some instances, he has outlined the design of a field agency, such as a peacekeeping force or a military observer group, simultaneously with his suggestion that it be created. Finally, the style employed by the secretary-general may have an important bearing on the outcome of executive actions. In some instances, the secretary-general has directed field work and headquarters activities in as detached a manner as possible from deliberative organs, reporting infrequently and sketchily. In other instances, he has made full and frequent reports and sought political guidance. In some cases, he has assumed a highly active style and made numerous interpretations of the broad policies given him by deliberative organs; in others, his executive work has been characterized by diffidence and restraint.

The most visible and complex executive action of the secretary-general comprised the peacekeeping efforts in the Congo from 1960 to 1964.[43] At some moments during this time, some twenty thousand armed men carried out military operations in the Congo under his supervision. Authority for these actions came from the Security Council and the General Assembly where a shifting consensus maintained enough cohesion so that with much difficulty the peacekeeping effort could be sustained. As with almost any large-scale (in terms of the capacity of the world organization) enterprise, the secretary-general's executive role merged with his other roles.

The peacekeeping effort in the Congo began late in June 1960 with the convening of the Security Council by the secretary-general acting under Article 99. The independence ceremonies in Leopoldville (now Kinshasa) had hardly ended when the Congolese army revolted against its Belgian officers. A widespread panic ensued among the thousands of Belgians still resident in the Congo as government servants and businessmen. The Belgian government, believing that a massacre impended, ordered troops still in the Congo under a treaty arrangement into action and supplemented them with paratroops from Europe. The Congolese government appealed to the United Nations for help in ending what it considered aggression.

Hammarskjöld seized the complaint as an opportunity for initiative under Article 99 and at the same time produced a legal formula that avoided calling the crisis a matter for enforcement. In part, he did this by unrolling before the Council a comprehensive plan for a peacekeeping force, made up of troops from small and supposedly disinterested countries who were to help restore law and order and not interfere with internal matters. The guidelines were explicitly modeled on the experience with the United Nations Emergency Force (UNEF) which was then on duty in the Sinai area; Hammarskjöld even referred to a study of the experience of UNEF, which he carried out under instructions from the General Assembly. The Security Council accepted his plan and gave him instructions to proceed accordingly. Thus he received a major executive assignment.

The subsequent activities in the Congo traced a tortuous and sometimes contradictory route through internal and external political quarrels, budgetary deficits, and ambiguities of direction to the secretary-general. The whole story is told elsewhere, but some outstanding points may be mentioned here. Hammarskjöld tried to use the Security Council as an instrument from which to get political guidance in changed situations. This procedure operated satisfactorily for a few weeks only until the coincidence of American and Soviet policy fell apart after the USSR opted for support of Premier Patrice Lumumba directly rather than working through the United Nations. The secession of Katanga province further complicated the problem of getting guidance because of the reluctance with which France, the United Kingdom, and Belgium viewed strong action by the United Nations force. After Lumumba was killed early in 1961, probably by agents of the Katangese government, the Security Council was galvanized into agreement and instructed Hammarskjöld to go even as far as the use of force to prevent civil war in the Congo. But, before this new policy had been tested, Hammarskjöld was killed while on a personal mediatory mission to Katanga. In general, from August 1960 until his death a year later, the secretary-general acted without the support of a comprehensive and logical framework of instructions. Therefore, he executed what instructions he had on the basis of his own assessment of the situation. He was quickly damned if he did and damned if he did not. In particular, he won the stout opposition of the Soviet Union whose rough-tongued Premier Khrushchev called on him to have the manhood to resign.

When U Thant succeeded Hammarskjöld, none of the earlier problems with the Congo disappeared, but perhaps the new secretary-general had the advantage of a more sober attitude among governments. He tried negotiations to end the secession in the Congo, long since the main problem, but failed as his predecessor had. By supporting the indisputably legal government, he took advantage of Hammarskjöld's hard and successful labor—largely through his field agents—to restore parliament to power (or nearly so, for the government always found opposition on the left).

Thant's support of the Leopoldville government led eventually to the publication of a coercive plan to deal with Katanga and to the use of the United Nations force to clear its own lines of communication and—surely not coincidentally—to topple the secessionist government.

With the Congo united, much of the task of the secretary-general in the security field was completed. The Congolese government dickered with Thant for the services of a military training mission—a perhaps odd request from an international peace organization, but one that dated back to the first days of United Nations involvement in the Congo—but failed to agree on which governments should do the training. Thant sought a wider spectrum of governments than the Congolese would accept. Thereupon, he withdrew the United Nations force entirely, blaming financial stringency for his action.

One part of the United Nations apparatus, however, which had developed a pervasive presence, continued to function.[44] This was the civil and technical assistance machinery put together to aid the tottering Leopoldville government. This government, inexperienced and ill informed, was to have a large number of Belgian technical advisers. When many of these fled during the initial disorders of 1960, the United Nations system tried to come to the aid of the floundering Congolese leaders. The specialized agencies—including the World Health Organization, the International Labour Organisation, the UN Education, Scientific and Cultural Organization, and others—furnished large numbers of advisers who, in fact, at various stages of the struggle acted as the top civil servants in the governments. They spread to every province and brought with them relief teams. They produced advice for officials and politicians, active decision-making capacity, and much information for the political directors of the United Nations mission in the Congo and for Thant himself at headquarters. Although the scale of this apparatus was reduced after the withdrawal of the military force, it continued to operate.

Thus the secretary-general played a highly influential role in determining the policy of the United Nations. Sometimes he did this by his own initiatives and at other times because no other authority would take any lead. He set out the guidelines at the beginning of the mission and took the decisions that ended it. He also organized a staff to give technical aid to the Congolese government and found himself with what amounted at certain times to dominant decision-making capacity in internal affairs.

For sheer size of executive structure, the only other comparable experience for the secretary-general came with the creation of the United Nations Emergency Force[45] which served in the Sinai area. As in the Congo, the secretary-general exercised much influence over the decision on his instructions. Once he received the instructions, Hammarskjöld moved ahead with remarkable speed to negotiate with Egypt the terms of deployment for the force and to put it into place. From that time onward, late in 1956, until the withdrawal of the force in 1967, the secretary-general clearly had almost autonomous direction of it. But it never involved

the pervasiveness of the Congo force; furthermore, there was neither
intention nor opportunity to create the broad governmental influences characteristic of the Congo operation.

The withdrawal of UNEF after the second Sinai Peninsula war in
1967 can be viewed as primarily executive action.[46] The Egyptian government demanded, first of the commanding officer of UNEF and later of the
secretary-general, that the force be withdrawn. Egyptian troops surrounded
the tiny units at their isolated posts facing Israel. Thant consulted his
advisory committee on UNEF, found that the principal contributors to
the force, India and Yugoslavia, flatly refused to allow their troops to
become engaged in any shooting action, although Canada wanted the force
kept in place. Nor was there any disposition to summon the General
Assembly. Thereupon, Thant abruptly announced withdrawal of the force
on the grounds that necessary permission for its deployment had been
denied by Egypt. It seems probable that he was impelled by the view that
UNEF's position was militarily and politically untenable and that a sharp
gesture might have some braking effect on the conflict on the horizon. It
did not, of course, and Thant fell under some heavy criticism from the
United States and the United Kingdom, demonstrating once again that
executive action has political implications.

The secretary-general has also been involved as executive agent in a
number of other ventures to maintain peace and security. He has directed
a peacekeeping force in Cyprus since 1964, sometimes with only three
months' authorization from the Security Council to which he has reported
frequently.[47] He headed an important observation mission in Lebanon
during disorders in 1958 and approved a report which in effect denied
allegations by Lebanon and the United States that large-scale infiltration
was occurring over the border with Syria.[48] He had responsibility for
sending an observation mission to the Dominican Republic to provide
another source of information to the Security Council in regard to the
landing of American troops during a governmental crisis in 1965.[49] In a
large number of instances, he or an agent named by him has served as
mediator in a dispute; the successful handling of the dispute between the
Netherlands and Indonesia over the territory in New Guinea known as
West Irian typifies this sort of executive action.[50]

The General Welfare

In many respects, the role of the secretary-general in the general welfare
functions of the United Nations parallels the categories of his activities
in the security field. But the style, the approach, and the range of permissible initiative differs rather sharply. In part, this divergence can be
traced to difference in immediate impact between a security crisis and a
long-term program for raising the standards of general welfare. The first
has dramatic qualities that capture public attention; it also lies within the

province of traditional diplomacy for which foreign office personnel are trained. The second lends itself to specialization and technical expertness which tends to obscure its significance from broad publics. It rarely blazes forth as a crisis.

Yet fostering the general welfare now constitutes far and away the most important function of international organization[51] if measured in terms of expenditures or in terms of number of staff personnel assigned to it. In the neighborhood of 80 percent of the resources of the United Nations are devoted to the general welfare and especially to economic development and social modernization. Around these programs a vast field network has grown; direct representatives of the United Nations system now operate in more than 130 countries and high-ranking resident representatives have been assigned to more than 90 capitals.

Coordinator. The United Nations serves as sponsoring organization and as a central point for reviewing a complex chain of intergovernmental agencies operating to foster the general welfare. These bodies, known as specialized agencies, have their own memberships, budgets, staffs, and chief administrative officers, comparable to the secretary-general in function and legal status. Their work sometimes tends to overlap and sometimes fails to be designed so as to be mutually reinforcing. Or important needs of the international community may be identified as appropriate for handling through this system of intergovernmental agencies. The Economic and Social Council [52] has the responsibility for coordinating the agencies, but this cumbersome and unevenly manned body of twenty-seven representatives of national governments could not operate without staff support. Here the secretary-general and his staff have assumed functions that influence the whole spectrum of programs.

The main instrument for coordination at "the working level" bears the splendidly bureaucratic title of Administrative Committee on Coordination.[53] It has given birth to a number of subcommittees with specialized subject matter. ACC consists of the secretary-general, as chairman, and the directors-general of the specialized agencies. Its agenda reflect the problems of coordination which arise from the extraordinarily sweeping programs and recommendations which issue from the Economic and Social Council. It tries to settle jurisdictional disputes and to deal with such matters as compatible statistics and staff practices. It resembles nothing so much as a meeting of ambassadors from several countries who are negotiating over some problem. The ACC, made up as it of representatives of autonomous organizations only loosely linked to each other, provides a negotiating table but not the capacity to enforce decisions.

The United Nations secretary-general furnishes staff work for ACC. As a result, the discussions almost inevitably tend to center around his proposals and analyses, although it would be a mistake to overlook the tenacity with which the concerned agencies battle for their positions. Over the years this coordinative machinery has functioned with increasing smoothness, although often it still cannot single out problems which should be given priority treatment. Because of the bargaining approach in the ACC, decisions on priorities tend to provide something for everyone.

Policy making. Formally, the secretary-general has much the same position in the general welfare field as he does in regard to peace and security. As chief administrative officer, he is an executive agent. Nor does he have any formal power of intervention analogous to Article 99. The vision of the secretary-general to be conjured from the United Nations Charter is that of the handmaiden of the organization.

In several ways, this formal view misleads even more than it does in the security field. Even in the League of Nations, the Secretariat, acting on behalf of the secretary-general, had exerted a leading influence in expanding the capacity of the organization to promote the general welfare. The functions of the United Nations in promoting the general welfare were based on this model but were far broader. The clear implication of the historical experience was that the secretary-general would have an even wider scope of operations than in the League.[54]

In fact, the welfare functions of the United Nations have expanded beyond the happiest dreams of the early planners. And with them the responsibilities of the secretary-general have widened. It is probably still fair to say that the main ideas of this expansion have come from the Secretariat and have been presented by the secretary-general or in his name.

Yet of the first three secretaries-general, only Hammarskjöld had much flair for the creation of a program or the development of ideas for the general welfare. In part, this came from his earlier experience as a high official of the treasury in Sweden and as director of the Swedish central bank. Even Hammarskjöld tended to become so involved with security matters that most of his activities in the welfare field had to be delegated to his subordinates. As a consequence, the style of policy making in the general welfare field is far less personal than in the security field. Moreover, so vast a network of cooperative machinery and operations has been created that it must of necessity be bureaucratized. Therefore, it lacks the vividness of a peacekeeping force or of a flying mission to mediate in a sudden outbreak of fighting.

The secretary-general usually exposes his ideas in speeches to the Economic and Social Council and other bodies, such as the United Nations regional economic commissions, whose meetings he attends at least for brief periods. The speeches sketch generally such programs as the United Nations Development Decade, the second of which is now in progress. Supporting papers, prepared by the Secretariat, as are the drafts of his speeches, flesh out the outline in the speech. The Secretariat officials act on behalf of the secretary-general within lines that they suggest and which he approves. Thus his policy leadership tends to have the character of that of a cabinet official explaining his program before a legislature. His staff has done the preparatory work.

Some causes in the general welfare field lend themselves to personal adoption by the secretary-general. Trygve Lie interested himself in technical assistance and urged its expansion on every occasion. Hammarskjöld is given credit for originating a scheme known as OPEX, by which high civil servants could be lent for service to national governments as if they were nationals of the country they were serving. This was an effort to spread the scarce resource of experienced management farther. Both Hammarskjöld and Thant have stoutly backed the two Development Decades,[55] first suggested by President John Kennedy, in an effort to focus the slender means of the United Nations in a more efficient manner.

Operations. The secretary-general has a lesser role in direct operations to foster the general welfare than do some of the heads of the specialized agencies. But his Secretariat does furnish technical assistance in such fields as public administration and the protection of human rights. In many instances, the United Nations serves as a contracting agency for the United Nations Development Program, the agency which provides funding for much of the field program.

The secretary-general also maintains an influence in the United Nations Development Program by reason of the fact that he appoints the administrator, although only after careful consultations with governments. The principal donors, especially the United States, receive much deference in this regard. The secretary-general long served as head of a consultative committee which included the head of the International Bank for Reconstruction and Development and the head of the Development Program. This committee was supposed to recommend general policies and no doubt had some effect from time to time.

Three relief agencies of some importance are also formally part of the Secretariat, although they operate largely autonomously. These are the United Nations Children's Fund, the High Commissioner for Refugees, and the Relief and Works Agency for Palestine Refugees. For new agencies, such as the United Nations Conference on Trade and Development, the United Nations Secretariat initially furnishes staff and thus is likely to reflect some influence from the secretary-general.

It is probably fair to say that the secretary-general personally has a rather passive role in promoting the general welfare. Usually, he speaks about the program only in a rather general way and delegates much authority to his Secretariat whose members tend to operate autonomously on the basis of professional standards. He has not neglected this work, however, but because of its nature and its susceptibility to handling in a bureaucratic manner it has taken second place to the work for maintenance of peace and security.

The Price of Leadership

On two important occasions when the secretary-general attempted to exert an unaccustomed degree of leadership, he incurred the savage enmity of the Soviet Union. To be denounced in Moscow is hardly a novel experience for non-Communist statesmen, but for the chief officer of the United Nations it betokens an imminent crippling. The Soviet Union, as one of the five permanent members of the Security Council, is in a position to prevent the reelection of a secretary-general; this being so, it is in a position to rob him of some of his effectiveness as he begins to approach the "lame duck" end of his term. Furthermore, the creditability of the secretary-general's role as a confidant of government depends on his having their ear. The denial of the Soviet ear reduces his general effectiveness. In addition, if a great power chooses to withhold its budgetary contribution, the financial effect on the Secretariat can be severe, even to the point of causing bankruptcy.

Although the Soviet Union produced the most visible and dramatic pressure on the secretary-general in return for his effort to lead United Nations activities opposed by the Kremlin, other governments have also protested his actions. The Nationalist Chinese government has acted coolly toward the first three secretaries-general after their espousal of seats in the United Nations for Peking. The United States government pressured the secretary-general to remove suspected subversives from the Secretariat in contradiction of its international status.[56] South Africa and Israel have reacted coolly to some initiatives from the secretary-general.

Nevertheless, the honor for the most violent public attacks still goes to Moscow. Trygve Lie let it be known in June 1950 that he supported the action taken by the Security Council—while the Soviet representative was boycotting its meetings to force the ejection of the Nationalist Chinese member—to turn back the Charter-violating attack by North Korea. Although the Soviet Union has never admitted having anything to do with the attack carried out by a government that received military aid from it, it denounced Lie's stand as violating the impartiality to be expected from him. When his term expired in 1951, the Soviet Union voted against his reappointment and pointedly let it be understood that it would accept absolutely anyone else. The United States, equally stubborn, would accept no one else. Eventually, the General Assembly simply voted to extend Lie's term of office. But, from 1951 onward, the Soviet Union would not address correspondence to Lie, refused to acknowledge his presence and with the ponderous militance of aging revolutionaries insulted him on every occasion.[57]

Lie endured the situation until 1953 when he resigned, protesting the humiliation he endured at Soviet hands. His successor, Dag Hammarskjöld,[58] was apparently expected to act as a mild and colorless civil servant who would keep out of the way and tend to meetings.

If that was the Soviet expectation, Hammarskjöld rather quickly gave cause for disappointment. His actions in Suez caused evident disquiet among the Soviet leadership which could not understand his insistence that the expenses of UNEF were those of the whole organization, not just the "imperialist aggressors." His intervention in Laos brought forth a mild protest. But the Congo was the straw that broke the Soviet back. Actions taken on the secretary-general's authority in September 1960 directly interfered with the flow of military supplies to Patrice Lumumba—Hammarskjöld said in violation of the Security Council's wishes. Hammarskjöld personally was blamed by the Soviet government for the turn of events, even though it was consistent with the secretary-general's announced policy of insulating the Congo from Great Power interference.

By the time that Lumumba's death became known in February 1961, Soviet denunciations of the secretary-general had become unmeasured. Then he was accused of complicity in Lumumba's death. Meantime, the Soviet government had trotted out its "troika" plan for the Secretariat. This called for reorganization of the office of secretary-general into a tripartite executive which would represent the socialist world, the Third World, and the Western world. It evoked little enthusiasm, except from the Soviet group, but it did give some measure of the depths of Soviet opposition to Hammarskjöld and to expansion of the activities of the office of secretary-general. It seems unlikely that Hammarskjöld could have been effective much longer in the office from which he was removed by death in September 1961.

It can be inferred from these two incidents and many comments from Soviet and other sources that the secretary-general has no guarantee that his leadership efforts will be long accepted or accepted at all in matters of peace and security. Clearly, the Great Powers have a strong check on him and he acts in full awareness that it can be brought to bear on him at any time. His defensive armor against attack is thin and undependable in an international milieu in which governments hesitate to make commitments to international causes. At best, the secretary-general operates under severe restraints.

Head of the Secretariat

As chief administrative officer of the United Nations, the secretary-general heads the Secretariat. He has formal responsibility for all of its work and represents its officials and their work in the major organs. He personally performs this staff function whenever and wherever he wishes within the United Nations system and delegates his officials to act for him when he cannot himself appear. The secretary-general appoints the subordinate officials of the Secretariat under staff rules that he proposes to the General Assembly. Furthermore, he proposes the budget for the organization, much of which is absorbed by salaries. In short, the secretary-general serves as manager of the Secretariat.

In many respects, these functions have a routine quality and are delegated. But, in other respects, management of the Secretariat has implications which affect the policy of the organization and touch on the member governments in sensitive places. Furthermore, the secretary-general can use his management functions to increase his own influence.

Budget proposals. The budgetary process probably has the widest overtones of all of the management functions. Preparation of a budget implies planning for the future. On the basis of his interpretation of the wishes of the deliberative organs of the United Nations, the secretary-general can emphasize certain activities and reduce others by suggesting budgetary figures. The main issues in the budget tend to be developed around proposals for new posts to be filled by international civil servants. Creation of new posts implies expansion of activities. The secretary-general can also try to restrict ongoing work—for example, a publication which has little appeal—by arguing that the expense of personnel assigned to it is too high and proposing to reduce the number of posts.

The budget is reported to the General Assembly, where it is examined and eventually adopted. The General Assembly has a budgetary watchdog in its Advisory Committee on Administrative and Budgetary Questions,[59] which invariably proposes a lower figure than that suggested by the secretary-general, who almost as invariably then compromises. A budgetary policeman, the Board of Auditors, ensures that money provided the secretary-general was spent according to instructions.

Some budgetary proposals have produced sharp political effects. Hammarskjöld always contended that peacekeeping enterprises had to be treated as part of the regular budget of the organization, but for clarity separate accounts of the costs of UNEF and the Congo force were maintained. If they were part of the regular budget, each member's contribution would then reflect the additional costs. The Soviet Union and France (in the Congo case) argued that they were not liable for such payments and began to hold back amounts equivalent to their increased share.[60] An advisory opinion of the International Court of Justice to the effect that all members were obliged to pay the expenses of the organization and that these were defined as anything falling within the purview of the powers of the General Assembly had little effect on the recalcitrants.[61] Eventually, the Soviet Union fell so far in arrears that the United States proposed barring its delegates from a vote in the General Assembly, as is possible under Article 19 of the United Nations Charter. This produced a sharp crisis in the nineteenth General Assembly in 1964, for the American position implied tough action against a major power which was hinting that it would retaliate in some unpleasant form. A large number of members proved reluctant to support the United States pressure on the Soviet Union but, before the issue was resolved by a relaxation of the American position, the General Assembly found itself proceeding through an entire session without taking votes. By this means, it avoided the final decision as to whether to bar the Soviet Union. In the end, the United States backed away from its tough position, announcing that it too would not be bound in the future to support automatically the budget for peacekeeping.

However much the financial crisis was talked about in technical terms, it was a political crisis. The issue could be found in the policies of the United Nations—designed in considerable part and strongly supported by the secretary-general—in the Suez area and in the Congo. The Soviet Union and France opposed delegation of the wide discretion required for UNEF and the Congo to the secretary-general. Their refusal to pay their contributions related to that objection, not to a financial difficulty or simply a question of administrative principle.

The financial crisis also demonstrated that the member states keep control of their own appropriations for United Nations expenses. The secretary-general may propose the budget of his organization, but the members can choose whether or not to respond to his lead. They have customarily supported an expansion of activities when they discuss the substance of United Nations work, but immediately afterward have adopted a cheese-paring stance in the budgetary committees. The United Nations budget has grown steadily from some $27 million in 1947 to some $183 million for 1971. In addition, voluntary pledges to the United Nations Development Program have exceeded $200 million per year. But it is a sobering fact that the United Nations mission in the Congo cost in the neighborhood of $10 million per month and failure of some members to pay for it and UNEF brought the organization close to bankruptcy.

The effect on the secretary-general of the difficulty in financing has been to limit the scope of his proposals. He has warned the General Assembly that if the financial problem continues it is bound to circumscribe United Nations capacity to respond to vital needs. Meantime, the organization limps along by borrowing, by paying bills late, and by depending on the generosity of its creditors.

Personnel questions. The Secretariat of the United Nations is an international civil service, arranged along the hierarchical lines of a national career service but with some special features. As a modern civil service, appointments to it, made entirely under the authority of the secretary-general, are supposed to be based on the highest standards of competence and efficiency; political considerations and rewards are not supposed to enter. But the instruction to the secretary-general to pay due regard to wide geographical distribution implies at least that in some manner appointment to the Secretariat has to take account of a "fair shares" test based on nationality.

Geographical distribution, in fact, turned into not only a nationality test but a political test. From the first steps in organizing the Secretariat, governments concerned themselves with whether they would be able to have their nationals at the top level of the international civil service. The Great Powers on the Security Council came to an understanding which gave each the opportunity to name one of their nationals to the under-secretary level, which comes immediately below that of the secretary-general. Posts in the next level also came under the scrutiny of governments, which put forward the candidacy of their nationals. After 1955, when a flood of new members began to enter the United Nations, their governments also began to press for the appointment of their nationals to leading posts in the Secretariat.

One consequence was that the secretary-general found it harder and harder to avoid making appointments on what amounts to a representational basis and found that the geographical distribution of the Secretariat created controversy in the General Assembly. Formulae were devised to match in a rough manner the number of posts given nationals of any country with its financial contribution, but it still proved difficult to find enough qualified candidates from some countries short of trained manpower. Others, especially the Soviet Union and its allies, permitted appointments only from lists presented by the government and also have rarely allowed a staff member to serve more than four years. Meantime, the machinery available to the secretary-general for seeking qualified applicants remained inadequate for scouring the world. Nor would it have been profitable to set up the large establishment that would have been required for such work. The result is that, increasingly, the secretary-general must depend on governmental nominations.

Some governments, especially the United States and the Soviet Union among the major powers, insisted on having some power of reviewing appointments under consideration. The Soviet Union accomplishes this by the device of presenting lists of candidates (while complaining that too few of its nationals are in the Secretariat). The United States, reacting to attacks from the late Senator Joseph R. McCarthy and his equally obscurantist followers on some individual Americans who were accused of subversive activities, organized an elaborate mechanism for investigating the backgrounds of American applicants for posts. The secretary-general makes appointments of American nationals only after receiving advice from the United States government. This is tantamount to saying that the United States applies a political test to its nationals working for the United Nations. Furthermore, the United States induced or forced Trygve Lie to dismiss the staff members accused by a senatorial subcommittee.

To some extent, these procedures rid the secretary-general of some embarrassing decisions, for he is able to place the onus for unsatisfactory appointments on the governments. Probably, he also needs some means of defending the Secretariat against its use as a shelter for active revolutionaries or spies. But the defense is not complete, for on a small number of occasions the United States has arrested Soviet nationals and some others on espionage charges and brought them to trial. The Soviet Union bitterly protested that such persons could not be arrested as they had immunity from process while they were international civil servants. The secretary-general followed the practice of suspending them while under accusation and dismissing those who were convicted on the grounds that their activities had nothing to do with their work as Secretariat members and constituted unbecoming conduct.

The appointment power can be used in a political manner by the secretary-general and there are some indications that appointments have been made to foster a favorable view of the Secretariat on the part of some governments. Furthermore, judicious appointments to give a broad geographical spread can build up the resources of knowledge present in the Secretariat and provide useful advisers for the secretary-general. But the secretary-general constantly faces the problem of appointing competent people from among names suggested primarily as a result of domestic political issues that are not directly relevant to the Secretariat.

THE FUTURE OF THE SECRETARY-GENERALSHIP

The future of the office of secretary-general has been partly shaped by its past, by the remarkable broadening of the scope of its activities, and by the ventures made by the secretaries-general into unanticipated lines in international politics. The quarter century of experience with the office suggests that the old question of whether the secretary-general is to serve as a handmaiden of the organization or whether he is to serve as a leader has been answered. Neither role is excluded. The emphasis on one or the other depends on a broader political configuration than that of the United Nations alone. It also depends on the views of the secretary-general about an active role for his office, and upon his personality.

Views of the Office

The activities of the three secretaries-general who served the organization during its first twenty-five years carry certain implicit views about the office. The most significant of these for future development holds that the office should be a center of influential activity and that the secretary-general should be involved in ceaseless initiatory effort to maintain the peace and to create underlying conditions for peace. Both Trygve Lie and Dag Hammarskjöld also made this conception of the office quite explicit in their speeches and statements. U Thant followed in precisely the same path and explicitly said he was doing so.

Of necessity, this view will be reexamined in 1972 as Kurt Waldheim begins his first term of office. The members of the Security Council will again have to work out limits of activity, either implicit or explicit, for their servant. Waldheim was well known in United Nations circles for his service as representative of Austria and came into office denying that he had been appointed for his rejection of an "activist" role. Whatever his intentions, he faced the formidable task of replacing the aged top level of his Secretariat and coping with a worsening financial crisis.

If the reading of the development of the office in this chapter is correct, it can be concluded that the active role of the secretary-general, his attempts at early warnings, at initiatives, and his policy-influencing style of executive action have become part of the standard institutional practice. Although the majority of the members appear to have accepted this practice without reservations in principle, neither the Soviet bloc nor France has relented in their opposition to delegating political functions to the secretary-general. Their positions tend to limit the effect of the institutionalization of the active role of the secretary-general.

The Secretariat of the United Nations and of the specialized agencies constitute strong supporters for the active secretary-general. Their own tasks and professional interests depend on the welfare of the international bureaucracy. The signs of this welfare, as is usual in any bureaucracy, are found in the expansion of tasks, greater specialization, and larger budgets. Their professional standards demand that they suggest improvements of the programs for which they are responsible. It is only an active secretary-general who effectively serves such ends. In a general way, they have the support of the majority of member states, whose governments seek additional services and assistance from any available source. International agencies and the United Nations particularly have the reputation, not always deserved, of impartial decisions and freedom from so-called neo-colonialism. But neither from the partisans nor opponents of higher national taxes is there a headlong rush to increase financial contributions.

Without support in principle for the active secretary-generalship, the present kind of office would have never developed. But the future of the office depends on the manner in which the principle is translated into specific actions. Here the secretary-general needs both a favorable international system and his own art as a political figure. Whenever the secretary-general has succeeded in playing an important role in the international system, he has had, as in the early days of UNEF and the Congo, either the support of the two superpowers, the United States and the USSR, or else their acquiescence. Any sharp expansion of tasks requires more than acquiescence because of the implication that more financial support would be required. Beyond this, application of the principle depends on which countries are involved, what sort of political tendencies they display, and whether the problem is in some way appropriate for treatment by the United Nations. Clearly, the secretary-general had no easy ticket to mediation in Budapest during the Hungarian revolt of 1956, despite General Assembly resolutions on the subject; Hungary is too sensitive a part of the Soviet system to permit much outside influence from the secretary-general. The same sort of statement might be made about the observer finally sent to the Dominican Republic; he went over the early opposition of the United States. Some problems—Vietnam is a notable example—seem ripe for United Nations handling except for the crucial fact that few of the members are prepared to face the implied responsibility. The turbulence of the Middle East and Israel's strife with its neighbors also seems an appropriate question for the United Nations because of the organization's long involvement and because it serves as a necessary channel of communication. Here the secretary-general has had a continuing role.

The art with which the secretary-general conducts his office depends to a considerable degree on his native qualities, his experience, and his ability to synthesize his impressions and information of the world around him into a coherent whole. Probably no individual in the world combines in just the right quantity all the qualities necessary for the perfect conduct of the office of secretary-general over a long period of time.

Both Lie and Thant brought to the office a certain forthrightness and dogged purposefulness. Lie had strong political inclinations, preferring diplomacy to bureaucratic work. He foresaw a rather grand role of the secretary-general and worked toward it as he saw it without fear for his position. But his fearlessness also betrayed a certain insensitivity of perception and may have led him to overlook significant opportunities for developing the organization. Thant has shown real skill for delegating diplomatic duties, as he did for instance in the West Irian case, but he has also spoken out strongly against some of the main policies of the Great Powers without ensuring first that his ideas were getting a hearing. Neither Lie nor Thant displayed much talent for putting together a coherent doctrine of their office or of their organization, but Thant has assumed the responsibility for serving, at least part of the time, as the spokesman of the less developed countries in the world forum.

Hammarskjöld contrasted with the other two secretaries-general in several ways. No one could doubt his brilliance and his ability to intellectualize the conflicting impressions that necessarily came his way. He showed a broad talent for improvising diplomatic formulae that left no party better off but no party perceptibly the loser. This made his participation in some negotiations, such as those after the Suez war of 1956, invaluable. He also had an eye on history and strove to place his work and his ideas in a framework that would endure. Therefore, he frequently spoke in a doctrinal vein so as to give continuing meaning to actions which were improvised for the moment. In particular, he defended with style and grace the active role so characteristic of his tenure. But he did so with subtlety and sometimes with contradiction, so that his area of maneuver remained wide. Although he became something of a popular hero whose movements were followed by an impressive public, he never strove for that role. Unlike his two colleagues, he seldom spoke to influence a broad public but usually directed his remarks to the foreign offices. They returned professional respect and courtesy (with the obvious exception of the Soviet group at the end of his tenure).

As would be expected, the backgrounds of all three secretaries-general contain experience with international relations. Lie had been foreign minister of Norway, Hammarskjöld a minister of state for foreign affairs, and Thant the permanent representative of his country to the United Nations. Only Thant had much direct involvement and experience with the

United Nations; Hammarskjöld had some important dealings with European international organization but little with the United Nations. Lie had come up a political ladder; so had Thant but in a colonial context. Hammarskjöld was by training a civil servant but, as happens in Sweden, was valued at the political level for his skills in forming national policy. Only Lie had been much in the public eye. The other two had been typically "backroom boys." Waldheim, however, has served both in the front office and the backroom, and his colleagues in his party in Austria thought highly enough of him to nominate him as their candidate for the presidency of the country.

From the characters and backgrounds of the four secretaries-general, it does not seem possible to draw up a prescription of personal qualities and formation for the office, aside from the obvious requirement of some experience in foreign affairs. Rather, the conclusion might be that the work of the office is likely to be conducted with a good deal of personal style, as in the case of the presidency of the United States.

Electoral Geography

The changes that have taken place in the membership of the United Nations since Hammarskjöld took office in 1953 have much to do with the selection of the secretaries-general of the future. The less developed countries, the former colonies, now have a majority of membership and, if the less developed and former colonial categories are fully stretched, have well over a two-thirds majority. These new or poor countries have also increased their representation on the Security Council and perhaps therefore their persuasiveness. In 1971 they created at least some interest in a secretary-general drawn from their ranks but eventually could agree on no candidate. Nor did the presence of representatives of the People's Republic of China, newly on the scene in the Security Council, appear to have a crucial influence on the appointment of Waldheim.

Yet in the future this configuration may differ from anything in the past, although it assumes that the major factor in earlier elections—the cold war—has changed enough so that the superpowers would at least acquiesce in the election of a secretary-general representative of the new majority. Both Lie and Hammarskjöld proved acceptable to the superpowers after the first-rank candidates were rejected for what amounted to tactical reasons in the cold war. After Hammarskjöld's death, the Soviet Union, which had not quite abandoned the "troika" plan for the office, bargained long with the United States before a formula was accepted by which the Burmese diplomat was named to the office on an acting basis. It was only a year later that he was able to win the office on a normal basis.

In part, Thant received the endorsement as secretary-general after the period of acting in the office because his incumbency permitted him to influence the terms under which he would continue. He made it clear that he would not accept appointment to a truncated office. He insisted and received the right to shape the Secretariat on his initiative, not on that of the Great Powers. On his reelection, he made a point of emphasizing his independence and has done so since.

This emphasis on independence has had the novel effect of turning the office into something of a platform for the views of the poor and former colonial countries. Thant has never hidden his sympathy for them and has adopted some of their positions as his own. His opposition to the policy of apartheid followed by the South African government is a case in point.[62] Thant also insists on the importance of a sharp rise in financial and technical aid to the less developed countries, even if some of the highly developed countries, including the United States and the Soviet Union, follow policies which demonstrate considerable skepticism about this approach to development. Despite these strong personal policies, Thant has never become the object of the bitterly antagonistic attacks to which Lie and Hammarskjöld were subject. In part, he may benefit from the popularity of his cause. But his safety may also, in part, be the result of wide understanding that strong views expressed by the secretary-general do not usually move governments, legislators, or taxpayers very far.

It did not follow from Thant's incumbency that the next secretary-general had to come from the Afro-Asian countries or from the less developed countries. Although this was certainly not excluded, it seems as in the previous elections that the particular political configuration of the moment had the strongest influence. If the United States, the Soviet Union, and China wish to cooperate in the United Nations, or proceed on the basis of indifference, it is conceivable that the secretary-general once again could come from a neutral country or from one which has little direct participation in the cold war. If the superpowers show strong antagonism, it is conceivable that one or the other will back a candidate from the Afro-Asian group who is strongly critical of the cold war and "imperialism." The Great Power backing such a candidate would be seeking political influence among the majority of members. Furthermore, it is possible that loosely defined regional interests could enter the considerations, especially if the Great Powers are indifferent. Latin America with more than twenty-five member governments has never furnished a secretary-general and might well submit candidates.

The Future

The doctrinal underpinnings of the office of secretary-general bear strong marks of the bonds of the past. The first twenty-five years of the United Nations saw the creation of the office, the testing of its limits, and its challenge by such events as Korea, Suez, the Congo, and the financial crisis. The Secretariat grew from slender beginnings to a functioning bureaucracy. The secretary-general developed the practices of trying to influence the policies espoused by his organization and of extending his administrative capacity into the territory of member states. In terms of sheer creativeness at the international level, what has happened to the office of secretary-general has many impressive aspects.

Although to some extent the future remains the projection of the past, it seems likely that further expansion of the scope of the office will be difficult if the international system retains its present emphasis on the nation-state and on the use of international organizations as adjuncts of governments, rather than as supervisors of governments. The member governments have already permitted the secretary-general to inject his presence into most international political troubles and to make his organization an integral part of international development activities. Governments also take for granted that the secretary-general and his staff have the capacity to mount administrative enterprises of various characters, ranging from peacekeeping forces and mediation attempts to the visit of a few days by a technical adviser. But, as the governments of the world become more experienced with international organization, they also no doubt become more and more aware of the limitations on the office of secretary-general.

No observer can mistake these limitations. The Great Powers do not favor an automatically influential role for the secretary-general. They determine their policies in the light of particular cases and situations, rather than on the basis of a general doctrine. Even the lesser powers have no intention of permitting international officials to assume a determining role in their affairs. Thus the secretary-general is limited by great and small alike. Furthermore, he depends on the members for finances for the enterprises he proposes to create and for the managing of those that already exist. Generosity in contributions toward international organizations has hardly been the hallmark of national policies. Therefore, even if the secretary-general identified the best interests of the people of the world faultlessly, he could not depend on the members of his organization to support his design for furthering those interests.

The frustrations that accumulate as the United Nations tries to deal with the intractable problems of remnant colonialism, as in Rhodesia, or gross violations of United Nations standards of human rights, as in South Africa, or of economic development, also dampen the effectiveness of the secretary-general. If his organization is treated with impatience, his ability to take a leading role will diminish accordingly. His staff, too, shows the effects of this frustration. Not only does it tend to become more sedate as a result of internal organization, but also it may attract fewer persons of outstanding quality, for they often hope to have a more immediate effect on the problems they want to solve. In the fact of frustration, the Secretariat may well grow more defensive rather than more imaginative.

To recognize that limits apply to the activities of the secretary-general must be a first requirement for a mature understanding. Yet the office retains its remarkable qualities. It continues to elevate an individual to the role of actor in the international system. It continues to serve as a center

NOTES   139

for discussion of organized efforts to meet world problems. Its capacity for making suggestions, for bringing new ideas under examination, for cautioning and warning of new problems, and for trying to solve old ones with wise suggestions and impartial administration remains. Its future will reflect that of the world around it more than the personality of its occupant or doctrine about its nature.

NOTES

1. Inis L. Claude, Jr., *Swords into Plowshares,* 3rd ed. (New York: Random House, 1964), pp. 12–13.
2. UN Charter, Articles 97 and 100. Preparatory Commission of the United Nations, *Report* (London, 1945), chap. VIII.
3. UN Charter, Articles 3 and 4; Leland M. Goodrich, Edvard Hambro, and Anne P. Simons, *Charter of the United Nations,* 3rd ed. (New York: Columbia University Press, 1969), pp. 84–85.
4. UN Charter, Article 7; Goodrich, Hambro, and Simons, *Charter of United Nations,* p. 10.
5. UN Charter, Article 97.
6. *Ibid.,* Article 98.
7. For further discussion see Leon Gordenker, *The UN Secretary-General and the Maintenance of Peace* (New York: Columbia University Press, 1967), pp. 150–152; and Goodrich, Hambro, and Simons, *Charter of United Nations,* p. 585.
8. UN Charter, Article 98. For additional comment see Gordenker, *UN Secretary-General* pp. 330–331; and Goodrich, Hambro, and Simons, *Charter of United Nations,* pp. 585–587.
9. For comment see Goodrich, Hambro, and Simons, *Charter of United Nations,* pp. 588–593; Gordenker, *UN Secretary-General,* chap. VII; and Stephen M. Schwebel, *The Secretary-General of the United Nations* (Cambridge: Harvard University Press, 1952), pp. 23–26.
10. For comment on these and other administrative matters, see Gordenker, *UN Secretary-General,* pp. 89–103.
11. *Ibid.,* chap. III.
12. On budgeting and financing see J. David Singer, *Financing International Organization: The United Nations Budget Process* (The Hague: Nijhoff, 1961); and John G. Stoessinger and Associates, *Financing the United Nations System* (Washington, D.C.: Brookings Institution, 1964). For accounts of current situations, see the annual "Issues before the General Assembly" number of *International Conciliation.*
13. Goodrich, Hambro, and Simons, *Charter of United Nations,* p. 69; and Georges Langrod, *The International Civil Service* (Leyden: Sijthoff, 1963), pp. 87ff.
14. Cf. Walter R. Sharp, *The United Nations Economic and Social Council* (New York: Columbia University Press, 1969), pp. 259–262, 271–276.
15. General Assembly, *Official Records* (16th sess.), Suppl. 1A, *Introduction to the Annual Report of the Secretary-General on the Work of the Organization.*
16. For their history and function, see Frederick S. Dunn, *The Practice and Proceedings of International Conferences* (Baltimore: Johns Hopkins Press, 1929).

17. Jean Siotis, *Essai sur le Secrétariat International* (Geneva: Droz, 1963), pp. 52–64.

18. Egon F. Ranshofen-Wertheimer, *The International Secretariat* (Washington, D.C.: Carnegie Endowment for International Peace, 1945), pp. 13–16.

19. On Thomas and his ideas and their influence on the ILO, see Edward J. Phelan, *Yes and Albert Thomas* (London: Cresset Press, 1949).

20. Schwebel, *Secretary-General,* pp. 4–8. For an unusually close look at how Drummond operated, see James Barros, *The League of Nations and the Great Powers: The Greek-Bulgarian Incident, 1925* (Oxford: The Clarendon Press, 1970), pp. 23–26, 43–44.

21. On Avenol, see James Barros, *Betrayal from Within: Joseph Avenol, Secretary-General of the League of Nations, 1933–1940* (New Haven: Yale University Press, 1969); Schwebel, *Secretary-General,* pp. 216–224.

22. For the most complete version of this planning, see Ruth B. Russell, *A History of the United Nations Charter* (Washington, D.C.: Brookings Institution, 1958).

23. See, for example, Royal Institute of International Affairs, *The International Secretariat of the Future: Lessons from Experience by a Group of Former Officials of the League of Nations* (London, 1944).

24. See his account in Trygve Lie, *In the Cause of Peace* (New York: The Macmillan Company, 1954), pp. 4–10.

25. UN Charter, Article 24.

26. *Ibid.,* Articles 11 and 12.

27. As Hammarskjöld always emphasized, often to gain support for policies that created a mild suspicion of his willingness to remain only a servant. For an extended exposition of his views, see his "The International Civil Servant in Law and Fact," reprinted in Wilder Foote (ed.), *The Servant of Peace* (London: Bodley Head, 1962), pp. 329–348. See also Gordenker, *UN Secretary-General,* chap. IV.

28. General Assembly, *Official Records* (3rd sess.), Suppl. 1, *Annual Report of the Secretary-General on the Work of the Organization,* pp. ix–x. It was stated even more emphatically the following year in the same document of the 4th sess., pp. xii–xiii.

29. General Assembly, *Official Records* (5th sess.), Suppl. 1, *Annual Report of the Secretary-General on the Work of the Organization,* pp. xiii–xiv.

30. "A hard core of actual colonialism still exists, particularly in Africa. It is coupled with the kindred problem of racial discrimination." General Assembly, *Official Records* (25th sess.), Suppl. 1A, *Introduction to the Annual Report of the Secretary-General on the Work of the Organization,* p. 14.

31. General Assembly, *Official Records* (18th sess.), Suppl. 1A, *Introduction to the Annual Report of the Secretary-General on the Work of the Organization,* pp. 1–2. See also the same document for the twenty-first session, pp. 2–4.

32. *Ibid.,* pp. 4–6.

33. UN Press Release SG/1387, 2, December 1962.

34. General Assembly, *Official Records* (15th sess.), Suppl. 1A, *Introduction to the Annual Report of the Secretary-General on the Work of the Organization,* pp. 1–2.

35. See his account in *In the Cause of Peace,* pp. 327–330; and comment in Gordenker, *UN Secretary-General,* pp. 143–145.

36. Preparatory Commission of the United Nations, *Report.*

37. Address at Oslo, June 3, 1958.

38. See Security Council Resolution S/4300, April 1, 1960, and Document S/4635 on South Africa; on the Middle East, Security Council Resolution S/3575 and S/3605.

39. Gordenker, "Multilateral Aid and Government Policies," in Robert W. Cox (ed.), *International Organization: World Politics* (London: The Macmillan Company, 1969), pp. 142–144.

40. For fuller discussion see Gordenker, *UN Secretary-General,* Part III.

41. Hammarskjöld urged more attention to the peaceful uses of atomic energy in his *Annual Report* for 1953–1954. General Assembly, *Official Records* (9th sess.), Suppl. 1, *Annual Report of the Secretary-General on the Work of the Organization,* p. xii. For a skeletal account of the major conference that followed, see UN, Department of Public Information, *Yearbook of the United Nations 1955* (New York, 1956), pp. 13–17.

42. For fuller discussion see Alan James, *The Politics of Peace-Keeping* (London: Chatto & Windus, 1969).

43. Writing on the Congo experience is almost endless. For useful introductions see King Gordon, *The U.N. in the Congo.* (New York: Carnegie Endowment for International Peace, 1962); Ernest W. Lefever, *Crisis in the Congo: A UN Force in Action* (Washington, D.C.: Brookings Institution, 1965); and Gordenker, *UN Secretary-General,* chaps. X, XI, and XII.

44. This entire mode of executive action gets less attention and is less well known than it deserves to be. It could perhaps be used much more to promote peaceful settlements of disputes. Gordenker, *UN Secretary-General,* chap. XII.

45. The standard work is Gabriella Rosner, *The United Nations Emergency Force* (New York: Columbia University Press, 1963). The most convenient documentation along with penetrating legal comments may be found in Roslyn Higgins, *United Nations Peace-Keeping,* I, *The Middle East* (London: Oxford University Press, 1969), Part II.

46. This was a highly controversial incident. Higgins argues that Thant had legal grounds for delay, but others would contend that he had little chance of effective action even if he played for time. Higgins, *Peace-Keeping,* pp. 366–367. For Thant's version see United Nations Document A/6672, July 12, 1967.

47. On the Cyprus force see James A. Stegenga, *The United Nations Force in Cyprus* (Columbus: Ohio State University Press, 1968). The operations appeared differently from the field from where part of the story is recounted in Michael Harbottle, *The Impartial Soldier* (London: Oxford University Press, 1970).

48. The documents can be found in Higgins, *Peace-Keeping,* Part III.

49. Brief accounts can be found in General Assembly, *Official Records* (20th sess.), Suppl. 1, *Annual Report of the Secretary-General on the Work of the Organization,* pp. 42–49, and the same document for the twenty-first session, pp. 31–35.

50. Background and comment can be found in Arend Lijphart, *The Trauma of Decolonization: The Dutch and West New Guinea* (New Haven: Yale University Press, 1966).

51. The most informative recent description and analyses can be found in Lester B. Pearson, *Partners in Development* (New York: Praeger, 1969) and the report of Sir Robert Jackson, *A Study of the Capacity of the United Nations Development System,* UN Document DP/5 (Geneva, 1969). See also Sharp, *Economic and Social Council.*

52. *Ibid.,* chaps. V–VII.

53. *Ibid.*, pp. 20–24; and Martin Hill, "The Administrative Committee on Coordination," in Evan Luard (ed.), *The Evolution of International Organization* (London: Thames & Hudson, 1966), pp. 104–137.

54. F. P. Walters, *A History of the League of Nations* (London: Oxford University Press, 1960), chap. LX.

55. For the first Development Decade the main document is *The United Nations Development Decade: Proposals for Action* (New York: United Nations, 1962) (Sales No. 62.II.B.2). For the second decade, the key document is United Nations General Assembly Resolution 2626 (XXV), which sets forth a development strategy for the period of the 1970s.

56. Gordenker, *UN Secretary-General*, pp. 107–110.

57. Lie, *Cause of Peace*, chap. XX.

58. The best brief biography of Hammarskjöld is Joseph P. Lash, Dag Hammarskjöld: *Custodian of the Brush-Fire Peace* (Garden City, N.Y.: Doubleday, 1961).

59. The committee also works closely with Secretariat budget officers and consequently can make informed criticisms.

60. Stoessinger and Associates, *Financing United Nations*, p. 77.

61. *Ibid.*, chap. VI.

62. Repeated annually in his *Annual Reports*.

David A. Kay

THE UNITED NATIONS AND DECOLONIZATION

A major factor in the post-1945 political arena has been the process of decolonization.[1] The potential extent of the decolonization problems facing the United Nations in 1945 were enormous. At the beginning of World War II there were more than eighty separate colonial territories, including approximately one-third of the population and covering one-third of the land area of the world. In 1939 seven countries—Great Britain, the Netherlands, France, Belgium, Portugal, Italy, and Spain—with a combined population of only 200 million people controlled almost 700 million people in their colonial possessions.[2]

THE LEAGUE OF NATIONS AND THE COLONIAL SYSTEM

In common with all of the Charter, those provisions dealing with colonial territories were strongly influenced by the similar provisions and experiences of the League of Nations. The rush in the last quarter of the nineteenth century to divide up Africa among European powers left a double legacy that had to be faced by the drafters of the League Covenant.[3] A number of writers, including J. A. Hobson, had identified the competitive struggle of states for colonies as a principal cause of war as well as being destructive of the interests of the native populations. Unless this policy of imperialism was brought to a halt and colonies put under some form of international supervision, so the argument ran, colonies would serve as a perpetual source of international conflict.[4] The more immediate legacy of the grand era of imperialism that faced the drafters of the Covenant was what should be done with the colonies detached from the defeated Central Powers of Germany and Turkey.

In the negotiations at the Paris Peace Conference, the more general problem of all colonial territories was quickly downgraded. The dominant question, and the one to which the League mandate system responded, quickly became the manner of disposal and administration of the former German and Turkish colonies.[5] American resistance, forcefully led by Woodrow Wilson, prevented the victorious powers from simply dividing the colonies among themselves. The result was that the colonial possessions of Germany and Turkey were mandated to more advanced states, usually the same states that would have been given them if the victors had simply divided the spoils, to be administered according to internationally agreed standards and with a minimal level of international supervision. This League mandate system applied only to the former colonies of Germany and Turkey and completely failed to touch more numerous colonial territories of the victorious Allied powers. With regard to the colonial possessions of the victorious powers, the League Covenant contained only a weak injunction that League members agreed to "undertake to secure just treatment of the native inhabitants of territories under their control." [6]

In the League system the mandatory power agreed to administer the territory it held under a mandate agreement according to international obligations set forth in the Covenant. The Covenant attempted to provide a flexible framework suitable to the wide range of conditions in the mandated territories by dividing the territories into three categories and imposing different obligations on the mandatory power according to the category of its mandate. In Class A mandates, the most advanced territories, the mandatory powers were obligated: to assist the territory to achieve full independence; to guarantee to the native peoples certain minimum rights and to protect them against specific abuses and evils; and to secure equal opportunities for the trade and commerce of all nations.[7] In Class B mandates, the mandatory powers were obliged: to guarantee to the native peoples certain minimum rights; to protect them against specific abuses and evils; and to secure equal opportunities for the trade and commerce of all nations.[8] In Class C mandates, the least advanced territories, the mandatory powers were obligated only to guarantee to the native peoples certain minimum rights and to protect them against specific abuses and evils.[9]

The principle established by the Covenant of international accountability for those territories held under mandate was supervised by the League Council and the Permanent Mandates Commission.[10] Annual reports on the mandated territories were required of the mandatory powers by the League Council. These reports were examined by the Permanent Mandates Commission—composed of colonial experts appointed by the Council to serve in their private capacity (i.e., not as representatives of any government)—and served as the basis for the commission to advise the Council on whether the mandatory powers were fulfilling their obligations under the mandate agreements. Although the Permanent Mandates Commission gained considerable recognition for its competence, its primary dependence upon the mandatory powers for information on conditions in the mandates was a severe restriction upon the League's development of a real capacity for supervising the conduct of the mandatory powers. Also, in the final analysis, the League lacked an effective means for enforcing its standards even if it could be demonstrated that they were being consistently violated by a mandatory power.[11]

In summary, Goodrich's judgment on the result of the League's mandate system appears convincing.

> While failing to live up to the expectations of its more idealistic proponents, it did achieve substantial benefits both in the quality of administration of dependent territories and in changing prevailing attitudes and expectations regarding the treatment of dependent peoples. One mandated territory (Iraq) was brought to independence during the League period, and Syria and Lebanon were on the threshold of independence when the Second World War broke out. There is evidence that standards of administration in dependent territories generally were favorably affected by League practices. Certainly the League mandate system gave encouragement and support to those who, more conscious of the evils of colonialism than of its benefits, were working for its termination and for the realization by dependent peoples of the benefits of self-government.[12]

THE UNITED NATIONS AND DECOLONIZATION

Political Context

While the provisions and experience of the League were significant factors in shaping the United Nations system for handling colonial problems, the changed political environment of 1945 was of even greater importance.[13] Actively engaged in drafting the Charter were a number of non-European countries overtly hostile to the prewar colonial system. Among the sources of this hostility was the fact that twenty-seven of the fifty-one founding members of the United Nations had won their independence after some form of colonial rule (63 of the present 131 members of the organization have gained their independence in the last twenty-six years). In their opposition to this system, this group enjoyed the support of one of the great powers, the Soviet Union. Another critical change in the political environment was that World War II had severed for the duration of the war the connections between the colonial powers and their possessions. At the time of San Francisco only the most tenuous of connections had been reestablished, in many cases, and in these colonial territories nascent revolutionary movements could usually be found struggling to prevent the reimposition of the prewar colonial order. The result of this new political environment has been ably summarized by Emil J. Sady:

> Since the earliest days of the San Francisco Conference, the principal colonial powers have been on the defensive in the Organization. Their attitude, in general, was that they had nothing to gain and much

to lose from the activities of the United Nations in the field of trusteeship and non-self-governing territories. Their opposition at the San Francisco Conference was formidable and their posture was weak.[14]

Charter Framework and Development 1945–1960

The United Nations Charter provides a two-pronged approach to colonial
problems.[15] First, in Chapters XII and XIII of the Charter the trusteeship
system, the direct successor of the League's mandate system, is set forth.
This system, which was to cover "(a) territories now held under mandate; (b) territories which may be detached from enemy states as a result
of the Second World War; and (c) territories voluntarily placed under the
system by states responsible for their administration," [16] offered the greatest amount of direct United Nations supervision. A Trusteeship Council,
operating under the authority of the General Assembly and composed of
governmental representatives drawn equally from administering and nonadministering states, was established by the Charter to exercise the functions of the organization with respect to trust territories. It was given the
power to consider reports submitted by the administering power, to accept
petitions without prior submission to the administering authority, and to
make periodic visits to the trust territories. The main emphasis of the
trusteeship system, as set forth in the Charter, was on the promotion of
"the political, economic, social and educational advancement of the inhabitants of the Trust Territories and their progressive development toward
self-government or independence as may be appropriate to the particular
circumstances of each Territory and its peoples and the freely expressed
wishes of the peoples concerned, and as may be provided by the terms of
each Trusteeship Agreement." [17]

By 1950 ten trusteeship agreements had been approved by the General Assembly. The agreements covered Nauru, administered by Australia,
New Zealand, and the United Kingdom; New Guinea, administered by
Australia; Cameroons and Togoland, administered by France; Somaliland
administered by Italy; Western Samoa administered by New Zealand;
Cameroons, Tanganyika, and Togoland, administered by the United Kingdom; and Ruanda-Urundi, administered by Belgium. An eleventh territory,
the Trust Territory of the Pacific Islands, composed of the former Japanese
mandated islands, is a strategic trust territory administered by the United
States under an agreement approved by the Security Council in 1947.[18]
It is important to note that one territory held under a League mandate,
South-West Africa which was administered by the Union of South Africa,
was not transferred by the administering power to the trusteeship system.
Also it is worth noting that not a single colonial territory which had not
been held under a mandate was voluntarily placed in the trusteeship sys-
tem.

As the organ principally responsible for examining conditions in the trust territories, the Trusteeship Council established the practice of conducting a yearly review of conditions in each territory. This review was drawn up on the basis of the following: an annual report submitted by each administering power in reply to an annual Trusteeship Council questionnaire requesting detailed political, economic, social, and educational information; periodic visiting missions sent by the Trusteeship Council to the trust territories; and any petitions received by the Council from the inhabitants of the trust territories. Beginning in 1952, the General Assembly requested the trust territories to submit information to the Council on the measures taken or contemplated that would lead the territories to self-government or independence within the shortest possible time and on the time that it would take the trust territories to attain self-government or independence.

In terms of the scope of application, the task of applying the elaborate provisions of the trusteeship system met with only limited success. In only eleven territories were the provisions of Chapters XII and XIII ever applied. At its height there were more than eight times as many non-self-governing territories, containing over ten times as many people, outside the trusteeship system as in it.[19] As of 1970 only two territories—New Guinea and the Trust Territory of the Pacific Islands—remain in the trusteeship system.

As a counterpoint to the trusteeship system, the Charter in Chapter XI embodied a commitment by the members controlling non-self-governing territories to "accept as a sacred trust the obligation to promote to the upmost . . . the well-being of the inhabitants of these territories." [20] Further, to achieve this goal these members agreed to develop self-government, to assist in the progressive development of free political institutions, and to transmit regularly to the secretary-general information on the economic, social, and educational conditions in these territories. The undertaking by the member states of international responsibilities for their colonial possessions was a significant departure from the traditional order. It was in the declaration of Chapter XI that one could most clearly glimpse the fundamental forces that were at work to change the colonial order. It embodied the first assertion, admittedly inchoate, of an international responsibility for the management of colonial territories outside the mandate or trusteeship system. It is from this acceptance of international responsibility that the later assertion of institutionalized international accountability has developed.

The Charter provisions for the United Nations supervision of the non-self-governing territories not placed under trusteeship are vague. It is only in Article 73e with its provisions for the transmission of certain information about these territories that a possible basis for institutionalized supervision can be discerned. In the period 1946–1949 the General Assembly took actions to define the scope, nature, and procedures relating to the transmission of information under Article 73e. During the period 1949–1955, the General Assembly proceeded to establish its competence to examine the information transmitted by the administering powers and to make specific recommendations on conditions in the non-self-governing territories. During this second period, the Committee on Information from Non-Self-Governing Territories, composed equally of administering and nonadministering members, had the burden of initially examining the information received. Between 1955 and 1960, the General Assembly increasingly asserted its competence to decide when the obligation to transmit information had ceased and also to decide when there existed an obligation to transmit information under Article 73e. Unlike the situation regarding the trust territories, the United Nations by 1960 had found no effective means for establishing direct contact with the vast majority of colonial territories falling under Chapter XI. With the significant exception of the Portuguese territories, the administering powers had largely accepted the obligation to supply the United Nations with technical information, but this fell far short of the organization's right to receive petitions from and send visiting missions to trust territories.

For reasons partly related to the small number of countries under the trusteeship system and more directly related to the strength of anticolonial forces in the General Assembly, the period 1946–1960 was marked by a steady shift of active concern with colonial problems to the General Assembly.[21] The Assembly during this period often took the Trusteeship Council to task for its timidity in dealing with the colonial powers. The Assembly also did not hesitate to consider colonial disputes that the Security Council dodged. Thus by the start of 1960 the General Assembly through a decade and a half of active probing concern with colonial problems had established for itself a dominant position in the organization with respect to these problems.

Precise assessment of the role of the United Nations in the profound changes that occurred in the colonial areas from 1946 to 1960 is impossible. In some instances the ideological support derived from the principles of the Charter may have aided to a limited extent the growth of nascent nationalist movements in these territories. Quite possibly, the Trusteeship Council's activities and/or the possibility of United Nations concern with a particular colonial situation may have hastened the willingness of colonial powers to undertake reforms aimed at independence. However, these same activities by the organization may have hardened the resolve of some colonial powers not to grant reforms under international pressure. The clearest contribution of the United Nations during this period was to provide an arena for the marshalling of a majority opinion hostile to a prolonged continuation of colonial rule in Africa and Asia.

Decolonization, 1960–1970

In 1960 the successful efforts of the anticolonial forces in the General Assembly to gain approval of a Declaration on Colonialism marked the start of a new phase in the United Nations role in the decolonization process.[22] Only a very little political acumen would have been required in the spring and summer of 1960 to foresee that the fifteenth session of the General Assembly convening in September 1960 would be decisively affected by the increased tempo of the disintegration of the colonial empires of Africa. Seventeen colonial territories were scheduled to gain their independence in time for admission to the organization at that session; of this prospective batch of new members, only Cyprus was a non-African country and it was in Africa that the colonial revolution was then at its acme. From past experience with newly independent states, it was easy to guess that these states would be almost totally mesmerized by the compulsion to hasten the total end of colonialism in the underdeveloped world. In a body as politically oriented as the United Nations, the shifting voting balance in the Assembly resulting from this rush to independence of a whole continent could not go unnoticed.

This, then, was the political context in which the Union of Soviet Socialist Republics decided to seize the initiative on September 23, 1960, by requesting that an additional item, a "declaration on granting of independence to colonial countries and peoples," be added to the agenda of the fifteenth session.[23] The Soviet draft declaration stridently proclaimed that in the colonial territories "the swish of the overseer's lash is heard; there heads fall under the executioner's axe." [24] In order to remove the multitude of injustices which the Soviets saw as flowing from the Western colonial system, the Soviet declaration went on to proclaim that all colonial countries "must be granted forthwith complete independence" and that all foreign bases in other states must be eliminated.

There was no reticence on the part of the Soviet Union in divulging to the General Assembly the strategy that underlay the formulation of its draft declaration. Nikita Khrushchev, chairman of the Council of Ministers of the Soviet Union, who was in personal attendance at the fifteenth session, explained the strategy very concisely when he said,

> I very much like the words of August Bebel, the social-democrat and leader of the German workers, who said, more or less, this: If the bourgeoisie praises you, Bebel, think, in that case, what a stupid thing you must have done. If the bourgeoisie reviles you, it means that you are truly serving the working class, the proletariat! If the colonialists now revile me, I am proud of it, because it means that I am truly serving the peoples which are struggling for their independence, for their freedom.[25]

And the Soviet declaration was indeed formulated according to this precept. The operative paragraphs of the Soviet draft, phrased as "demands," were not in the bland diplomatic language of the Assembly best suited to encompass the widest divergency in views and garner the largest number of affirmative votes.

Once the decision had been taken to place the Soviet item on the agenda, informal talks began within the Afro-Asian group which at that time included all the new nations in the United Nations except Israel. In spite of a wide range of opinion on the Soviet draft, a consensus was reached that the Afro-Asian group should try to formulate, without prejudice to the Soviet draft, its own draft resolution on this item. There was a general fear among the Afro-Asian states that Soviet sponsorship would result in a "cold war" vote in which the Latin Americans would join the West in opposing the Soviet draft with the result that the draft might fail to achieve the votes necessary for adoption in the Assembly. There was also an emotional belief that, as the nations with the most direct concern and experience with colonialism, they should be the ones to introduce and sponsor any Assembly resolutions on colonialism.

Having decided to propose its own draft resolution on colonialism, the Afro-Asian group was next faced with the task of coming up with a text which would encompass the diversity of opinion within its own membership.[26] During this period in which the struggle over a provisional text was taking place, no attempt was made to consult groups outside the Afro-Asian group as to their views on the alternative texts, the feeling being that such consultations would tend only to splinter the Afro-Asian group itself. On the whole, the new nations of Africa, the majority of which favored a draft close to the Soviet proposal, lost more battles than they won during the intragroup negotiations. For example, the specific mention of Algeria's right to independence was deleted from the final version. As one of the more moderate members of the group explained it later,

> There is no doubt, for example, that many of the co-sponsors of this draft declaration who have suffered greatly from the ravages of colonialism would have preferred a more expressive text, including clauses condemning colonialism in its most culpable aspects. However, in order to rally all currents of opinion in the Assembly in favour of a text acceptable to all the Members of the United Nations, they have, in a spirit of conciliation, accepted certain phrases of a much more moderate nature.[27]

In its preamble, the final Afro-Asian draft drew heavily upon the resolutions previously approved by the Afro-Asian conferences at Bandung in 1955, Accra in 1958, and Addis Ababa in 1960 because they represented previously agreed-upon phraseology which could be accepted without extensive negotiation. The operative paragraphs of the final draft fluctuated between easily accepted platitudes and ambiguous phrases into which each sponsor could inject its own interpretation. First, an example of the former:

> The subjection of peoples to alien subjugation, domination and exploitation constitutes a denial of fundamental human rights.

Of the latter:

> Inadequacy of political, economic, social or educational preparedness should never serve as a *pretext* for delaying independence.[28]

This Afro-Asian draft differed from its Soviet counterpart in both tone and substance. Whereas the Soviet draft was both anticolonial and anti-Western, the Afro-Asian text was only anticolonial and strenuously avoided attacks on specific Western countries. The tone was as measured, although slightly shrill, as the platitudes were general. Instead of proclaiming "the following demands," as in the Soviet draft, this draft only "declares." The substance of the operative paragraphs also differed. While the Soviet text had demanded that all colonial territories "be granted forthwith complete independence and freedom," the Afro-Asian draft spoke of "immediate steps" to be taken to transfer power, implying that the transfer could proceed according to an orderly timetable. In contrast to the Soviet draft, no mention is to be found in the Afro-Asian draft of any prohibition upon foreign bases.

During the debate on the drafts which opened on November 28, the Western states, in their effort to depict the more constructive aspects of colonialism, received considerable support from Latin America. Appealing to the new nations to take a more balanced account of their colonial past, the Latin American representatives pointed to the constructive cultural and educational benefits of the system. They aptly noted that in many cases it was the language of the ex-colonial power which provided a major bond uniting the new nations.

Neither the West nor the Latin Americans found a willingness among the new nations to concede the possibility of some beneficial effects resulting from colonialism. Almost as one, the new nations depicted the colonial era as

> nothing other than a stormy succession of wars and expeditions waged by Powers intoxicated by their economic and military potential, seeking to gain strategic positions and hankering for wealth and prestige.[29]

Although the Latin Americans had presumed to speak on colonialism as fellow products of the system, the new nations would not accept this relationship and defended their exclusive right to speak as experts on colonialism. As the delegate from Mali said,

> The delegations which speak in this Assembly of their colonial experience or proclaim the benefits of colonialism can unfortunately only speak of the empire of their fathers' day; they speak of it as a heritage.
> If their countries were colonized at some time in history, they know it only from history books. Therein lies the fundamental difference between those delegations and ours, who have personal experience of colonial rule. Our knowledge is not based on hearsay or on what we learnt in school; we were for decades the living embodiment of that system.[30]

The Soviet bloc was far from silent during the debate on the agenda item that it had proposed. The Soviets maintained a withering fire against all forms of Western colonialism. Foreign military bases and North Atlantic Treaty Organization (NATO) assistance to countries engaged in colonial wars were favorite subjects of this often vitriolic attack. However, despite the ferocity of this attack, the Soviet bloc was able to avoid incurring the odium of the new nations for injecting cold war politics into the debate because it shared with those nations a common target: Western colonialism. The Soviets continued to press publicly for the adoption of their own draft resolution. The Afro-Asians were quite happy to have the Soviet Union continue to urge its own more far-reaching resolution rather than publicly embrace their milder resolution. This happy configuration, which has been repeated often on colonial issues since 1960, enabled the new nations to appeal to their Western and Latin American colleagues as a voice of reason and restraint which if not supported would result in the victory of the more odious Russian draft.

When the General Assembly on December 14 turned to voting on the drafts before it, the Soviet text as well as two Soviet amendments to the Afro-Asian draft were quickly defeated.[31] By this time there was certainly no doubt as to the vote's outcome, and the only element of suspense was provided by the uncertainty as to how the United States would vote. During the Assembly debate the United States delegation had displayed a disquieting ambivalence. It had only the strongest praise for the struggle of the colonial areas toward nationhood and was most solicitous toward their problems, but a strange reticence prevailed as to how it would finally vote on the resolution.[32] It was common knowledge in the Assembly that the United Kingdom and Portugal, two NATO allies of the United States, were exerting great pressure on the United States not to vote in favor of this draft. Thus, on the final vote more than on any of the minor decisions preceding it, the United States was being asked to choose between its old ally, the United Kingdom, and the new nations of Africa and Asia.

By a roll call vote of 89 in favor, none against, and with 9 abstentions, the Afro-Asian draft became General Assembly Resolution 1514 (XV), the Declaration on the Granting of Independence to Colonial Countries and Peoples.[33] Those abstaining were Australia, Belgium, the Dominican Republic, France, Portugal, Spain, the Union of South Africa, the United Kingdom, and the United States.

The disquietude of the United States delegation at finding itself in the company of this group of colonial powers was not helped by the fact that the only Negro member of the delegation, Mrs. Zelma Watson George, stood up and applauded the adoption of the draft. In explaining its vote, the United States justified its abstention on the grounds that the resolution was "completely silent on the important contributions" which the administering powers had made in the colonial areas and was so "heavily weighted toward complete independence as the only acceptable goal." [34] While this was the formal explanation given for the United States abstention, the actual reason appears to have been a direct appeal from British Prime Minister Harold Macmillan to President Dwight D. Eisenhower to avoid placing the United Kingdom in an awkward position. The final decision that the United States should abstain was made by Eisenhower against the advice of the entire United States delegation.[35]

An important element contributing to the success of the new nations in obtaining Assembly adoption of the Declaration on Colonialism was the strong feeling in the Assembly that the victory of the decolonization movement was inevitable and the accompanying unwillingness to sacrifice developing relations with the new nations in defense of a system which most states admitted was doomed. And, while the principal colonial powers did abstain, that in itself was a form of victory in that the draft in question, *inter alia,* proclaimed "the necessity of bringing to a speedy and unconditional end colonialism in all its forms and manifestations." This unwillingness to be clearly stigmatized as being against the lofty principles enunciated in the draft is testimony of sorts to the political influence of the new nations. Few had supposed in any case that the new nations had a great deal of influence on Portugal, Spain, and the Union of South Africa. The United Kingdom, probably the most progressive of all colonial powers, had again demonstrated its testiness on the issue of international responsibility for the administration of colonial possessions. It was really only with the United States that the new nations could have been disappointed with the results of their exercise of political influence. When the issue came down to a choice between fidelity to the principal ally of the United States and support for the new nations on an anticolonial declaration in the United Nations, the Eisenhower administration supported Britain. But the loss was not without profit for the Afro-Asian states. The abstention of the United States had focused attention on the nature of the choice and made clear that many even within the administration would have preferred to support the new nations. And, perhaps most hopeful from the standpoint of the new nations, a new administration that spoke eloquently of a new role for the United States in support of the national aspirations of the colonial and former colonial parts of the world was about to assume power in Washington.

In 1961, with the initial push again coming from the Soviet Union but with the major source of influence being supplied by the new nations, the General Assembly established a special committee on colonialism to examine the implementation of the declaration passed the previous year.[36] Whereas nine countries had abstained on the 1960 declaration, four of these states—the United States, Belgium, Australia, and the Dominican Republic—voted in favor of the establishment of the Special Committee. The ranks of those willing to stand against overwhelming Assembly majorities on the question of a general commitment to end colonialism had substantially dwindled since the Charter was written in 1945. Concerned as the new nations were with accelerating the final demise of colonialism and possessed of sufficient votes in the organization to make this national concern the concern of the United Nations, in 1960 and 1961 they were able to move all but a remnant of colonial powers to join publicly in singing the funeral dirge of colonialism.

Considerable political sophistication was shown by the new nations in 1961 in pushing for a subsidiary organ with a predominant anticolonial bias as a means of achieving their aims. Though cloaked in moderate terms, General Assembly Resolution 1654 (XVI) which established the Special Committee on Colonialism provided the new nations with a vehicle to push for the end of colonialism without any necessity of kowtowing to the administering powers as in the Trusteeship Council or the Committee on Information from Non-Self-Governing Territories. Both of the latter bodies were organized on the basis of parity of membership between the colonial powers and the noncolonial states. From its beginning, however, the Special Committee on Colonialism had an automatic anticolonial majority, with eight of its seventeen members Afro-Asian states, initially, two from the Soviet bloc plus Yugoslavia, two from Latin America, and two from Western Europe plus the United States and Australia. In 1962 the Special Committee's membership was given an added anticolonial bias with the addition of seven members: four Afro-Asian states, one Soviet bloc state, one Latin American state, and one Scandinavian state.

The first task faced by the Special Committee was to decide exactly what its broad General Assembly mandate meant in terms of operational procedures.[37] In the context of parliamentary diplomacy, the Special Committee's operation would be governed by rules of procedure "subject to tactical manipulation to advance or oppose a point of view," [38] hence the determination of its operating procedures could decisively affect its future role. Over the objections of its Western members, the Special Committee decided to resort to voting procedures "whenever any member felt that procedure was necessary" and that territories should be considered on a country-by-country basis with priority given to the territories of Africa.[39]

THE CASE OF RHODESIA

Rather than attempting to cover the Special Committee's activities with regard to the more than sixty territories it has considered between its first meeting on February 10, 1962, and the middle of 1966, the case of Southern Rhodesia will be used to illustrate the use to which the new nations have put the Special Committee in their drive to abolish colonialism. As the first territory considered by the Special Committee and the one which has received the most sustained attention of this body, Southern Rhodesia is particularly suited to this purpose.

Situated in south central Africa, Southern Rhodesia is the northern bastion of the white-dominated third of Africa. With the Zambezi River as its northern frontier, it sprawls over 150,000 square miles populated by approximately 3,600,000 Africans and only about 222,000 Europeans. Although first seized as a private venture by Cecil Rhodes in the late nineteenth century, Southern Rhodesia passed in 1923 to the United Kingdom as a self-governing territory with control of the territory's foreign relations resting with Britain. From 1953 until 1963, white-dominated Southern Rhodesia was part of an uneasy federation with Northern Rhodesia and Nyasaland. This British-sponsored federation broke up in 1963, partly over the antagonistic racial policies of the Southern Rhodesian government. With the dissolution of the federation, Northern Rhodesia continued as a self-governing but nonindependent British territory. The Southern Rhodesian constitution of December 6, 1961, which had eliminated most of the residual powers formerly held by the United Kingdom while holding only the most tenuous of promises for any meaningful African participation in the government, served as the constituent document of the territory until its unilateral declaration of independence in 1965.

After devoting fifteen of its first twenty-six meetings to Southern Rhodesia, the Special Committee established, with Western acquiescence, a Subcommittee on Southern Rhodesia. This subcommittee—composed of India, Mali, Syria, Tanganyika, Tunisia, and Venezuela—immediately undertook to establish contact with the United Kingdom government to discuss the future of the territory. After holding talks in London with the British government between April 7 and April 14, 1962, the subcommittee recommended that "the situation in Southern Rhodesia should be considered by the General Assembly . . . as a matter of urgency." [40] The Special Committee, over the objections of Australia, Italy, the United Kingdom, and the United States, not only endorsed this recommendation but also recommended Assembly adoption of a draft resolution which declared Southern Rhodesia to be a non-self-governing territory within the meaning of Chapter XI of the Charter and requested Britain to take immediate steps to set aside the 1961 Southern Rhodesian constitution, to restore civil liberties in Southern Rhodesia, to immediately apply there the 1960 Declaration on Colonialism, and to repeal all Southern Rhodesian laws which sanctioned racial discrimination. [41]

Over sustained Western objections, the Assembly in June 1962 took up the Special Committee's recommendations. The United Kingdom's position, which had been placed previously before the subcommittee and the Special Committee, was reiterated before the Assembly. Resting on the nuances of the United Kingdom's constitutional practices, the British contended that they had no power to annul the Southern Rhodesian constitution and that because of its status as a self-governing territory neither the United Kingdom nor the United Nations had a right to discuss its internal affairs. A thirty-nine-power Afro-Asian draft was offered to the Assembly as a moderate alternative to the more sweeping draft recommended by the Special Committee. While this draft affirmed that Southern Rhodesia was a non-self-governing territory within the meaning of Chapter XI of the Charter, it avoided calling directly upon the United Kingdom to annul the Southern Rhodesian constitution. However, the thirty-nine-power draft did request Britain

to undertake urgently the convening of a constitutional conference . . .
which would ensure the rights of the majority of the people in conformity
with the principles of the Charter of the United Nations and the Declaration on the granting of independence to colonial countries and peoples.[42]

The Assembly debate revealed that a clear majority of the membership
felt that Britain had a moral obligation which should transcend any constitutional limitations to protect the African majority from the white-
dominated government of Southern Rhodesia. The compromise draft was
overwhelmingly approved by a vote of 73 in favor to 1 against, with 27
abstaining, and Portugal and the United Kingdom present but not voting.[43]

Neither the British nor the Southern Rhodesian whites were moved
to change their previously announced positions by the Assembly's action.
Faced with this intransigence, the anticolonial forces decided upon seeking
another Assembly resolution before the first elections could be held at
the end of 1962 under the 1961 constitution. In a display of power that
both angered and awed many delegates, the Afro-Asian states forced a
closure of Fourth (Trust and Non-Self-Governing Territories) Committee
debate on their draft on October 31, 1962, only one day after its introduction and before all states had had an opportunity to speak, and brought
the draft before the Assembly that night. This draft called upon the United
Kingdom to secure "the immediate convening of a constitutional conference," and "the immediate extension to the whole population without
discrimination of the full and unconditional exercise of their basic political
rights." [44] In both its tone and substance, this draft went further than the
resolution on the same subject approved by the Assembly four months
earlier, but the Assembly approved it on the same evening it was brought
before the plenary session. In fact, the vote this time was even more lop-
sided, with 81 in favor, 2 opposed, 19 abstaining, and the United Kingdom
not participating. Again there was no response from the United Kingdom
other than the standard reply that Southern Rhodesia had been self-governing since 1923 and neither Britain nor the United Nations had a right to
intervene in its internal affairs.

In March 1963 the Special Committee returned to the question of
Southern Rhodesia and again dispatched a subcommittee to London for
talks with the British. On the basis of its London visit this subcommittee,
composed of Mali, Uruguay, Syria, Sierra Leone, Tanganyika, and Tunisia,
recommended consideration of the question of Southern Rhodesia at a
special session of the General Assembly, drew the attention of the Security
Council to the deteriorating situation in Southern Rhodesia, and requested
the secretary-general to draw the attention of the United Kingdom to the
seriousness of the situation.[45] On June 23, 1963, the Special Committee—
with Australia, Denmark, Italy, and the United States abstaining and Britain not participating—approved its subcommittee's report and recommendations and also requested Britain to abrogate the 1961 constitution.[46]
The chairman of the Special Committee transmitted its report to the Security Council, and this was quickly followed by the request of thirty-two

African states for an urgent meeting of the Security Council on the grave threat posed to the peace and security of the African continent by Southern Rhodesia.[47] When the Security Council convened on September 9, 1963, Ghana, Morocco, and the Philippines submitted a draft resolution which requested the United Kingdom not to grant independence to Southern Rhodesia until a fully representative government had been established.[48] This draft was vetoed by the United Kingdom—France and the United States abstained—and the Security Council was forced to adjourn without adopting any resolution.

Having failed to obtain Security Council approval of their demands, the new nations brought them before the eighteenth session of the Assembly and quickly obtained their adoption.[49] With the Assembly decisions in hand, the Special Committee—minus the Western states—on March 23, 1964, drew the Security Council's attention to "the explosive situation" in Southern Rhodesia.[50] At the same time the Special Committee asked the United Kingdom to declare that independence would not be granted to Southern Rhodesia except on the basis of universal adult suffrage and also requested all states to voluntarily refrain from supplying arms and ammunition to Southern Rhodesia. In May 1964 the Special Committee decided to send to London a third subcommittee—composed of Ethiopia, Mali, Sierra Leone, and Yugoslavia—to discuss with the British the implementation of the previously adopted United Nations resolutions. This subcommittee concluded that further discussions with the United Kingdom were "unlikely to yield fruitful results" and called upon the Security Council to again consider the question of Southern Rhodesia "as a matter of urgency." [51] After considering its subcommittee's report, the majority of the Special Committee adopted a resolution on June 26, 1964, deploring "the persistent refusal" of Britain to cooperate in the implementation of the United Nations resolutions on Southern Rhodesia.[52] This resolution also endorsed the conclusions and recommendations of the subcommittee and reiterated the call for Security Council action. On October 27, 1964, the Special Committee drew "once again . . . the attention of the Security Council to the question of Southern Rhodesia." [53] On November 17, 1964, the Special Committee authorized its subcommittee to keep the situation under review and to maintain close contact with the United Kingdom with a view to achieving the implementation of the United Nations resolutions.[54]

The Southern Rhodesian case illustrates vividly the circuitous policy that the new nations have followed in attempting to influence the course of events in the remaining colonial areas. Secure in their control over the Special Committee of Twenty-Four, the new nations have used it and its subcommittees as originating points for new initiatives and as organs of constant surveillance of these colonial areas.[55] Subcommittees, which lack even the token Western representation of the parent body, have borne the main burden of conducting initial investigations and formulating recommendations. Usually over Western opposition, the Special Committee endorses the reports of its subcommittees, although sometimes toning down their draft resolutions. Next, the Special Committee's recommendations are forwarded to the General Assembly. Within the Assembly, as the case of Southern Rhodesia illustrates, the dominant anticolonial majority ensures a sympathetic hearing for the Special Committee's recommendations although some modification is usually introduced in order to obtain the largest possible majority. Simultaneously, the Special Committee has called for Security Council action on its reports. In 1964 three separate pleas were addressed to the Security Council for action on Southern Rhodesia. The Special Committee has not been altogether successful in obtaining even a hearing, much less action, from the Council on its proposals. This circuitous policy has been most successful in maintaining continuous United Nations involvement with the colonial areas and increasing the verbal intensity of the resolutions adopted. By the end of 1964 it had been successful in obtaining broad and repeated censure of the remaining recalcitrant colonial regimes. However, this circuitous policy had not yet produced any change in the policy of these hard-core regimes or any operational role for the organization in bringing about some change in this area.

Ironically, through their threats of a unilateral declaration of independence from the United Kingdom and finally with such a declaration on November 11, 1965, the Southern Rhodesian government brought about the direct involvement of the United Nations which the new nations had been unable to achieve. In the early autumn of 1965, as the signs of an early unilateral declaration of independence multiplied, forty Afro-Asian states rushed a draft resolution through the Fourth Committee and the General Assembly condemning any attempt by the Southern Rhodesians to seize independence and calling upon the United Kingdom to use all possible means to prevent a unilateral declaration of independence.[56] On November 5, 1965, the Assembly again appealed for British action to prevent a Southern Rhodesian declaration of independence.[57] This resolution was in stronger terms than the October resolution and, in fact, called upon the United Kingdom "to employ all necessary measures, including military force" to prevent a unilateral declaration of independence. In reaction to the Southern Rhodesian declaration of independence on November 11, the Assembly in near unanimity adopted a resolution which condemned "the unilateral declaration of independence made by the racialist minority in Southern Rhodesia" and recommended that the Security Council consider the situation as a matter of urgency.[58] This resolution, sponsored by thirty-six African states, was adopted by 107 in favor, 2 against, and 1 abstaining. As was the case with the October resolution, only Portugal and South Africa voted against this resolution, while France abstained.

At the behest of the United Kingdom, the Security Council met on November 12, 1965, to consider the Southern Rhodesian situation. With this meeting the principal locus of United Nations concern with Southern Rhodesia shifted from the General Assembly to the Security Council where it remains at the time of this writing. In requesting a Security Council meeting on Southern Rhodesia, the British were finally abandoning their position that neither the United Kingdom nor the United Nations had the right to interfere in the territory's internal affairs. During November 1965 the Security Council passed resolutions which condemned the unilateral declaration of independence, called upon all states to refrain from recognizing or assisting the regime, requested all states to break economic relations with Southern Rhodesia, and requested the establishment of an embargo on oil and petroleum products to Southern Rhodesia.[59]

In defiance of the Security Council's request for an embargo on the shipment of oil and petroleum products to Southern Rhodesia, two oil tankers were discovered in April 1966 to be nearing the port of Beira in Portuguese Mozambique with cargoes rumored for transshipment to Rhodesia. At the request of the British government, the Security Council met, declared that the "situation constitutes a threat to the peace," and authorized the British to prevent "by the use of force if necessary" oil from reaching Rhodesia through the port of Beira.[60] This marked the first time that a specific state had been authorized to carry out a decision of the Security Council.

The tempo of United Nations action against Southern Rhodesia was again increased in December 1966 after the collapse of renewed negotiations between London and the Ian Smith regime. Under strong African pressure, the United Kingdom asked the Security Council to approve for the first time since its founding selective, mandatory sanctions against a regime.[61] During a week of discussion, the African states made a concerted attempt to alter drastically the British draft to include more commodities and to provide enforcement provisions to ensure that the Council's edict was carried out. The African states also sought to have the Security Council deplore the British refusal to use force against Southern Rhodesia and to call upon the United Kingdom to withdraw all previous offers to the Southern Rhodesian regime and to declare flatly that it would grant independence to Southern Rhodesia only under majority rule.[62]

In this attempt the African states largely failed although the final resolution contained eight African amendments, including a ban on the supply of oil and oil products to Rhodesia.[63] On December 16, by a vote of 11 to 0, with Bulgaria, France, Mali, and the Soviet Union abstaining, the Security Council approved a ban on the purchase of twelve of Southern Rhodesia's chief exports and on the supply to Southern Rhodesia of oil and oil products. Not only did this mark the first use of mandatory sanctions by the Security Council, but the Council itself emerged as a new instrument in the politics of decolonization. The success or failure of these developments will, moreover, have a profound effect upon the organization's relations with the remainder of southern Africa.

Thus, by the beginning of 1967, the Southern Rhodesians by their own actions had provided the occasion for the United Nations to initiate mandatory sanctions against the regime. This was an action long desired by the new nations but one which even their adroit use of political influence had been unable to obtain prior to the Southern Rhodesian unilateral declaration of independence.

In December 1966, following the breakdown of renewed negotiations between Great Britain and the regime of Ian Smith, the Security Council declared that the situation in Southern Rhodesia constituted a threat to international peace and security and for the first time since the founding of the United Nations called for selective mandatory sanctions under Chapter VII of the Charter. Included in these sanctions were petroleum products. In total, the selective sanctions covered about 15 percent of Rhodesian imports and 60 percent of her exports. Almost a year and a half later, May 19, 1968, the Security Council unanimously imposed comprehensive and mandatory economic sanctions against Southern Rhodesia. This was the first time in United Nations history that such action had been taken.

The use and effectiveness of sanctions has become a key issue in the United Nations involvement in Southern Rhodesia. Selective sanctions have now been in effect for approximately four years and comprehensive sanctions for over two years. However, the Smith regime has been able to maintain itself in the face of these sanctions.

SOUTH AFRICA

South Africa presents two different problems to the United Nations although in practice the African states have often blurred this distinction. One problem concerns the application by the Republic within South Africa of a constellation of racial policies, going under the rubric of apartheid, designed to maintain separation of the races and also to preserve white domination of the government, economy, and society of South Africa. There is, however, a second problem which concerns the administration and future of the mandated territory of South-West Africa. First seized from the Germans in 1915 and then placed under a League mandate in 1920, this mandated area has been administered by South Africa for approximately fifty years as an integral part of its territory although South Africa grudgingly admits a limited international responsibility for its administration.

Commencing in 1960, largely through the pressure of the African states, various United Nations organs produced a steady stream of reports, recommendations, and denunciations of the apartheid policies of the South African government. During this period these efforts went significantly beyond previous efforts by the organization to force an alteration in this policy. In November 1962 the General Assembly issued a call for member states to take a specific list of diplomatic and economic measures, ranging from the breaking of diplomatic relations to the boycotting of all South African products, in order to bring about the abandonment of the policy of apartheid.[64] This resolution also established a Special Committee on Apartheid to monitor South Africa's compliance with United Nations resolutions.

In the face of South Africa's refusal to modify its apartheid policy, the African states beginning in 1963 turned their attention to gaining Security Council adoption of a program of mandatory sanctions against South Africa. Although it refused to emulate the Africans' zeal for adopting mandatory sanctions against South Africa, the Security Council under continuous pressure from the African states made limited moves in that direction. In August 1963 the Security Council adopted a voluntary arms embargo which requested all states to halt "the sale and shipment of arms, ammunition . . . and military vehicles" to South Africa. In December 1963 the Security Council adopted a Norwegian proposal that a group of experts be established "to examine the methods of resolving the present situation in South Africa." [65] The report of this expert group in April 1964 urged the creation of a national convention, representative of all the people of South Africa, to set a new course for the future. It also recommended an expert examination of the "economic and strategic aspects of sanctions." [66] The Security Council agreed to establish an Expert Committee on Sanctions and it reported to the Security Council in March 1965. In its report this Expert Committee concluded that while economic and diplomatic sanctions could do damage to South Africa, such sanctions would have extensive economic repercussions in many other member states as well and be very difficult to enforce.[67]

In spite of repeated General Assembly resolutions calling for drastic Security Council action against South Africa to force a change in its apartheid policy, the Security Council failed to meet formally since 1964 on the situation created in South Africa as a result of apartheid. As of 1970 the African states have been unable to energize the power of the United Nations into a frontal assault backed by mandatory collective measures on South Africa. In fact, the voluntary arms embargo and voluntary economic sanctions called for by the Security Council and the General Assembly in 1962 have been publicly flaunted by France and quietly circumvented by other states.[68]

The second problem presented by South Africa to the United Nations —the future of the League mandated territory of South-West Africa— more clearly fits into the category of decolonization than the apartheid problem discussed above. After having its 1946 proposal for the annexation of the territory rejected by the General Assembly, South Africa rebuffed all suggestions that it follow the lead of the other League mandate-administering powers and conclude a trusteeship agreement with the United Nations. Acting on the basis of a 1950 advisory opinion of the International Court of Justice, the General Assembly began to attempt to exercise the supervisory functions of the League with respect to the mandate.

Between 1946 and 1960 the main scene of United Nations concern with South-West Africa was the General Assembly and its committees. More than sixty resolutions concerning South-West Africa were passed by these bodies between 1946 and 1960. An important new scene was added when it was decided at the Second Conference of Independent African States meeting at Addis Ababa in June 1960 to sponsor a submission to the International Court of Justice for adjudication of South Africa's responsibilities to South-West Africa under the mandate. As the only two African members of the League, Ethiopia and Liberia initiated this proceeding in November 1960. The Court was asked to find that South Africa had violated the mandate by its extension of apartheid to South-West Africa, its unilateral changes in the legal status of the territory, and its failure to submit reports on the territory to the General Assembly.

The legal proceedings surrounding this case were extremely long and complex and the final decision was not rendered until July 18, 1966. While the case was before the Court, the anticolonial majority in the General Assembly continued to press for additional resolutions condemning South African policy in the territory. These resolutions produced no concessions on the part of South Africa. On the other hand, these seemingly redundant resolutions did serve to provide a basis for future action if South Africa were to be faced—as everyone expected—with an unfavorable International Court of Justice opinion and chose to flout the opinion. The hope among the African states was that the long-delayed Court opinion would provide the opportunity to use the moral consensus expressed in these resolutions as the foundation for enacting a program of mandatory sanctions against the regime of South Africa.

However, to the great surprise of almost all observers, in July 1966 the Court dismissed the claims of Liberia and Ethiopia without ruling on the merits of the case.[69] In an eight-to-seven decision, the Court ruled that the applicants had no legal right or interest in the subject matter of their claim and this, hence, made it unnecessary for the Court to rule on the merits of the case. This decision was reached after the Court had taken 336 hours of oral testimony, 3,756 pages of evidence, and in six years had held 112 court sessions devoted largely to the merits of the case.

This decision came as a particular setback to the African states. From 1960 to 1966 their strategy had been premised upon an eventual International Court condemnation of South Africa which would provide the needed leverage to gain some form of direct United Nations presence in South-West Africa. A sense of profound bitterness at this session was directed by these states at the Court and at the Western states that had supported six long years of Court proceedings as the reasonable procedure to obtain a redress of grievances.

As could be expected, the twenty-first session of the General Assembly in 1966 was marked by a venting of much of this bitterness and by a search for a new strategy for asserting United Nations authority over South-West Africa. The strategy hit upon was for the General Assembly by a resolution to terminate the mandate and set up an ad hoc committee to recommend means by which South-West Africa should be administered.[70] The following year the Assembly established a United Nations Council for South-West Africa to administer the territory until it achieved independence, renamed South-West Africa "Namibia" after the Namibian Desert along its Western shore, and created the post of United Nations

Commissioner for Namibia.[71] While this resolution was approved by the General Assembly, the vote was far from decisive. The eighty-five states supporting the resolution were from the expected quarters of Africa, Asia, the Caribbean, and Latin America plus Cyprus, Greece, Israel, Spain, and Yugoslavia. While no one should have been surprised by the negative votes of Portugal and South Africa, the large number of abstentions—thirty— was a disappointment to the sponsors. This was particularly so in the case of the United States, where the final decision rested on a judgment that the course which the resolution set, if followed, would lead either to chaos and bloodshed in southern Africa or more likely to complete frustration of the United Nations efforts.

By late 1970 the Council for Namibia had still been unable to enter the territory. South Africa has maintained that any attempt by the United Nations to terminate its mandate for the territory was clearly illegal. Prodded by the Council for Namibia and the African states, the Security Council in 1969 began to take a more active role on the issue. On March 20, 1969, the Security Council called on South Africa "to immediately withdraw its administration from the territory" and set October 4, 1969, as the deadline for the withdrawal.[72] The deadline was not met. The Security Council responded by outlining steps of a political and economic nature that might be taken by members to assert the illegality of the continued control of Namibia by South Africa.[73] The Security Council also requested an advisory opinion of the International Court on the question of legal consequences for states of South Africa's continued presence in Namibia.[74]

PORTUGUESE TERRITORIES

While in no sense attracting the same attention as South Africa and Southern Rhodesia, Portugal's territories in Africa are also a focus of United Nations efforts at decolonization. In fact, of all the European colonial powers, Portugal has managed to hold its grip on its African possessions —the major ones being Angola, Mozambique, and Portuguese Guinea— the longest and with the most determination. In July 1963 the Security Council called upon Portugal to (1) recognize immediately the right of the territories to self-determination and independence; (2) cease repressive measures and withdraw all military forces; (3) grant unconditional political amnesty; and (4) negotiate with nationalist groups with a view to the transfer of power leading to immediate independence.[75] Portugal's refusal to accept the resolution or even to recognize United Nations competency in this area is based upon its claim that it is constitutionally a unitary state and hence its African territories are really provinces, not colonies.

Portugal's insistent refusal to yield its position on this issue has been met by a steady stream of United Nations declarations and resolutions of condemnation and calls for further United Nations action. In 1965, at its twentieth session, the General Assembly called upon member states to break off or refrain from establishing diplomatic and consular relations with Portugal; to close ports to ships flying the Portuguese flag or in the service of Portugal; to prohibit their ships from entering ports in Portugal and its colonial territories; to refuse landing and transit facilities to all Portuguese aircraft; and to boycott all trade with Portugal. This resolution also called on NATO members to stop the sale of arms to Portugal and to refrain from providing any assistance that could be used by Portugal to continue its repression of the African populations in its territories.[76]

The ultimate impact of the numerous United Nations resolutions on Portuguese policy toward its African territories appears most uncertain. Indeed, much of the United Nations attention to the Portuguese territories has been diverted to Southern Rhodesia since that regime declared its independence in 1965. It appears that the greatest pressure for a modification of Portugal's colonial policy is likely to come from the economic burden on Portugal of the defense and security costs involved in suppressing various guerrilla movements in the territories. It is now estimated that approximately 40 percent of Portugal's national budget is spent on such defense costs.

THE UNITED NATIONS AND DECOLONIZATION—LIMITS, LESSONS, AND PORTENTS

As the United Nations begins its twenty-sixth year of operation, there remain forty-four territories with more than 28 million inhabitants under colonial rule. Of these forty-four territories, five (Southern Rhodesia, Namibia, and the Portuguese-administered territories of Angola, Mozambique, and Guinea) represent critical problems of decolonization that have so far defied solution by the organization. The other thirty-nine territories represent in the most literal sense "the remnants of empire." Representative of this latter group are the Cocos (Keeling) Islands with an area of 5 square miles and a population of 684; the Falkland Islands with an area of 4,618 square miles and a population of 2,000; American Samoa with an area of 76 square miles and a population of 31,000; and Gibraltar with an area of 2 square miles and a population of 25,000. In only a few cases have these small territories attracted the sustained attention of the United Nations.

United Nations activity in the area of decolonization has developed a recognizable pattern. The General Assembly has become a source of constantly escalating demands for immediate independence directed toward the administering powers. In order to maintain constant pressure on the recalcitrant colonial regimes, the anticolonial forces have succeeded in creating a number of subsidiary United Nations organs to focus exclusively on one or several aspects of decolonization. Figure 1 outlines the current United Nations organs active in this area. These subsidiary bodies have

FIGURE 1

UNITED NATIONS ORGANS AND BODIES DIRECTLY DEALING WITH
VARIOUS ASPECTS AND MANIFESTATIONS OF
APARTHEID, RACIAL DISCRIMINATION, AND COLONIALISM

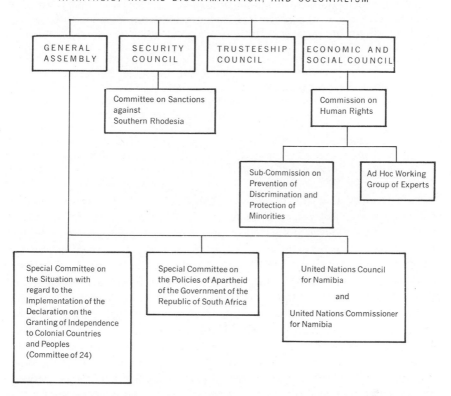

generally had memberships composed of even a greater proportion of anti-colonial states than the general membership of the United Nations. Two of the subsidiary organs, the Committee of 24 and the Special Committee on the Policies of Apartheid, have repeatedly demanded Security Council action, including mandatory sanctions and the consideration of the use of armed force as a means of bringing the colonial powers of southern Africa to account. These demands have then been endorsed, although usually after some moderation, by the General Assembly and then referred to the Security Council. To date, the Security Council has only partially—principally in the case of Southern Rhodesia—acceded to these demands for action.

With regard to the hard-core problems of southern Africa, coercive action of the Security Council has become fixed as the goal of the anti-colonial forces within the United Nations. However, the Western members of the Security Council, particularly the United Kingdom and the United States, appear determined to block with their vetoes any further escalation of the confrontation between the United Nations and the regimes of

southern Africa. The secretary-general's comments in reviewing progress
in decolonization since 1969 appear particularly relevant.

> Since that time (1969), some constitutional progress has been
> registered in certain of the dependent Territories. The fact remains, how-
> ever, that, on the whole, the intervening period has been one of con-
> tinuing disappointment and frustration. The complete achievement of
> the goals for colonial peoples laid down in the Charter appears to be
> beyond immediate reach, and is still eluding peaceful realization in
> several Territories. In southern Africa, for instance, the expectations
> aroused by the adoption, nine years ago, of the Declaration on the
> Granting of Independence to Colonial Countries and Peoples have so far
> met with utter disappointment. Indeed there are disquieting signs that
> those expectations may soon be turning into scepticism of the inter-
> national community's readiness to assist effectively the dependent peo-
> ples in that part of the world to translate into reality their legitimate
> aspirations to freedom and independence.[77]

It is clear that the major remaining decolonization crisis involves
southern Africa. The issues at stake for the United Nations in this crisis
exceed any previous decolonization crisis. Pushed by a majority of the
organization's members, the United Nations has clearly staked its prestige
behind the early independence with black rule for this region. The African
states continue to proclaim the colonial problem to be the number one
international problem. More importantly for the organization, they have
repeatedly demonstrated that they intend to judge the value of the United
Nations according to how successful it is in eliminating the colonial regimes
of southern Africa. For their part, the regimes of southern Africa have
convincingly demonstrated that they have no intention of yielding their
positions to mere United Nations resolutions or even mandatory economic
sanctions. In the near future there appears to be no prospect for the United
Nations changing the nature of the regimes in southern Africa unless its
members are willing to sanction the use of a large measure of military
force. France, United Kingdom, and United States appear ready to repeatedly use their veto in the Security Council to block just such a confrontation.

In short, if this analysis is correct, the United Nations is faced with
the problem of being forced, by a majority of its members, to deal with the
problems of southern Africa with little prospect for success. And since
these same members view the success of the United Nations in removing
colonialism from southern Africa as the principal criteria of the United
Nations' success, this impasse is likely to pose a serious threat to their
commitment to the United Nations. The most immediate test of the prestige
of the United Nations is in regard to Southern Rhodesia and Namibia. If
Southern Rhodesia is able to continue to thrive in the face of United Nations sanctions or if the United Nations remains unable to exercise its
self-proclaimed writ in Namibia, the organization's credibility will have
suffered a major blow.

The African states' continued belief in the primacy of the colonial problem at a time when virtually no one else would rank it first, coupled with the United Nations inability to successfully grapple with the problem, poses a serious threat to the viability of the institutional processes of the United Nations. Frustrated by the lack of progress in decolonization, the African states have now begun to attempt to delay and manipulate the international community's response to more crucial issues of survival—such as nonproliferation of nuclear weapons—in order to gain marginal bargaining power on colonial issues. If the colonial question comes to dominate every United Nations organ, as it may, then a significant incentive will have been created for avoiding, where possible, United Nations consideration of major issues.

The unresolved colonial problems of southern Africa and the very intense feelings on the issue held by a majority of the United Nations membership holds the real prospect of poisoning the United Nations political process. Unless new methods of modifying the racial policies of the white regimes of southern Africa are discovered, one can confidently predict a growing disenchantment on the part of the African with the United Nations. That this struggle will inevitably take on racial overtones only increases its destructive potential.

NOTES

1. The author wishes to acknowledge the assistance of the Graduate Research Committee of the University of Wisconsin, Madison, in supporting the research covered in this study.

2. Emil J. Sady, *The United Nations and Dependent Peoples* (Washington, D.C.: Brookings Institution, 1956), p. 3.

3. One striking measure of the drive to colonial empire in the latter part of the nineteenth century is that before 1875 less than one-tenth of Africa had been claimed by European states whereas by 1895 less than one-tenth remained unclaimed by European states. C. J. H. Hayes, *A Generation of Materialism, 1871–1900* (New York: Harper & Row, 1944), p. 236.

4. R. N. Chowdhuri, *International Mandates and Trusteeship Systems* (The Hague: Nijhoff, 1955), pp. 22–24.

5. James N. Murray, Jr., *The United Nations Trusteeship System* (Urbana: University of Illinois, 1957), p. 9.

6. League of Nations Covenant, Article 23(b).

7. The mandatory powers and the Class A mandates under their administration included United Kingdom: Iraq and Palestine; France: Syria and Lebanon.

8. The mandatory powers and the Class B mandates under their administration included United Kingdom: Tanganyika, Togoland, Cameroons; France: Togoland, Cameroons; Belgium: Ruanda-Urundi.

9. The mandatory powers and the Class C mandates under their administration included United Kingdom, New Zealand and Australia: Nauru; New Zealand: Western Samoa; Australia: New Guinea; Japan: North Pacific Islands; Union of South Africa: South-West Africa.

10. Detailed accounts of the operation of the mandate system can be

found in Chowdhuri, *International Mandates;* Quincy Wright, *Mandates Under the League of Nations* (Chicago: University of Chicago Press, 1930); Hessel Duncan Hall, *Mandates, Dependencies and Trusteeship* (Washington, D.C.: Carnegie Endowment for International Peace, 1948).

11. These limitations became most obvious in the case of the Japanese mandate of the North Pacific Islands. Serious suspicions, later proved well founded, that the Japanese were placing fortifications on these islands in violation of the mandate could never be clearly proved by the Permanent Mandates Commission because the Japanese tightly controlled access and information on these territories.

12. Leland M. Goodrich, *The United Nations* (New York: Crowell, 1959), p. 296.

13. The debate at the San Francisco Conference that swirled around the extent to which the United Nations was to be concerned with colonial problems is cogently set forth in Ruth B. Russell, *A History of the United Nations Charter. The Role of the United States, 1940–1945* (Washington, D.C.: Brookings Institution, 1958), pp. 808–842.

14. Sady, *Dependent Peoples,* p. 824.

15. David A. Kay, *The New Nations in the United Nations, 1960–1967* (New York: Columbia University Press, 1970), pp. 147–150.

16. UN Charter, Article 77(1).

17. *Ibid.,* Article 76. For a full exposition of the trusteeship system of the United Nations, see Chairman Edwards Toussiant, *The Trusteeship System of the United Nations* (New York: Praeger, 1956), and Murray, *United Nations Trusteeship System.*

18. The Charter provides in Articles 82 and 83 for the designation by an administering power of all or part of a trust territory as a strategic area. In such a case the supervisory functions of the United Nations are exercised by the Security Council rather than the General Assembly or Trusteeship Council. Only the United States availed itself of the right to declare its trust territory as a "strategic area."

19. Harold Karen Jacobsen, "The United Nations and Colonialism: A Tentative Appraisal," *International Organization,* XVI, No. 1 (Winter 1962), 45.

20. UN Charter, Article 73. Also Article 1(2) declares that one of the purposes of the United Nations is "to develop friendly relations among nations based on respect for the principle of equal rights, and self-determination of peoples." Significantly, for later developments, this provision was sponsored at the San Francisco Conference by the Soviet Union.

21. Kay, *New Nations,* pp. 149–150.

22. David A. Kay, "The Politics of Decolonization: The New Nations and the United Nations Political Process," *International Organization,* XXI, No. 4 (Autumn 1967), 786–811.

23. UN Document A/4501, September 23, 1960.

24. UN Document A/4502, September 23, 1960.

25. General Assembly, *Official Records* (15th sess.), 902nd plenary meeting, October 12, 1960, p. 687.

26. This account of the negotiations leading to the adoption of the declaration on colonialism draws on contemporary press reports in the *New York Times* of November 1960 and the many revealing remarks made by the delegates during the debate on the question.

27. Mehdi Vakil (Iran), quoted in General Assembly, *Official Records* (15th sess.), 926th plenary meeting, November 28, 1960, pp. 995–996.

28. UN Document A/L.323, November 28, 1960. Emphasis added.

29. General Assembly, *Official Records* (15th sess.), 945th plenary meeting, December 13, 1960, p. 1250.

30. General Assembly, *Official Records* (15th sess.), 931st plenary meeting, December 1, 1960, p. 1065.

31. General Assembly, *Official Records* (15th sess.), 947th plenary meeting, December 14, 1960, pp. 1272–1273.

32. For the view of the United States delegation see Senator Wayne Morse (Oregon), "The United States in the United Nations: 1960—a Turning Point," *Supplementary Report to the Committee on Foreign Relations, United States Senate* (Washington, D.C.: Government Printing Office, 1961), pp. 20–21.

33. General Assembly, *Official Records* (15th sess.), 947th plenary meeting, December 14, 1960, pp. 1273–1274.

34. *Ibid.*, p. 1283.

35. *New York Times,* December 16, 1960, p. 4; Thomas J. Hamilton, "Colonialism at the U.N.," *New York Times,* December 18, 1960, sec. 4, p. 9; and Morse, "Turning Point," pp. 20–21. According to Arthur Schlesinger,

> Our delegation even had the concurrence of the State Department in Washington in its desire to vote for the resolution. But the British were opposed, and Harold Macmillan called Eisenhower by transatlantic telephone to request American abstention. When an instruction to abstain arrived from the White House, James J. Wadsworth, then our ambassador to the UN, tried to reach Eisenhower to argue the case. Eisenhower declined to accept his call.

Arthur M. Schlesinger, Jr., *A Thousand Days: John F. Kennedy in the White House* (Boston: Houghton Mifflin, 1965), pp. 510–511.

36. General Assembly Resolution 1654 (XVI), November 27, 1961. In the idiom of the UN, the formal title of this body is the Special Committee on the Situation with Regard to the Implementation of the Declaration on the Granting of Independence to Colonial Countries and Peoples, often referred to as the Special Committee on Colonialism or the Special Committee of Twenty-Four (after 1962).

37. General Assembly Resolution 1654 (XVI), operative paragraph 5, under which the Assembly "directs the Special Committee to carry out its task by employment of all means which it will have at its disposal within the framework of the procedures and modalities which it shall adopt for the proper discharge of its functions."

38. Dean Rusk, "Parliamentary Diplomacy—Debate vs. Negotiations," *World Affairs Interpreter,* XXVI, No. 2, (July 1955) 122.

39. UN Document A/5238, October 8, 1962, p. 18.

40. UN Document A/5124, May 21, 1962, Annex I.

41. *Ibid.,* Annex III.

42. UN Document A/L.386/Rev. I and Add. 1–4, June 18–19, 1962.

43. General Assembly, *Official Records* (16th sess.), 1121st plenary meeting, June 28, 1962, p. 1549. The draft was adopted as General Assembly Resolution 1747 (XVI), June 28, 1962.

44. UN Document A/C.4/L.753, October 31, 1962.

45. UN Document A/5446/Add.3, July 30, 1963, Appendix.

46. *Ibid.*

47. UN Document S/5409, August 30, 1963.

48. UN Document S/5425, September 11, 1963.

49. General Assembly Resolutions 1883 (XVIII), October 14, 1963, and 1889 (XVIII), November 6, 1963.

50. UN Document A/Ac. 109/61, March 23, 1964.

51: UN Document A/Ac. 109/L.128, June 17, 1964.

52. UN Document A/Ac. 109/88, June 26, 1964.

53. UN Document A/5800/Add. I, Part II, December 22, 1964.

54. UN Document A/Ac. 109/SR. 315, November 19, 1964.

55. For example, during the period 1962–1964 Southern Rhodesia was considered at the following meetings of the Special Committee: 9, 11, 13–26, 37, 44–49, 53, 71, 107, 130–140, 143, 144, 146, 168, 171–177, 223–233, 245–249, 252, 254, 255, 258, 259, 262, 263, 268, 269, 271–273, 278, 286, 294–296, 315.

56. General Assembly Resolution 2012 (XX), October 12, 1965.

57. General Assembly Resolution 2022 (XX), November 5, 1965.

58. General Assembly Resolution 2024 (XX), November 11, 1965.

59. Security Council Resolutions 216, November 12, 1965, and 217, November 20, 1965.

60. Security Council Resolution 221, April 9, 1966.

61. *New York Times,* December 9, 1966, p. 22.

62. *New York Times,* December 17, 1966, p. 9.

63. Security Council Resolution 232, December 16, 1966.

64. General Assembly Resolution 1761 (XVII), November 6, 1962.

65. UN Document S/5471, December 4, 1963. For a full account of the political bargaining surrounding United Nations involvement with South Africa, see Kay, *New Nations.*

66. UN Document S/5658, April 20, 1964.

67. UN Document S/6210, March 2, 1965.

68. For an analysis of the issues surrounding the possible use of sanctions against South Africa, see Amelia C. Leiss (ed.), *Apartheid and United Nations Collective Measures: An Analysis* (New York: Carnegie Endowment for International Peace, 1965).

69. For a discussion of the legal issues and reasoning surrounding this decision, see John R. Stevenson, "Judicial Decisions," *American Journal of International Law,* LXI, No. 1 (January 1967), 116–210; Richard A. Falk, "The South-West Africa Cases: An Appraisal," *International Organization,* XXI, No. 1 (Winter 1967), 1–23; Ernst A. Gross, "The South-West Africa Case: What Happened?", *Foreign Affairs,* XLV, No. 1 (October 1966), 36–48.

70. General Assembly Resolution 2145 (XXI), October 27, 1966.

71. General Assembly Resolution 2248 (S-V), May 19, 1967.

72. Security Council Resolutions 264, March 20, 1969, and 269, August 12, 1969.

73. Security Council Resolution 283, July 29, 1970.

74. Security Council Resolution 284, July 29, 1970.

75. Security Council Resolution 180, July 31, 1963.

76. General Assembly Resolution 2107 (XX), December 21, 1965.

77. U Thant, "Dissappointment and Frustration," *Objective: Justice,* II, No. 2 (April 1970), 4.

Leo Gross

THE DEVELOPMENT OF INTERNATIONAL LAW
THROUGH THE UNITED NATIONS

INTRODUCTION

It is proposed to focus attention in this essay on the contribution of two
of the six principal organs of the United Nations to the development of
international law—the General Assembly and the International Court of
Justice. This is done for reasons of economy, and there is no intention
to imply that the other principal organs would not have to be considered
if a more comprehensive treatment of the subject were attempted. Certainly, the practice of the Security Council is a rich mine for legal exploration, but in principle and given its limited jurisdiction, the Council's
contribution would be chiefly in the area of the interpretation and application of the Charter. The work of the other two councils, the Economic and
Social Council and the Trusteeship Council, has largely been channeled
to the General Assembly. The Secretariat, through the legal opinions of
the secretary-general, has made a notable contribution to the interpretation
of the Charter and is also relevant from the point of view of general
international law. But it is the General Assembly which is charged by
Article 13(1) of the Charter with the task of initiating studies and making
recommendations for the purpose of "encouraging the progressive development of international law and its codification." The inclusion of the Court
hardly needs explanation or justification as traditionally international lawyers have looked to tribunals of arbitration and the predecessor of the
Court of the United Nations, the Permanent Court of International Justice
of the League of Nations, for substantial contributions to the development
of the law.

Before discussing the work of the Assembly and the Court, it may be
useful to trace briefly the development of international law prior to the
establishment of the United Nations. The final section will be concerned
with the prospects for the future.

THE DEVELOPMENT OF INTERNATIONAL LAW PRIOR TO THE UNITED NATIONS

The development of modern international law may be conveniently related
to the final stage of the wars against Napoleon in 1814–1815. During the
preceding period the doctrine of the classical writers including Vitoria,
Suarez, and Grotius, and the practice of states were concerned with laying
the foundations of the law of nations, the problems arising from the age of
discoveries, and the emergence, following the settlement of Westphalia of
1648, of a multiplicity of sovereign states which recognized no common
superior authority other than that of the fledgling law of nations. It seems
fitting, therefore, that the era of legal positivism and continuous technological progress marked initially by the Industrial Revolution was ushered in
by two significant acts of deliberate law creation: the provision in the
Final Act of the Congress of Vienna of June 9, 1815, concerning freedom
of navigation on international rivers, and the regulation signed at Vienna
on March 19, 1815, concerning the classification of diplomatic agents.
The latter was designed to clarify the ranking of diplomatic officials through
which the official business between states is conducted, their immunities
and privileges having been based on customary international law. The
former was intended, as the Permanent Court of International Justice
was to say a hundred years later in its advisory opinion in the *Jurisdiction
of the European Commission of the Danube* case, to do away with monop-
olistic controls by the riparian states which "not only hampered the
development of commerce but also tended to prevent the growth of international relations appropriate to a state of peace." [1] It may be noted in
passing that international regulation of the navigation on international
rivers such as the Rhine and the Danube was continued at several inter-
state conferences, including the Paris Peace Conference of 1919 following
World War I, and, insofar as the Danube is concerned, at the Peace
Conference of Paris in 1947 following World War II. The Statute on the
Regime of Navigable Waterways of International Concern adopted at
Barcelona in 1921 is a landmark in the efforts of liberalizing navigation
from oppressive national control. It may also be noted that the work
begun in Vienna in 1815 concerning diplomatic agents was substantially
completed at the United Nations conference held in Vienna in 1961, which
on April 16 adopted the Convention on Diplomatic Intercourse and Immunities. This convention, declares the preamble, is to contribute "to the
development of friendly relations among nations, irrespective of their differing constitutional and social systems." [2] The 1815 regulation was adopted
by eight monarchical powers (Austria, France, Great Britain, Portugal,
Prussia, Russia, Spain, and Sweden) which invited "the representatives of
other crowned heads to adopt the same regulations," whereas the 1961
conference was attended by representatives of eighty-one (seventy-five

members of the United Nations) states with widely differing political systems.

International lawmaking continued throughout the nineteenth century at an impressive pace. Relative political stability in Europe, the center of the then prevailing international system, may well have been a factor in the process but probably no more than that. The technological exploitation of scientific discoveries and the expanding commerce involving movement of goods and persons and communications of all sorts across national boundaries called for international regulation by means of treaties. The sovereign state, then as now, knows of no other way for transcending its own limitation—namely, that its writ runs only as far as its national boundaries and that any movement of persons, goods, or communications across its boundaries required the cooperation of its neighbors and its neighbors' neighbors. Customary international law relating to traffic across the seas solved the problem when it gradually gave scope and some precision to the principle of freedom of the high seas. But a more comprehensive and explicit regulation was achieved only in 1958 when the United Nations Conference on the Law of the Sea, attended by eighty-five states, adopted four conventions, two of which, the Convention on the High Seas and the Convention on the Territorial Sea and the Contiguous Zone, deal with various aspects of navigation.[3] However, the pressing demands for freer movement of goods, persons, and communication across the land, later across the air, and in the future across outer space could not and can not wait for principles and rules to develop through the usually slow process of customary law. An alternative method had to be adapted and adopted. The method of negotiating and adopting multilateral conventions —that is, treaties binding on more than two states—was selected. Bilateral treaties, treaties binding on two states only, have been used prior to and along with multilateral conventions but their usefulness as a tool of regulation in an increasingly interdependent world is limited. Where general problems require general regulation, the multilateral treaty is the instrument chosen by governments. As a supplement to such a treaty or where specific matters affecting the interests of and intercourse between two states are concerned, the bilateral treaty will continue to be used.

An example or two will illustrate the process. Postal communications had been the subject of numerous bilateral agreements which came to exhibit certain common features. A conference held in 1863 did not succeed in framing a multilateral convention but a conference of twenty-two states held in Berne in 1874 did and created the General Postal Union which in 1878 was expanded into the Universal Postal Union which is now one of the specialized agencies of the United Nations. It counts 135 participating states, more than any other international instrument and organization. The discovery and practical application of the telegraph led first to bilateral arrangements, but very soon the states responded to the need for a more comprehensive and uniform legal regulation by concluding the International Telegraph Convention in Paris in 1865. Initially, the treaty and the organization based on it comprised twenty states. As new discoveries were made—telephone and broadcasting—they too were brought under an international regime. A series of treaties led in 1932 to the creation of the International Telecommunications Union which has become a specialized agency of the United Nations and has a membership of 133 states.

During the fifty-year period 1864 to 1914, the year of the outbreak of World War I, numerous multilateral conventions were concluded on topics of relevance to the growing volume of transactions such as weights and measures, trademarks, copyrights, patents, and others where uniformity of law appeared desirable. To borrow a term from the United Nations International Law Commission, the states engaged on an unprecedented scale in the progressive development of international law.[4] During the same period states also attempted to codify certain aspects of customary international law, particularly the law of war and neutrality. This is a process which had its start with the Paris Declaration of 1856, which formulated four rules on naval warfare and which continued at several conferences, the latest of which is the Geneva Conference of 1949, which adopted four conventions.[5] The most important of these conferences were the first and second Hague Peace Conferences of 1899 and 1907, respectively, which, in addition to several conventions dealing with the law of war, also produced the Convention for the Pacific Settlement of International Disputes of 1899, revised in 1907. This convention provided for establishment of the still existing Permanent Court of Arbitration.[6] The Hague conferences mark the beginning of periodic conferences for both the codification and the progressive development of international law.[7] One of the most ambitious attempts at codification was the London Naval Conference of 1908–1909, growing out of The Hague Conference of 1907. This conference was remarkable for three reasons: first, it was intended to formulate the law of naval warfare and thereby make possible the establishment of the International Prize Court; second, it was the first major conference which had the benefit of thorough preparation; and, third, it was confronted with the problem of distinguishing between the codification of the "common law of nations" and its development.[8] Thorough preparation has come to be accepted as prerequisite for the subsequent activities of the League of Nations and the United Nations. The separation of codification from development has been accepted in principle, but abandoned in practice, by both the League and the United Nations.

The establishment of the League of Nations provided the first opportunity for a sustained effort for both the development and codification of international law. Unlike the conventions of the nineteenth century which were linked to functional organizations with a single purpose, like the postal and telegraph agencies, the League was a multipurpose institution with an elaborate infrastructure including a highly efficient and sophisticated Secretariat. The League provided the auspices for many conferences which resulted in over one hundred twenty international instruments covering a wide array of subjects: arbitration and security, unification of commercial law, agricultural credit, counterfeiting currency, customs, bones, hides and skins, unification of river law, railways, road traffic, humanitarian and social questions (traffic in women and children, obscene publications, slavery), and narcotics. Many of these instruments failed to enter into force, others merely served as models, and some continue in force, and the secretary-general of the United Nations has taken over the depository function with respect to them.[9]

Several League treaties which are still in force were amended by protocols or were further developed by additional treaties concluded under United Nations auspices. This was the case in the fields of control of narcotics and other dangerous drugs,[10] traffic in persons,[11] obscene publications,[12] economic statistics,[13] and slavery.[14] Partly as a result of the war in Vietnam, the United Nations gave prominence to the Geneva Protocol for the Prohibition of the Use in War of Asphyxiating, Poisonous or other Gases and of Bacteriological Methods of Warfare of June 17, 1925, which resulted from the work of the League in the field of security. The General Assembly on December 16, 1969, adopted Resolution 2603 (XXIV), in which it noted that (1) a majority of the states existing in 1925 adhered to the protocol; (2) since then further states have become parties to it; (3) other states have declared that they will abide by its principles and objectives; (4) those principles and objectives have commanded broad respect in the practice of states; and (5) the General Assembly, in its Resolution 2162B (XXI) of December 5, 1966, "without any dissenting vote, has called for the strict observance by all States of the principles and objectives of the Geneva Protocol."[15]

The League of Nations, after what seemed to be very careful preparation, failed in its one and only effort to codify substantial and controversial parts of customary international law. The topics selected were nationality, territorial waters, and responsibility of states for damage to the persons and property of aliens. A diplomatic conference of forty-seven governments, members and nonmembers of the League, was held at The Hague in 1930. No agreement was reached on territorial waters and responsibility of states. With respect to nationality, no agreement was reached on the main question, the principles which govern the acquisition of nationality. The delegates were able, however, to draft instruments relating to certain conflicts of nationality laws, to military obligations in certain cases of double nationality, and to certain cases of statelessness.[16] One of the factors generally believed to have caused difficulties was disagreement as to what the law actually was as well as the desire of certain governments to modify existing law which they considered unsatisfactory.[17] However, the "bases of discussion" drawn up by the Preparatory Committee for the conference enriched the literature on the subjects concerned. A by-product of the League's officials effort was the unofficial Harvard Research on International Law, organized by Professor Manley O. Hudson, which resulted in several draft conventions, the first three of which were devoted to the topics selected for The Hague conference.[18] Used all over the world by scholars and tribunals, the Harvard Research continues to serve as a standard work on the subjects with which it dealt and as a monument to Manley O. Hudson.

Even a short survey of the League's activities in the development of international law would be incomplete without mentioning the International Labor Organization which up to 1946 formed an integral though autonomous part of the League. Since then it has become an independent institution and a specialized agency of the United Nations which in 1971 had 121 members. The mission of the organization is to promote international peace through social justice and improvement of conditions of labor. During the period of its connection with the League, it adopted 67 International Labor Conventions and, since 1946, 63 more conventions were adopted. The organization also addressed 134 recommendations to the member states which were intended to influence their domestic legislation in the direction of social welfare. While the International Labor Conventions enter into force when ratified by two member states, some have received a very large number of ratifications: thus the Forced Labor Convention of 1930 was ratified by 106 members, the Freedom of Association and Protection of the Right to Organize Convention of 1948 by 77 members, and the Right to Organize and Collective Bargaining Convention of 1949 by 89 members. Altogether, the International Labor Conventions received 3,500 ratifications.[19] The United States of America is the champion nonratifier of International Labor Conventions, having ratified 2 out of some 130 conventions: the Minimum Age (Sea) Convention (Revised) of 1936, and the Certification of Able Seamen Convention of 1946.[20]

THE UNITED NATIONS

Concern with the Fundamental Bases of a New International Legal Order

The contributions of the United Nations to the development of international law have exceeded all expectations. Beginning with its first session in 1946, there has been a steady stream of resolutions, declarations, and conventions adopted by the General Assembly or by diplomatic conferences convened under its auspices. While there can be no doubt, after five and twenty years, about the Assembly's enthusiasm amounting almost to a passion for the progressive development of international law and through it of branches of municipal law, there has been and there remains a lingering doubt about its consistency and methodology in pursuing this task. It would seem that the Assembly selected whatever organ appeared most serviceable for a particular purpose or created a new one as convenience dictated, and cast the results of its work in whatever form—resolution, declaration, convention—was acceptable to its members. This process was bound to create problems—if not for the Assembly then at least for scholars who felt the need for evaluating, from the legal point of view, the significance of the new forms in which a good deal of the Assembly's contribution was cast, namely, resolutions and declarations, in preference to or in anticipation of the traditional form of conventions.

The first actions of the Assembly at the second part of its first session appear, in retrospect, to have set the pattern. Recognizing that the Charter in Article 13, paragraph 1 (a) laid an obligation upon it to initiate studies and make recommendations for "encouraging the progressive development of international law and its codification," the Assembly adopted on December 11, 1946, Resolution 94 (I) instituting a Committee of Seventeen Members to study the methods for carrying out this obligation.[21] However, without awaiting the recommendations of the committee, the assembly proceeded at once to the adoption of two resolutions which were neither in the nature of studies nor explicitly in the nature of recommendations as laid down in paragraph 1 (a) of Article 13. In Resolution 95 (I), adopted on the same day, the Assembly "*affirms* the principles of international law recognized by the Charter of the Nürnberg Tribunal and the judgment of the Tribunal." [22] In Resolution 96 (I) of the same day, the Assembly "*affirms* that genocide is a crime under international law . . . for the commission of which principals and accomplices . . . are punishable." The Assembly perceived no inconsistency in proceeding to request the Economic and Social Council, one of the principal organs of the United Nations, to undertake the necessary studies with a view to drawing up a draft convention on the crime of genocide.[23] The Council discharged its task and the Assembly two years later, on December 9, 1948, approved the Genocide Convention or, to give its full title, Convention on the Prevention and Punishment of the Crime of Genocide, by Resolution 260 (III).[24] Some seventy-five states have ratified or acceded to the convention in the usual manner, some with reservations, and some governments made objections to some of the reservations.[25] Here the Assembly affirmed the crime by resolution and in anticipation of the adoption of the convention. What was the legal significance of the resolution prior to the adoption of the convention? Suppose that for one reason or another the convention would never have been drafted or, if drafted, failed of adoption in the Assembly?

The further course of the Nuremberg principles is illustrative of the relevance of the latter question.

Having first committed itself to the affirmation of the principles of international law recognized by the Charter and the Judgment of the International Military Tribunal, the Assembly on November 21, 1947, adopted Resolution 177 (II) in which it entrusted the International Law Commission, whose members were to be elected in 1948, with the

formulation of the principles of international law recognized in the charter of the Nürnberg Tribunal and in the judgment of the Tribunal.[26]

The International Law Commission itself was established by Resolution 174 (II), adopted on the same day, and it did not begin to function until April 12, 1949, when it held its first session. The commission first debated the question "whether or not the Commission should ascertain to what extent the principles contained in the Charter and in the judgment constituted principles of international law." [27] Had the commission, some of whose members were out of sympathy with the post-World War II war crimes trials, particularly the crimes against peace, embarked on ascertaining what, if any, the principles of customary international law were which had found expression in the Charter and Judgment of the Tribunal, the result would have been in doubt. A finding supported only by a majority of the commission might well have been regarded as disavowing the Assembly's confident affirmation that there were indeed some principles of customary international law contained in the Charter and in the judgment. Some jurists may have been tempted to point out that the Assembly *appeared* to say one thing but meant another. What the Assembly appeared to declare and what the resolution was generally understood to imply, was that in the Assembly's view the Charter and the judgment were based on principles of customary international law; that, in other words, the 1945 Charter in formulating some principles which were highly controversial— such as individual responsibility for crimes against peace and humanity, denial of immunity for acts of state or acts done in conformity with national law, and others—merely gave expression to existing law. Others may have been inclined to interpret the resolution as implying that *if or to the extent that* the Charter and the tribunal contained principles of customary international law, they were affirmed by the Assembly. The decision of the commission, in the light of these alternatives, was becomingly diplomatic, namely that "since the Nürnberg principles had been unanimously affirmed by the General Assembly in Resolution 95 (I) of 11 December 1946, the task entrusted to the Commission was not to express any appreciation of those principles as principles of international law but merely to formulate them." [28]

The subsequent course taken in the Assembly with regard to the Nuremberg principles was anticlimactic. The commission formulated seven principles in 1950 and transmitted them to the Assembly.[29] The Assembly, having lost its initial fervor, neither adopted nor rejected them. Instead, it decided by Resolution 488 (V), adopted on December 12, 1950, to send them to the member states for comments and instructed the commission to take such comments into account in drafting the Code of Offences against the Peace and Security of Mankind.[30] Thus the Nuremberg principles became linked with the major project of the code which still gathers dust in the archives of the United Nations because this code in turn was linked with yet another project—namely, that of defining aggression— which is still under the active consideration of a committee of the Assembly.

Pursuant to Resolution 488 (V), referred to above, the commission submitted a draft in 1951, a draft Code of Offences against the Peace

THE DEVELOPMENT OF INTERNATIONAL LAW

and Security of Mankind, but this was not considered at the 1951 session nor was it considered at the 1952 session of the Assembly. In the meantime, the Assembly by Resolution 378 (V) of November 17, 1950, had, at the behest of the Soviet Union, requested the commission to define the concept of aggression. The commission, after some hesitation, included a definition in the draft code which it submitted to the Assembly in 1954 in the following terms:

> The following acts are offences against the peace and security of mankind:
>
> (1) Any act of aggression, including the employment by the authorities of a State of armed forces against another State for any purpose other than national or collective self-defence or in pursuance of a decision or recommendation of a competent organ of the United Nations.
>
> (2) Any threat by the authorities of a State to resort to an act of aggression against another State.[31]

It is certainly not surprising that the Assembly was not satisfied with this definition. It proceeded, beginning in 1952, with the establishment of special committees which were charged with the task of defining aggression. None of them succeeded in reaching a consensus on the definition of this elusive concept.[32] The latest Special Committee, established in 1967, was urged to submit a definition to the twenty-fifth anniversary session. This the committee failed to do, but it did report that "it did not have sufficient time to complete its task" and recommended to the Assembly that it be invited "to resume its work as early as possible in 1971." [33] No doubt the Assembly will accept the Special Committee's recommendation. It remains to be noted that by Resolution 1186 (XII) of December 11, 1957, the General Assembly transmitted the 1954 draft code of offences to the member governments for comment. Since then the draft code did not appear on the agenda of the Assembly.[34]

To round out the picture of the several interlocking efforts of the Assembly stemming from its 1946 affirmation of the Nuremberg principles, mention should be made of the work on the question of an international criminal court. This was initiated by Resolution 260B (III) adopted by the Assembly on December 9, 1948. In it the Assembly requested the International Law Commission

> to study the desirability and possibility of establishing an international judicial organ for the trial of persons charged with genocide or other crimes over which jurisdiction will be conferred upon that organ by international conventions.[35]

The Assembly also requested the commission to consider the possibility of establishing "a Criminal Chamber of the International Court of Justice." Fortunately, the commission did not pursue this idea and generally did not manifest much enthusiasm for the project. Accordingly, a committee was

established, by Resolution 489 (V) of December 12, 1950, which produced
a draft statute for an international criminal court. Consideration of it,
however, was postponed in 1954 and again in 1957 since this project related to the draft Code of Offences and the task of defining aggression.[36]
Thus, nearly twenty-five years after the adoption of the initial resolution
affirming the Nuremberg principles, the Assembly has failed to carry out
the several projects to which it was impelled by a certain internal logic.
It was certainly logical for the Assembly to want to be sure what the principles were to which it had subscribed, although if logic had been the guide
of the Assembly in the first place it would have considered the formulation
of the principles before affirming them. However, having reversed the
order of formulation and affirmation, it was logical to want to place the
principles in the larger framework of a Code of Offences against the Peace
and Security of Mankind including, as the 1954 draft does, the crime of
genocide. The desire for a definition of aggression and the statute for a
permanent international criminal court already envisaged in the 1948
Genocide Convention[37] was a logical outgrowth of the related projects.
In a larger sense, so was the project for a formulation of a draft declaration
on the rights and duties of states, which the International Law Commission
was instructed to prepare by Resolution 178 (II) of November 21, 1947.
The draft elaborated by the commission at its first session in 1949 consists
of fourteen articles, some of which are restatements of principles contained
in the Charter of the United Nations and the 1928 Kellogg-Briand Pact, or
generally found in textbooks on international law. The most remarkable
and therefore probably the most objectionable principle is contained in Article 14:

> Every State has the duty to conduct its relations with other States in ac-
> cordance with international law and with the principle that the sover-
> eignty of each State is subject to the supremacy of international law.[38]

This principle is as elementary as it is self-evident, and the wonder is that
the commission found it necessary to make it explicit. Any normative conception of international law as a law governing relations between states can
settle for no less but the General Assembly, which obviously had second
thoughts about this matter as about the Nuremberg principles, the draft
Code of Offences, and international criminal jurisdiction was quite willing
to settle for the rather lame statement in Resolution 375 (V) of December
6, 1949, in which it deemed the draft declaration

> a notable and substantial contribution towards the progressive develop-
> ment of international law and its codification and as such commends it
> to the continuing attention of Member States and of jurists of all na-
> tions.[39]

If the project of a draft declaration of the rights and duties of states
needs to be excused and explained, it can be excused and explained by

the relative immaturity of the Assembly and perhaps of the commission as well. The Assembly cannot invoke this ground, however, when it embarked on a somewhat analogous project in 1962 by resolving

> to undertake, pursuant to Article 13 of the Charter, a study of the principles of international law concerning friendly relations and co-operation among States in accordance with the Charter with a view to their progressive development and codification, so as to secure their more effective application.[40]

For all except one of the seven principles eventually selected for study, progressive development and codification, are contained in the Charter[41] and several of them were included, albeit in a somewhat different form, in the draft Declaration of Rights and Duties of States. Nonetheless, in 1963 the Assembly established a Special Committee on Principles of International Law concerning Friendly Relations and Co-operation among States which labored for six years. Under continuous prodding of the Assembly, the Special Committee finally submitted in 1970 a draft Declaration on Principles of International Law concerning Friendly Relations and Co-operation among States "as expressing the consensus of the delegations' members of the Drafting Committee." [42] This draft declaration "on" rather than "of" principles—a subtle nuance—reached the twenty-fifth anniversary session of the United Nations in the nick of time. By Resolution 2625 (XXV) adopted on October 24, 1970, the "draft declaration" became simply the "declaration" in which the Assembly declared *inter alia:*

> *Deeply convinced* that the adoption of the Declaration on Principles of International Law concerning Friendly Relations and Co-operation among States in accordance with the Charter of the United Nations on the occasion of the twenty-fifth anniversary of the United Nations would contribute to the strengthening of world peace and constitute a landmark in the development of international law and of relations among the States, in promoting the rule of law among nations and particularly the universal application of the principles embodied in the Charter,
>
> Considering the desirability of the wide dissemination of the text of the Declaration,
>
> 1. *Approves* the Declaration on Principles of International Law concerning Friendly Relations and Co-operation among States in accordance with the Charter of the United Nations, the text of which is annexed to the present resolution;
>
> 2. *Expresses its appreciation* to the Special Committee . . . for its work resulting in the elaboration of the Declaration;
>
> 3. *Recommends* that all efforts be made so that the Declaration becomes generally known.[43]

Thus came to end another effort to come to grips with fundamental problems of international law and relations. The very title of the declaration represents a victory for the United States and its supporters who were determined to sidetrack the original Soviet proposal for a codification of the principles of peaceful coexistence. The action of the Assembly in 1970 closely parallels its action in 1949 with respect to the draft Declaration of the Rights and Duties of States: it approves the declaration and it recommends that it become generally known. More innocuous words could not have been chosen. Whatever intrinsic merit the declaration of 1970 may have was further diminished by the words "in accordance with the Charter of the United Nations" which did not appear in the title given to the declaration by the Special Committee.[44] Thus the principles of international law must be read in conformity with the Charter as the overriding law. That this is so appears from the formulation of some of the principles themselves. Thus the principle on the nonuse of force—Article 2(4) of the Charter—is elaborated in several paragraphs, the last of which reads:

> Nothing in the foregoing paragraphs shall be construed as enlarging or diminishing in any way the scope of the provisions of the Charter concerning cases in which the use of force is lawful.[45]

The second and third principles on the settlement of disputes and nonintervention in matters of domestic jurisdiction, respectively, contain similar clauses safeguarding the law of the Charter.[46]

To make doubly sure that the protracted labor of the Special Committee has no impact upon the Charter, the 1970 resolution, in a section entitled "General Part," declares:

> Nothing in this Declaration shall be construed as prejudicing in any manner the provisions of the Charter or the rights and duties of Member States under the Charter or the rights of peoples under the Charter, taking into account the elaboration of these rights in this Declaration.

The Assembly further declares:

> The principles of the Charter which are embodied in this Declaration constitute basic principles of international law, and consequently appeals to all States to be guided by these principles in their international conduct and to develop their mutual relations on the basis of the strict observance of these principles.[47]

It is obvious that the declaration is the product of contradictory policies with respect to the Charter and its elaboration by means other than the formal amendment provided for in Article 108. Hence the ambiguity in the formulation of the principle of interpretation and the paradoxical proposition that, on the one hand, the Charter principles are principles of international law and that, on the other hand, these principles should guide all states in their conduct. One may legitimately wonder whether the description of the Charter principles as "guides" was intended to raise or diminish their binding force as principles of international law.

To return to the starting point of this necessarily brief and incomplete analysis of one phase of the efforts to promote the development of international law, what is the nature of the contribution in legal terms? I suggest the affirmation of the Nuremberg principles by the Assembly, the further resolutions of the Assembly, the work of the International Law Commission on the draft Declaration of Rights and Duties of States and the draft code of Offences against the Peace and Security, and finally the work of the Special Committee on Principles of International Law and its qualified endorsement by the General Assembly have enriched the legal literature on some basic problems of international law and relations. The hesitant attitude of the Assembly, reflecting the divergent policies of members, rules out any confident statement that the various principles, other than those embodied in the Charter itself, are legally binding. They may become legally significant, even legally binding, but that will depend on the conduct of the member states.

We would be living in a different world if the various projects dealing with fundamental aspects of a new legal order had been brought to fruition, but it seems that we shall have to live in a different world in order to be able to bring them to fruition.

The Development of International Law through International Conventions

On the more mundane level of the work of the International Law Commission there has been impressive progress indeed. Created in 1947 with a membership of 15, raised to 21 and 25 in 1956 and 1961, respectively, the commission's mandate has been both progressive development and codification of international law.[48] Broadly representative of the membership of the United Nations, of old and new states, of the main forms of civilization, of the principal legal system and geographic regions, the commission's members are elected and serve for terms of five years in their individual capacities. Nonetheless, several members of the commission are officials of their governments, while others are selected from law faculties and the bar. Far from detracting from the efficiency of the commission, this mixture of independent and official experts has been regarded as one of its assets, along with the fact that members of the commission serve only in a part-time capacity. The commission usually holds one session annually, lasting for several weeks. The latter feature has been regarded as a shortcoming by those who found the pace of work disappointingly slow and therefore advocated that the commission be transformed into a full-time body. On the other hand, the part-time character of the commission, in the words of one of its members,

> seems to have encouraged the type of professional representation which has been found in the Commission almost since its initiation—academic lawyers working harmoniously alongside professional diplomats with some general legal training and much practical experience, a goodly

number of experienced legal advisers of Ministries for Foreign Affairs, and some experienced general lawyers, including national judges. This has provided the Commission with sufficient expertise on the specific topics of international law which it was considering at a given moment, an adequate leavening of impractical legal philosophizing, and a similar adequate leavening of the chronic impatience of the shrewd practical lawyer and diplomat at scholasticism, pedantry and mere academic brilliance.[49]

Apart from its composition, the method of work adopted by the commission deserves a great deal of credit for its accomplishments. The statute of the commission lays down the general guidelines for both progressive development and codification. The feature common to both is the provision for submission of draft articles to the governments directly for their comments as well as to the General Assembly. There is a degree of overlapping here as the governments may make their comments directly to the commission in response to its request but they also, and much more frequently, comment on the draft articles and the underlying conceptions in the Legal (Sixth) Committee of the General Assembly, which is composed of all members of the United Nations. The result has been a "marriage of governmental reaction and professional expert investigation by the International Law Commission" and an awareness of the political as well as juridical implications of the commission's work at various stages.[50] This process ensures the success of the diplomatic conferences which were convened by the Assembly to adopt the draft articles prepared by the commission with a minimum of amendments. The formulation of the draft articles accompanied by extensive commentaries reflects the opinion of governments as expressed in comments and debates in the Assembly. Although the commission appoints one of its members as rapporteur for each of the projects, who is responsible for the research and the initial drafting, the result is probably as much due to his scholarship, drafting skill, and tact as to the collective wisdom of the commission. Further refinements of the commission's method of work have been to entrust a large measure of responsibility for the substantive formulation of the draft articles to a Drafting Committee, to shun formal voting, and to seek consensus instead.[51] It was a simplification if not a refinement of its work for the commission to gradually emancipate itself from the distinction laid down in the statute, as noted earlier, between progressive development and codification of international law. That distinction had already complicated the work of the London Naval Conference of 1908 [52] and of the League of Nations Codification Conference of 1930.[53] Only one of the products of the International Law Commission, the Geneva Convention on the High Seas, of April 29, 1958, declares in the preamble that the parties to that convention desired "to codify the rules of international law relating to the high seas." [54] The other conventions are silent on this point, although the last three conventions contain language which may be construed as an indirect reference to codification.[55] There are certainly good reasons for minimizing the distinction between progressive development and codification, no matter how sound the distinction may be on theoretical grounds, in the practice of the commission. Any statement which the commission or a convention may make about the nature of the rules would certainly not be conclusive, although it would be relevant. The evaluation of the conventions drafted by the commission as progressive development or codification is best left to the writers, the practitioners, and the courts.[56]

In discussing the work of both the International Law Commission and the General Assembly in the development of international law, it is essential not to lose sight of an imponderable by-product: namely, the participation of new states. Many of them entered the international community with a negative or, at the very least, highly critical attitude with respect to the inherited body of customary international law. The view has often been expressed by their spokesmen that this body of law reflected not their interests but the interests of the dominant colonialist powers and that, in any event, it was not attuned to the needs of a changed and still changing international society, a society multiracial in character and exhibiting different constitutional and social systems. Through participation in the debates in the commission, particularly since its enlargement to twenty-five members in 1961, in the General Assembly and its Sixth Committee, and finally in the diplomatic conferences on the law of the sea in Geneva in 1958 and 1960, on diplomatic relations, consular relations, and the law of treaties in Vienna in 1961, 1963, and 1968–1969, respectively, they have had a full opportunity to state their positions, defend their interests, and make the weight of their votes felt. Statistical evidence of their participation in debates on international law questions may not be a reliable indication of their interests. Other governments friendly and sympathetic to their views may have taken up the cudgel for them. Moreover, dissatisfaction with the law is by no means limited to new states. And, finally, some of the new states may still be short of qualified personnel both at home and abroad.

The topics selected by the commission, it must fairly be noted, were not of especial interest to the new nations. The year 1960 was the year in which a substantial number of formerly colonial territories were admitted to membership in the United Nations. Prior to that the commission was engaged in drafting articles on the law of the sea, a project which is of considerable interest to a number of new states, but the diplomatic conference on the law of the sea took place in 1958, that is, before their admission. The second and unsuccessful Law of the Sea Conference took place in 1960 for the purpose of defining the extent of the territorial sea and thus to complete the work of 1958. That conference, however, also was held prior to their admission. The subsequent topics—diplomatic and consular relations and the law of treaties—are of general interest and the new states took a particularly active part in the elaboration of the law of treaties. The subjects of the responsibility of states and succession of states and governments may offer a better test of the interest and participation of new states. In the meantime, it is natural that they should concentrate their resources on matters such as decolonization and economic development which are "bread and butter" issues to them.[57]

At its first session in 1949, the sense of the commission was "that while the codification of the whole of international law was the ultimate objective, it was desirable for the present to begin work on the codification of a few of the topics, rather than to discuss a general systematic plan, which might be left to later elaboration." [58] This has, so far remained the policy of the commission. However, at its 1969 session the commission confirmed "its intention of bringing up to date in 1971 its long-term programme of work, taking into account the General Assembly recommendations and the international community's current needs." [59] At its first session the commission reviewed twenty-five topics and drew up a provisional list of fourteen topics for codification. Five of these topics have so far not been dealt with and some or all of these may be discarded in 1971. These are recognition of states and governments, jurisdictional immunities of states and their property, the right of asylum, the treatment of aliens, and jurisdiction with regard to crimes committed outside national territory. Of the nine topics selected for codification three were given priority—the law of treaties, arbitral procedure, and the regime of the high seas—and rapporteurs were appointed. The remaining six topics were succession of states and governments; the regime of territorial waters; nationality, including statelessness; diplomatic intercourse and immunities; consular intercourse and immunities; and state responsibility. The result of the commission's work on these nine topics can be summarized briefly.

It may be convenient to begin with a topic which was not crowned with success—namely, arbitral procedure. In 1953 the commission submitted to the General Assembly a draft on arbitral procedure which received a largely hostile reception. This was due in substance to the basic conception of the draft—namely, that once states have voluntarily agreed to submit a dispute to arbitration they were legally bound to take all the subsequent steps required for the arbitration to take place (appointment of arbitrators and of an umpire, etc.), and that if either party failed to take any of those steps they would be taken by a third party. As interpreted by the Rapporteur, the Assembly rejected what it considered an attempt to deprive traditional arbitration of its diplomatic character and transform it into a "quasi-compulsory jurisdictional procedure." [60] A revised draft was prepared and adopted by the commission in 1958, and the Assembly took note of it. This is known as "Model Rules on Arbitral Procedure" and no further action was taken by the commission or the Assembly.[61]

The commission's work on nationality, including statelessness, fared somewhat better. No work was done on nationality as another organ of the United Nations, the Commission on the Status of Women, took in hand the question of the nationality of married women which had already appeared on the agenda of the League of Nations 1930 Codification Conference. Accordingly, the Commission on the Status of Women drafted a Convention on the Nationality of Married Women which was adopted by the

General Assembly in 1957.[62] With respect to statelessness, the commission prepared two drafts, one on the elimination and another on the reduction of future statelessness. The drafts were based on what turned out to be an erroneous impression, that the object in view was elimination and reduction of future statelessness. Since statelessness is the product of autonomous and conflicting national legislations and practices, changes in such legislations and practices were required in the drafts. The governments, however, seemed not disposed to make the necessary modifications in their legislation.[63] The Assembly, by Resolution 896 (IX) of December 4, 1954, left the door open for a diplomatic conference if at least twenty states expressed an interest in it. The United Nations Conference on the Elimination or Reduction of Future Statelessness was eventually held in Geneva in 1959 and thirty-five states participated. It adopted the commission's drafts as bases of discussion. This conference failed to reach agreement and another conference was held in New York City in 1961 which adopted the Convention on the Reduction of Statelessness on August 30, 1961. It may be noted that if in the interval no progress was made on the reduction of statelessness, progress was achieved on reducing the number of interested states. Only thirty states were represented at the second conference, only five states signed it, and only one of those (United Kingdom) ratified, and one (Sweden) acceded to it.[64]

The means for reduction of future statelessness are essentially two in number. According to Article I (1) of the convention, "a Contracting State shall grant its nationality to a person born in its territory who would otherwise be stateless." And, according to Article 8 (1), subject to stated exceptions, "a Contracting State shall not deprive a person of its nationality if such deprivation would render him stateless." [65] Unrelated to the International Law Commission are three instruments with respect to refugees and statelessness in the making of which the General Assembly or one of its subsidiary organs was involved.[66]

The work of the International Law Commission on the law of treaties and the regime of the high seas, given priority in 1949, was crowned with success. The work on the law of the high seas was expanded to include the regime of territorial waters, which was selected for codification without being accorded priority. In drawing up articles on these topics, the commission had the benefit of the advice of outside groups of experts.[67] The final report of the commission—covering, along with the traditional law of the high seas and territorial waters, the continental shelf and conservation of living resources of the sea—served as a basis of discussion of the United Nations Conference on the Law of the Sea held in Geneva in 1958, pursuant to General Assembly Resolution 1105 (XI) of February 21, 1957. It was attended by eighty-six states, including seventy-nine members of the United Nations. The conference adopted four substantive instruments: the Convention on the Territorial Sea and the Contiguous Zone, the Convention on the High Seas; the Convention on Fishing and Conservation of the Living Resources of the High Seas, and the Convention on the Continental Shelf.

The conference also adopted an Optional Protocol of Signature concerning the Compulsory Settlement of Disputes.[68] The question of the free access to the sea of landlocked countries was before the conference but not fully resolved. In 1965 the United Nations Conference on Transit Trade of Land-Locked Countries was held, and it adopted a convention under the same title.[69]

All four conventions of 1958 as well as the optional protocol entered into force. Thirty-seven states are parties to the Convention of the Territorial Sea, forty-four to that on the high seas, twenty-eight to that on fisheries, and forty to that on the continental shelf. Many states attached reservations to their ratifications and many states objected to some or all of them.[70] It will be recalled that only one of the conventions, that on the high seas, purports to codify the existing rules of international law. The rather low proportion of ratifying states to the number of states which had a hand in the drafting of the four conventions could be interpreted as an indication that the conventions are not fully responsive to the needs of many states. The optional protocol is binding on only twenty states which have ratified one of the four conventions and signed or ratified the optional protocol.[71]

As noted earlier, the 1958 Conference on the Law of the Sea was unable to agree on the breadth of the territorial sea. Therefore, a second conference was held in 1960 which was attended by eighty-two states. This conference failed by a narrow margin to adopt a proposal to fix the width of the territorial waters at six miles and the width of exclusive fishing rights at twelve miles.[72] The 1960 conference merely confirmed the existence of a firmly held position on the width of the territorial sea which first came into the open at the League of Nations Conference of 1930. Since then the international community has been functioning under the regime of what might be called "free-floating" boundaries of the territorial waters and fishing rights. A somewhat similar regime was adopted by the 1958 conference with respect to the delimitation of the continental shelf. As stated in Article 1 of the Convention on the Continental Shelf:

> For the purpose of these articles, the term "continental shelf" is used as referring (a) to the seabed and subsoil of the submarine areas adjacent to the coast but outside of the area of the territorial sea, to a depth of 200 metres, or, beyond that limit, to where the depth of the superjacent waters admits of the exploitation of the natural resources of the said areas; (b) to the seabed and subsoil of similar submarine areas adjacent to the coasts of islands.

The convention thus lays down a fixed limit—a depth of 200 meters—and a "moving" or "creeping" limit determined by the technological feasibility of exploitation. Inasmuch as by Article 2, "the coastal State exercises over the continental shelf sovereign rights for the purpose of exploring it and exploiting its natural resources," the "creeping" limit appeared to offer a privileged position to states with advanced technology and to penalize the so-called developing nations. At the very least, it seemed to deprive them of the benefits of the last source of mineral and other resources and a share in the produce of the exploitation of the seabed and the subsoil.

Thus the absence of agreement on the limit of the territorial sea and the "creeping" limit for the continental shelf [73] become entwined with the new problem of a politically acceptable legal regime for the seabed. In 1968 the Assembly established a committee with the somewhat long-winded title Committee on the Peaceful Uses of the Sea-Bed and the Ocean Floor beyond the Limits of National Jurisdiction. As a result of the committee's work and further debates in the Assembly's Political Committee, the General Assembly in 1969 adopted four resolutions. Only the first of these, Resolution 2574A (XXIV), is relevant in this context. It was adopted on December 15, 1969, by 65 votes to 12, with 30 abstentions, and requests the secretary-general

> to ascertain the views of Member States on the desirability of convening at an early date a conference on the law of the sea to review the regimes of the high seas, the continental shelf, the territorial sea and contiguous zone, fishing and conservation of the living resources of the high seas, particularly in order to arrive at a clear, precise and internationally accepted definition of the area of the sea-bed and ocean floor which lies beyond the limits of national jurisdiction, in the light of the international regime to be established for that area.[74]

The terms of the projected conference are very comprehensive indeed. The regime to which reference is made, as described in another resolution adopted on the same day, is to ensure the exploitation of the resources of the seabed and ocean floor "for the benefit of mankind, irrespective of the geographical location of States, taking into account the special interests and needs of the developing countries, whether land-locked or coastal." [75] As guideline for the conference which is scheduled for 1973, the Assembly adopted at its 1970 session a declaration according to which the resources of the seabed and ocean floor are "the common heritage of mankind" and their exploitation "shall be carried out for the benefit of mankind as a whole." And the president of the Assembly, Dr. Edvard Hambro (Norway), was quoted as having observed at the conclusion of the twenty-fifth session that "the seabed is being decolonized before it is colonized." [76] As a forecast for the projected conference, this does not sound unlikely at all given the present composition of the United Nations. The vast majority of its 127 members consists of new states, a large number of which were admitted since the 1958 Conference on the Law of the Sea and therefore had no share in its outcome.

In this context it may be conveniently noted that the 1970 session of the General Assembly, by 104 votes to 2, with 2 abstentions, adopted by Resolution 2660 (XXV) the Treaty on the Prohibition of the Emplacement of Nuclear and Other Weapons of Mass Destruction of the Sea-Bed and Ocean Floor. This treaty was drafted in substance by the United States and the Soviet Union and was submitted to the Assembly by the Geneva Conference of the Committee on Disarmament. Under its terms

> States which become parties would undertake not to place nuclear or
> other weapons of mass destruction on the floor of the sea outside of a
> zone beginning 12 miles off shore. Facilities for storing, testing or using
> such weapons would also be prohibited from that area. The Treaty contains provisions for verification under which any party may observe the
> activities of any other party carried out on the sea-bed.[77]

Surely this treaty marks a milestone in the efforts of the United Nations to ensure that the seabed and ocean floor are used essentially, though not exclusively, for peaceful purposes. Under the terms of the treaty not all military uses of the seabed and ocean floor are excluded. In this respect there is some analogy with the regime for outer space.[78]

The third topic accorded priority in 1949 by the International Law Commission, the law of treaties, was successively in the hands of four rapporteurs. The completion of work on this topic will probably rank as one of the great accomplishments of the commission. The draft articles with expert commentaries were discussed at two diplomatic conferences in Vienna in 1968 and 1969, convened pursuant to resolutions of the General Assembly of 1966 and 1967. In the same resolutions the Assembly had also decided that the results of the work of the conferences should be embodied in an international convention.[79] The Vienna Convention on the Law of Treaties of May 23, 1969, is the first comprehensive though not exhaustive "codification and progressive development of the law of treaties." [80] Some aspects of the law which have not been included in the Vienna convention will be handled by the commission separately. One of them is the succession in respect of treaties and the other is the question of treaties concluded between states and international organizations or between two or more international organizations.[81] The Vienna conference itself adopted a resolution recommending that the General Assembly refer the latter question to the International Law Commission inasmuch as the Vienna convention's scope is limited to treaties between states.

The Vienna Convention on the Law of Treaties is the product of an impressive collaboration between a very substantial number of states—103 attended the first and 110 the second session of the conference—of different social, political, and economic systems and varying stages of development. Success was made possible by the very thorough expert work of the commission and several consultations with governments and discussions in the Assembly's Sixth Committee. Since treaties are and will remain in the foreseeable future the main tool for conducting business between states and for developing international law, the importance of the Vienna convention can hardly be overestimated. As Rosenne put it: "With the law of treaties the codification effort is entering the core of the law." [82] The convention in its eighty-five articles represents a consensus and accommodation of a large variety of viewpoints for "no part of the Vienna Convention of 1969 was adopted by a bare two-thirds majority, but always by one well in excess of two-thirds." [83] Any attempt by the majority to dictate to the minority would obviously have jeopardized the ratification of the convention by important states.

It is not possible within the scope of this essay to provide more than a very brief reference to some of the more significant features of the convention. First of all, it must be noted that the convention is not retroactive; that is, it applies only to treaties concluded after its entry into force (Article 4). It includes both the *pacta sunt servanda* rule[84] and an elaborate formulation of the controversial *rebus sic stantibus* doctrine (Article 62). With regard to the relation between treaties and municipal law, the convention provides that "a party may not invoke the provisions of its internal law as justification for its failure to perform a treaty." This makes explicit one of the implications of the supremacy of international law over municipal law. With respect to the controversial question of the relevance of internal law regarding the competence of governments to conclude treaties, the convention reflects clearly the position of the internationalists although it makes allowance for the constitutionalists.[85] The desire for a more incisive formulation had to be compromised by the desire for accommodation.

The use of force against a state in procuring its consent to a treaty (duress) has traditionally *not* been regarded as vitiating its validity. In accordance with the prevailing trend to eliminate the use of force in international relations, the convention provides that "a treaty is void if its conclusion has been procured by the threat or use of force in violation of the principles of international law embodied in the Charter of the United Nations" (Article 52). To many of the new states, and others as well, this did not go far enough. To them any use of force, even in the more subtle form of economic coercion, is unacceptable. In a spirit of accommodation, the conference adopted a declaration included in its Final Act, in which it "solemnly condemns the threat or use of pressure in any form, whether military, political, or economic, by any State in order to coerce another State to perform any act relating to the conclusion of a treaty in violation of the principles of the sovereign equality of States and freedom of consent." [86] The declaration as such is not legally binding but it is relevant as an expression of international public policy.

Probably the most controversial and in a sense perhaps progressive principle incorporated in the convention is that of the so-called *jus cogens*. treaties insofar as their subject matter is concerned. In the future, this Traditionally, states enjoy a virtually unlimited autonomy in entering into autonomy is to be curtailed by the following principle in Article 53 of the Vienna convention:

> A treaty is void if, at the time of its conclusion, it conflicts with a peremptory norm of general international law (i.e., *jus cogens*). For the purpose of the present Convention, a peremptory norm of international law is a norm accepted and recognized by the international community of States as a whole as a norm from which no derogation is permitted

and which can be modified only by a subsequent norm of general international law having the same character.[87]

The inclusion of this new principle was strongly resisted by some states, particularly France. Article 53 does not contain a substantive definition of *jus cogens* norms, although the commission's commentary provides examples of what is sometimes thought to be a peremptory norm.[88] The inclusion of Articles 53 and 64 was made acceptable to a powerful minority only by providing a measure of compulsory settlement with regard to disputes concerning their application or interpretation. If a dispute is not settled through the means indicated in Article 33 of the Charter of the United Nations,[89] any one of the parties to the dispute may, in virtue of Article 66(a), submit it to the International Court of Justice by a written application. They may also by common consent agree to submit the dispute to arbitration. Article 66(a) is not free from ambiguity as it does not stipulate that the Court shall have compulsory jurisdiction if a unilateral application is made by one of the parties to the dispute.

The prevailing reluctance to accept the compulsory jurisdiction of the Court can also be seen in Article 65 which lays down the procedure to be followed with respect to invalidity, termination, withdrawal from or suspension of the operation of a treaty on any of the grounds stated in the convention including fundamental change of circumstances (*rebus sic stantibus*). If a party invokes any of these grounds and the other party raises objections within three months, the parties are bound to seek a solution through the means indicated in Article 33; that is, through mutual consent or unilaterally, by setting in motion the procedure for conciliation specified in an annex to the convention. The Commission of Conciliation shall first seek an amicable settlement of the dispute and, failing that, make a nonbinding recommendation for consideration of the parties. The convention is silent about the consequences of a failure of the parties to settle the dispute amicably with or without the assistance of the Conciliation Commission, thus leaving a gap in the progressive development of international law.

Of the other six topics selected in 1949 for codification without being accorded priority, two more have been completed: diplomatic intercourse and immunities and consular intercourse and immunities. Held in Vienna in 1961, the United Nations Conference on Diplomatic Intercourse and Immunities was attended by eighty-one states of which seventy-five were members of the United Nations.[90] On April 18, 1961, the conference adopted the Vienna Convention on Diplomatic Relations which entered into force in 1964, and to which ninety-one states have become parties.[91] This convention is concerned only with regular diplomatic relations, as was the 1815 Vienna regulation.[92] The question of "*ad hoc* diplomacy" was on the agenda of the conference but work on it was not completed. At the recommendation of the conference, the General Assembly referred the topic back to the International Law Commission which completed its work in 1967. The draft articles prepared by the commission on "*ad hoc* diplomacy" or "special missions" were discussed in the Assembly's Sixth Committee, and the Assembly itself adopted the Convention on Special Missions by Resolution 2530 (XXIV) of December 8, 1969. In Article 1 this convention defines *special missions* as follows:

> A "special mission" is a temporary mission, representing the State, which is sent by one State to another State with the consent of the latter for the purpose of dealing with it on specific questions or of performing in relation to it a specific task.[93]

In view of the rapid increases of ad hoc diplomacy since the end of World War II, the clarification of the status, immunities, and privileges of such special missions will be welcomed by both the sending and receiving states. The Vienna Convention on Diplomatic Relations and the Convention on Special Missions emphasize in their respective preambles that the "purpose of such privileges and immunities is not to benefit individuals but to ensure the efficient performance of the functions of diplomatic (special) missions as representing States." [94] Both conventions have thereby pronounced themselves in favor of the functional theory of immunities and privileges.

The Vienna Conference on Diplomatic Relations also adopted an Optional Protocol concerning the Compulsory Settlement of Disputes arising from the application or interpretation of the convention. Only thirty-eight states are parties to this protocol as compared with ninety-one parties to the convention itself. A similar protocol was adopted by the General Assembly with respect to the Convention on Special Missions.

The draft articles on consular relations prepared by the International Law Commission formed the basis of discussion at the United Nations Conference on Consular Relations held in Vienna in 1963. It was attended by ninety-five states. The work of this conference of plenipotentiaries resulted in the Vienna Convention on Consular Relations and an Optional Protocol for the Compulsory Settlement of Disputes of April 24, 1963.[95] The convention has become binding on thirty-eight states and the optional protocol on fifteen states.[96]

The three instruments, the conventions on diplomatic and on consular relations and on special missions, are an important contribution to both the codification and the progressive development of international law governing the intercourse between states. They should facilitate peaceful relations between members of the international community which has grown so much in number and in diversity. There remains one gap to fill, namely, the law applicable to representatives of states to international organizations. In connection with its work on diplomatic relations, the International Law Commission considered the question of the "relations between States and international organizations and the privileges and immunities of such organizations." [97]

While some aspects of this matter are covered by existing conventions,[98] the General Assembly requested the commission to continue its work on the legal position of representatives of states to international organizations. The commission expects to complete work on this topic in 1971. The draft articles will also cover permanent missions of member states to international organizations; their conduct, facilities, privileges, and immunities; and permanent observers of nonmember states.[99]

Two of the six subjects selected for codification in 1949 are still on the agenda of the International Law Commission: responsibility of states and state succession. Active work on state responsibility was started in 1955 and continued until 1961. As the special rapporteur who was in charge of the subject was not reelected, a new special rapporteur was appointed in 1963. The original intention was to deal with the traditional subject of responsibility of states for injury to the person or property of aliens. The resumed work started from a "fresh viewpoint," namely, the responsibility of states for "internationally wrongful acts," in which, the commission agrees, "progressive development would be particularly important." [100] This topic is of special interest to new states and, in spite of several resolutions of the General Assembly urging the commission to try to achieve results, progress to date has been exceedingly slow, even making allowance for a change in the direction and the preoccupation during the sixties with the law of treaties. Whichever way the topic is approached, it is likely to prove highly controversial. If the commission's codification work entered "the core of the law," with the law of treaties, it will complete, with the law of state responsibility, "this hard core of obligational law, and thus provide the trunk from which all other branches of the law will draw their strength." [101] However, the trunk needs roots and the roots need a fertile soil and in 1971 the election of members of the commission will take place.

In connection with the succession of states and governments, the work proceeded very slowly but since 1967 it has been receiving more active consideration. It was decided to deal with the topic under three headings: (1) succession in respect of treaties, (2) succession in respect of matters other than treaties, and (3) succession in respect of membership of international organizations. Active work was started on the first two topics; the third was deferred.[102] Members of the commission

> stressed the importance which State succession had at the present time for new States and for the international community in view of the modern phenomenon of decolonization, and agreed . . . that special attention should be given in the study to the problems of concern to new States.[103]

A report on the second topic (succession of states in respect to matters other than treaties) ran into trouble because it proposed to deal first with the question of acquired rights, a well-known but always controversial principle of customary international law.[104] Progress may well be expected on the first topic (succession in respect of treaties) because the initial proposal supported unanimously by members of the commission is designed to take it out of the context of succession—namely, the transmission of rights and obligations from the old to the new state—and to consider it "as a particular problem within the general framework of the law of treaties." [105] As provisionally defined, succession means "the replacement of one State by another in the sovereignty of territory or in the competence to conclude treaties with respect to territory." The provisions of the Vienna Convention on the Law of Treaties of 1969 will be taken "as an integral part of the legal foundations of the law relating to succession in respect of treaties." [106] The principle on which the provisional draft articles are based that there is no "general obligation on a new State to take over the treaties of its predecessor" found support among members of the commission[107] and will appeal to the new states generally.

Currently, in addition to the topics just discussed, the commission's agenda includes the question of treaties concluded between states and international organizations or between two or more international organizations, and the study of the most-favored-nation clause.[108] It has already been noted that at its 1971 session the commission intends to bring up to date its long-range program.[109] There is every hope that the partnership between the Assembly and the commission will continue to be fruitful but progress in the core and controversial areas of international law may be slow.

To round out the survey of the progressive development of international law by the General Assembly by means of conventions, two areas must be mentioned: outer space and human rights. By Resolution 1721 (XVI) of December 20, 1961, the Assembly established the Committee on the Peaceful Uses of Outer Space. The first result of the committee's work was Resolution 1962 (XVIII), entitled Declaration of Legal Principles Governing the Activities of States in the Exploration and Use of Outer Space, which was adopted unanimously on December 13, 1963. This was followed by the Treaty on Principles . . . Outer Space, including the Moon and Other Celestial Bodies, which was negotiated outside the United Nations but "commended" by the Assembly in Resolution 2222 (XXI) of January 25, 1967, to which the text of the treaty was annexed. The third major step was the Agreement on the Rescue of Astronauts, the Return of Astronauts and the Return of Objects Launched into Outer Space, which was "commended" by Assembly Resolution 2345 (XXII) of December 19, 1967.

The treaty follows generally the Declaration of Legal Principles. It provides for peaceful exploration of celestial bodies "on a basis of equality"; it lays down the principle of nonappropriation;[110] and bars the use of nuclear and other kinds of weapons of mass destruction in space or on celestial bodies.[111] This treaty, like the seabed treaty, does not, however, exclude all military activity in outer space such as reconnaissance. The treaty also provides for mutual inspection.[112]

While it is possible to arrive at agreement on the principles applicable to distant celestial bodies, no agreement has yet been reached on such down-to-earth matters as a delimitation of outer space and a convention "to establish international rules and procedures concerning liability for damage caused by the launching of objects into outer space and to ensure, in particular, prompt and equitable compensation for damage." [113] This is of direct concern to all people whereas the exploration of outer space is of direct interest to a handful of states. It may be noted that the preparatory work with respect to outer space is carried out in the Committee on the Peaceful Uses of Outer Space, its legal subcommittee, and the First (Political) Committee of the Assembly.

In the field of human rights, the General Assembly has from the outset manifested profound concern and has engaged in continuous and far-ranging activities. Reference has already been made to the 1948 Genocide Convention.[114] The basic act is the Universal Declaration of Human Rights, adopted without a dissenting vote by the Assembly in Resolution 217 (III), of December 10, 1948. It was proclaimed, as stated in the preamble, "as a common standard of achievement for all peoples and all nations." The declaration did not claim and does not have binding character. It contains, along with the usual political and civil rights, social and economic rights such as the right to social security, to work, to education, and others which have become associated with the social welfare state and have already been outlined in Article 55 of the Charter. Work on human rights was continued in the Economic and Social Council, in its Human Rights Commission, in the Assembly's Third Committee (Social, Humanitarian, and Cultural Questions), and, of course, in plenary meetings of the Assembly itself. The Assembly voiced its concern with human rights in innumerable resolutions, sometimes called declarations, some of which achieved the stage of conventions.

The most important achievement of the United Nations is without a doubt the two human rights covenants—the International Covenant on Economic, Social and Cultural Rights and the International Covenant on Civil and Political Rights—and the optional protocol to the latter. All three instruments were adopted by Resolution 2200 (XXI) of December 16, 1966.[115] Neither of the two covenants has yet entered into force. They have become binding on eight states (Colombia, Costa Rica, Cyprus, Ecuador, Libya, Syria, Tunisia, and Uruguay); they will enter into force after the deposit of the thirty-fifth ratification or accession. The optional protocol had been ratified by four states (Colombia, Costa Rica, Ecuador, and Uruguay) and will enter into force three months after the deposit of ten ratifications or accessions.[116]

It is impossible to indicate even in outline the substantive content of the covenants. Both instruments provide in Article 1 for the right of political and what is sometimes called economic self-determination.[117] The paucity of acceptances of the covenants indicates that although the members were able and willing to accept compromise formulas to accommodate different political and socioeconomic systems, they are reluctant to adjust their domestic systems to the rights included in the covenants. This reluctance accounts also for the weakness of the procedures for international supervision. In the Covenant on Economic, Social and Cultural Rights, they have been reduced to reports which the contracting parties agree to submit, in Article 16, "on the measures which they have adopted and the progress made in achieving the observance of the rights recognized herein." In this fashion the "rights" have become indistinguishable from the standards of achievement formulated in the 1948 Universal Declaration.

The procedures laid down in the Covenant on Civil and Political Rights are more explicit. They also include for the parties the duty to make reports on measures taken to give effect to the various rights. In addition, the parties have the option of conferring upon the Human Rights Committee provided for in Part IV of the convention the competence to receive complaints from a state party that another state party "is not fulfilling its obligations under the present Covenant" (Article 41[1]). The committee shall, under certain conditions, "make available its good offices to the State Parties concerned with a view to a friendly solution" (Article 41[1][e]). Failing this, the committee shall make a report without any recommendation. The Optional Protocol to the Covenant on Civil and Political Rights opens up the possibility for individuals to address communications to the Human Rights Committee in cases in which they "claim to be victims of a violation by that State Party (i.e., the State Party which has ratified the Protocol or has acceded to it) of any of the rights set forth in the Covenant" (Article 1). The procedure before the committee is limited to written communications which shall be examined in closed meetings. The committee "shall forward its views to the State Party concerned and to the individual" (Article 5). How much all these enforcement procedures lag behind an acceptable model can be gleaned by comparing them with those established under the European Convention on Human Rights of 1950. These include the right of individual and group petition, a commission, and a Court of Human Rights.[118] The European convention, like the international covenant, contains escape clauses which permit the imposition of restrictions in the interest of national security or public order or other overriding considerations. However, the factual justification of the invocation of such contingencies is subject to judicial control in case of the former, whereas in the case of the latter it does not seem to be subject to any review whatever.[119]

The United Nations, from its inception, has been concerned particularly with one human right: the right not to be subjected to racial discrimination. One of its chief preoccupations has been the policy of racial discrimination, known as apartheid, practiced in South Africa and by South Africa in the former mandate of South-West Africa.[120] On the general level the Assembly adopted, by Resolution 1904 (XVIII) of November 20, 1963, the United Nations Declaration on the Elimination of All Forms of Racial Discrimination, in which it affirmed the necessity of speedily eliminating racial discrimination throughout the world. This was followed by the International Convention on the Elimination of All Forms of Racial Discrimination, adopted by the Assembly in Resolution 2106A (XX) of December 21, 1965.[121] This is a very elaborate instrument with enforcement procedures which appear much stronger than those included in the covenant discussed above. The convention is in force for thirty-eight states.[122] A draft convention on the elimination of all forms of intolerance and discrimination based on religion or belief is on the agenda of the Assembly.[123]

The consideration of the Nuremberg principles by the General Assembly may appropriately be recalled in the context of human rights inasmuch as crimes against humanity are punishable as crimes under international law.[124] An issue which pertains to this matter relates to the application of national statutes of limitation to the prosecution of war criminals. The issue arose concretely in the Federal Republic of Germany and was generally discussed in the Economic and Social Council. Acting on its recommendation, the General Assembly by Resolution 2391 (XXIII) of November 26, 1968, adopted the Convention on the Non-Applicability of Statutory Limitations to War Crimes and Crimes against Humanity. The convention has been ratified by ten socialist states and has entered into force on November 11, 1970.[125] The preamble of the convention recalls the resolutions of the Assembly relating to war criminals, including Resolution 95 (I) of December 11, 1946, in which it affirmed the Nuremberg principles. Article I provides that "no statutory limitation shall apply to the following crimes, irrespective of the date of their commission," namely, war crimes and crimes against humanity "as they are defined in the Charter of the International Military Tribunal, Nürnberg, of 8 August 1945, and confirmed by resolutions 3(I) of 13 February 1946 [126] and 95(I) of 11 December 1946 of the General Assembly of the United Nations, particularly the 'grave breaches' enumerated in the Geneva Conventions of 12 August 1949 for the protection of war victims."

It is interesting to note that, in the context of this convention, the possibility of establishing an international criminal court has again come up for consideration.[127] This was to be accomplished by means of an optional protocol to the convention. A draft optional protocol was submitted to the Assembly, but the Assembly decided by Resolution 2392 (XXIII) of November 26, 1968, to defer its consideration until "it resumes consideration of the question of international criminal jurisdiction." Thus the Assembly continues to be involved in the consideration of the bases of a new international legal order.

Numerous instruments relating to special activities of the United Nations, such as control of traffic in narcotic and other dangerous drugs, traffic in persons, and other areas, need not be discussed here.[128]

The Development of International Law by the General Assembly through Resolutions and Declarations

Having considered the progressive development of international law by means of conventions or treaties adopted by the General Assembly or plenipotentiary conferences held under its auspices or convened at its behest, it remains to consider its contribution to the growth of law through resolutions. It is universally recognized that conventions or treaties are a source of international law or a source of legal obligation. There is no agreement but a good deal of controversy with respect to the question whether resolutions, even if called declarations, are a source of law or of legal obligation. The fact that international conventions are specifically listed in Article 38 (1) of the Statute of the International Court of Justice, which is usually regarded as a statement of sources of international law, and resolutions of organs of the United Nations are not, is certainly not of critical importance as this article was inherited from the Statute of 1920 of the Permanent Court of International Justice and antedates contemporary developments. International custom, however, is listed in Article 38 (1) and it was natural that those who are inclined to the view that resolutions have legal significance tend to look upon them as a means, a new means, of creating customary international law.

Probably the strongest endorsement of the latter view came from the pen of Judge Tanaka. In his dissenting opinion in the *South-West Africa* case, Judge Tanaka stated that individual resolutions or declarations "have no binding force upon the members of the organization"; that they must be repeated frequently since "what is required for customary international law is the repetition of the same practice"; and that with respect to the issue at hand—the existence of a rule of equality of treatment or nondiscrimination—"the accumulation of authoritative pronouncements such as resolutions, declarations, decisions, etc., concerning the interpretation of the Charter by the competent organs of the international community can be characterized as evidence of the international custom referred to in Article 38, paragraph 1 (b)." [129] Judge Jessup, on the other hand, in his dissenting opinion in the same case, rejected the argument "that the so-called norm of non-discrimination had become a rule of international law through reiterated statements in resolutions of the General Assembly, of the International Labor Organization, and of other international bodies." He based this rejection on the ground that "since these international bodies lack a true legislative character, their resolutions alone cannot create law." [130] Elsewhere, he stated the view that "the accumulation of expressions of condemnation of apartheid . . . as recorded in the resolutions of the General Assembly of the United Nations are proof of the pertinent contemporary international community standard." [131]

There are some flaws in Judge Tanaka's proposition. If individual resolutions have no binding force for the members, this must be due to the absence of legislative authority. If this is so, then how can it be explained that an accumulation of such nonbinding resolutions results in a binding norm of international law? To say that this results from practice, which is an element of customary international law, is to confuse the practice of organs with the practice of members of the United Nations. The accumulation of the resolutions is evidence of the former and not of the latter. Customary international law is the product along with *opinio juris* of the practice of states and not the practice of organs. Moreover, there is the open question, how large the accumulation must be, and the further question of the size of the majority, its composition, and so on.

Another flaw seems to be the attribution of resolutions to the members instead of to the United Nations. It is universally recognized that the United Nations has an international legal personality;[132] it acts through its various organs in a corporate capacity. Therefore, the resolutions which it adopts are resolutions of the corporate body, the United Nations, and not of the members, although they may be and usually are addressed to them.

Still another flaw appears in the attribution to the General Assembly of the power or competence to give authentic interpretations of the Charter.[133] The Charter has deliberately conferred no such authority on the Assembly, not even on the Court.[134] It is, to put it no higher, doubtful whether such an authority has been acquired by the Assembly though there is no doubt that the General Assembly often seems to have claimed this authority or proceeded on the assumption that it was indeed endowed with it. It is another but, in the present submission, relevant question whether it would be wise or desirable to attribute the competence of authentic—that is, binding—interpretation to so highly political and politicized a body as the Assembly.[135]

To accept Judge Tanaka's conclusions would be tantamount to accepting the Assembly as a world legislature, operating on the basis of the one-state-one-vote principle, and promulgating binding acts by a two-thirds majority which a simple majority could conceivably reduce to a simple majority.[136] The circumstances that a single act would not be binding but would have to be repeated—how many times?—is of some but minor significance. Considering that in the *Expenses* case, the Court attributed to the Assembly a virtually unlimited power with respect to expenditure which can be imposed upon the members,[137] the United Nations would seem to be possessed of some powers of a world government. It is scarcely conceivable that the members or even the organs of the United Nations intended this to happen.

If the major proposition, that the Assembly has competence to create "customary" international law by the process of the reiteration of resolutions, must be rejected, the minor proposition that the Assembly may play a role in the development of customary international law is unobjectionable. It is a factual proposition and depends merely upon proof that, in fact, this or that resolution initiated the process culminating in the emergence of a new rule of customary international law.[138] To be sure, the adoption of a resolution or declaration may create, may indeed be based on, the expectation that the members generally or particular members will act in accordance with the resolution or declaration. But this is a far cry from saying that they are legally bound to do so or that expectations as to the conduct of states are identical with legal norms governing the conduct of states in the particular subject matter.[139] It is trite to say that many expectations, whether expressed in international conventions or in resolutions of international or national assemblies, have remained unfulfilled.

However, if it is right to say that resolutions may be the initial step in the formation of custom, its existence would still depend upon the usual requirements: practice of states (objective element) and sense of legal obligation (*opinio juris,* the subjective element). This has been confirmed many times by the International Court of Justice, most recently in the *North Sea Continental Shelf* case. Referring to the *opinio juris* requirement, the Court said that two conditions must be fulfilled:

> Not only must the acts concerned amount to a settled practice, but they must also be such, or be carried out in such a way, as to be evidence of a belief that this practice is rendered obligatory by the existence of a rule of law requiring it. The need for such a belief, i.e., the existence of a subjective element, is implicit in the very notion of the *opinio juris sive necessitatis*. The States concerned must therefore feel that they are conforming to a legal obligation. The frequency, or even habitual character of the acts, is not in itself enough.[140]

The Court's concept and application of customary international law has been criticized,[141] and obviously there is room for differences of opinion, but the Court, like other organs of the United Nations, is dealing with sovereign states and states do not easily assume legal obligations.

In any event, the reiteration of resolutions setting forth certain goals may say something about the attitude of the organ, but the real question is whether or not the member states—not merely in words spoken in the General Assembly and in votes—respond to the resolution and, in particular, whether in responding they do so out of a sense of legal obligation and not merely because they find it convenient or inevitable to bow to public opinion or to pressures in and out of the United Nations. There are benefits to be reaped in conforming to Assembly resolutions and costs are involved in opposing them. Thus conduct conforming to resolutions may be the outcome of a "costs-benefits" calculation and, apart from the rhetoric of law so popular in the Assembly, there need be no reason to analyze such conduct in terms of law.[142] However, if such an analysis is attempted, it would have to be not in terms of expectations but along the lines of the usual concept of customary international law—that is, practice of states and sense of legal obligation. Since writers concerned with the legal effect of Assembly resolutions usually start out by attributing such effect to them, there has not been sufficient analysis of specific resolutions or declarations to determine whether they have "by custom become recognized as laying down rules binding upon States." [143] In a study which offers such an analysis, Resolution 1514 (XV) of December 14, 1960, entitled Declaration on the Granting of Independence to Colonial Countries and Peoples, one of the most frequently reiterated resolutions, it is concluded that it "is as much a part of our international law as any of the familiar traditional doctrines." [144] This conclusion is based on the "confirmed re-citation" of the resolution, the "fixed and universal expectation" that colonialism will be terminated, and that "no State could be unaware of this expectation or that the resolution was merely a 'recommendation' with no normative force as an authoritative interpretation of the United Nations Charter, and few colonial Powers have attempted to permanently obstruct decolonization." [145] No doubt, a few colonial powers have so far, at any rate, held on to their colonial territories or their "overseas" metropolitan territories. That the resolution has created expectations is hardly open to doubt, though the expectation seems—so far, at any rate—less than universal. That the resolution *in toto* or some of its parts constitutes an authoritative interpretation rather than a revision of the Charter is by no means clear, even if it were granted, for the sake of the argument, that the Assembly has the competence to make such interpretations. [146] Be that as it may and granted that many dependent and colonial territories were given independence both before and after the adoption of Resolution 1514 (XV), no evidence has been offered that the states concerned have done so out of a sense of legal obligation. Decolonization and the application of the principle of self-determination to colonial and other peoples have been a continuing process for several decades and owe their dynamics to forces of nationalism rather than to law.

Looking at the practice of states, one finds that forty-five territories with approximately 28 million people still remain under colonial rule, despite the reiteration "of their fundamental and inalienable right to self-determination and independence," [147] and the assiduous activity of the Special Committee which was set up by the Assembly in 1963 to speed up the implementation of the 1960 declaration. As before, it is the administering authority and not the Assembly which determines when its obligations under Chapter XI are satisfied and its obligation to transmit information has come to an end. To be sure, this is deplored by the Special Committee. Thus the United Kingdom has simply informed the Assembly's Fourth Committee that certain territories under its administration "having achieved the status of Associated States, they had achieved 'a full measure of self-government' and that information on them would not be transmitted in the future." This occurred in 1967 and the attitude of the United Kingdom has not changed since then. [148] France seems to have taken a similar attitude with two of its remaining territories. [149]

If, then, some members take the attitude that they and not the Special Committee or the Assembly determine the fulfillment of their obligations under the Charter, Portugal rejects the authority of the Assembly to determine that its overseas possessions are non-self-governing territories within the meaning of Chapter XI of the Charter and that it is bound to transmit information with respect to them. For this it has been repeatedly condemned. [150] Still less does Portugal admit that these territories are entitled to self-determination and independence. The conditions in southern Africa are bleak indeed, but the secretary-general is probably right in saying that Portugal must be convinced by the members "of the wisdom of acknowledging the right to freedom and independence of the peoples of the Territories under its administration." [151] It will be particularly necessary not merely to convince Portugal that these territories have a right to independence but it will be even more imperative to change the factors in its "costs-benefits" calculations.

Finally, it would seem that even the General Assembly itself does not consider that it has authority to create what has sometimes been called "instant" international law by means of resolutions or declarations. In several cases the passage of a declaration—as in connection with human rights, outer space, and racial discrimination—was merely a first step. This was followed by the elaboration and adoption of international conventions along similar or identical lines—that is, the normal procedure for the creation of norms of international law. Such conventions are, however, binding on the contracting states. If the preceding resolution or declaration had already binding legal character for the members, why incorporate the same or essentially similar content in an international convention which is binding only on the contracting states? [152] The inference seems inescapable that the declarations have not created new international law. Referring to the 1966 Covenants on Civil and Political and on Economic, Social and Cultural Rights, the secretary-general of the United Nations stated that their ratification "will *complement* the Universal Declaration of Human Rights with *legally binding provisions,* including measures of implementation, and it will give a much firmer basis to the role of the United Nations in the protection of human rights." [153] This, it is submitted, seems an accurate perception of the relation between declarations and resolutions, on the one side, and international conventions, on the other. This leaves open the question which is beyond the scope of this essay, whether some resolutions have or have not entered into the process from which customary law emerges.

The Contribution to the Development of International Law by the International Court of Justice

The contribution of the International Court of Justice to the progressive development of international law has been very modest but significant. The Court had very few cases to decide—only twenty-four contentious cases—and even fewer requests for advisory opinions—only thirteen, of which one is pending.[154] Several cases and requests were of a very narrow compass, requiring perhaps no more than the interpretation of a contested clause in a treaty. It is, incidentally, in this area that the Court made a decisive contribution inasmuch as the rules concerning the interpretation of treaties in the Vienna Convention on the Law of Treaties (Articles 31 and 32) are based on the jurisprudence of the Court as well as of its predecessor, the Permanent Court of International Justice. In some cases

the Court made pronouncements of a general character which were inci-
dental to the contested issue. Some examples will illustrate the point.

In several cases the Court had occasion to express its views on the
nature of customary international law. The Court's pronouncement in the
North Sea Continental Shelf case was referred to above. The Court expressed a similar view in the *Asylum* case.[155] In the *Right of Passage*
case, the Court recognized the existence of a local custom binding on only
two states.[156] These pronouncements clarified the concept substantially
and stimulated scholarly discussion.

More directly, the Court made contributions to the progressive development of international law in the *Corfu Channel* and *Fisheries* cases.
In the former case, the Court held "that States in time of peace have a
right to send their warships through straits used for international navigation between two parts of the high seas without the previous authorization of a coastal State, provided that the passage is innocent." [157] This
holding facilitated the work of the International Law Commission on the
law of the high seas and was incorporated in the 1958 Geneva Convention on the Territorial Sea and Contiguous Zone (Article 16[4]).

In the *Fisheries* case, the Court found that the drawing of straight
base lines for the delimitation of the territorial sea was not contrary to
international law and that the traditional ten-mile rule for the closing line
of bays "has not acquired the authority of a general rule of international
law." [158] Again, the Court cleared the way for the International Law Commission, and the relevant articles in the 1958 Geneva Convention on the
Territorial Sea and Contiguous Zone are based on the Court's holdings
(Article 4).

Still another contribution to the development of international law
was made by the Court in the advisory opinion concerning *Reservations
to the Genocide Convention*. In this case the Court rejected both the "absolute integrity" theory—namely, that a reservation to a multilateral convention must be accepted by all states in order to permit the reserving
state to become a party to it—as well as the sovereignty theory—namely,
that a reserving state, in virtue of its sovereignty, may become a party to
the convention without the consent of other controlling parties. Instead,
the Court held that a state "which has made . . . a reservation which has
been objected to by one or more of the parties to the Convention but not
by others, can be regarded as being a party to the Convention if the reservation is compatible with the object and purpose of the Convention." [159]
The International Law Commission initially preferred, in opposition to
the Court, the integrity theory but it reversed itself in connection with its
work on the law of treaties, and the Vienna Convention on the Law of
Treaties incorporated the Court's holding in its Articles 19–23 on reservations.

Several cases may be included here because they contain significant
pronouncements which clarify contested points of law although they have
not contributed directly to its codification. In the *Reparation* case, the

Court not merely affirmed the international legal personality of the United Nations but also developed a theory of the functional protection by the United Nations of its agents and of the implied powers of the organization.[160] In the hotly contested issue of the status of *South-West Africa,* the Court laid the juridical foundations for its subsequent consideration in the General Assembly by holding that the mandate survived the dissolution of the League of Nations, that the supervisory function of the League Council passed to the United Nations General Assembly, and that South Africa as the mandatory was under the continuing obligation to administer the mandate in accordance with Article 22 of the Covenant of the League, and to transmit petitions from the inhabitants of the territory. The Court, however, also held that South Africa was under no obligation to place the territory under the trusteeship system of the United Nations.[161] This being an advisory opinion, it was legally not binding upon South Africa. Attempts to obtain from the Court a binding judgment, the execution of which could ultimately be enforced by the Security Council, failed. The Court, "by the President's casting vote—the votes being equally divided," decided "to reject the claims of the Empire of Ethiopia and the Republic of Liberia." [162] The judgment provoked strong, almost intemperate criticism in and out of the United Nations, and it was gratifying that the secretary-general of the United Nations rose to the defense of the Court against political pressures.[163]

In the *Nottebohm* case, the Court recognized that international law leaves it to the state to determine who are its nationals, but the state "cannot claim that the rules it has thus laid down are entitled to recognition by another State unless it has acted in conformity with this general aim of making the legal bond of nationality accord with the individual's genuine connection with the State which assumes the defence of its citizens by means of protection as against other States." [164] This "genuine bond" or "genuine link" theory has aroused much discussion in the literature. However, in spite of it, the theory was adopted into Article 5 of the 1958 Geneva Convention on the High Seas. It provides that "each State shall fix the conditions for the grant of its nationality to ships . . . and for the right to fly its flag," but "there must exist a genuine link between the State and the ship." The provision is intended to curb the use of so-called "flags of convenience."

This brief survey is by no means exhaustive of the contribution which the jurisprudence of the Court has made to the development of international law. A more extensive analysis would be of interest primarily to specialists.

CONCLUSION

By all criteria, the contribution of the United Nations to the progressive development of international law has surpassed all expectations.

It would be surprising if the pace set in the first twenty-five years of the United Nations will be matched by that of the next quarter of a century. As indicated above, the International Law Commission has some very difficult topics on its agenda. The interest of the members of the United Nations seems increasingly concentrated on economic development, abolition of racial discrimination, and decolonization. The problem of the exploitation of the seabed for the general welfare rather than for the exclusive benefit of technologically highly developed states remains to be solved. The treaty on liability for damage caused by space objects remains to be drafted. The question of direct broadcast satellites has been on the agenda of the United Nations for some years. Problems of human environment will require for their solution technical skill and statesmanship in order to safeguard the interests of the developing countries. The growing interdependence in trade will require regulation by international conventions. For this purpose the General Assembly, by Resolution 2205 (XXI) of December 17, 1966, established the United Nations Commission on International Trade Law.[165]

The role of science and technology in the development of nations is and will be a major problem. The Assembly requested the secretary-general, by Resolution 2658 (XXV) of December 7, 1970, to undertake a study of the ways and means for strengthening international cooperation in the new applications of science and technology.

In all of these fields one may expect some action by the United Nations. It may take the form of international convention or of declarations and resolutions. So far the energies of the United Nations have been focused on substantive law. The field of adjective or remedial law to ensure that the substantive law is properly applied and enforced has been sorely neglected. The optional protocols to the Geneva and Vienna conventions have not been widely ratified. None has been ratified by the Soviet Union and the United States. The remedies provided for in the Human Rights Covenants are merely halting steps in the right direction. A proposal for the creation of the post of United Nations High Commissioner for Human Rights was on the agenda of the 1969 and 1970 sessions of the General Assembly but it was not adopted.[166] The General Act for the Pacific Settlement of International Disputes, originally adopted by the League of Nations in 1928 and revised by the General Assembly of the United Nations in 1949, has been entirely accepted by five members (Belgium, Norway, Denmark, Luxembourg, and Upper Volta) and partially by one (Sweden).[167] This act provides for the settlement of political and legal disputes by conciliation, adjudication (the International Court of Justice), and arbitration. The disappointing fate of the work of the International Law Commission on a draft Code of Arbitral Procedure may be recalled in this context as further evidence of the neglect of remedial procedures by the United Nations.

The use, or perhaps the nonuse, of the International Court of Justice has already been indicated. There is no contentious case pending before the Court and since 1961 there has been only one request for an advisory opinion. Only forty-six states—forty-four members and two nonmembers —have accepted the jurisdiction of the Court as compulsory under Article 36 (2) of its statute.[168] The reasons for this neglect of the principal judicial organ of the United Nations by its organs and its members are too complex to be discussed here.[169] Fortunately, there have been some indications lately of concern about the future of the Court. At the 1970 session of the General Assembly, several members submitted a proposal entitled "Review of the Role of the International Court of Justice." In their view such a review "is urgently needed." And they proposed the study "of obstacles to the satisfactory functioning of the International Court of Justice, and ways and means of removing them." They also proposed that the Assembly authorize an *Ad Hoc* Committee to undertake this study.[170] The General Assembly did not adopt this proposal. It decided, however, by a resolution adopted on December 15, 1970, to begin with a request to the members for their comments and suggestions concerning the future role of the Court, an invitation to the Court to state its views, and a request to the secretary-general for a comprehensive report.[171] It is to be hoped that this will mark the beginning of a new era in the fortunes of the Court and in the elaboration of procedures designed to secure the application of substantive law. Substantive and remedial are interdependent, there is no need to further one at the expense of the other, for if the states and their peoples are to reap the benefits of the substantive law they need to have at their disposal adequate means for obtaining redress. It is time to restore a balance between the two interdependent branches of the law.

NOTES

1. Publications of the PCIJ Series B, No. 14 (1927), p. 38; also in Manley O. Hudson, *World Court Reports* (Washington, D.C.: Carnegie Endowment for International Peace, 1935), II, 164.

2. Ian Brownlie (ed.), *Basic Documents in International Law* (Oxford: Clarendon Press, 1967), p. 112.

3. See Brownlie, *Basic Documents,* pp. 70, 80.

4. M. O. Hudson, *International Legislation,* I (1931), IX (1946), counted 257 multilateral conventions for the period 1864–1914 (I, p. xxxvi) and 670 for the period 1919–1945 (IX, p. xvi). However, not all of these instruments entered into force.

5. These are: Convention for the Amelioration of the Condition of the Wounded and Sick in Armed Forces in the Field; Convention for the Amelioration of the Condition of Wounded, Sick and Shipwrecked Members of Armed Forces at Sea; Convention Relative to the Treatment of Prisoners of War; and the Convention Relative to the Protection of Civilian Persons in Time of War. *U.S. Treaties and Other International Acts Series* 3362–3365.

6. J. B. Scott (ed.), *The Hague Conventions and Declarations of 1899 and 1907* (New York: Oxford University Press, 1915).

7. For a survey see this writer's study prepared for the Division for the

Codification of International Law of the Secretariat of the United Nations and distributed as UN Document A/AC.10/5, April 29, 1947; republished in 41 AJIL Suppl. 29–111 (1947). This study is entitled "Historical Survey of the Development of International Law and its Codification by International Conferences" (Henceforth cited: "Historical Survey").

8. *Ibid.*, p. 44f.

9. See *Multilateral Treaties in respect of which the Secretary-General Performs Depository Functions.* List of Signatures, Ratifications, Accessions, etc., as at December 31, 1969. UN Pub. Sales No.: E.70.V.3. Document ST/LEG/SER. D/3 (1970). Part II of this publication lists twenty-seven League of Nations multilateral treaties. (Will henceforth be cited: *Multilateral Treaties.*)

10. *Ibid.*, chap. VI.

11. *Ibid.*, chap. VII.

12. *Ibid.*, chap. IX.

13. *Ibid.*, chap. XII.

14. *Ibid.*, chap. XVIII.

15. General Assembly, *Official Records* (24th sess.), Suppl. 30 (A/7630), p. 16. The General Assembly reiterated its call for strict observance of the protocol in Resolution 2662 (XXV) which was adopted by a vote of 113:0:2. *Ibid.* (25th sess.), Suppl. 28 (A/8028), p. 14.

16. "Historical Survey," p. 82.

17. *Ibid.*, pp. 84–86.

18. For a list of the topics covered by the Harvard Research, see "Note on the Private Codification of Public International Law," 41 AJIL Suppl. 138–147 (1947), pp. 146–147.

19. See Summary of Reports on Ratified Conventions: International Labor Conference, 53rd sess., 1969, 3rd item on the Agenda (Report III, Part I), Nos. 29, 87, 98; and C. Wilfred Jenks, *Social Justice in the Law of Nations* (New York: Oxford University Press, 1970).

20. Summary Report, *ibid.*, Nos. 58, 74. In fairness it should be pointed out that in many matters legislation in the United States is up to the standards of the ILO conventions.

21. Resolutions adopted by the General Assembly (1st sess.), Part II, Document A/64/Add. 1, p. 187.

22. *Ibid.*, p. 188.

23. *Ibid.*

24. General Assembly, *Official Records* (3rd sess.), Part I, Resolutions (A/810), p. 174.

25. *Multilateral Treaties,* pp. 61–67.

26. General Assembly, *Official Records* (2nd sess.), Resolutions (A/519), pp. 111–112. In the same resolution the Assembly also directed the commission to prepare a draft code of offenses against the peace and security of mankind.

27. *The Work of the International Law Commission,* UN Pub. 67.V.4 (1967), p. 21. Henceforth cited as: *Work of the ILC.*

28. *Ibid.*

29. *Ibid.*, pp. 63–64.

30. *Ibid.*, p. 21.

31. Article 2 of the draft code, the text of which is reproduced *ibid.*, pp. 64–65.

32. On the history of attempts by the League of Nations to define the concept and for a thorough analysis of the problems involved in working out a definition, see Julius Stone, *Aggression and World Order* (London: Stevens & Sons, 1958) and my review of it in 34 *British Year Book of International Law* (1958), pp. 421–425.

33. General Assembly, *Official Records* (25th sess.), Suppl. 19 (A/8019),

Report of the Special Committee on the Question of Defining Aggression, July 13–August 14, 1970, p. 4.

34. For a short history of the draft code, see *Work of the ILC,* pp. 26–28.

35. *Ibid.,* p. 21.

36. *Ibid.,* pp. 21–22.

37. Article 6 of the convention provides for trial of persons charged with genocide by national tribunals "or by such international penal tribunal as may have jurisdiction with respect to those Contracting Parties which shall have accepted its jurisdiction." For an analysis of the crime of genocide, see the article "Genocide as a Crime under International Law" by the "father" of the Genocide Convention, the late Raphael Lemkin, in 41 AJIL 145–151 (1947).

38. *Report* of the International Law Commission to the General Assembly on the work of the 1st sess., Document A/CN.4/13, June 9, 1949, p. 21; also in *Work of the ILC,* p. 62.

39. General Assembly, *Official Records,* Resolutions (A/1251), p. 66. The reaction of one jurist, Hans Kelsen, was a textual critique "The Draft Declaration on Rights and Duties of States," 44 AJIL 259–276 (1950), and that of another, Herbert W. Briggs, the editor of a rightly highly regarded case book, was as follows: "The utility of manifestoes like the Draft Declaration . . . , which appears to reflect the natural law approach of inherent ('basic') rights of States, seems doubtful to many international lawyers, including the Editor." *The Law of Nations, Cases, Documents, and Notes,* 2nd ed. (New York: Appleton-Century-Crofts, 1952), p. 15. Such an attitude overlooks the enormous debt which positive international law owes to natural law.

40. Resolution 1815 (XVII) of December 18, 1962, noted in *Report* of the Special Committee on Principles of International Law concerning Friendly Relations and Co-operation among States. General Assembly, *Official Records* (25th sess.), Suppl. 18 (A/8018), p. 3.

41. The exception being the principle numbered (c): "The duty not to intervene in matters within the domestic jurisdiction of any State, in accordance with the Charter." The reference to the Charter is somewhat misleading as there is no directly analogous clause in the Charter. Article 2(7) of the Charter is concerned with intervention by the United Nations and not with intervention by states in matters essentially within the domestic jurisdiction of any state.

42. See *Report* of the Special Committee (*supra,* n. 40), p. 62, paragraph 83.

43. General Assembly, *Official Records* (25th sess.), Suppl. 28 (A/8028), p. 121.

44. That title was, it may be recalled, Draft Declaration on Principles of International Law concerning Friendly Relations and Co-operation among States. *Report* of the Special Committee, p. 62. paragraph 83.

45. *Supra,* n. 43, p. 123.

46. *Ibid.* The final clause in the formulation of the non-intervention principle reads as follows: "Nothing in the foregoing paragraphs shall be construed as affecting the relevant provisions of the Charter relating to the maintenance of international peace and security." This is a curious statement inasmuch as the maintenance of peace and security is the business of the organization and not of individual states, and the exception from Article 2(7) is contained in the final clause in that provision.

47. *Ibid.,* p. 124.

48. As stated in Article 15 of the commission's statute, "the expression 'progressive development of international law' is used for convenience as meaning the preparation of draft conventions on subjects which have not yet

been regulated by international law or in regard to which the law has not yet been sufficiently developed in the practice of States. Similarly, the expression 'codification of international law' is used for convenience as meaning the more precise formulation and systematization of rules of international law in fields where there already has been extensive State practice, precedent and doctrine." *Work of the ILC,* p. 57.

49. Shabtai Rosenne, "The Role of the International Law Commission," *Proceedings of the American Society of International Law,* 24–37 (1970), p. 27.

50. *Ibid.,* p. 29. The commission's draft articles on the law of treaties have been debated at five sessions of the Assembly between 1962 and the opening of the Vienna Conference on the Law of Treaties in 1968.

51. For further analysis of the commission's organization and method of work, in addition to the article by Rosenne, see the book by a former member of the commission, Herbert W. Briggs, *The International Law Commission* (Ithaca, N.Y.: Cornell University Press, 1965); and Luke T. Lee, "The International Law Commission Re-Examined," 59 AJIL 545–570 (1965).

52. See *supra,* p. 174.

53. See *supra,* p. 175.

54. *Work of the ILC,* p. 104.

55. Thus in the preamble to the Vienna Convention on Diplomatic Relations of April 18, 1961, the parties affirm "that the rules of customary international law should continue to govern questions not expressly regulated by the provisions of the present Convention." *Ibid.,* p. 121. The Vienna Convention on Consular Relations of April 24, 1963, *ibid.,* p. 142, and the Vienna Convention on the Law of Treaties of May 23, 1969, 63 AJIL 875 (1969) contain substantially identical language.

56. The complexity of the problem is well illustrated by the recent judgment of the International Court of Justice in the *North Sea Continental Shelf* case of February 20, 1969. In that case the Court had to examine the argument of the Netherlands and Denmark that the equidistance principle in Article 6(2) of the Geneva Continental Shelf Convention of 1958 was or has become a principle of customary international law; and that, consequently, it was binding on the Federal Republic of Germany even though the latter had not become a party to the convention. ICJ *Reports* (1969), p. 3, at 28ff.

57. David A. Kay, *The New Nations in the United Nations, 1960–1967* (New York: Columbia University Press, 1970), pp. 49, 182. For statistics on speeches made by new nations during the fifteenth to twenty-first sessions in plenary and committee meetings see pp. 191–199. On p. 48 Kay writes: "Similarly, 69.7% of the new nations did not speak on any of the international law topics before the 15th Assembly, and at the 21st session 32.6% of these nations did not speak on this subject." Insofar as topics are concerned which were actively under consideration of the International Law Commission and of the Assembly at those sessions, the statement must be read in the light of the observations made in the text above.

58. *Report* of the ILC to the General Assembly on the Work of its First Session, A/CN.4/13, p. 6.

59. *Report* of the ILC on the Work of its twenty-second Session, General Assembly, *Official Records* (25th sess.), Suppl. 10 (A/8010/Rev. 1), p. 40.

60. *Yearbook of the ILC* (1958), II, 80.

61. *Ibid.,* pp. 83–88. The text of the model rules is also printed in *Work of the ILC,* p. 69. See also Leo Gross, "The United Nations and the Role of Law," 19 *International Organization* 537–561 (1965), at 545.

62. *Work of the ILC,* p. 28. The Commission on the Status of Women was also responsible for two other conventions: the Convention on the Political

Rights of Women adopted by the Assembly in 1952 and the Convention on Consent to Marriage, Minimum Age for Marriage, and Registration of Marriages adopted by the Assembly in 1962. All three conventions are in force. See *Multilateral Treaties,* pp. 305, 311, 313.

63. *Work of the ILC,* p. 29.

64. *Multilateral Treaties,* p. 101.

65. For text of the convention see *Work of the ILC,* p. 135.

66. The Convention relating to the Status of Refugees of 1951 was adopted by a conference convened pursuant to Assembly Resolution 429 (V) of December 14, 1950. *Multilateral Treaties,* p. 83; The Convention relating to the Status of Stateless Persons of 1954 was adopted at a conference held pursuant to a resolution of April 26, 1954, of the Economic and Social Council; *ibid.,* p. 94; the Protocol relating to the Status of Refugees of 1967 was approved by ECOSOC in 1966 and transmitted to interested states in virtue of Assembly Resolution 2198 (XXI) of December 16, 1966, p. 103.

67. For a brief history of the commission's work on this topic, see *Work of the ILC,* pp. 31–35.

68. For text of these instruments see *Work of the ILC,* pp. 97–121.

69. *Ibid.,* p. 34, n. 26.

70. For ratifications, reservations, and objections see *Multilateral Treaties,* pp. 345–362.

71. *Ibid.,* p. 363. The interlocking provision is in Article V of the optional protocol.

72. For a first-hand account by the chairman of the U.S. delegation to the conference see Arthur H. Dean, "The Second Geneva Conference on the Law of the Sea: The Fight for Freedom of the Seas," 54 AJIL 751–790 (1960); for a comment on this by the chairman of the Mexican delegation to that conference see Alfonso Garcia Robles, "The Second United Nations Conference on the Law of the Sea—a Reply," 55 AJIL 669–675 (1961); and a response by Mr. Dean, *ibid.,* pp. 675–680.

73. There may be some limit to the "creeping" limit but this depends on how narrowly or how broadly the term "adjacent" in Article 1 will be interpreted in practice. Louis Henkin, "The United Nations and the Rules of Law," 11 *Harvard International Law Journal* 428–436 (1970), p. 432. See *ibid.,* p. 443, n. 4.

74. General Assembly, *Official Records* (24th sess.), Suppl. 30 (A/7630), p. 10.

75. General Assembly Resolution 2574B (XXIV), *ibid.,* at 11.

76. *New York Times,* December 18, 1970, p. 1. Resolution 2749 (XXV), December 17, 1970, General Assembly, *Official Records* (25th sess.), Suppl. 28 (A/8028), p. 24.

77. United Nations Press Release WS/480, December 11, 1970, p. 3, and *ibid.,* pp. 11, 12.

78. See *infra,* p. 195.

79. General Assembly, *Official Records* (22nd sess.), Suppl. 16(A/6716), p. 80.

80. Preamble of the convention, the text of which is reproduced in 63 AJIL 875–903 (1969). The Final Act of the UN Conference on the Law of Treaties is in Doc. A/Conf./39/26.

81. *Report* of the ILC on the Work of its Twenty-second Session, May 4–July 10, 1970, *supra,* n. 59, pp. 31, 41.

82. Rosenne, "Role of International Law Commission," p. 33.

83. *Ibid.,* p. 34.

84. Article 26: "Every treaty in force is binding upon the parties to it and must be performed by them in good faith."

85. Article 46: "1. A State may not invoke the fact that its consent to be bound by a treaty has been expressed in violation of a provision of its internal law regarding competence to conclude treaties as invalidating its consent unless that violation was manifest and concerned a rule of its internal law of fundamental importance. 2. A violation is manifest if it would be objectively evident to any State conducting itself in the matter in accordance with normal practice and in good faith."

86. Final Act, UN Conference on the Law of Treaties (A/Conf./39/ii/ Add. 2), p. 285.

87. Another article, Article 64, deals with the contingency of the emergence of *jus cogens* in the future: "If a new peremptory norm of general international law emerges, any existing treaty which is in conflict with that norm becomes void and terminates."

88. In one place the commentary refers to "the hypothesis that in international law today there are a certain number of fundamental rules of international public order from which no State may derogate even by agreement with another State." In another, reference is made to suggested examples such as treaties "contemplating or conniving at the commission of acts such as trade in slaves, piracy or genocide," or "treaties violating human rights, the equality of States or the principle of self-determination," or treaties "contemplating an unlawful use of force contrary to the principles of the Charter," or treaties "contemplating the performance of any other act criminal under international law." General Assembly, *Official Records* (21st sess.), Suppl. 9 (A/6309/Rev.1), *Report* of the ILC on the second part of its 17th sess. January 3–28, 1966, and on its 18th sess. May 4–July 19, 1966, p. 77, paragraph 3, and p. 89, paragraph 1.

89. These include negotiations, inquiry, mediation, conciliation, arbitration, judicial settlement, resort to regional agencies or arrangements, or other peaceful means chosen by parties.

90. It is the standing practice of the General Assembly to invite to conferences held under its auspices members of the United Nations or of specialized agencies or of the IAEA or parties to the Statute of the Court. By means of this formula, Communist China and the Communist regimes of North Korea, North Vietnam, and East Germany are excluded from participation in the codification and progressive development of international law. See, for example, par. 3 of Resolution 2166 (XXI), December 5, 1966, General Assembly, *Official Records* (21st sess.), Suppl. 16 (A/6316), p. 95.

91. *Multilateral Treaties*, p. 44.

92. See *supra*, p. 173.

93. General Assembly, *Official Records* (24th sess.), Suppl. 30 (A/7630), p. 99.

94. For the text of the Vienna Convention on Diplomatic Relations, see *Work of the ILC*, p. 121, and the text of the Convention on Special Missions, the annex to the resolution referred to above in n. 93. A similar clause is included in the Vienna Convention on Consular Relations. See *infra*, p. 193.

95. Text in *Work of the ILC*, p. 142. It may be noted that the Vienna Conferences of 1961 and 1963 also adopted optional protocols relating to the acquisition of nationality. See *ibid.*, pp. 132, 164. The purpose of these protocols is to exclude the acquisition of nationality by members of the mission or the counsular post solely by the operation of the law of the receiving states. This applies to those members who are not nationals of the receiving states.

96. *Multilateral Treaties*, pp. 53, 57.

97. *Work of the ILC*, p. 38.

98. The chief instrument is the Convention on the Privileges and Immunities of the United Nations which was adapoted by Resolution 22A(1) of

February 13, 1946. The host country of the United Nations, the United States, acceded to this convention only in 1969, subject to some reservations. Altogether, 102 states are parties to the convention. General Assembly, *Official Records* (25th sess.), Suppl. 1 (A/8001), *Report of the Secretary-General on the Work of the Organization,* June 16, 1969–June 15, 1970, p. 229f. On November 21, 1947, the General Assembly adopted the Convention on the Privileges and Immunities of the Specialized Agencies, to which seventy-two states are parties. *Ibid.,* p. 230. In 1947 the United Nations concluded the Headquarters Agreement with the United States.

99. Permanent observer missions to the headquarters of the United Nations are maintained by the Federal Republic of Germany, the Holy See, the Republic of Korea, Monaco, Switzerland, and the Republic of Vietnam. *Report of the ILC on the Work of its Twenty-second Session,* Document A/8010, p. 5.

100. *Ibid.,* p. 36, paragraph 64, p. 37, paragraph 66(b), and p. 38, paragraph 71.

101. Rosenne, "International Law Commission," p. 33.

102. Report of the ILC, *supra,* n. 99, p. 29.

103. *Work of the ILC,* p. 50.

104. As reported, in the view of most members of the commission, "the topic of acquired rights was extremely controversial and its study, at a premature stage, could only delay the Commission's work on the topic as a whole. The efforts of the Commission should, therefore, be directed to finding a solid basis on which to go forward with the codification and progressive development of the topic, taking account of the differing legal interests and current needs of States." *Report* of the ILC (supra, n. 99), p. 30, paragraph 33.

105. *Ibid.,* p. 32, paragraph 38, and p. 34, paragraph 49.

106. *Ibid.,* p. 32, paragraphs 38 and 39.

107. *Ibid.,* p. 34, paragraph 54.

108. *Ibid.,* p. 41.

109. *Ibid.,* p. 40. In the meantime the General Assembly adopted Resolution 2669 (XXV) recommending that the commission take up the study of the law relating to the non-navigational uses of international watercourses, with a view to codification and progressive development. General Assembly, *Official Records* (25th sess.), Suppl. 28 (A/8028), p. 127.

110. Article 2: "Outer space, including the Moon and other celestial bodies, is not subject to national appropriation by claim of sovereignty, by means of use or occupation, or by any other means." Brownlie, *Basic Documents,* p. 106.

111. Article 4: "States Parties to the Treaty undertake not to place in orbit around the Earth any objects carrying nuclear weapons or any other kind of weapons of mass destruction, install such weapons on celestial bodies, or station such weapons in outer space in any other manner." *Ibid.* There is no corresponding provision in the declaration of the General Assembly.

112. Article 12: "All stations, installations, equipment and space vehicles on the Moon and other celestial bodies shall be open to representatives of other States Parties to the Treaty on a basis of reciprocity. Such representatives shall give reasonable advance notice of a projected visit, in order that appropriate consultations may be held and that maximum precautions may be taken to assure safety and to avoid interference with normal operations in the facility to be visited." *Ibid.,* p. 109. There is no corresponding provision in the Assembly declaration.

113. Paragraph 5 of General Assembly Resolution 2061B (XXIV) of December 16, 1969. This resolution recalls the Assembly resolutions since 1961 relating to the question of liability. Resolution 2601A (XXIV) refers to the

definition of outer space. General Assembly, *Official Records* (24th sess.), Suppl. 30 (A/7630), pp. 12–13.

114. See *supra*, p. 177. For conventions on rights of women, see *supra*, p. 186, and refugees and stateless persons, see *supra*, p. 187.

115. General Assembly, *Official Records* (21st sess.), Suppl. 16 (A/6316), p. 49. The text of the three instruments is annexed to the resolution. They are reproduced along with the Universal Declaration in Brownlie, *Basic Documents*, pp. 132–175.

116. General Assembly, *Official Records* (25th sess.), Suppl. 1 (A/8001), *Report of the Secretary-General on the Work of the Organization*, June 16, 1969–June 15, 1970, p. 112.

117. Article 1: "1. All peoples have the right of self-determination. By virtue of that right they freely determine their political status and freely pursue their economic, social and cultural development. 2. All peoples may, for their own ends, freely dispose of their natural wealth and resources without prejudice to any obligations arising out of international economic co-operation, based upon the principle of mutual benefit, and international law. In no case may a people be deprived of its own means of subsistence."

118. For text and literature see Brownlie, *Basic Documents*, p. 194.

119. For a case before the European Court of Human Rights, see the *Lawless* case, 56 AJIL 171–211 (1962), Judgments of November 14, 1960 and July 1, 1961.

120. The practice of racial discrimination in South-West Africa was the very issue in the case between *Ethiopia and Liberia* v. *South Africa* before the International Court of Justice. The Court's judgment of July 18, 1966, rejected the claims of the applicant governments on the ground that they failed to establish "any legal right or interest appertaining to them in the subject-matter of the present claims." ICJ *Reports* (1966), p. 6, at 51.

121. For text see Brownlie, *Basic Documents*, pp. 178–192.

122. General Assembly, *Official Records* (25th sess.), Suppl. 1 (A/8001), *Report of the Secretary-General on the Work of the Organization*, June 16, 1969–June 15, 1970, p. 106.

123. *Ibid.,* p. 112.

124. On the Nuremberg principles, see *supra*, p. 177.

125. *Report of the Secretary-General (supra*, n. 122), p. 112.

126. This resolution is concerned with the extradition and punishment of war criminals. For Resolution 2391 (XXIII), see General Assembly, *Official Records* (23rd sess.), Suppl. 18 (A/7218), p. 40.

127. For earlier consideration see *supra*, p. 179.

128. For a listing of such instrument see *Multilateral Treaties*, passim.

129. ICJ *Reports* (1966), p. 292. Judge Tanaka explained this process saying: "Briefly, the method of the generation of customary international law is in the stage of transformation from being an individualistic process to being a collectivistic process. This phenomenon can be said to be the adaptation of the traditional creative process of international law to the reality of the growth of the organized international community. It can be characterized, considered from the sociological viewpoint, as a transition from traditional custom-making to international legislation by treaty." *Ibid.,* p. 294. Judge Tanaka did not explain how the highly individualistic "international legislation by treaty" can result, seen sociologically or otherwise, from the new collectivistic customary law-creating process.

130. *Ibid.,* p. 432. Judge Jessup also invoked another consideration which is not material here.

131. *Ibid.,* p. 441. In this context he declared that this conclusion "does

not rest upon the thesis that resolutions of the General Assembly have a general legislative character and by themselves create rules of international law."

132. See the advisory opinion of the International Court of Justice in the *Reparation for Injuries* case. ICJ *Reports* (1949), p. 174, at 179.

133. See Judge Tanaka's dissenting opinion, *supra*, n. 129, p. 294. Judge Tanaka surely overshot the mark when he attributed retroactive effect to the authentic interpretation.

134. See Gross, "Role of Law," p. 538f.

135. This argument is of a general character and does not address itself to the question of the powers of the Security Council under chap. VII of the Charter.

136. See Article 18(3) of the Charter.

137. ICJ *Reports* (1962), p. 151. See also Leo Gross, "Expenses of the United Nations for Peace-Keeping Operations: The Advisory Opinion of the ICJ," 17 *International Organization* 1–35 (1963).

138. This seems to be the view of the memorandum of the Office of Legal Affairs of the United Nations Secretariat. Commenting upon the distinction between "recommendation" and "declaration," the memorandum states that "in view of the greater solemnity and significance of a 'declaration,' it may be considered to impart, on behalf of the organ adopting it, a strong expectation that Members of the international community will abide by it. Consequently, insofar as the expectation is gradually justified by State practice, a declaration may by custom become recognized as laying down rules binding upon States." Document E/CN.4/L. 610, April 2, 1962, pp. 1–2.

139. With reference to numerous resolutions of the Assembly calling for the termination of colonial situations, Dr. Rosalyn Higgins said, "I would have thought that cumulatively, even if individually they are not 'binding' on these countries (viz., Portugal and South Africa), they do create a community expectation about what is and is not lawful behavior." "The United Nations and Law-making: The Political Organs," *American Society of International Law, Proceedings,* 64 AJIL 37–48 (1970), at 42. In the absence of an independent norm of conventional or customary international law, the conduct of the states concerned cannot be qualified as lawful or unlawful unless it is assumed that the relevant resolutions cumulatively have created the norm requiring states to divest themselves of their colonial holdings. This is Judge Tanaka's line of reasoning which I cannot accept.

140. ICJ *Reports* (1969), p. 3, at 44.

141. C. Wilfred Jenks, *The Prospects of International Adjudication* (Dobbs Ferry, N.Y.: Oceana, 1964), p. 237.

142. Professor R. Falk is very close to this position when he says: "The degree of authoritativeness that the process of law-creating by Assembly action comes to enjoy depends upon the extent to which particular resolutions influence behavior and gain notoriety in legal circles and the extent to which this process is incorporated into the developing framework of an evolving system and science of international law." "On the Quasi-Legislative Competence of the General Assembly," 60 AJIL 782–791 (1966), p. 786. The difference is that Professor Falk starts out by positing the process of "law-creating" by the Assembly whereas in my view it would be appropriate to speak of the process of "resolution-creating." To speak of "law-creating" anticipates the outcome which depends upon the states and, to a much lesser degree, the science of international law.

143. See the memorandum of the Office of Legal Affairs, n. 138.

144. Samuel A. Bleicher, "The Legal Significance of Re-Citation of General Assembly Resolutions," 63 AJIL 444–478 (1969) at 475. For the fre-

quency of the citation of this and a few other resolutions, see *ibid.*, pp. 455–456.

145. *Ibid.*, p. 475.

146. A more discriminating view will be found in Hanna Bokor-Szegö, *New States and International Law* (Budapest: Akademiai Kiado, 1970). In her opinion the declaration interprets the Charter in defining the right of self-determination but in several respects, "when it condemns all forms of colonial rule," disregards the distinction between trust and non-self-governing territories and when it "demands the immediate granting of independence to all dependent territories," it goes beyond the Charter. "These provisions of the Declaration . . . cannot be considered interpretation of the Charter. They amend and develop it in a progressive sense. As, however, amendments to the Charter are governed by its provisions in Chapter XVIII, the Declaration in question could not validly modify the appropriate articles of the Charter." *Ibid.*, pp. 28–29.

147. *Supra*, n. 122, Suppl. 1A (A/8001/Add. 1), *Introduction to the Annual Report of the Secretary-General*, p. 14, paragraph 113.

148. *Report* of the Special Committee on the Situation with Regard to the Implementation of the Declaration on the Granting of Independence to Colonial Countries and Peoples (covering its work during 1970), Document A/8023/Add. 8, Annex, p. 5. On pp. 6–8 there is a list of non-self-governing territories, the total number of which is somewhat less than forty-five.

149. *Ibid.*, p. 6. The last territory, New Hebrides, is a condominium with the United Kingdom.

150. *Ibid.*, p. 4.

151. See *supra*, n. 147, *Introduction to the Annual Report of the Secretary-General*, p. 15, paragraph 122.

152. See Gross, "Role of Law," p. 555f.

153. See *supra*, n. 147, *Introduction to the Report of the Secretary-General*, p. 12, paragraph 103. Italics supplied.

154. This is the request of the Security Council of July 29, 1970, for an opinion on the "Legal Consequences for States of the Continued Presence of South Africa in Namibia (South West Africa) notwithstanding Security Council Resolution 276 (1970)." ICJ *Yearbook* (1969–1970), p. 5.

155. *Asylum* case (Colombia/Peru), ICJ *Reports* (1950), p. 266, at 276, 277.

156. Case concerning *Right of Passage over Indian Territory* (*Portugal* v. *India*), ICJ *Reports* (1960), p. 6, at 39.

157. *Corfu Channel* case (*United Kingdom/Albania*), ICJ *Reports* (1949), p. 4, at 28.

158. *Fisheries* case (*United Kingdom v. Norway*), ICJ *Reports* (1951), p. 116, at 129 and 131.

159. ICJ *Reports* (1951), p. 15, at 24, 29.

160. Advisory opinion: ICJ *Reports* (1949), p. 174, at 179, 182, 184.

161. Advisory opinion: ICJ *Reports* (1950), p. 128, at 143–144.

162. *South West Africa* Cases (*Ethiopia* v. *South Africa; Liberia* v. *South Africa*), Second Phase, Judgment, ICJ *Reports* (1966), p. 6, at 51.

163. General Assembly, *Official Records* (22nd sess.), Suppl. 1 (A/6701/Add. 1), *Introduction to the Annual Report of the Secretary-General on the Work of the Organization*, June 16, 1966–June 15, 1967, p. 19, par. 155.

164. *Nottebohm* case (*Liechtenstein v. Guatemala*), ICJ *Reports* (1955), p. 4 at 23.

165. For the history of the commission, its functions, and composition, see General Assembly, *Official Records* (22nd sess.), Suppl. 1 (A/6701), *Annual Report of the Secretary-General on the Work of the Organization*, June 16, 1966–June 15, 1967, pp. 180–182.

166. For a brief history of the proposal, see *supra,* n. 122, *Annual Report of the Secretary-General,* p. 115.

167. *Ibid.,* p. 229.

168. ICJ *Yearbook* (1969–1970), p. 51.

169. For a brief analysis, see Leo Gross, "The International Court of Justice and the United Nations," Hague Academy of International Law, *Recueil des Cours,* I, 1967 (Leyden: Sijthoff, 1968), 319–435, particularly 422–435.

170. Document A/8042, August 14, 1970, p. 3.

171. Resolution 2723 (XXV), in General Assembly, *Official Records* (25th sess.), Suppl. 28 (A/8028), p. 128.

Robert W. Gregg

UN ECONOMIC, SOCIAL, AND TECHNICAL ACTIVITIES

International organizations are only one of the many channels through which the issues making up international relations flow. The overwhelming preponderance of international relations continues to be bilateral in character. In the sea of world affairs, international organization as a generic form of interstate relations does not loom particularly large. Moreover, there are many who seem ready to write the obituary for the most prominent of international organizations, the United Nations. Bereft of dramatic accomplishments for a decade or more and unable to demonstrate a capacity for sustained task expansion, the UN seems to have declined in importance.

But, if international organization is only an iceberg in a vast sea of global relations, and perhaps a melting one at that, it might be well to recall that icebergs display but a small fraction of their bulk above the water lines. It is submitted that we have been too mesmerized by the visible fraction of international organization activity, the part charged with peace-keeping and peace-restoring. In this realm of high politics, there is no doubt that the United Nations has faltered and fallen into relative desuetude.

However, international organizations do many things; the issues which crowd their agenda include aid and trade, transportation and communication, science and technology, health and welfare, modernization and industrialization, food and population. Although these issues may at times generate a substantial amount of heat, they tend to be less volatile and urgent than the issues which are the stuff of headlines. They also command the attention of more limited publics. These economic, social, and technical issues are of course political issues, but some issues are less conspicuously political than others and they are the ones that make up the invisible bulk of the iceberg of international organization activity.

What they lack in drama and urgency, these issues make up in magnitudes of several kinds. They dominate the phenomenon of international organization. Most international agencies could reasonably be characterized as primarily economic, social, and technical, as opposed to political and security, in purpose. The budgets of international agencies are similarly weighted toward "nonpolitical" issues, and the overwhelming majority of international staff have credentials and assignments which involve them in those issue areas. According to virtually all indices of size and scope, if not of influence and importance, international organization is preponderantly international economic, social, and technical organization. It is not inconceivable that the quantitatively larger sector of international organization may prove to be the qualitatively more significant as well.

The very scale of the organizational activity in economic, social, and technical sectors requires more detailed analysis, not so much to make the point more convincing as to lend some shape and substance to that mass below the surface of our attention. One could begin by leafing through a recent edition of the *Yearbook of International Organizations*. Remove the pages devoted to public international agencies which are primarily concerned with questions of clear and present danger to peace and security, and neither length nor heft of the book is diminished sufficiently to make the difference noticeable. Among global organizations, all a part of the United Nations system, the disproportion between "political" and "economic/social/technical" agencies is even more pronounced. Only the UN itself is specifically enjoined to concern itself with the larger issues of war and peace, and its attention—as well as its structure, staff, and budget —is divided, with a major emphasis on economic and social questions. When one adds to the UN the specialized agencies, the bank group, the International Atomic Energy Agency, and major UN operational programs and organs, the resulting United Nations system is overwhelmingly oriented toward that cluster of issues which we have labeled economic, social, and technical.

The roll call of UN system agencies and operational programs reveals the scope of international organizational activity in these sectors: the UN's own Economic and Social Council (ECOSOC); the International Labour Organization (ILO); the Food and Agriculture Organization (FAO); the United Nations Educational, Scientific, and Cultural Organization (UNESCO); the World Health Organization (WHO); the International Civil Aviation Organization (ICAO); the Universal Postal Union (UPU); the International Telecommunications Union (ITU); the World Meteorological Organization (WMO); the International Maritime Consultative Organization (IMCO); the International Bank for Reconstruction and Development (IBRD); the International Monetary Fund (IMF); the International Development Association (IDA); the International Atomic Energy Agency (IAEA); the United Nations Development Program (UNDP); the United Nations Conference on Trade and Development (UNCTAD); the United Nations Industrial Development Organization (UNIDO); and the World Food Program (WFP). On paper this may be a mind-numbing list of memorable acronyms and forgettable titles, but in practice it represents an enormous commitment to the proposition that economic and social and technical problems deserve a high priority on the global agenda, and that multilateral, institutionalized approaches to these problems are highly valued and may in some cases be essential.

If one takes the assessed budgets of the UN and the specialized agencies (excluding the bank group) *and* the voluntary contributions to UNDP for 1969, the total is $557.3 million.[1] Of this amount, $406.1 million represents the budgets of the agencies and contributions to UNDP,[2] *all* by definition earmarked for economic, social, and technical purposes or the administration of programs serving those purposes. That is nearly three-quarters of the total. Moreover, a substantial portion of the UN's own budget is used for these categories of activities. Very conservatively, at least 85 percent of the $557.3 million was spent for economic, social, and technical purposes, leaving no more than 15 percent for peacekeeping and maintenance of the elaborate machinery of the "parliament of nations." The administrative expenses of the bank and IDA for the fiscal year ending June 30, 1970, were another $62.9 million;[3] although bank loans and IDA credits are not comparable to UNDP and UN system technical assistance expenditures, totals would be enormously higher if we added the $2.29 billion of loans and credits for 1970.[4] These figures represent a lumping together of many different kinds of programs and strategies for international cooperation, but they do suggest the extent to which international organizations operate outside the spotlight of crisis diplomacy.

Similarly, the profile of international officialdom points in the same direction. The secretary-general and his more familiar emissaries on peace missions may command our attention, but they are a minute fraction of the UN system staff, and the total number of persons in political and security posts within the UN system is relatively small. Of the 10,565 professional personnel financed by the regular budgets of the UN system agencies as of January 1969, 8,177, or more than three-fourths, were directly or indirectly involved in economic, social, or technical activities.[5] If we include project personnel, and particularly the professionals employed in the field under UNDP auspices, the total of UN system professional staff climbs to 18,451 for that date, of which approximately 16,000 or 87 percent may be said to have had their assignments as a result of the international organization's mandate in the economic/social/technical sector.[6] Once again, Bank Group personnel add substantially to the total.

The preceding recital of magnitudes is not intended to convey the impression that the UN system is either enormous or enormously successful. Compared with the bilateral machinery for conducting international relations, the UN system is very modest in scale. However, the point we wish to make is that there is "another UN" and a large one at that. In fact, the focus of the United Nations system upon investment, development planning, transfer of knowledge, and technological revolution has become so important—perhaps to the world and certainly to the UN—that it may not be hyperbole to claim that the future of the United Nations and the historical judgment upon it may be more closely related to what it accomplishes in these spheres of action than to what it does or does not do in the realm of war and peace.

II

It is not an easy task to find a handle by which to take hold of this "other United Nations." It is a many-sided phenomenon, a grab bag of issues and agencies and programs, each with different origin, history, clients, rationale, and decision style. Under what rubric do we subsume all of this variety? What organizing principle can we employ which will permit generalizations about UNCTAD and ICAO, narcotic drugs and reforestation, locust control and social welfare? Simply to lump together economic, social, and technical matters, as we have been doing in the first pages of this essay, is not a very felicitous way of classifying international organizational activities.

There is probably no single conceptual device which will permit us to speak systematically, coherently, and generally about this large, amorphous, and little publicized United Nations. But there are several characteristic features of the economic and social and technical UN which, if identified and analyzed, may facilitate understanding of what it is and what it does without the necessity of treating each of its many issue areas seriatim in a long catalog of individually limned programs and agencies. These several salient characteristics will also provide a framework for examining the historical development of the United Nations system in this sphere and for assessing its future prospects.

There are at least six such salient characteristics of that sphere of UN activity under discussion. They are not at all mutually exclusive, but are rather mutually reinforcing as well as overlapping. They do not all pertain to all aspects of UN activity in this sphere, but their reach is wide enough and deep enough to permit the observation that they do in fact characterize the UN system as a whole.

1. The activities of this sector of the UN system are rooted in part in the proposition that knowledge and its widespread dissemination and application to practical problems is intrinsically desirable and very probably instrumental in the creation of a more stable, peaceful world. There is here the echo of Wilsonian idealism, the notion that peace will remain elusive until all peoples better understand each other and their environment. The constitution of UNESCO makes the point very explicitly: "Since wars begin the minds of men, it is in the minds of men that the defenses of peace must be constructed." The sharing *and* the creation of knowledge have been the special province of international organizations of an economic, social, and technical character almost from their inception, whether consequences for war and peace can be demonstrated or not. The United Nations system is a research complex, a data-gathering enterprise; it is an elaborate clearing house of information as well as a generator of new information. It seeks to chart the economic and social and technical dimensions of the world in order to better understand them, cope with them, and ameliorate them. All international organizations perform these functions;

when the UN Security Council is seized of a situation described as a threat to the peace or when the General Assembly is debating questions of racial discrimination, part of the problem is to ascertain the facts. But this is a problem so different in degree as to be virtually different in kind. In the realm of high politics, facts are likely to be a matter of perspective. In the less politically volatile world of food and agriculture, health and disease, resources and development, the prescriptions may be controversial but there remains a widespread acceptance of the need to define the problem, give statistical specificity to its dimensions, and share expertise which may help to overcome it.

This research task of the UN system commands the services of economists, statisticians, and experts from literally dozens of fields. It produces regular reports in a variety of areas, such as the annual *World Economic Report* (UN), *Statistical Yearbook* (UN), *Year Book of Labor Statistics* (ILO), *World Survey on Education* (UNESCO), *The State of Food and Agriculture* (FAO), *Epidemiological and Vital Statistics Report* (WHO), *International Financial Statistics* (IMF), *Direction of International Trade* (UN, IBRD, IMF), and *Report on the World Social Situation* (UN). Moreover, a number of justly famous research reports have been produced on special topics by the UN system, such as *Towards a New Trade Policy for Development,* authored by Raúl Prebisch, former executive secretary of the United Nations Economic Commission for Latin America (ECLA) and secretary-general of UNCTAD. These and related publications add up to an immeasurably valuable assessment, and in many cases continued reassessment, of the world's economic, social, and technical problems, as well as a commentary, sometimes quite explicit and at other times implied, upon the speed and efficiency with which they are being addressed. The resulting wealth of information is of course incomplete and contains its share of errors. But the UN's contribution to knowledge in these areas has been so great and so fundamentally important as a basis for future efforts of both a multilateral and bilateral character, that if the United Nations system should cease to exist tomorrow, at least these research and informational services would have to be reinstituted at once.

2. A second salient characteristic of the UN system in these fields is closely related to the first. It is the functionalist orientation of the activity. Functionalism as a prescription for peace and for the organization of the international system has been explained and reexplained by a series of advocates and interpreters.[7] Its fundamental premise is that nation-states are not the most promising instrumentalities for achieving enduring peace, nor are conflict-laden issues of high politics the most promising vehicles for developing habits of cooperation. Eschewing states and statesmen, the functionalist emphasizes an incremental approach to peace which would be based upon the collaborative efforts of experts in relatively noncontroversial areas of shared interest and need. By a process of spillover, the penchant for cooperation developed in one functional sector would lead to cooperation in other sectors. In the long run, states would atrophy and

a nexus of cooperative relationships based upon function would be the characteristic feature of the international system.

This millennial view of international relations patently overstates the capacity of experts, in the absence of benevolently active governmental support, to transform the world. It also assumes a kind of automaticity of spillover of cooperative habits from one sector to another, when in fact there is much evidence of the separability of issue areas. However, the emphasis upon the development of strategies of cooperation in nonsecurity areas, as well as the preponderant use of nongovernmental professionals in these endeavors, gives the UN system a functionalist dimension. If ECOSOC, FAO, and UNCTAD are organized in the traditional fashion, with governments represented in their assemblies, their agenda is at least the agenda of functionalism. One of the oldest of the specialized agencies in the UN system, ILO, has taken a further step toward the functionalist model, giving representation to labor and management as well as to government in its celebrated tripartite system. And in all of the agencies and programs concerned with economic, social, and technical questions, although to varying degrees, the assemblies, secretariats, and field projects are populated with persons who do not fit the stereotype of politician-diplomat. They may have the skills of the statesman; but their primary credentials in most cases are their competence and experience as economists, public health officials, agronomists, engineers, and experts in a host of other lines normally deemed apolitical.

The UN system is, in brief, a hybrid version of the functionalist prescription, for one of the major characteristics of UN activity is its emphasis on welfare rather than security and its emphasis on professionalism rather than politics.

3. A third characteristic of the UN system in this area is that it is regulatory. This is, of course, an inflated generalization about the United Nations, a caricature of reality. But there is much more than a kernel of truth in the observation that UN system agencies have regulatory responsibilities which are almost totally lacking in more conspicuously political and security sectors of their mandates.

Regulation implies legislation and its enforcement. International organizations have very little rule-making authority; they do define the rules for their own internal functioning but they do not, with but a very few exceptions, legislate with respect to the issue areas which make up their agenda. When they do, enforcement is left to sovereign states. This is merely a reflection of the fact that power and authority are decentralized within the international system. The exceptions which prove this rule are for the most part clustered in the economic and social and technical sectors under review here. This is not surprising, given the less politically sensitive character of nonsecurity issues.

The regulatory thrust of the UN system is based upon the widely shared perception that minimally effective functioning of the international system requires some regulation in some fields. This need for relatively predictable and relatively smoothly functioning relationships in some areas has been responsible for much of existing international law. It has also spawned a number of international organizations which are a part of the UN system and which through their regular machinery or through special conferences adopt conventions or otherwise make rules for the regulation of international activities which can remain unregulated only at an intolerable cost to member states of the system.

The full spectrum of UN agencies and programs is not engaged in regulatory activity.[8] It is the more technical agencies that regulate, notably those in the fields of communication and to a lesser degree those concerned with transportation and diseases and other phenomena which are no respecters of political boundaries. Some of this activity is indisputably regulatory; the rules are binding and they are observed, almost reflexively. In other cases the regulatory activity is more tentative; the UN system makes rules but they are less comprehensive within the "regulated" field and their acceptance and enforcement are more problematic. The former case is exemplified by the Universal Postal Union and the International Telecommunications Union, neither of which looms large in terms either of size or attention in most assessments of the UN system, but both of which have more authority to create and administer regulations than most other global organizations. Similarly, the World Health Organization and the International Civil Aviation Organization have limited regulatory capability. It can hardly be claimed that the ILO is a regulatory agency; but its conventions prescribe labor standards and practices and have a force greater than that of the hortatory and recommendatory resolutions which are the principal output of the deliberative process of most international organizations.

It would appear that regulation by international agencies is likely to be most ambitious in those areas where it is urgently needed *and* where political sensitivity is not controlling. The allocation of international high-frequency radio channels by an international agency remains the most instructive illustration of this proposition.

4. One of the most insistent facts about the United Nations, especially in this area, is its redistributive character. Virtually all resources are available in insufficient supply to satisfy all states, much less all of the world's population. This is true for intangible resources such as attention and influence and for tangible resources such as wealth, goods, and services. International organization is continuously engaged in the redistribution of these resources or at least in providing a forum in which their distribution is the announced or tacit subject of debate.

Nowhere, however, is the redistributive character of interstate relations more openly acknowledged or more conspicuously focused than in the economic, social, and technical aspects of United Nations activity. Aid and trade are bilateral phenomena as well as multilateral, and in fact bulk much larger outside of the UN system than within it. But the UN has undertaken to make the claims of developing or disadvantaged states matters of right, not of privilege, and the response of developed or better-endowed states a matter of obligation, not of discretion. The very range of UN system programs and projects in economic and social fields is testimony to the capacity of the have-not majority of states to compel attention to its arguments and to gain legitimacy for its position. The crucial feature of the UN effort is not, however, that the UN and the specialized agencies have addressed themselves to questions of welfare and development, but that a substantial commitment of financial and human resources has been made toward the realization of a more equitable distribution of economic and social well-being.

This redistributive effort is made explicit in the case of the World Bank and its related agencies, the International Finance Corporation (IFC) and IDA. It is the rationale for the UNDP and its component parts, the Expanded Program of Technical Assistance (EPTA) and the Special Fund, both of which antedated the creation of UNDP by many years. It explains UNCTAD and UNIDO, two of the most recent UN creations, which are expressions of a desire to restructure world trade and to hasten industrial development. The whole panoply of UN agencies, as well as the UN itself, send forth a steady stream of both dollars and experts. This redistributive thrust of the agencies is brought into focus by a few statistics. In 1968 technical assistance expenditures constituted 71 percent of the total net expenditures of FAO, 49 percent in the case of UNESCO, and 47 percent, 46 percent, and 42 percent in the cases of WHO, ILO, and the UN, respectively.[9] The flow of experts is also a conspicuous form of redistribution, and in 1968 the UN system dispatched a total of 10,317 experts to developing states; the number had been only 1,733 as recently as 1952.[10] If World Bank loans and IDA credits are regarded as redistributive even if repayment is expected, we find seventy loans and fifty-six credits made by the Bank and IDA, respectively, in 1970. They aggregated $1,680 million and $606 million and brought the cumulative total of Bank/IDA support in the form of loans and credits to $17,047 million as of June 30, 1970.[11] There are many other ways of making this point, but it is not really in dispute—the UN is engaged in an ambitious redistribution of resources which are in chronically short supply, notably money and expertise.

5. Another important characteristic of the UN effort is that it is to a large and growing extent operational. The UN system is not only conference machinery and research capability; nor is it only confined to New York, Geneva, and other headquarters sites. Associated with the shift of attention to economic and social questions, and especially with redistribution of resources, is an impulse to leave the offices and laboratories, the polished corridors and conference rooms, and get out into the field. Inexorably, the UN system has been drawn by the logic of its agenda and of its research findings away from postures of detached discussion, fact-finding, analysis, and prescription, and toward action. The UN has "gone operational." [12]

The operational thrust of the UN system means a number of things in practice. In the first place, it means that international agencies under the UN umbrella have had to develop a whole new set of administrative skills and practices. It is one thing to stage conferences and process resolutions which are in the main enforced by nation-states, if they are enforced at all. It is quite another to assume responsibility for negotiating technical assistance, preinvestment projects, or loans and then implementing the agreements. International administration has been transformed by the operational character of its economic and social activities. Another aspect of this trend has been the growth of funding schemes other than assessment. The annual pledging conference is now an important phenomenon, swelling as it does the capacity of the UN system to provide goods and services in the developing regions of the world. In 1969, for instance, voluntary contributions to the UNDP totaled nearly as much as the regular budgets of all of the specialized agencies, exclusive of the Bank Group and IMF, and much more than the regular budget of the UN itself. Over $1.6 billion has been contributed through pledging to the Expanded Program of Technical Assistance, the Special Fund, and UNDP since 1950.[13] These monies would not have been forthcoming, nor perhaps would the regular budgets of agencies such as WHO displayed such growth, had the UN remained rooted at headquarters and in conference and research endeavors.

There are other facets to the operational trend. Paralleling the growth of nonassessed budget resources has been the development of a large group of UN system personnel who are not a part of the regular staff of the UN or the agencies, but who are recruited on a relatively short-term basis to staff the various projects which make up the operational program. As of January 1969, such personnel totaled nearly eight thousand, and in the case of the agencies actually exceeded the number of professional personnel on the regular budget.[14] All of these feautres of the operational United Nations have either induced or accelerated a trend toward regionalization and decentralization within the UN system. If UN programs are field-oriented, so increasingly are UN structures and decision-making authority. To a degree undreamed of, much less attempted, in the days of the League of Nations, not only has the UN system dirtied its hands with action programs, but it has also transferred more and more of its people and its authority to locations far from New York and Geneva and closer to the recipients of the goods and services which it is redistributing. This shift in the organizational center of gravity of the UN system has been most pronounced in the case of WHO, which is highly decentralized and which has long used the largest percentage of its regular budget for technical assistance of any of the agencies, and in the case of the UN itself, whose Regional Economic Commissions are one of the more interesting features of the economic and social sphere of the UN system. In general, the UN is closer to the grass roots in these issue areas, at least geographically, than in any other.

6. One final feature of the "other UN" would appear to be its integrative character. It seems to be the consensus of the literature that the regional approach to integration, rather than the global, is most promising. If global integration is to take place, it will presumably follow upon regional integration, the global edifice being built with regional blocks.[15] One may search long and hard for evidence of truly integrative as opposed to more modestly cooperative activity within the UN system. But, consciously or not, the ultimate goal of the United Nations is probably an integrated world in which disputes are invariably resolved by peaceful means, a world in which decision making as opposed to merely recommendatory power resides in the global organization and in which the judgments of those central organs enjoy legitimacy and command confidence. This is the logical extension of the very meaning of the United Nations, whether it is the acknowledged goal or not. In the shorter run, however, the integrative quality of the United Nations efforts is of a decidedly different order.

If the record does not support the conclusion that the UN system is an integrating system, it does suggest that the activities of the UN and the specialized agencies display on occasions a kind of incipient integrative quality which ought to be noted. And that quality is most apparent in the economic sector. Although the acceptance by nation-states of global norms is quite limited, certain ideas are legitimated as a result of UN efforts or, more precisely, as the result of persistent pressures which are channeled through the UN and the agencies.[16] As noted earlier, the view that developed states have an obligation to provide tangible support for the economic development of new and poor states has in effect been legitimated by the United Nations, although no capacity to compel the developed states to provide that support yet exists. However modest this and related accomplishments in the economic, social, and technical sectors may be, they point toward a more integrated world in which members begin to act systematically on the time-worn but tenacious proposition that no man is an island.

Within the UN system, the most significant efforts with an avowedly integrative thrust have probably been those of the UN regional economic commissions, especially the Economic Commission for Latin America. A transfer of authority from nation-states to international agencies has been consciously sought by ECLA, which has played the catalytic role in launching common market schemes in Latin America (the Latin American Free Trade Association and the Central American Common Market). It is interesting that the most conspicuously integrative efforts of the global organization have been made at the regional level by regional units of the UN. It is probably no accident that regionalism began to flourish within the UN system at the very time that regional schemes for economic cooperation and integration outside of the global organization, such as the European Common Market, were beginning to display vigor.

It is the thesis of virtually all of the literature on integration that the economic sector would be the one most likely to generate momentum. The assumption is that economic activity is sufficiently important to bear the weight of integration, but not as sensitive as military and security activity and hence more likely to be allowed to serve as a vehicle for integration. At their most ambitious, UN activities in the economic and technical sectors have been less tied to preservation of the present international system than have UN activities in the areas of peace and security; moreover, they have followed regional paths in important instances. Thus these activities appear to possess some integrative potential, at least enough to warrant the statement that one of the distinctive characteristics of the UN system in its economic, social, and technical aspects is that relative to the UN of high politics it is modestly integrative.

III

The six salient features of UN activity which have been outlined here are closely related to each other. They did not all manifest themselves simultaneously, however. Nor have they developed evenly. The history of this aspect of international organization reveals a close relationship between the changing international environment, on the one hand, and the creation of international agencies, task expansion within such agencies, and the development of these several characteristics of the UN system, on the other.

It may be useful, in viewing the evolution of UN economic, social, and technical activity, to treat the UN system as a phenomenon which began in 1865 with the establishment of the Union télégraphique internationale.[17] This fiction, which takes liberties with historical facts but not with historical trends, adopts the present UN system as our point of departure and enables us to project it backward in time to its origins and forward to its still dimly perceived future. Whereas the Concert of Europe is the antecedent of the UN Security Council, the Union télégraphique internationale is the lineal ancestor of, and still (as the ITU) an integral part of, the economic, social, and technical component of the United Nations system. The ITU, together with the Universal Postal Union, founded in 1874 as the General Postal Union, constitutes the beginning of global international organization in areas other than peace and security. Although it was to be a long time before this entering wedge was expanded to any appreciable extent, the UN system as we know it today had been launched. ITU and UPU were (and are) conspicuously characterized by a functionalist orientation, a commitment to the creation and dissemination of information in these specialized areas, and a mandate to regulate these important media of international communication. Other characteristic features of the "nonpolitical" UN were subsequently grafted on or grew naturally, under appropriate environmental conditions, from these roots in the public international unions of the nineteenth century.

Both in terms of growth in the numbers of UN system agencies and programs and in terms of task expansion among those agencies and programs, the subsequent history of international organization activity in these sectors may be divided somewhat arbitrarily into four phases. In each of these periods of time the role of global international organization in the economic, social, and technical sectors has been greater than in the previous period. The several periods are distinguished from each other by specific events or by an acceleration of trends so pronounced as to create a new thrust or emphasis within the UN system.

The first phase is that of the public international unions. In terms of international politics, this epoch in the history of international organization encompassed several different periods: the Bismarckian, the turn-of-the-century period of imperialist nationalism, and finally World War I. But the UN system-to-be was a very limited one during this period, its mandate narrowly technical, the reach of its activities cautiously circumscribed. The international organization habit had not yet been cultivated, although the unions were a proving ground for the development of some of the principal ingredients of contemporary international organization. Their survival and the presence of continued support for them through major changes in the international system were evidence of the viability of formal machinery for international cooperation in politically less sensitive areas.

A second phase in this evolutionary trend coincides with the creation of the League of Nations and the International Labour Organization at the end of the war. It lasted through the breakdown of the tenuous stability which states thought they had achieved at Versailles and ended with World War II, another watershed for international organization. The importance of ILO to the evolution of international organization cannot be overstated.[18] Albert Thomas created a model of international executive leadership and the tripartite system a model of representation at variance with traditional assumptions about the role of the nation-states in international decision making. The proposition that economic conditions may breed war or contribute significantly, if indirectly, to it was given serious and prominent attention. A major and frequently delicate matter of intrastate relations was recognized as a matter of interstate concern in about as dramatic a way as possible: the creation of a major new international organization at the peace conference which was terminating the most devastating war in modern history.

The establishment of the League of Nations itself was also an event of great importance, but the consequences for economic and social cooperation were primarily latent; although the League had an Economic and Financial Organization, a Communications and Transit Organization, an Intellectual Cooperation Organization, a Health Organization, and, in the realm of social issues, an Advisory Committee on Traffic in Women and Children and in Opium and Other Dangerous Drugs, it was not until the latter days of the League's existence that its economic and social respon-

sibilities began to receive the prominent and creative attention that they
have been accorded in the UN era. The League mandate was modest; its
performance was comparably modest. Although the several organizations
and committees in economic, social, and technical fields were prototypes
for subsequently developed UN system agencies, they labored primarily
(and not very productively) in the realm of text drafting, hoping to elaborate a network of agreements, binding upon governments, which would
prescribe state behavior in a variety of economic, financial, and related
matters. Whatever the limitations of the international organization effort
in these fields, the League period was one of marked growth in the number
of issues under global purview and in the institutional mechanisms established to cope with them.[19]

It was in the last years of the League's existence, however, that the
third phase in this facet of UN system history had its beginnings. The
third phase is the initial UN phase, the period of the creation and early
development of the United Nations itself and the more important of the
specialized agencies. But the League's Bruce Commission pointed to this
new chapter with its call for a reorientation of the focus of the 1920s and
1930s. As stated in the Report of the Bruce Commission in 1939, deep
in the gathering shadow of World War II, "the primary object of international cooperation should be rather mutual help than reciprocal contract." [20] Without really abandoning the established concerns of the preceding years, the founders of the UN system took their cue from the Bruce
Commission and created a set of agencies with a commitment to positive
action with a functionalist bias. They also created in the UN's Economic
and Social Council a body which was intended to be the counterpart in
the economic sector of the Security Council and the coordinating center-
piece of the UN system. Earlier committees and organizations were transformed into FAO, WHO, and UNESCO; the debacle of World War II
imparted to the agencies impetus to address a wide range of urgent problems, and the UN itself assumed extensive residual responsibility with
respect to economic and social questions. Although an operational thrust
had yet to be developed, and a self-conscious mission of integration was
lacking, the UN system had extended the reach of its concern and its
capacity far beyond the tentative beginnings in the public international
unions or the faltering League experiment. This third phase was brief; it
was not terminated, but rather was overtaken early in the UN's history by
pressures to make international organization an active partner in the developmental and modernization process.[21]

President Truman's enunciation of what came to be called the Point
Four doctrine probably marked the beginning of the fourth phase in this
process. The World Bank had been established at the Bretton Woods Conference in 1945, and the business of economic development with the aid
of international organization was under way. But the main thrust of the
UN system was not, in the early postwar years, developmental or operational. The Expanded Program of Technical Assistance changed that,

bringing together donors and recipient states to effect a transfer of technology under the aegis of the UN and the specialized agencies.

Just as the third phase was characterized by the establishment of the UN and a large number of coordinate specialized agencies, as well as by the cultivation and assertion by each of its own expertise, style, and role, the fourth phase has been characterized by a quest for effective and politically acceptable development strategies by the UN system. The principal thrust of the UN system outside of the Bank Group has been in the realm of technical cooperation. Experts have gone by the thousands to developing countries, fellowship recipients by the thousands from developing to developed countries for training. This incremental approach to development has generated its own problems and led to corrective efforts to increase the impact of technical assistance as well as the volume of it. Thus this fourth and most recent phase of UN history has produced the Special Fund to channel more funds into fewer projects of longer duration in order to improve the investment climate of recipient countries; UNDP to merge the Expanded Program and the Special Fund into a more efficient and well-coordinated aid-distributing instrumentality; UNIDO to overcome the dispersion of UN industrial development resources and efforts among a large number of agencies and programs within the UN system; a growing emphasis upon development plans within recipient countries and upon joint planning and execution of projects within the UN system; a field network, far from New York and the European capitals of the agencies, consisting of regional offices, resident representatives, and experts, with attendant devolution of authority and responsibility; and, with the creation of UNCTAD, an assertion that trade more than aid is the key to more rapid economic development and that it should be restructured in ways favorable to the so-called LDCs.

These trends and organizational events have brought into being the full set of characteristics described as salient in UN economic, social, and technical activity earlier in this chapter. In fact, two of the six characteristics are virtually peculiar to this most recent period: the redistributive nature of the activity and its operational dimension. The sixth attribute, its integrative quality, while present in latent form earlier, has become overt in recent years with respect to both the identification of new norms and the establishment of new "unions" or integrating organizations.

These several phases in the history of the UN system reflect the changing international environment. Inasmuch as it continues to change, and at an accelerating rate, it should not be surprising to discover that we are at the threshold of yet another period—if, indeed, we have not already crossed it. Such environmental factors as the distribution of wealth; volume and patterns of world trade; channels of international communication and transportation; number and variety of states which are members of the international system; demographic trends; levels of literacy; economic and social content of ideological movements; war and war-induced dislocation; status of technological innovation and application—these and a host of other environmental factors have shaped the UN system since its inception, and as they shift the organizational response to them shifts, eventually if not at once.

The contrast between the environment of today and that of a century ago, approximately the time when the first public international unions were established, is so dramatic and obvious as to require virtually no documentation. The world than was Eurocentric; indeed, it was an almost exclusively European world as far as international organization was concerned. It may be that the Concept of Europe had broken down, but the residual need to regulate communications and to exchange information basic to the efficient functioning of the state system persisted, and it seemed to be an essentially European need. Wealth was not equitably shared, but the disparities in wealth among states which are so glaringly apparent in the 1970s were not approached a century ago. The second half of the nineteenth century was, in the long view of history, very much a part of the modern era; but so nearly exponential has been the rate of growth of technology, transportation, and communication that, in the brief history of international organization, that period is part of another very remote era. Europe was then enough one world to sustain the cautious functionalism of the ITU and UPU; it was far enough into the age of industrialization, with its attendant pressures on routine inter-state relations, to require that these and other agencies be established to help facilitate routinization of those relations.

The informational and routine regulative activities of international organizations flourished first. They were and they remain immune to all but the most extreme ideological currents. They are fed by technological revolution and respond to increases in literacy and a general capacity to absorb and use knowledge. The most advanced states, the heaviest users of the world's arteries of communication and transportation, have the greatest stake in these services. They initiated them and have sustained them. The functionalist character of these activities has also been present from the beginning, but more in the form of specialized attention to specific problems than of self-conscious pursuit of "peace in pieces." Both of the great wars resulted in experiments in modified functionalism. In addition to political and peacekeeping apparatus, both wars prompted creation of machinery in the economic, social, and technical sectors, and it was more extensive, more ambitious, and its mandate more specific after World War II than after the first war.

In effect, what has happened with respect to the UN system is that the world has closed in. Population has risen dramatically; the communications revolution has brought the various elements of that population into a much greater and more immediate awareness of each other than would have been thought possible when ITU was established; resources are being depleted at a savage rate. Spaceship earth, in Barbara Ward's felicitous phrase, requires conscious and constant tending. These trends have been accompanied by a proliferation of agencies and programs and an expansion of their terms of reference. This would probably have happened had international politics remained primarily a European or Western phenomenon, its members relatively few and all of them relatively affluent, whether conflicts of interest degenerated into conflicts of ideology or not.

But, of course, the world of the UN system has not remained so geographically limited and so economically and culturally homogeneous. The quantitative *and* qualitative changes in the membership of the nation-state system, combined with the revolution in technology and communication and the political and economic legacy of two world wars, have wrought a transformation in the UN system. They have contrived to give the UN's economic and social activities a redistributive character. They have led to a pronounced shift in the direction of more operationally active international organizations. They have intensified the politicization of the functional attributes of the UN system without impeding the trend toward ever-more specialized programs to deal with ever-more technical transnational problems. They have created new incentives for integration and new and somewhat more self-conscious strategies for its realization.

These changes, which have produced such a modification of the thrust of the UN system, have frequently been summed up in the observation that the main axis of conflict within international organization in recent years has been North-South rather than East-West. Although an oversimplification of the reality of UN politics, the assertion of the primacy of North-South or developed-developing state issues does correspond to a major long-term trend. At one time or another, a total of sixty-three states belonged to the League of Nations; fifty-one were charter members of the United Nations. The overwhelming percentage of both groups were European, North American, and Latin American. Athough the Latin American states were during the League and early UN period (as they are today) LDCs, that distinction had not acquired currency and the tendency was to view them as Western states. Still Western in some important senses of the word, today the Latin American states are readily classified as underdeveloped and hence an integral part of the larger "bloc" of Southern states within the UN system. Nothing better illustrates the shift from East-West to North-South politics within the UN than this acknowledged migration of the Latin American republics.

Quantitatively, the UN membership has vaulted from 51 to 128 in twenty-five years; the membership of the specialized agencies has kept pace. This membership explosion alone reflects environmental changes which were bound to affect the economic, social, and technical mandates of the UN system. But it is the qualitative change that has been critical. During the League era, a majority of states could probably have been classified as poor and lacking the essential attributes of modern industrial states. But the Eurocentric character of the League and the ILO smothered the welfare and development issues and contributed to the somewhat legalistic approach to the economic and social agenda. From a modest beginning of fewer than ten conspicuously underdeveloped member states from Africa, the Middle East, and Asia, these regions of "new" states now constitute better than 50 percent of UN membership and include nearly seventy of that organization's members. Coupled with the Latin American states in the first UNCTAD in 1964, those African and Asian states which were then independent produced the much publicized "75," a bloc committed to the proposition that the gap between rich and poor nations has been widening and that it is of utmost urgency that the United Nations address itself forcefully and immediately to the closing of that gap.[22]

At the time EPTA was launched, a majority of UN system member states were LDCs by most standards of measurement, but the redistributive and operational tides were running slowly. Throughout the decade of the 1950s, the shift in these directions continued, but only incrementally. Thirty-two states had joined the UN from 1946 through the late 1950s, of which eighteen were non-European. Thus reconstituted, the UN was seized with the issue of SUNFED, the movement for a capital development fund; it failed and the Special Fund was established in its stead.[23] IDA was set up as a subsidiary of the World Bank to provide development financing on more flexible terms than was possible with conventional loans. The first rumblings of the campaign for decentralization to the UN regional economic commissions were heard, as the LDCs were generally becoming restless with an unrepresentative ECOSOC and with traditional theories of economic development propounded by Western economists both on delegations to international conferences and as members of international secretariats.

Inexorably, the center of gravity of the UN and the agencies shifted southward. When the dam broke in 1960, producing over the next several years a flood of forty-odd new states, all demonstrably underdeveloped and many only marginally viable, the pressure for new approaches to the economic and social agenda quickened. The status gap was too great, the UN's programs for ameliorating the problem were proving inadequate, frustrations with the situation were increasing, and the votes were now present within the UN to force the issue. The results were UNCTAD, UNIDO, and UNDP; they also included the enlargement and modified composition of ECOSOC and the intensification of decentralization efforts within the UN and ILO.

Trends in the global environment have thus been reflected in the creation of new agencies and programs and in the responsibilities assigned to them and the results expected from them. More states, and more diverse states, have become involved in a competition for inadequate resources at a time when the reality of inequitable distribution is impossible to conceal. Increasingly, the UN system has been viewed not only as an instrumentality for economic and social change but also as a set of agencies and programs the control of which is intrinsically desirable. What is at issue is not only a larger piece of the pie but a hand on the knife as well. In part, this contest for control of the UN process is the product of a stubborn hope that the UN will, in the "right" hands, be able to work the miracles of which its Charter speaks. But it may also, paradoxically, be a product of nagging doubts about the efficacy of the UN system and a suspicion that the only significant gains from the UN system for disadvantaged states may lie in the exercise of authority and influence, however sterile, within the UN process itself. In any event, part of the story of the UN's economic, social, and technical endeavors is that the recipients of aid, the states most vulnerable to changing conditions in world trade, the nations where illiteracy and other indices of lag in modernization are most conspicuous, are demanding and playing an increasingly important role in the UN effort in these sectors. Equally important to note is that Western states and Western nationals continue to exercise ultimate control. Majorities of new, small, and underdeveloped states have made little headway against the grain of obdurate opposition by the large and relatively more important middle powers, most of which are Western and developed; this has been particularly true of the economic sector in which the funds, the trade concessions, the loan terms, the skills and expertise are largely within the power of the developed countries—and especially the Western countries—to give or withhold.

Take, for instance, the case of the IBRD. Voting power within the Bank is proportional to the capital subscriptions of member nations. In this system of weighted voting, the United States casts 63,750 votes in the Bank and 64,558 in IDA, 24.53 percent and 25.28 percent of the total, respectively.[24] There are 113 Bank members, but five industrial powers (the United States, the United Kingdom, France, the Federal Republic of Germany, and Japan) cast exactly half of the votes. Quite obviously, this is a far cry from the United Nations, with its one-state-one-vote formula in both the General Assembly and ECOSOC. Then, too, there is the matter of leadership. In 1971 the president of the Bank and IDA was an American national (Robert S. McNamara). So was the administrator of the United Nations Development Program (Paul G. Hoffman). The higher echelons of officialdom in both cases, Bank and UNDP, are predominantly Western; the practices governing Bank loans and Special Fund allocational decisions within UNDP have been predominantly Western. Too much can be made of the backgrounds of both McNamara and Hoffman as one-time highly successful American industrial leaders, but their occupancy of the key posts in the Bank and UNDP symbolizes the reality of Western control, however benevolent and constructive, of international organization in these critical sectors.

The twin facts of LDC numerical control of the UN decision-making process and Western state control of the goods and services toward which those UN decisions are directed have produced a growing disparity between what the UN system purports to do and what it actually accomplishes. This performance gap may in time undermine the credibility of the organization in the field of some of its most impressive accomplishments and of its most sustained impact. That rhetoric outdistances performance is not surprising; but so does institutional change. Designation of the 1960s as the United Nations Development Decade was an act of exhortation rather than the launching of a carefully articulated development plan tied to serious commitments by nation-states. But the Development Decade could hardly have been more than "an ordering principle" or, as Philippe de Seynes characterized it, "a symbol of the collective responsibility of the international community for the development of the Third World." [25]

But it has been in the realm of institution building and manipulation of the constitutional authority of the UN itself that the changing political environment has produced the greatest disjunction between appearance and reality and, indeed, the greatest threat to the spirit of cooperation so essential if the UN is to make a difference in the field of economic development. That today global international organizations are composed of states which do not all subscribe to the same rules of conduct and to the same understanding as to the purposes and limits of the UN system is obvious. Evidence is readily available in the economic sector, demonstrating that economic development is after all a fundamentally political matter. The creation of the UN Capital Development Fund supplies some of that evidence. Not only did the majority override adamant Western opposition to an institution which Western states would have to support through voluntary contributions for it to be effective; they also directed that administrative expenses be borne out of the regular budget. Although not "unconstitutional" in any sense, this decision can hardly be described as politically or economically constructive. Similarly, the UNCTAD efforts to impose obligations on the minority of developed Western states—that is, to legislate in areas where the UN has recommendatory but not legislative authority—can only be described as doubtfully conducive to cooperation for development. UNCTAD, moreover, represents an attempt to replace ECOSOC as the coordinating agency for the UN system; it is also a conscious invasion of the well-populated development field. UNIDO provides further evidence. When it was created, the UN General Assembly specified that the Governing Council of the UNDP would not provide any guidance or direction for the UN's technical assistance program in industrialization. A UNIDO Industrial Development Board would assume that assignment. There is at work here an overriding suspicion on the part of the LDCs of the older and presumably more Western and less malleable UN organs and programs.

These are only a few manifestations of the determination of LDCs to shape and reshape the United Nations. They are not the first group of states to seek to do this. The United States and her European allies were relatively successful at precisely this exercise in the UN's earlier and formative years, and what we are now witnessing is in part an explicit rejection of the institutions and principles which are the legacy of those earlier Western initiatives. In effect, the Soviet Union and other Communist states boycotted many UN system activities in the economic and social sectors during the early years out of a conviction that they reflected an alien economic philosophy and should not be given the blessing of Soviet participation or the boon of Soviet financial contributions. Later, when the USSR saw an opportunity to influence these UN activities and a chance to demonstrate its support for the growing number of LDCs, it reversed its position and plunged actively into the total UN development effort.[26]

In spite of the fact that the capture of the UN decision-making process by underdeveloped, non-Western states is but the latest turn of events in a struggle for domination of the global organization, it may, in this instance, lead to an overloading of UN system circuits. The UN seems incapable of heeding Richard Gardner's warning against "the tendency to think that every new proposal requires a new institution to carry it out." [27] Available resources, both in staff and dollar terms, are being stretched thin in an effort to mount viable programs, staff them without loss of efficiency while achieving equitable geographical distribution, satisfy strong and persistent pressures to locate new programs away from New York, and create special funds, usually through pledging conferences, to meet the costs of these activities. Those with the resources to tip the development scales are not prepared to make that commitment, calling as it does for such a restructuring of priorities, and many are resentful both of the demands made upon them and the manner in which those demands have been made. In the meanwhile, the recent spate of program building has further complicated an old and increasingly serious problem which is most acute in these sectors of UN system activity, the problem of coordination. To borrow from the vernacular, each component of the system has seemed bent on "doing its own thing."

IV

As we have observed, the history of the UN system in economic, social, and technical sectors has been a history of uneven growth. Inevitably, that century of growth has proceeded without a master plan. Although two global wars very nearly wiped the slate clean and hence provided opportunities to build anew and in a more systematic fashion, today the UN system is large, unwieldy, and hard to manage. At a time when a well-orchestrated assault on a multitude of nagging and even deepening development problems would seem to be in order, the UN system remains, in large part, what it has always been—a congeries of agencies and programs that are part of a common effort more in name than in reality. This is a harsh judgment. But it is true that the phrase "United Nations system," like the phrase "community of nations," begs the question and papers over the reality of scattered, frequently unfocused, and only minimally coordinated effort.

Each of the UN agencies and programs is to some extent a modest empire, jealously nurtured and defended against reorganization of the

total UN system. There has been a certain amount of functional paro-
chialism which is hardly surprising, given the manner in which the UN's
activities have evolved. Each UN activity developed in response to a
specific problem or set of problems which seemed ripe for institutionalized
attention; once in being, the agency or program attracted a staff of specialists and gradually became linked, both through its bureaucracy and
the national representatives on its governing bodies, to particular government agencies and interests within member states. In Sir Robert Jackson's
words, the agencies, with the support of governments, have "become the
equivalent of principalities, free from any centralized control. Over the
years, like all such institutions, they have learnt to safeguard and increase
their powers, to increase their independence, and to resist change." [28]
The Jackson Report suggests that the UN machinery for promoting development might very well be doomed to extinction if it cannot adapt to
meet the challenge of an increasingly taxing environment.

> Governments created this machine—which over the years has
> grown into what is probably the most complex organization in the world.
> What is it exactly? Briefly, it is built up of the administrative structures of
> the United Nations and its component parts, such as UNDP, UNICEF,
> UNIDO and UNCTAD, etc., and of about a dozen Specialized Agencies.
> In theory, it is under the control of about thirty separate governing
> bodies; in the past, much of their work in dealing with administrative
> problems has been self-defeating. At the headquarters level, there is no
> real "Headpiece"—no central co-ordinating organization—which could
> exercise effective control. Below headquarters, the administrative ten-
> tacles thrust downwards into an extraordinary complex of regional and
> sub-regional offices, and finally extend into field offices in over ninety
> developing countries. This "Machine" now has a marked identity of its
> own and its power is so great that the question must be asked "Who
> controls this 'Machine'?" So far, the evidence suggests that governments
> do not, and also that the machine is incapable of intelligently controlling
> itself. This is not because it lacks intelligent and capable officials, but
> because it is so organized that managerial direction is impossible. In
> other words, the machine as a whole has become unmanageable in the
> strictest sense of the word. As a result, it is becoming slower and more
> unwieldy, like some prehistoric monster. [29]

Sir Robert was speaking only of the technical cooperation and preinvestment effort of the United Nations, and he specifically excluded the
World Bank and IMF from his indictment. However, it is within the economic, social, and technical sectors generally that the problems of un-
planned growth and inadequately coordinated activity are most acute.
The latter-day redistributive and operational thrust of the UN system
has been responsible for bringing the issue of the relationships among the
parts of the UN system to a head; coordination in the area of high politics
has been a matter of relationships between the League and the UN, on
the one hand, and regional organizations such as the Organization of
American States (OAS), on the other. In addition, in a world character-

ized by the decentralization of power and authority, it has been a matter of the relationships between international organizations and nation-states. In either case the coordination problem has been a vertical one.

In the fields under discussion in this essay, however, the problem has a horizontal as well as a vertical dimension. It is not merely a question of global-regional relations, or international organization–nation-state relations. The vast array of agencies and programs *within* the UN system compounds the problem of coordination. When the League was created, UPU and ITU were already in existence, as were prototypes for other specialized agencies. Establishment of the ILO as a separate organization was an entirely understandable, even an inevitable, act. There was and still is a pervasive sentiment that specialized organizations, while related to the general purpose body with peacekeeping responsibilities, should have a somewhat independent existence to avoid becoming infected by the debilitating virus of intensely partisan political issues. As it was, the ILO was technically quite closely tied to the League; membership in the latter meant membership in the former, and the League's general funds were used to meet ILO's expenses.

Article 24 of the League Covenant stated that all international bureaus already established by general treaties should be placed under League direction if the parties to such treaties consented, and that all subsequently established international bureaus should also be placed under the direction of the League. However, Article 24 proved to be a weak instrument for purposes of either control or coordination. The UN Charter in this area, as in most others, is much more detailed than the Covenant. But, whereas the Charter is more explicit, it is actually less ambitious and concedes the multiplicity of international economic and social agencies. Article 57 of the Charter employs the language "shall be brought into relationship with the United Nations" in describing the specialized agencies, as contrasted with the Covenant's phrase "shall be placed under the direction of the League." During World War II, with the League moribund and the United Nations organization itself only dimly perceived by the wartime coalition of the same name, the specialized agencies were already taking shape independently of any central controlling mechanism. This process began with the Hot Springs Conference on Food and Agriculture in 1943; the system that emerged has been characterized as one of "functional federalism." [30]

Primus inter pares among the independently created and quite independent agencies of the United Nations system was to be the UN itself. Although specific responsibilities in economic, social, and technical sectors are allocated to ILO, FAO, UNESCO, WHO, and the other specialized agencies, the UN, as the general international organization, also has a general mandate in these sectors. Article 55 makes this clear, just as it also makes it inevitable that coordination problems and jurisdictional disputes would develop within the UN system. They follow from Charter language that the UN shall promote "higher standards of living, full em-

ployment, and conditions of economic and social progress and development," "solutions of international economic, social, health, and related
problems," and "international cultural and educational cooperation." The
vehicle for sorting out the relationships between the UN and the specialized agencies was to have been the Economic and Social Council, a principal organ of the UN. Coordination was to be directed by one of the
organizations to be coordinated and, what is more, by the one with the
least precise mission in an unevenly developed world. It is not surprising
that the UN generalists have encountered resistance from the agency
specialists.

However, coordination is generally conceded to be necessary, not
so much in the negative sense of avoiding overlap as in the positive sense
of maximizing effectiveness by developing concerted plans for attacking
complex problems. In the final analysis, development and modernization
seem to happen in the manner of a syndrome, a set of a closely interlocking
and not fully understood relationships among a whole series of economic,
social, *and* political phenomena. Awareness that this mesh must be ap-
proximated if the results for which both governments and international
organizations are striving are to be enduring and cumulative has produced
a great deal of concern in UN circles for coordination and for overall plans
or approaches. This, ostensibly, has been ECOSOC's responsibility, and
ECOSOC has not been adjudged a successful organization.[31]

ECOSOC probably had an impossible assignment from the very
beginning. It was one which could not be accomplished alone by an intergovernmental body of eighteen nation-states meeting twice a year, alter-
nately in New York and Geneva. A part of the problem has been its scale.
In 1947 the number of units reporting regularly to ECOSOC was twenty-
two: eight specialized agencies, one special UN program (United Nations
International Childrens Emergency Fund (UNICEF)), an interagency
Committee on Coordination, and twelve subsidiary bodies of ECOSOC
itself, including nine functional commissions and subcommissions, two
regional commissions, and a committee on Non-Governmental Organizations (NGOs). By 1967 this roster, already dangerously inflated if more
than perfunctory attention were to be paid to the reports of these bodies or
very much coordination achieved, had grown to a total of thirty-eight reporting units, now including fourteen specialized agencies, six special UN
programs, two interagency bodies, and no fewer than sixteen subsidiary
bodies of ECOSOC.[32] Part of this large array of units to be coordinated
are in existence, at least in part, because of disappointment with ECOSOC
performance. Part reflect an attempt on the part of ECOSOC to enhance
its coordinating capability. Virtually all tend to define agenda broadly and
deliberate on matters with which other units are also seized or which others
have previously belabored. Virtually all have grown and expanded along
with the UN itself until most are rather too large for expeditious consideration of the items before them.

ECOSOC's role as the guiding engine of UN system efforts has been complicated by three other factors, all interrelated. It has had, according to the Council's unofficial biographer, Walter Sharp, a multiple *raison d'être*.[33] It has been charged with interagency and interunit coordination, with establishing and controlling various programs directly under the aegis of the UN, and with providing a general forum for discussing world economic and social issues. With respect to these responsibilities, it has not made decisions as to priorities which might save it from overload, diffusion of energy, and resultant loss of confidence. A second factor in the saga of ECOSOC has been the membership problem. As the UN acquired new members, and as new members were increasingly and finally exclusively LDCs, an eighteen-member ECOSOC constituted according to a "gentleman's agreement" reached when the UN was founded became a frustrating straitjacket for the LDCs. For some time expansion was blocked by the quarrel over Chinese representation in the UN and when in 1965 the Charter was amended to enlarge the Council to twenty-seven members the drift away from ECOSOC was already quite pronounced. Of the additional nine seats, seven were to go to African and Asian states and one to Latin American states. Thus the balance was decisively shifted southward. But, even with seventeen seats in the enlarged Council, only one in five LDCs may serve at any given time, so rapidly has the UN grown. Representativeness may have come too late; the Assembly habit had already been established and is a third important factor accounting for ECOSOC's problems. Particularly with respect to its roles as world policy forum and creator of dynamic new programs, the Council has to a large extent been preempted by the Second and Third Committees of the General Assembly. Here *all* states—and this is significant when an overwhelming majority are consumers of UN system development assistance—can shape official policy if not results in economic and social sectors. At best, the Council and the Assembly are embarked upon repetitive efforts, wasteful of UN funds and of the time of both Secretariat and delegation personnel.

This trend to involve all members in decision-making processes or, at the very least, to create decision-making bodies which replicate the General Assembly is now widespread within the UN, but nowhere more conspicuous than in the economic and social sectors. The functional commissions of ECOSOC, set up as representative rather than expert bodies to the dismay of many and contrary to the Dumbarton Oaks proposals, have grown in size and, except for the Commission on Narcotic Drugs, have had their membership redistributed according to explicit geographical formulas. As Assembly discussion is repetitious of Council discussion, so is Council discussion repetitious of that in the commissions. Similarly, UNCTAD's Trade and Development Board, the key organ of this important UN component, has a membership of no fewer than fifty-five states, and the principal committees of UNCTAD have forty-five members each.

It is apparent that the urge to participate directly and the obsession with equitable distribution have produced a dramatic escalation in the size of special purpose bodies within the UN.

All of these developments have contributed to lack of focus in the UN development and welfare efforts. ECOSOC has been unable to play its Charter role of providing such a focus. There are, however, two other vehicles available for the job. One is the Administrative Committee on Coordination (ACC) and the other is the UN resident representative.

Whereas ECOSOC is a governmental body, ACC is a staff body. It is also, as ECOSOC is not, an interagency body. It has the obvious advantage for interagency cooperation and coordination of having a foot in each agency. Conversely, it has the disadvantage of having no intergovernmental body which is also an interagency body to lend political muscle to its recommendations. It serves ECOSOC and serves it well but ECOSOC, as we have noted, is not an interagency body. Although devoid of collective responsibility to any single policy control body, the ACC has been likened to an "administrative quasi-cabinet." [34]

The value of this committee to the economic, social, and technical agenda of the UN system is that it brings together the executive heads of the UN and the agencies, *all* of which have mandates in these sectors. Although the ACC is concerned with many administrative matters that are only indirectly relevant to substantive issues of welfare and development, the periodic meetings of highly placed agency officials have increasingly focused attention of the disparate parts of the UN system on the need to engage in concerted action. To cite but a few of the many subsidiary bodies currently working under the aegis of the ACC, there is a Sub-Committee on Education and Training, another on science and technology, and yet a third on water resources development; there are working groups on housing and urbanization and on rural and community development, and other bodies, variously titled, in such fields as population, industrial development, agrarian reform, the economic and social consequences of disarmament, and the evaluation of programs of technical cooperation. In every case they address themselves to questions which are on the agenda of several of the UN system agencies, and frequently they work at the cutting edge of international organization involvement in new fields, such as oceanography, peaceful uses of outer space, and urbanization.

The ACC complex has grown large, but in fields where specialization is rampant and in which the UN effort is rapidly expanding, the machinery of the ACC brings to a whole range of problems an awareness of the totality of the UN effort, so essential to the realization of maximum impact. If it is still hard to see the forest for the trees, at least the ACC achieves some rough approximation of common purpose among the responsible international officials at headquarters level.

At the opposite end of the operational spectrum, out in the field where UN programs take effect, another instrumentality of system-wide coordination exists in the person of the UN resident representative. This has been one of the most important institutions developed by the UN. It has given the UN a "presence" in many countries which project staff alone could not have provided. The resident representative symbolizes the UN development effort and the UN system's commitment to fit the several pieces of that effort together into a rational plan for the development of the country concerned. He has been—where the post is held by a person possessing in full measure the attributes of diplomat, economist, and administrator—a UN ambassador to the host country.[35]

The resident representative has not, of course, been an unalloyed success, any more than ECOSOC and the ACC have been. One man, working in Accra or LaPaz or Delhi, can hardly be expected to knit together the many threads of development activity, each representing a different program or ministry of the receiving state's government as well as different international agencies. The resident representative approaches the assignment of getting the many individuals involved in the development process to work purposefully together as an agent of UNDP. This would seem to give him status as spokesman for all of the participating agencies. However, the resident representative is widely perceived to be the UN's man; the specialized agencies frequently maintain their own country mission chiefs and negotiate independently with the national governments. Moreover, the presence in the developing regions of the UN's Regional Economic Commissions, each with a professional staff of between one hundred and two hundred and each very desirous of playing a pivotal role in the development process, weakens the resident representative's representational role even with respect to the United Nations itself.

It is clear that the multiplicity of agencies and programs produces competitiveness and inefficiency which sharply reduces the capacity of the UN system to serve. Instead of a cooperative approach, the UN effort is frequently marred by "agency salesmanship." As one frustrated resident representative states the case,

> The selection and allocation of projects, coupled with the fullest assessment of a given country's ability to absorb it, are the key issues to the whole question of development aid and must be resolved before we even think of carrying out a greatly expanded programme, but what exists today is "inter-Agency rivalry for projects," each Agency insisting, almost as a matter or right, to get a slice of the country pie, regardless of the value and propriety of the project from the country's point of view, at its particular stage of development.[36]

Nor is this simply a reflection of the frustration of the resident representative who is not in command of the situation. Governments echo this view and seem also to find the crazy-quilt pattern of field offices and agency missions confusing. One observed that

the various specialized agencies with representation in some developing
member countries are housed separately. They communicate separately
not only within the UN system but also within the system of government
in the country. . . . The end result is that the activities of UNESCO,
WHO, ILO, etc., are not properly harmonized within the UN system on
the one hand and on the other the government system. These series of
parallel actions towards a single objective unnecessarily prolong the ultimate aim of reaching effective decision with the minimum of cost and
inefficiency.[37]

Another government called for "better coordination among Specialized
Agencies to avoid tribal fighting on matters of common interest."[38] The
remarkable thing is that these indictments are still heard, more than fifteen
years after the substitution of country programming for agency shares as
the primary desideratum in allocating EPTA funds. Everyone talks about
concerted action to expedite development, but the view from the field
suggests that the total UN effort continues to be a fragmented one. The
resident representative by himself cannot put the pieces together. But,
ironically, the very proliferation of programs and projects and points of
contact between agencies and government ministries may make the resident representative an essential broker in every capital of the Southern
Hemisphere.

The thrust of the last several pages has been to analyze the efforts
of the parts of this complex and disjointed enterprise to become a whole.
That the promise of a "United Nations system" has not been fully realized
may be the inevitable consequence of the decision to create autonomous
international bodies in each of several functional fields such as health,
agriculture, and education. When the principal components of the UN
system were established and their relationships with each other fixed, the
pressures for rapid development and multilateral aid to help achieve it
were unknown or merely incipient. Subsequent increases in the responsibilities loaded upon the system have not been accompanied by fundamental institutional adaptation, although the modifications in this sphere
of UN activity far exceed those in the political sphere. The efforts to pull
the several parts of the UN system together,

to weave them into a tough and durable fabric, adorned with a harmonious pattern, have, at best, led to patchwork. One could argue that,
in the context of the original and fundamental role of the Specialized
Agencies to promote cooperation and foster the exchange of ideas in
their respective spheres, such a state of constant ebullition was by no
means a bad thing; that diversity, of itself, ensured a varied approach,
stimulated imaginative thinking and staved off fossilization. That may
well be so, but it is equally incontrovertible that such a system was not
conducive to the efficient management of one of the most complicated
operational programmes ever conceived, involving rapid and effective
action on a worldwide scale to resolve complex problems varying greatly
from one country to another.[39]

V

So the UN has fallen short of perfection in this, as in the more publicized political and security sphere. Rhetoric has not been matched by performance and the principal losers, as the Jackson Report tells us, have been the developing countries. But where are the successes of "the other UN"? And what are the criteria by which we measure success? It would be as silly to find the UN at fault for the failure of many developing states to achieve takeoff as it is to credit the UN with having prevented a global war in the quarter century since its inception. There is, however, a conventional wisdom about the UN system's work in economic, social, and technical areas, and it identifies a number of successes. These successes include agencies, programs, projects, and individuals. What they have in common is that (1) they have accomplished what they set out to accomplish, and (2) what they have set out to accomplish is in itself substantial and significant—not necessarily of system-transforming magnitude, but important enough to make a pronounced impact either on the environment or on the role of international organizations within that environment.

These somewhat elusive criteria of success suggest several things to look for in assessing performance across the full spectrum of UN activities, and they call to mind the canons advanced by Ernst Haas for judging the organizational ideology of international officials.[40] Haas is concerned with an international organization commitment to transform the international system, and he worries about the tendency to get bogged down in minutiae and to fail to develop programs which have the capacity to achieve systemic transformation. His commentary on the problems of programming by international organizations sheds light on our assessment of the success of the UN system in economic and related sectors.

> They cannot simply proceed to feed the world's poor, educate its illiterate, or cure its cripples. The objective of plenty contains, by definition, subgoals involving coffee and wheat, land tenure and tax rates. The objective of education contains subgoals regarding literacy, school construction, teacher placement, and taxes. The subgoals of security defy simple enumeration. In order to meet overall objectives, appropriate sections of the bureaucracy must address themselves to programs directed at these subgoals. Subgoals beget specialists with primary interests in subgoals. They also beget alliances between these specialists on the one hand, and groups and governments on the other, these latter being more concerned with the narrow aim than with the broad organizational objective. Can bureaucratic leadership overcome this drag on dynamic programming? Can it subordinate the specialist with his ideological commitment to subgoals? The answer involves the knotty question of consensus, and the danger that programming will become part of a tacit general objective of mere survival.[41]

Part of the indictment of the UN of high politics and crisis diplomacy is that its first concern has become that of mere survival. In some quarters of the nonpolitical or less political UN, routine performance of routine tasks is probably all that is expected or needed. But, on the whole, success is contingent upon more than that. There must, presumably, be task expansion; the routine and noncontroversial must be done well, and out of the satisfaction that comes from doing it well must come a willingness to do more and a capacity to mobilize a coalition of support for doing it.

The emphasis upon task expansion is simply a call for realistic recognition that the mountain of world problems is very large and that the UN has barely begun the treacherous ascent. One can take satisfaction in establishing a good base camp but that is clearly not enough, especially in view of the ambitious goals trumpeted in such places as the Charter of the UN and the resolution announcing the UN Development Decade. By its very nature, the UN system carries the burden of great expectations. To realize them, viable coalitions of nation-states and international bureaucracies, committed to dynamic programs, must be forged and sustained.

Where do the several aspects of the UN system's economic, social, and technical endeavors fit into this prescription? In the first place, it should be noted that UNDP, in spite of criticisms voiced in the preceding pages, is in a relative sense an important success story. Its problem, as we have noted, has been that it is slow and is not making the best use of its resources, and the explanation offered has been that development cooperation has been thrust on a structure not designed for that purpose, a structure characterized by sectoral autonomy. But, for all of its weaknesses, UNDP is an important and massive effort. If it has scored low, that is a relative failure, for it has aimed high. In the words of the Jackson Report,

> The UN system has taken its first groping steps along the road to world order. Almost unnoticed, it has moved into *action*—a development of profound significance—and in so doing it has demonstrated its aptness for cooperating with the Third World. Lacking both capital resources and an organization specifically designed for the purpose, it has yet improvised a major international service, that of technical cooperation and pre-investment. In this process, the UN system and the developing countries have laid the foundations of a vital and universal partnership.[42]

The very fact that it has acquired redistributive and operational characteristics, and on a large scale, is evidence of significant task expansion in the evolution of the UN system from its more modest beginnings.

Working on the other side of the street of economic development has been the World Bank, considered a highly successful component of the UN system.[43] Here, too, it may be argued that more capital should have been made available to developing states and that the terms on which it was offered should have been less rigorous. The Bank has been vulnerable to criticism that it has had an ideological bias against lending to state-owned manufacturing and mining industries.

The problem is, in part, that the IBRD has insisted on being a "sound" bank, a posture which follows logically upon its overwhelmingly Western, market-economy character. Its soundness is not in dispute nor is its efficiency. The Bank is viewed with respect in most quarters, whatever the misgivings or even resentment felt about its weighted voting, limited membership, and relatively stiff loan requirements. In effect, the success of IBRD is closely related to each of these "liabilities." The Bank enjoys the luxury of independence of action—it can set financing policy and then implement it without the need to accommodate the divergent interests and aims of many UN system agencies. It is easier to achieve and maintain consensus as to purposes and procedures given the relative homogeneity of the voting majority and of the top-level administrative personnel.

What the Bank does, even on its own terms, is critically important to the development process; although only about one-tenth of total public and private capital flows to developing countries are through the World Bank Group, the amount is not insubstantial and it constitutes a major multilateral alternative to bilateral development financing.[44] One student of international finance has claimed that "the Bank's greatest contribution probably has been to make economic development lending respectable." [45] To do this, it has developed methods to ensure proper and efficient use of funds; by its insistence on sound projects and by its imposition of conditions on recipient states, it has helped to rescue development financing from wasteful practice and political manipulation. Nor has the Bank Group, for all its reputation as one of the conservative elements in the UN system, remained static. It has contributed to the renaissance of agricultural development after a period of Third World obsession with industrial development; the Bank's agricultural projects in 1969 and 1970 totaled half as many as in the entire previous history of the Bank.[46] It has also given every indication of making population one of its major concerns in the years ahead. It has begun lending in that field, and it is of more than passing interest that population has been a major theme of some of Mr. McNamara's most important recent addresses.[47] On balance, the Bank has been and promises to continue to be a pillar of strength in the UN's economic, social, and technical endeavors.

Another success story, but of a rather different kind, has been the Regional Economic Commissions of the United Nations. Perhaps it should be observed that the regional commissions are not so much successful as they are an important adaptation of the UN system to environmental needs and pressures. Their most significant contribution has been their very presence and their sustained growth and development at those points where the global international system intersects several prominent regional systems.[48] If the growth of the UN system has proceeded at an accelerated rate, the growth of regional organizations has been even more remarkable. There are now regional common market schemes on three continents; regional development banks in Asia, Africa, and Latin America; such general purpose organizations as the Organization of American States, the

Organization of African Unity (OAU), and the Arab League; and a large
number of subregional or more limited bodies devoted to specific purposes.
The regional impulse has many explanations which need not detain us
here. But whatever the explanation for it, the result has been a vigorous
challenge to the UN and the specialized agencies, inasmuch as the global
and regional systems have not evolved as part of a common plan but almost invariably share a welfare and development agenda. The lateral decentralization of autonomous specialized agencies has been joined by the
vertical decentralization of global and regional organizations. The economic commissions are interesting precisely because they are a part of
the UN system and the regional challenge to it.

The commissions are not unique. The World Health Organization
has six regional offices with comprehensive responsibility for planning and
execution of programs in their respective regions. FAO and ILO have
elaborate but less authoritative regional components. But it is the UN's
Regional Economic Commissions which are of special interest because
the scope of their substantive concerns is nothing less than the totality
of country and regional development. They have taken the lead in doing
something that the Bank Group and the UN and the agencies and UNDP
have not been equipped to do or disposed to do, except quite incidentally:
developing a sense of regional consciousness with the objective of solving
some of the many problems in these sectors of the UN's mandate at the
regional level but with the support of global resources and talent.

In a sense, the commissions have become the *de facto* agents for
integrative initiatives within the regions. The Economic Commission for
Latin America (ECLA), Economic Commission for Africa (ECA), and
Economic Commission for Asia and the Far East (ECAFE) had much to do
with creating the regional development banks; ECLA launched the Latin
American Free Trade Area (LAFTA) and the Central American Common Market. The Asian region, largely devoid of forces conducive to regional cooperation, much less integration, has received most of what impetus it has had toward joint planning from ECAFE. ECA has helped to
provide the economic and social staff work for the OAU and has, more
than any of the other commissions, experimented with a subregional approach to a wide range of African issues. The subregionalization efforts
of ECA and ECLA's emphasis upon common market schemes in Central
and South America are part of a pragmatic search for the appropriate
level or arena for development action. The commissions may contribute
to realization of some of the advantages of the regional approach cited
in the UN's Capacity Study, among them the essentiality of economic
integration for effective development among small states with limited
ranges of production and insignificant domestic markets, the preferability
of analysis of regional requirements to an aggregate of individual country
analyses in building a global development strategy, and the utility of the
regional channel for adapting global policy to local circumstances.

One of the distinguishing features of the regional commission experience has been the leadership provided by two executive secretaries of the commissions, Gunnar Myrdal and Raúl Prebisch. Both have long since moved on to other assignments, but both left a dramatic mark on the UN system. It may be that the "success" of the regional commission concept is attributable to their vision and dynamic stewardship on behalf of carefully articulated philosophies of economic cooperation and development. Myrdal used the Economic Commission for Europe as a bridge of functional cooperation between East and West during the darkest days of the cold war.[49] Prebisch provided ECLA and especially its Secretariat with a sense of purpose and of élan which has been rare in international organization anywhere at any time. He promulgated and promoted development doctrine which raised ECLA's performance out of the level of routine and gave the regional approach to development a status which it still enjoys, in spite of the many vicissitudes through which the commission and the Latin American common market schemes have since passed.

Reference to Myrdal and Prebisch is a reminder that successes may be personal as well as institutional, and that the only saint in the UN's hagiography is not Dag Hammarskjöld. The relative obscurity in which "the other UN" functions is underscored by the very limited public awareness of leaders other than the secretaries-general of the UN and peace mission lieutenants such as Bunche and Jarring. Any listing of those officials who have made a real difference in the evolution of the UN system would have to include Eugene Black of IBRD and Paul Hoffman of the Special Fund and UNDP, as well as Prebisch and Myrdal. More important than any other, however, was Albert Thomas, first director of the International Labor Office of the ILO. Thomas did not "succeed," any more than ECLA, the Bank, or the UN Development Program has succeeded. But like them he stands out for what he attempted, for what he made of his opportunities.

The Thomas story has been told many times.[50] The concept of office held by the distinguished French socialist leader is invariably contrasted with that which Sir Eric Drummond brought to his assignment as the first secretary-general of the League of Nations. It was Thomas, not Drummond, the ILO, not the League, which provided the model for the secretary-general in the UN Charter and for the more successful international officials in the more recent states of the UN system's evolution. Thomas left a legacy of activism, of strong policy initiatives, of personal missions throughout the world, of systematic efforts to cultivate constituencies for his office and his organization. He also contributed to the autonomy of the ILO, both by his vigorous resistance to a stronger role for the League's Assembly in ILO affairs and by the sheer force of his personality and style. His is a case of a preeminently political leader of an international organization providing an example of politically attuned functionalism for a whole generation of international officials to follow. While Thomas was *sui generis,* the UN's approach to security and economic issues alike has been influenced by the experience of the formative years of ILO.

The range of activities in economic, social, and technical sectors of the UN system's mandate is so broad as to make it impossible to do more than sketch brief vignettes of a few of the many notable organizations and programs and people which have constituted that system. It ought to be noted, however, before turning to the future of the "other United Nations," that many of the agencies which have been swept along on a tide of generalizations in this chapter have registered singularly important accomplishments by themselves. They are, after all, specialized agencies, and within their fields of specialization some have done remarkably well. Frequently they have not had a central purpose which gives meaning to their more specific accomplishments. But, as Haas indicates in his discussion of Julian Huxley's call through UNESCO for a world culture based on scientific humanism, and of John Boyd Orr's plan for a World Food Board under FAO to stabilize prices by buying up surplus in times of glut and disposing of it in times of famine, a central purpose which is at all specific is a very difficult thing to implement. Hence we are usually left with more limited achievements in more limited areas.

The regular programs of FAO and WHO fall into this category, as do some of the major technical cooperation projects with which they have been identified. Both have been solid organizations performing valuable services. Neither has been spectacular, but, given the balance between populations and the resources to sustain them, the former seemingly increasing more rapidly than the latter, they have occupied and can expect to occupy a crucial position in the panoply of UN agencies and programs.

WHO has a dismal record with respect to population problems but in those areas where it has undertaken to exert its influence, health services and disease control, it has made its mark. Its budget is by far the largest among the specialized agencies (second only to the UN itself within the UN system), and it has been used in a highly professional manner to bring communicable diseases under control; promote environmental health through control of water sewerage and food; collate, codify, standardize, and disseminate data and information in fields where national boundaries cannot contain problems but can severely complicate their amelioration; and maintain one of the most elaborate educational and training programs within the UN system. WHO has been earliest into the technical assistance field with its own resources, least involved in UNDP, most self-consciously professional, and aloof from and critical of the "political" United Nations. It may be that, among UN agencies, WHO has been the example par excellence of preoccupation with subgoals which are noncontroversial, such as eradication of malaria or maternal and child health; but, if this attitude has precluded significant task expansion, few can deny that the human condition, if not the human environment, is being affected importantly by WHO's work program.

Finally, the Food and Agriculture Organization merits at least passing mention in an essay on the economic and social aspects of United Nations activities because it is concerned with making the planet habitable in the

most fundamental sense—improving the capacity of our soils and our seas
to sustain a large and growing population. This is development for survival,
and it is FAO's business. FAO has long labored in the shadows of other
agencies, with the UN, UNESCO, ILO, and WHO all attracting more attention. And yet the population-food squeeze places FAO very much in the
front line of the UN system effort. In a recent and sympathetic book, the
problem is described in almost apocalyptic terms:

> People in most other organizations can read the facts about the popula-
> tion explosion, enjoy a few moments of fright, sigh, and turn to more
> comfortable subjects. Not so FAO. For 60 million people added to
> the world's population each year, most of them in the poorer countries
> where hunger and malnutrition are already national afflictions, must
> somehow be fed. This steady, fantastic increase in food consumers neces-
> sarily enters into all FAO calculations. If FAO spokesmen at times
> sound strident, it is because they are aware that existing efforts in most
> of the countries of Asia, Africa, and Latin America, where populations
> are growing at 2 to 4 percent a year, are doing little more than feed the
> new mouths without making much inroad upon the backlog of poverty,
> ignorance, hunger, and malnutrition. They know that in many countries
> and regions food supply is not even keeping up with population growth.[51]

FAO has accepted this challenge at the level of global policy and
more localized projects alike. An Indicative World Plan for Agricultural
Development has taken shape under FAO's supervision; it seeks to "set
goals, indicate alternative policies, describe the inputs, economic incentives,
and institutional changes they would require, and state the implications for
investment and manpower needs," [52] first for 1975 and then for 1985, of a
comprehensive program of agricultural planning. This world plan is part of
a general reassertion of the critical character of the agricultural sector.
Former Secretary-General U Thant sought to place production in this sector
in perspective by insisting that "there is no conflict between the priorities
of farming and industry, and the need to reemphasize farming springs not
from any desire to 'keep developing economies dependent' but simply to
counteract the glamour of factory chimneys which may all too often be
smoking above products which no one in the community can afford to
buy." [53]

The claim of FAO to some share in the UN system's success to date
is not based exclusively on urgent forecasting or adamant insistence that
we neglect agricultural production at our peril. FAO has annually had the
largest expenditure financed from EPTA, Special Fund, and UNDP resources of any of the UN system agencies and some of the projects with
which FAO has been involved have been singularly important to the causes
of food abundance and restoration of the "good earth." One such project,
widely publicized, has been the Desert Locust Project, aimed at sparing
Africa, the Middle East, and South Asia from the ravages of a plague as
old as the Bible. Another, with roots in the agency's regular program, is
the Mediterranean Project, an ambitious effort to devise an integrated de-

velopment plan for a once rich region of the world which has suffered from
deforestation, soil depletion, and erosion, with poor states and poor regions
of more developed states sharing the decline of the wine dark sea and its
littoral.[54]

VI

This is the United Nations which functions beyond the reach of headlines, attracting the attention only of specialists because its work is
specialized and its crises are protracted affairs lacking single moments of
truth. It is not all of it because it is too vast to comprehend in a single
volume, much less in a single chapter.

What of the future? The problem to which the UN must address itself
more systematically is the quality of life on this planet or, rather, the
prospect of its further decline and the necessity for reversing that decline.
The future of the United Nations system in the economic, social, and technical sectors of its mandate is intimately bound up with this issue. To date,
the UN has done very little which warrants optimism. This is not surprising;
the UN quite accurately mirrors the configuration of forces and interests in
the world at large and, generally, there has been less concern around the
globe for the qualitative than for the quantitative aspects of life. But we
are now entering a fifth phase in the evolution of the United Nations system,
already signaled by accelerating attention to population. As with previous
phases, there will be no clean break with the past. Old programs and
projects will continue but new emphases will emerge—are now emerging, in
fact, however tentatively.

This entire chapter is laden with evidence that the quality of life
has not been the UN's basic concern heretofore. The main emphasis has
been on economic development. Although it has been impossible to touch
upon every UN component from the Advisory Committee on the Application of Science and Technology to Development (ACASTD) to the World
Meteorological Organization, the record on the whole sustains the selec-
tivity practiced by the author. The emphasis of the UN system itself has
been economic and developmental.

To assert that the UN's effort has been quantitative rather than qualitative is not to suggest that economic development is unconcerned with the
quality of life. To increase the annual rate of growth of an LDC, to improve
the per capita income and level of living of the citizens of less well endowed or late-starting countries, to promote planned industrialization and
diversifications of the economies of states that have been too dependent on
one or two commodities, to build up a solid infrastructure that can sustain
future development in the LDCs—to do these things, and they are what the
UN system is doing or helping to do, is to bring to the least developed
states the benefits of modernization. That, presumably, is a qualitative
thing. But, of course, it is in the main something else. What is being sought
is more income for more people to buy more goods and more services, as

well as the production of more goods and services for them to consume. Some elements of the UN effort are more directly concerned with this process than others; some work directly on the problem, others have or hope to have a trickle-down (or percolate-up) effect. They share, however, a common objective: the closing of the status gap between rich and poor states and the realization of economic well-being, by states and by individuals within those states.

Although it is generally understood that modernization is a mixed blessing, and although some conscious efforts are being made to prevent homogenization in the industrialized Western mold and to preserve that which is distinctive in different modernizing cultures, it has been difficult to focus sustained or significant attention on the qualitative aspects of the UN effort. The reason is that social and technical change and development are even more political than economic change and development. Covey T. Oliver has described the problem as the taboo of "Inviolable National Privacy." [55] He quite accurately observes that economic development practices and doctrines, on the whole, have been removed from the proscribed zone. This permits a global consensus among the developed, developing, and underdeveloped that it is necessary and desirable to get on with economic development. The respective roles and obligations of the several parties may be in dispute, and resources for the task may not be forthcoming. But the developing states want to share in the good life, and the developed states agree in principle and to a considerable extent in practice that this would be a very good thing.

Not so with social and technical development; cooperation in these spheres is more problematic. Resistance to change is greater here because it threatens the social fabric of the country more directly, in the one case, and compromises the security of states or deprives them of present or prospective advantage, in the other. Social development is "modernization of the norms and processes for sharing burdens and benefits," inevitably a hazardous undertaking in which governments are loath to have international agencies interfere. Technical development embraces the capacity of the technological revolution to harness the atom, the oceans, and outer space on behalf of all mankind—in other words, to bend the unknown, the not yet fully known, and above all the unappropriated to general and cooperative as opposed to parochial and conflictual uses. The UN system labors in all of these fields, but not as successfully as in the field of economic development.

The problem may be posed quite simply by referring once more to the impact of the changing environment on international organizations and the tasks they perform. The rate of shrinkage of the earth is so great that the taboo of "inviolable national privacy" must yield, not because some people at UNESCO or the UN or WHO know best, but simply because we are moving inexorably toward the global village where unilateral decisions are not only intellectually indefensible but physically indefensible as well. This is what is meant by the qualitative dimension of the UN's mandate. It is not enough to develop economically. Life itself is becoming precarious, and not only from the threat of nuclear war. If there are too many people to enjoy it, economic development will have proved a snare and a delusion. The problem, we are told, can be solved in part by harvesting the sea and increasing the yield of the earth; but we are beginning to discover that our waters are dangerously polluted and our lands mindlessly stripped of their capacity to sustain life.

We are, in brief, confronted with the deeply disturbing prospect that progress may enslave man rather than free him.[56] There is little that man cannot do; increasingly, he is the master of his physical environment. But to master it is not necessarily to use it wisely. More than three and a half billion people and nearly one hundred fifty independent nation-states, functioning without central control and often without systematic attention to the environmental costs of progress at those levels where control is exercised, are an invitation to disaster. The United Nations system is needed here as much as it is in peacekeeping and economic development fields, but thus far it has moved cautiously. In the field of development, the UN and the specialized agencies and the development programs have been saying "yes": yes to money, experts, welfare, health care, urbanization, industrialization, education, and a host of other things. Now they have to say "no": no to population growth, no to this land use and that resource policy, no to pollution, no to untrammeled freedom of choice (be it by state or by individual) to live, consume, dispose, waste, create, experiment, and destroy at will.

In effect, the United Nations must now press ahead in its role as a regulatory body. The task of development is far from completed. In fact, the gap between affluence and want is widening, which seems to suggest that we shall continue to witness a major development effort involving the Bank Group, UNDP, UNCTAD, UNIDO, the UN, and the agencies in their individual capacities. But the penchant of both have and have-not states to despoil the global village and rob economic well-being of its meaning dictates that the next phase in the UN's history must be characterized by much more emphasis on regulation, even while development continues. Inevitably, this means that the next phase will be a much more difficult one than those that have preceded it. It means that the separation of political from nonpolitical issues, never perfectly realized but often urged and defended, must be set aside in favor of a responsible realization that the major economic, social, and technical issues still on the agenda are inextricably intertwined with political issues.

C. Wilfred Jenks, a long-time student of international organization, has urged our consideration of a whole series of lawmaking treaties which would regulate man's manipulation of his environment and the scientific and technological tools which have come into his possession.[57] Among these regulatory instruments, analogous perhaps to the Treaty on Principles Governing the Activities of States in the Exploration and Use of Outer Space and to the Antarctic Treaty, might be an ocean depths treaty (an inner space equivalent of the outer space treaty); a center of the earth treaty (governing experiments and deep-drilling operations in the earth's interior); a world pollution treaty (designed to protect "air, water, crops, wild life and ecological balance of nature generally against the havoc of scientific and technological vandalism"); a sonic boom treaty (protective of health, property, and amenities against the dangers of intolerable noise levels); a cybernetics treaty (minimizing the dangers of cybernetic error); and a world weather treaty (governing weather and climate modification experiments). This list could be expanded without much effort. Moreover, a number of existing regulatory treaties require more teeth. To cite one conspicuous example, a decade after the signing of the much heralded Single Convention on Narcotic Drugs, the cancerous spread of heroin addiction in the great urban centers has virtually made the regulatory strategy of that treaty obsolete.[58] It may be argued that Jenks, given his identification with international law and association with the ILO, is unduly sympathetic to the lawmaking treaty as a method of meeting international problems. Perhaps. But it is hard to imagine the United Nations system succeeding over the long term if its quantitatively oriented development efforts (and successes) are not soon matched with some qualitatively oriented regulatory achievements.

This will be a tremendous challenge for the UN system. It will have to display a capacity for task expansion not heretofore demonstrated. Already the UN has been hard at work on the problem of the oceans and the need to be foresighted in regulating their exploitation. Progress has been slow and the constraints placed upon national sovereignty by draft instruments in this field have not been especially dramatic. Nonetheless, there has been a marked shift in emphasis; an important beginning has been made; development now shares attention with regulation of who develops what and for whom on a crucial "last frontier." The most dramatic manifestation of this changing emphasis is the United Nations Conference on the Human Environment, to be held in Stockholm in 1972. The most publicized UN initiative since the first UNCTAD in 1964, the Stockholm Conference reflects an attempt to mobilize awareness and to commence concerted action on behalf of a beleagured planet and its life-sustaining capabilities. To date, the environmental issue has worried the developing states; they have tended to fear exploitation of this issue as a strategy for placing constraints upon their economic development which will relegate them to a permanently inferior status. Moreover, at the time this book went to press, the conference was threatened by a dispute over the participation of East Germany, one more reminder that the universality of a problem is no guarantee that the approach to its solution will not be parochial. As *The New York Times* editorialized, however, "The Baltic Sea cannot be salvaged without the cooperation of both East and West Germany. Ocean life cannot be saved for the Russians without the active aid of the British, the Americans, the Japanese." [59]

In any event, the next decade or two promise to be parlous times for the United Nations. The UN development effort will expand but, whether there is a major rechanneling of bilateral development assistance through the UN or not, the results will almost certainly fall short—and probably far short—of what is required to close the gap between affluent and disadvantaged states. This will produce more anger and frustration than we have yet witnessed. That anger and frustration will in turn produce further tinkering with the UN system. Experience to date suggests that such tinkering will probably not meet the performance criteria of the Pearson or Jackson reports. The machinery for development will probably remain imperfect, although subject to persistent and occasionally effective efforts at improvement. The likelihood is that the United Nations will continue to peck away at the problems of welfare, development, trade, nutrition, communication, transportation, and education, and that the degree of success will be related to the capacity of the UN to find a formula for ameliorating the enduring tensions between the many small states and the few large states and a majority of developing states and a minority of developed states, and among a host of agencies and programs, each with its own *raison d'être,* history, and approach to the major economic and social issues of the latter years of the twentieth century. It requires no great prescience to predict that a formula will not be found.

It is not this failure which is likely to be crucial, however. It will be a relative failure, and it will be shared by international agencies and bilateral aid programs. What will be crucial is the capacity of the United Nations to assume a leadership role in the conservation of spaceship earth. In the short run other things will loom larger, but such other successes as the UN may achieve will be hollow and transient if the world becomes increasingly inhospitable to life, much less the good life. Whether the requisite task expansion will occur is problematic, but there is no question of the appropriateness of the UN for the assignment. It is incontestably a global issue, the more so on a shrinking globe. If man as warrior does not trigger the apocalpyse, man as consumer may. In either event, the UN is entering upon the most important phase in its long and uneven history.

The Record of the World Bank and IDA for Ten Years, 1961–1970
(*Expressed in Millions of United States Dollars*)

	Fiscal Year									
	1961	*1962*	*1963*	*1964*	*1965*	*1966*	*1967*	*1968*	*1969*	*1970*
World Bank										
Loans: Number	27	29	28	37	38	37	46	44	84	70
Loans: Amount	$ 610	$ 882	$ 449	$ 810	$ 1,023	$ 839	$ 877	$ 847	$ 1,399	$ 1,680
Disbursements	398	485	620	559	606	668	790	772	762	772
Repayments to Bank	101	104	113	117	137	166	188	237	298	329
Gross Income	167	188	204	219	267	292	331	356	410	504
Net Income	63	70	83	97	137	144	170	169	171	213
Total Reserves	602	699	813	846	895	954	1,023	1,160	1,254	1,329
Borrowings: Gross	787	271	121	100	598	288	729	735	1,224	735
Borrowings: Net	300	104	−5	−32	250	64	503	215	698	299
Subscribed Capital	20,093	20,485	20,730	21,186	21,669	22,426	22,850	22,942	23,036	23,159
Member Countries	68	75	85	102	102	103	106	107	110	113
IDA										
Credits: Number	4	18	17	18	20	12	20	18	38	56
Credits: Amount	$ 101	$ 134	$ 260	$ 283	$ 309	$ 284	$ 354	$ 107	$ 385	$ 606
Disbursements	—	12	56	124	222	267	342	319	256	143
Subscribed Capital	906	917	969	987	996	999	1,000	1,000	1,013	1,014
Supplementary Resources and Special Contributions	—	—	6	679	756	763	768	773	1,054	1,950
Member Countries	51	62	76	93	94	96	97	98	102	105
Professional Staff	317	349	406	444	496	615	685	740	917	1,166

Source: *World Bank/IDA Annual Report 1970*, p. 3.

Bank Loans and IDA Credits 1969/70 by Purpose
(Expressed in Millions of United States Dollars)

	Bank	IDA	Total
Agriculture			
Afghanistan—Agricultural credit..................	$ —	$ 5.00	$ 5.00
Bolivia—Livestock..............................	—	1.40	1.40
Ceylon—Irrigation and drainage..................	13.60	5.10	18.70
Ceylon—Drainage.............................	—	2.50	2.50
Colombia—Livestock...........................	18.30	—	18.30
Ecuador—Livestock............................	—	1.50	1.50
Ethiopia—General agricultural development........	—	3.10	3.10
Ethiopia—General agricultural development........	—	3.50	3.50
Ghana—Fisheries..............................	—	1.30	1.30
Ghana—Cocoa production......................	—	8.50	8.50
Honduras—Livestock...........................	—	2.60	2.60
India—Irrigation...............................	—	35.00	35.00
India—Agricultural credit.......................	—	35.00	35.00
India—Agricultural credit.......................	—	27.50	27.50
Indonesia—Agricultural estates...................	—	17.00	17.00
Indonesia—Irrigation...........................	—	18.50	18.50
Iran—Agricultural credit........................	6.50	—	6.50
Ivory Coast—Cocoa production..................	7.50	—	7.50
Kenya—Forestry...............................	2.60	—	2.60
Malaysia—Land settlement and development........	13.00	—	13.00
Malaysia—Forestry.............................	8.50	—	8.50
Morocco—Irrigation...........................	46.00	—	46.00
Niger—Agricultural credit.......................	—	0.58	0.58
Pakistan—Irrigation............................	—	13.00	13.00
Pakistan—Irrigation............................	—	14.00	14.00
Papua and New Guinea—Oil palm, coconuts, and cattle.................................	—	5.00	5.00
Philippines—Irrigation..........................	34.00	—	34.00
Spain—Livestock..............................	25.00	—	25.00
United Arab Republic—Drainage.................	—	26.00	26.00
Uruguay—Livestock...........................	6.30	—	6.30
Zambia—Commerical farming....................	5.50	—	5.50
	$ 186.80	$226.08	$ 412.88
Education			
Cameroon.....................................	$	$ 10.50	$ 10.50
Chile...	1.50	—	1.50
Chile...	7.00	—	7.00
China..	9.00	—	9.00
Colombia.....................................	6.50	—	6.50
Ivory Coast...................................	11.00	—	11.00
Kenya..	—	6.10	6.10
Pakistan......................................	—	8.00	8.00
Sierra Leone..................................	—	3.00	3.00
Spain..	12.00	—	12.00
Zambia.......................................	5.30	—	5.30
	$ 52.30	$ 27.60	$ 79.90
Telecommunications			
Costa Rica....................................	$ 6.50	$ —	$ 6.50
Kenya, Tanzania and Uganda...................	10.40	—	10.40

Bank Loans and IDA Credits 1969/70 by Purpose (continued)
(Expressed in Millions of United States Dollars)

	Bank	IDA	Total
Nepal..	$ —	$ 1.70	$ 1.70
Pakistan...	—	15.00	15.00
Singapore..	11.00	—	11.00
Yugoslavia.......................................	40.00	—	40.00
	$ 67.90	$ 16.70	$ 84.60
Transportation			
Bolivia—Natural gas pipeline.....................	$ 23.25	$ —	$ 23.25
Brazil—Roads....................................	100.00	—	100.00
Cameroon—Roads.................................	12.00	7.00	19.00
Cameroon—Railways..............................	5.20	—	5.20
Central African Republic—Roads..................	—	4.30	4.30
Chile—Roads....................................	10.80	—	10.80
Colombia—Roads.................................	32.00	—	32.00
Congo, People's Republic of—Roads..............	—	1.50	1.50
Costa Rica—Roads...............................	15.70	—	15.70
Gambia, The—Port...............................	—	2.10	2.10
India—Railways.................................	—	55.00	55.00
Iran—Roads.....................................	42.00	—	42.00
Kenya—Roads....................................	23.50	—	23.50
Kenya, Tanzania and Uganda—Ports...............	35.00	—	35.00
Kenya, Tanzania and Uganda—Railways...........	42.40	—	42.40
Korea—Railways.................................	40.00	15.00	55.00
Malagasy Republic—Port.........................	—	9.60	9.60
Mali—Roads.....................................	—	7.70	7.70
Mexico—Roads...................................	21.80	—	21.80
Morocco—Roads..................................	7.30	7.30	14.60
Nigeria—Roads..................................	10.60	—	10.60
Nigeria—Roads, railways, and ports..............	25.00	—	25.00
Pakistan—Natural gas pipeline...................	19.20	—	19.20
Papua and New Guinea—Roads...................	4.50	4.50	9.00
Paraguay—Roads................................	6.00	—	6.00
Rwanda—Roads.................................	—	9.30	9.30
Senegal—Roads.................................	—	2.10	2.10
Tanzania—Roads................................	—	7.50	7.50
Uganda—Roads.................................	—	11.60	11.60
Yugoslavia—Roads..............................	40.00	—	40.00
	$ 516.25	$144.50	$ 660.75
Electric Power			
Argentina..	$ 60.00	$ —	$ 60.00
Brazil...	80.00	—	80.00
Ceylon..	0.90	9.40	10.30
Ceylon..	21.00	—	21.00
China...	44.50	—	44.50
Colombia..	52.30	—	52.30
Costa Rica......................................	12.00	—	12.00
Cyprus..	5.00	—	5.00
Honduras..	5.50	5.50	11.00
Indonesia..	—	15.00	15.00
Liberia..	7.40	—	7.40
Malawi..	—	5.25	5.25

Bank Loans and IDA Credits 1969/70 by Purpose (continued)
(Expressed in Millions of United States Dollars)

	Bank	*IDA*	*Total*
Mexico...	$ 125.00	$ —	$ 125.00
Panama...	42.00	—	42.00
Thailand...	46.50	—	46.50
	$ 502.10	$ 35.15	$ 537.25
Industry			
Brazil—Development finance company.............	$ 25.00	$ —	$ 25.00
Ceylon—Development finance company............	8.00	—	8.00
China—Development finance company............	18.00	—	18.00
Congo, Democratic Republic of—Development finance company...............................	—	5.00	5.00
Dominican Republic—Facilities for nickel mining project.................................	25.00	—	25.00
Greece—Development finance company............	20.00	—	20.00
India—Development finance company.............	40.00	—	40.00
Indonesia—Fertilizer plant........................	—	30.00	30.00
Israel—Development finance company.............	25.00	—	25.00
Morocco—Development finance company..	15.00	—	15.00
Pakistan—Development finance company..........	—	20.00	20.00
Pakistan—Small industries........................	—	3.00	3.00
Philippines—Development finance company........	25.00	—	25.00
Singapore—Development finance company..........	5.00	—	5.00
Tunisia—Development finance company............	10.00	—	10.00
Yugoslavia—Automotive and steel industries........	18.50	—	18.50
	$ 234.50	$ 58.00	$ 292.50
Project Preparation			
Botswana—Infrastructure for mining project........	$ —	$ 2.50	$ 2.50
Burundi—Road engineering and maintenance study...	—	0.38	0.38
Ghana—Road engineering........................	—	1.50	1.50
Pakistan—Agricultural engineering.................	—	0.80	0.80
Pakistan—Agricultural engineering.................	—	2.40	2.40
Pakistan—Port engineering........................	—	1.00	1.00
	$ —	$ 8.58	$ 8.58
Water Supply & Sewerage Systems			
Colombia—Water supply..........................	$ 18.50	$ —	$ 18.50
Ghana—Water supply and sewer system............	—	3.50	3.50
Tunisia—Water supply............................	—	10.50	10.50
	$ 18.50	$ 14.00	$ 32.50
Family Planning			
Jamaica..	$ 2.00	$ —	$ 2.00
General Development & Industrial Imports			
India—Industrial imports.........................	$ —	$ 75.00	$ 75.00
International Finance Corporation...................	$ 100.00	$ —	$ 100.00
TOTALS.................................	$1,680.35	$605.61	$2,285.96

SOURCE: *World Bank/IDA Annual Report 1970*, pp. 10–11.

REGULAR BUDGET OF THE SPECIALIZED AGENCIES[1] AND OF THE UNITED NATIONS FROM 1950 THROUGH 1969

Voluntary contributions to EPTA, SF and UNDP during the same period
(Expressed in $ million)

	1950	1951	1952	1953	1954	1955	1956	1957	1958	1959	1960	1961	1962	1963	1964	1965	1966	1967	1968	1969
FAO	4.5	4.6	4.8	5.1	5.5	6.0	6.4	7.0	9.1	10.5	10.6	11.1	14.4	16.8	18.0	23.6	27.8	29.7	34.1	33.6
UNESCO	7.2	8.0	8.7	8.0	9.0	9.2	11.4	10.6	12.3	12.6	13.8	15.8	18.2	19.7	21.3	27.6	28.6	32.9	37.3	42.1
WHO	6.1	6.3	7.9	8.1	8.1	9.3	10.0	12.1	14.0	15.4	17.1	19.2	24.2	29.8	33.9	42.1	48.2	56.3	62.5	67.4
ILO	5.3	5.8	6.4	6.5	6.6	7.0	7.3	7.7	8.5	9.1	9.6	10.4	11.6	14.5	17.0	21.5	23.5	26.5	29.1	31.1
IAEA	—	—	—	—	—	—	—	—	3.9	4.5	5.2	6.0	6.4	6.9	7.3	8.8	10.0	10.4	11.7	12.6
WMO	—	0.2	0.2	0.3	0.3	0.4	0.4	0.4	0.4	0.5	0.6	0.6	0.8	0.9	1.1	1.5	2.0	2.4	2.9	3.2
ITU	1.6	1.6	1.6	1.5	1.3	1.3	1.7	1.5	1.9	2.7	2.3	2.8	3.4	4.1	4.1	5.6	7.0	6.8	7.6	7.5
UPU	0.3	0.4	0.4	0.4	0.4	0.4	0.4	0.5	0.5	0.6	0.6	0.7	0.7	0.8	1.2	1.1	1.3	1.5	1.7	2.0
ICAO	2.9	3.2	3.2	3.2	3.1	3.3	3.3	3.9	4.0	4.5	4.6	4.8	5.5	5.8	6.1	6.4	7.5	7.0	7.7	8.0
IMCO	—	—	—	—	—	—	—	—	—	0.2	0.3	0.3	0.4	0.4	0.5	0.9	0.9	0.8	1.0	1.1
Total	27.9	30.0	33.3	33.1	34.3	36.9	40.9	43.7	54.6	60.6	64.8	71.8	85.6	99.7	110.4	138.7	156.7	174.3	195.4	208.7
UN[2]	43.7	48.6	50.3	49.3	48.5	50.1	50.5	53.2	62.5	61.9	65.8	71.1	84.5	92.2	102.9	107.1	118.6	130.5	140.4	151.2
Voluntary contributions to EPTA, SF & UNDP		20.0	18.8	22.3	25.0	27.6	28.8	30.8	31.1	55.2	72.6	89.1	105.6	122.7	136.9	145.3	154.8	172.0	183.5	197.4[3]

SOURCES: *Budgets*: Annual reports of ACABQ to the General Assembly.
Voluntary Contributions: (UNDP).
A Study of the Capacity of the United Nations Development System, Appendix 6, Table 4.
[1] Not including Bank Group, IMF and GATT.
[2] Including UNCTAD and UNIDO.
[3] As at 30 September 1969.

MAJOR ELEMENTS IN PRESENT STRUCTURE FOR UN DEVELOPMENT COOPERATION

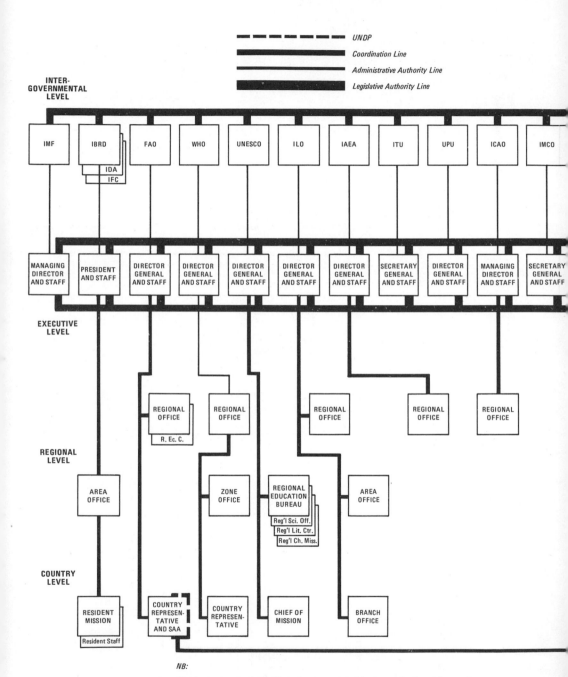

NB:

This chart has been prepared for illustration purposes only; it is not comprehensive and does not show, for instance, all connections between agencies and UNDP Resident Representatives.

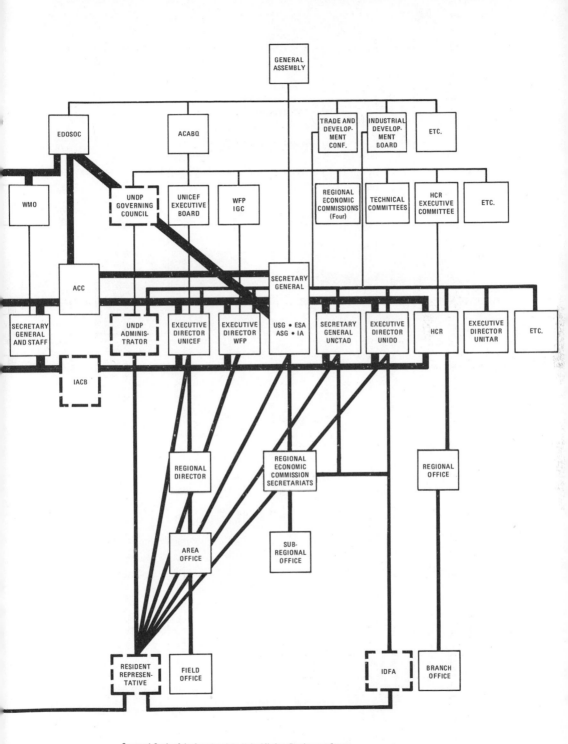

Source: *A Study of the Capacity of the United Nations Development System*

UN SYSTEM TOTAL NET EXPENDITURE IN ECONOMIC AND SOCIAL ACTIVITIES BY MAIN SOURCES OF FUNDS, 1965-1968

(Expressed in $ million)

Agencies or programmes	Total net expenditures				Part financed by UNDP[1] — Amounts				Part financed by UNDP[1] — Percentages of total net expenditures				Breakdown of total net expenditures: Financed by regular budget				Breakdown of total net expenditures: Financed by extra-budgetary funds			
	1965	1966	1967	1968	1965	1966	1967	1968	1965	1966	1967	1968	1965	1966	1967	1968	1965	1966	1967	1968
UN[2]	84.9	100.0	112.7	128.0	25.6	32.8	37.8	46.0	30	33	34	36	48.9	57.1	63.5	69.2	36.0	42.8	49.2	58.8
FAO	56.4	70.6	77.8	88.5	36.4	47.2	53.5	62.5	65	67	69	71	20.9	24.4	26.2	28.0	35.5	46.2	51.5	60.5
UNESCO	43.7	50.3	54.0	66.5	19.9	25.2	25.8	34.0	46	50	48	51	24.8	26.1	29.6	33.9	18.9	24.2	24.4	32.6
WHO	62.6	74.1	82.7	89.3	8.7	11.4	10.4	13.3	14	15	13	15	38.3	43.4	51.3	55.6	24.2	30.6	31.4	33.8
ILO	31.6	35.6	38.4	44.1	11.7	14.1	15.8	19.1	37	40	41	43	19.2	21.5	23.3	25.6	12.4	14.1	15.1	18.5
IAEA	10.8	12.9	10.6	11.4	1.1	2.0	1.2	2.1	10	15	11	19	7.7	8.7	8.8	9.5	3.2	4.2	1.7	1.9
WMO	3.5	4.7	5.0	7.5	1.8	2.8	2.6	4.5	52	59	52	59	1.3	1.8	2.2	2.7	2.2	2.9	2.8	4.8
ITU	9.5	11.1	11.1	12.3	3.4	4.8	4.8	5.5	36	43	43	44	5.1	5.9	5.7	6.1	4.4	5.2	5.4	6.2
UPU	1.6	2.1	2.2	2.5	0.4	0.6	0.5	0.6	22	27	22	23	1.2	1.4	1.6	1.7	0.4	0.7	0.6	0.8
ICAO	9.1	10.9	9.3	10.8	3.8	4.6	3.7	4.3	42	42	39	40	5.2	6.2	5.6	6.1	3.8	4.7	3.7	4.7
IMCO	0.9	0.9	1.0	1.0	—	0.1	0.1	0.2	3	8	17	20	0.9	0.9	0.8	0.8	—	—	0.2	0.2
Sub-total	314.6	373.1	404.7	462.0	112.9	145.6	156.2	191.7	36	39	39	42	173.6	197.5	218.7	239.3	141.0	175.6	186.0	222.7
UNDP adm.	10.8	13.2	14.7	17.1	10.8	13.2	14.7	17.1	—	—	—	—	—	—	—	—	10.8	13.2	14.7	17.1
UNICEF	30.3	36.2	40.0	45.9	—	—	—	—	—	—	—	—	—	—	—	—	30.3	36.2	40.0	45.9
WFP	18.2	32.0	30.7	50.7	—	—	—	—	—	—	—	—	—	—	—	—	18.2	32.0	30.7	50.7
UNRWA	37.6	37.5	40.5	44.0	—	—	—	—	—	—	—	—	—	—	—	—	37.6	37.5	40.5	44.0
Grand total	411.6	492.0	530.7	619.8	123.7	158.8	170.9	208.8	30	32	32	34	173.6	197.5	218.7	239.3	238.0	294.5	312.0	380.5

SOURCES: —Expenditures of the UN system in relation to programmes, Annual reports of the ACC (doc. E/4351, E/4501 and E/4702).
—UNDP statistics.
—A Study of the Capacity of the United Nations Development System, Appendix 6, Table 11.

[1] UNDP payments to Agencies include projects as well as overhead costs; note that UNDP funds are not always presented as extra-budgetary; a number of Agencies consider, for instance the overhead payments as part of their regular budget; this explains why in a few cases the part of TNE financed by UNDP is larger than the total of extra-budgetary funds expended. Also note that UNDP figures do not include payments to IBRD ($ 2 million in 1965, 3.6 in 1966, 5.1 in 1967 and 8.4 in 1968; therefore totals differ from those shown in Tables 6 and 7.
[2] Figures include only expenditures attributable to activities in the economic, social and human rights fields (as per definition adopted by ACC); see source below; total include UNIDO, UNCTAD and UNHCR expenditures.

UN SYSTEM PROFESSIONAL STAFF
as of January 1969

Shown by Agencies and Programmes, by source of funds and by location level

Agencies and Programmes	Personnel financed by regular budgets and overheads[1] payments			Project personnel			Total			Regional level (as included in total)		
	HQ[2]	Field	Total	HQ	Field	Total	HQ	Field	Grand total	RB+O	PP	Total
UN[3]	2 706	514	3 220	40	1 155	(1 196)[4]	2 746	1 669	(4 416)	439	187	626
UNHCR	58	44	102	2	2	4	60	46	106	—	—	—
UNICEF	79	134	213	—	—	—	79	134	213	72	—	72
UNWRA	2	115	117	—	—	—	2	115	117	—	—	—
UNDP	183	285	468	—	—	—	183	285	468	—	—	—
Sub-total UN	3 028	1 092	4 120	42	1 157	(1 200)	3 070	2 249	(5 320)	511	187	698
ILO[5]	759	165	924	6	691	(689)	765	856	(1 613)	35	52	87
FAO[5]	1 150	129	1 279	9	2 208	(2 223)	1 159	2 337	(3 502)	84	10	94
UNESCO	639	117	(754)	45	1 170	(1 225)	684	1 287	(1 979)	88	96	184
WHO[6]	653	313	(971)	115	1 572	(1 688)	768	1 885	(2 659)	189	182	371
IBRD	907		955	—	21	21	907	69	976	16	8	24
IMF	532	6	538	—	63	63	532	69	601	—	—	—
ICAO	170	51	221	19	186	(182)	189	237	(403)	39	2	41
UPU	62	—	62	6	19	25	68	19	87	—	7	7
ITU	130	—	130	17	196	(211)	147	196	(341)	—	7	7
WMO	102	—	102	—	98	98	102	98	200	—	—	—
IMCO	31	—	31	—	4	4	31	4	35	—	—	—
GATT	83	—	83	—	—	—	83	—	83	—	—	—
ITC	33	—	33	5	—	(7)	38	—	(40)	—	—	—
IAEA	352	10	362	—	250	250	352	260	612	—	—	—
Sub-total other agencies	5 603	839	(6 445)	222	6 478	(6 686)	5 825	7 317	(13 131)	451	364	815
Grand total	8 631	1 931	(10 565)	264	7 635	(7 886)[7]	8 895	9 566	(18 451)	962	551	1 513

SOURCES: —A Study of the Capacity of the United Nations Development System, Appendix 6, Table 18.
—Annual CAAQ list of regular and project personnel posts of the UN and related agencies as of January 1969 (doc. CAAQ/S.30/R.42 [PER]), 14.VII.69.

(Notes continued on following page.)

[1] The following definitions have been used:

Regular and overhead posts
(a) continuing posts financed under the regular budgets and included in the regular manning tables; plus
(b) continuing posts financed from voluntary funds but used to provide or to supplement the "overhead" administration of the field programmes financed by the same voluntary funds.

Project posts
a) posts in country, regional or special projects to provide technical assistance financed from voluntary funds (UNDP, UNICEF, trust funds etc.);
(b) similar technical assistance posts financed from regular budget appropriations.

[2] "Headquarters" refers to the following locations, for the agencies mentioned only:
Vienna: UN (UNIDO) and IAEA; Montreal: ICAO; Paris: UNESCO; Rome: FAO;
Bern: UPU; London: IMCO; Geneva, New York, Washington: UN and all other Agencies.

"Field" refers to all other locations.

[3] Including posts for all functions (political and security affairs, finance and management, public information, conference and general services, etc.). As far as *economic and social affairs* are concerned, the following figures illustrate the respective importance of the various administrative units concerned: figures do not come from the source used for the main table; they relate only to non-project personnel; it was not possible to obtain them according to the same pattern:

Department of Economic & Social Affairs	
ECA	544
ECAFE	205
ECE	169
ECLA	107
UNESOB	160
	26
Sub-total ESA	1211
UNCTAD	206
UNIDO	289
UNITAR	26

SOURCES (for note 3 only):
—United Nations, *Work programme of the United Nations, in the economic, social and human rights fields and its budgetary requirements*, (doc. E/4612).
—United Nations, *Budget estimates for the financial year 1969 and information annexes* (doc. A/7205, Vol. II).
—UNITAR, Report of the Executive Director (doc. A/7263).

[4] Figures obtained from different tables do not always coincide; figures between brackets are those given in the source's aggregate table and differing from the total of other columns, which were obtained through the use of country tables.
[5] Including WFP posts (some 130, of which about 50 in the field).
[6] Including PAHO.
[7] N.B. comments to Table 10.

NOTES

1. *A Study of the Capacity of the United Nations Development System,* United Nations Publications Sales No. E.70.I.10, Appendix 6, Table 4.

2. *Ibid.*

3. World Bank/International Development Association, *Annual Report 1970,* Appendix 3, p. 114.

4. *Ibid.,* p. 3.

5. *United Nations Development System,* Appendix 6, Table 18.

6. *Ibid.*

7. See especially David Mitrany, *A Working Peace System* (Chicago: Quadrangle Book, 1966), and, for a critique of functionalist theory, Ernst B. Haas, *Beyond the Nation State* (Stanford: Stanford University Press, 1964).

8. For a summary analysis and classification of United Nations system agencies according to types of tasks performed and primary procedures for reaching decisions, see Willian D. Coplin, *The Functions of International Law* (Chicago: Rand McNally, 1966), chap. IV.

9. *United Nations Development System,* Appendix 6, Table 12.

10. *Ibid.,* Table 10.

11. World Bank, *Annual Report 1970,* p. 3, and Appendix 2 p. 113.

12. The evolution of an operational UN is well chronicled in Walter R. Sharp *Field Administration in the United Nations System* (New York: Praeger, 1961).

13. *United Nations Development System,* Appendix 6, Table 5.

14. *Ibid.,* Table 18.

15. For a sampling of the literature on this theme, see *International Political Communities* (Garden City, N.Y.: Doubleday, 1966).

16. This theme is developed in Inis L. Claude, Jr., "Collective Legitimization as a Political Function of the United Nations," *International Organization,* XX, No. 3 (Summer 1966), 367–379.

17. For a comprehensive treatment of the history of the UN system and its antecedents through the early 1950s, see Gerard J. Mangone, *A Short History of International Organization* (New York: McGraw-Hill, 1954); for a more recent but briefer survey of the history of the UN system and its antecedents, see C. Wilfred Jenks, *The World Beyond the Charter* (London: George Allen & Unwin, 1969).

18. A brief historical review of ILO, written by its former director-general, is to be found in David A. Morse, *The Origin and Evolution of the I.L.O. and Its Role in the World Community* (Ithaca, N.Y.: Cornell University Press, 1969); a more systematic critique of ILO is found in Haas, *Beyond the Nation State.*

19. The standard treatment of the League experience is F. P. Walters, *A History of the League of Nations* (London: Oxford University Press, 1952); for a review of League activities in the sectors under discussion here, see Martin Hill, *The Economic and Financial Organization of the League of Nations* (Washington, D.C.: Carnegie Endowment for International Peace, 1946).

20. Quoted in Walters, *League of Nations,* p. 752.

21. The early efforts in this field are chronicled in Robert E. Asher et al., *The United Nations and Promotion of the General Welfare* (Washington, D.C.: Brookings Institution, 1957; an updating of this work is to be found in many of the essays in Richard N. Gardner and Max F. Millikan (eds.), *The Global Partnership: International Agencies and Economic Development* (*International Organization*), XXII, No. 1 (Winter 1968).

22. For an account of the UNCTAD confrontation, see Richard N.

Gardner, "The United Nations Conference on Trade and Development," in Gardner and Millikan (eds.) *Global Partnerships,* pp. 99–130; and Irving Louis Horowitz, *The Three Worlds of Development* (New York: Oxford University Press, 1966), chap. VI.

23. For an analysis of the creation of the Special Fund, see John G. Hadwen and Johan Kaufmann, *How United Nations Decisions Are Made* (Leyden: Sijthoff, 1961), chap. V.

24. World Bank, *Annual Report 1970,* Appendix 5, p. 117.

25. Quoted in Walter M. Kotschnig, "The United Nations as an Instrument of Economic and Social Development," in Gardner and Millikan (eds.), *Global Partnership,* p. 23.

26. Changing Soviet views of UN economic and social activities are analyzed in Harold K. Jacobson, *The USSR and the UN's Economic and Social Activities* (Notre Dame: University of Notre Dame Press, 1963); and Alvin Z. Rubinstein, *The Soviets in International Organizations* (Princeton: Princeton University Press, 1964).

27. Quoted in Kotschnig, "Economic and Social Development," p. 41.

28. *United Nations Development System,* Foreword, p. v.

29. *Ibid.,* p. iii.

30. C. Wilfred Jenks, quoted in Walter R. Sharp, *The United Nations Economic and Social Council* (New York: Columbia University Press, 1969), pp. 3–4.

31. For a comprehensive treatment of ECOSOC, see Sharp, *United Nations Economic and Social Council.*

32. For a more detailed review of this machinery, see *ibid.,* chap. II.

33. *Ibid.,* chap. 1. This theme is developed in subsequent chapters of Sharp's book.

34. For an analysis of ACC's coordinating role, see Martin Hill, "The Administrative Committee on Coordination," in Evan Luard (ed.), *Evolution of International Organizations* (New York: Praeger, 1966); and Sharp, *United Nations Economic and Social Council.*

35. The most extensive analysis of the resident representative is Gerard J. Mangone, "Field Administration: The United Nations Resident Representative," in Mangone (ed.), *UN Administration of Eocnomic and Social Programs* (New York: Columbia University Press, 1966). See also *United Nations Development System.* passim.

36. *United Nations Development System,* p. 76.

37. *Ibid.,* p. 87.

38. *Ibid.*

39. *Ibid.,* p. 22.

40. Haas, *Beyond the Nation State,* p. 119.

41. *Ibid.,* pp. 113–114.

42. *United Nations Development System,* p. 6.

43. For an analysis of the Bank see James Morris, *The Road to Huddersfield* (New York: Pantheon Books, 1963); James Patrick Sewell, *Functionalism and World Politics* (Princeton: Princeton University Press, 1966); and Roy Blough, "The World Bank Group," in Gardner and Millikan (eds.), *Global Partnership,* pp. 152–183.

44. Blough, "World Bank Group," p. 156.

45. *Ibid.,* p. 181.

46. Robert S. McNamara, *Address to the Board of Governors* (Copenhagen), September 21, 1970, p. 3.

47. See, for instance, Robert S. McNamara, *Address to the University of Notre Dame,* May 1, 1969 and *Address to the Board of Governors* (Copenhagen), September 21, 1970.

48. For elaboration upon this theme see Robert W. Gregg, "The Role of the UN Regional Economic Commissions in Multinational Cooperation," in Robert Jordan (ed.), *Multinational Cooperation* (New York: Oxford University Press, 1972).

49. This theme is developed in Jean Siotis, "The Secretariat of the United Nations Economic Commission for Europe and European Economic Integration: The First Ten Years," *International Organization*, XIX, No. 2 (Spring 1965), 177–202.

50. The standard reference is E. J. Phelan, *Yes and Albert Thomas* (London: Cresset Press, 1936).

51. Joseph M. Jones, *The United Nations at Work* (London: Pergamon Press, 1965), p. 218.

52. Roger Revelle, "International Cooperation in Food and Population," in Gardner and Millikan (eds.), *Global Partnership,* p. 384.

53. "The United Nations Development Decade at Mid-Point: An Appraisal by the Secretary-General" (UN (Document E/4071, June 11, 1965), p. 32.

54. This project is described in Jones, *United Nations at Work,* pp. 157–173.

55. Covey T. Oliver, "New Problems of Social Development," *Foreign Service Journal,* XLVII, No. 11 (November 1970), 43.

56. Jenks, *World Beyond the Charter,* p. 131.

57. *Ibid.,* pp. 170–171.

58. For a brief review of the UN effort in this issue area, see Leland M. Goodrich, "New Trends in Narcotics Control," *International Conciliation,* No. 530 (November 1960); and Robert W. Gregg, "The United Nations and the Opium Problem," *International and Comparative Law Quarterly,* January 1964, pp. 96–115.

59. *The New York Times,* January 14, 1972, p. 30.

Index